Colonialism Experienced

Colonialism Experienced

Vietnamese Writings on Colonialism,
1900–1931

Truong Buu Lam

Ann Arbor
THE UNIVERSITY OF MICHIGAN PRESS

Copyright © by the University of Michigan 2000
All rights reserved
Published in the United States of America by
The University of Michigan Press
Manufactured in the United States of America
∞ Printed on acid-free paper

2003   2002   2001   2000   4   3   2   1

A CIP catalog record for this book is available from the British Library.

Library of Congress Cataloging-in-Publication Data

Lâm, Truong Buu.
    Colonialism experienced : Vietnamese writings on colonialism, 1900–1931 / Truong Buu Lam.
        p.   cm.
    Includes bibliographical references and index.
    ISBN 0-472-09712-1 (cloth : alk. paper) — ISBN 0-472-06712-5 (pbk. : alk. paper)
    1. Vietnam—Politics and government—20th century—Souces. I. Title.
DS556.8.L25   2000
959.703—dc21   99-058296

Acknowledgments

Book writing is a collective undertaking. This book is no exception. Many collaborators contributed to its making. First of all, my colleague and friend Jagdish P. Sharma has patiently stood by me for many years, consistently prodding me to complete this project. Furthermore, he has read and edited every page of the manuscript. Without him I am certain to have taken much more time to achieve this task, if I were ever to finish it. I hereby offer Professor Sharma my most profound gratitude. Maivan Clech Lam and Damaris A. Kirchshoffer have generously given their time to sift through the first two chapters. I would like to convey to both my heartfelt thanks. In the fall semester of 1995 I solicited suggestions from students in my class on Indo-china modern history, to whom I had distributed chapter 2. Brian Cassity and Gerry McDonald made numerous comments for which I am thankful. I would like to express my deep appreciation to Vo-Le Thanh Diep, who has provided me with many insightful interpretations of certain aspects of Vietnamese culture and particularly of Vietnamese literature. Three anonymous scholars have made such sharp and appropriate criticisms that I followed practically all of their suggestions. To all three I present my warmest thanks. Finally, I owe a great debt of gratitude to Ingrid Erickson and Christina Milton of the University of Michigan Press, who have presided over the making of this book with expertise, understanding, and thoughtfulness.

Contents

Abbreviations

ANSOM   Archives Nationales de France. Section d'Outre Mer.

ICP   Indochinese Communist Party. Dang Cong San Dong Duong or Dong Duong Cong San Dang.

SLOT   Archives Nationales de France. Section d'Outre Mer. Service de liaison avec les originaires des territoires d'Outre Mer.

TVVN   *Hop Tuyen Tho Van Viet Nam.* 2d ed. in 6 vols. Vol. 4, 1858–1920. Vol. 5, 1920–45. Hanoi, 1978.

TVYNVCM   *Hop Tuyen Tho Van Yeu Nuoc. Tho Van Yeu Nuoc va Cach Mang: Dau The Ky XX (1900–1930).* Hanoi, 1976.

VNQDD   Viet Nam Quoc Dan Dang. Vietnamese Nationalist Party.

VTCM   Dang Thai Mai. *Van Tho Cach Mang Viet Nam Dau The Ky XX, (1900–1925).* Hanoi, n.d.

Introduction

Vietnam's colonial history in modern times can be divided into three distinct phases. The first phase began with the French attack against Da Nang in 1858 and ended with the appointment in 1897 of Paul Doumer, who, as governor-general of Indochina, completed the imposition of French rule over Vietnam. A mere five years after his arrival in Indochina, Doumer was able to proudly report to the French minister of colonies that, from 1897 to 1901, not a single French soldier had died in any battlefield on the entire territory of the Indo-chinese colony. In less than a half-century France has, indeed, fought its way into the territory of Vietnam, Cambodia, and Laos, which it has reduced to the status of colony and protectorates. The spontaneous reactions of the indigenous peoples who took up arms in the defense of their country and of their kings died out before the end of the century. The first colonial possession of France in Southeast Asia took its definite shape and form in 1897, when Governor-General Doumer implemented an old decree to institute the French Indochina Union. The pacification campaign had brought about good results for the French, and in the entire union only a small pocket of resistance remained under the command of a military officer of the old regime by the name of De Tham, whose supporters occupied a strip of land located in the province of Yen The, in the northwestern part of northern Vietnam. They, however, represented no threat to the French, for they had struck a deal with the new colonial authorities whereby they could live undisturbed in their base provided that they did not export their resistance.

The first forty-five years of the twentieth century constituted the second phase in Vietnam's colonial history. These years delineated the contours of a colonial society in which successive governors-general deployed their efforts to devise the best methods to keep the native population submissive and to design the most effective means to exploit the local resources. It was also in that same colonial milieu that Vietnamese patriots thought up the most con-vincing arguments aimed at mobilizing their fellow countrymen against French colonialism and concocted secret plans to stimulate the Vietnamese against French rule. This second phase ended with the declaration of independence and formation of the first government of independent Vietnam on 2 September 1945.

The armed struggle for unity and total independence, which started in 1946 and terminated with the reunification of the country thirty years later, constituted the third and last phase of Vietnamese modern colonial history.

The second phase, in its turn, can be subdivided into two periods. From 1900 to 1931 anticolonial activities manifested a clear progression toward a more systematic organization into political parties that reflected the practice of modernized polities. From the formation of the rudimentary *Dong Du* (Going East) movement of Phan Boi Chau in 1905, that social and political effervescence culminated with the founding of the Vietnamese Nationalist Party (Viet Nam Quoc Dan Dang, or VNQDD) in 1927 and the Indochinese Communist Party (Dong Duong Cong San Dang, or ICP) in 1930. The transition to the next period was provided by the years 1930–31 during which the rebellion that began in Yen Bai, fomented by the Nationalist Party, the strike-demonstrations and work stoppages of the industrial workers which took place almost on a daily basis, and finally the peasants' armed uprisings that resulted in the formation of local soviet governments under the leadership of the Indochinese Communist Party shook the Vietnamese colony from the one end to the other. The strife elicited extremely harsh repression from the French colonial authorities. No political formations could survive the persecution: many of their leaders were arrested, some of them executed; the survivors went into exile, while rank-and-file members had to adopt a low profile. It was not until the beginning of the 1940s that the Viet Minh was able to merge the main political factions into one united front to fight against both Japanese fascism and French imperialism. It was the same Viet Minh that led the resistance against the French attempt at colonial reconquest, which began in 1945.

This book introduces the first period of the second phase, the years between 1900 and 1931. It will present the history of those years in the same way as I did its first phase (1858–1900) in my book *Patterns of Vietnamese Response to Foreign Intervention,* published in 1968 by Yale University's Southeast Asian Studies Monograph Series. Now, after almost thirty years, I have not changed the way I want to present Vietnamese colonial history—that is, through the translation of the more expressive writings authored by Vietnamese patriots who have formulated ideas concerning the colonial situation of their country. The twenty documents translated here represent a vast array of opinions, and all of them, in varying degrees, have exerted some influence over the people of Vietnam. They belong to a variety of genres: propaganda pamphlets, open letters to government officials, texts to be used in private or clandestine classrooms, manifestos of political or cultural organizations, newspapers columns, public proclamations, petitions to international agencies, and poems. They were written in Vietnamese, French, or classical Chinese. Some of the documents have been published into booklets; some original texts are still preserved in archival depositories; still some others have been reprinted generally as excerpts in anthologies or studies in literature or history. For readers who are slightly familiar with Vietnamese history, these documents are all well-known texts, quoted in every publication that examines the period under consideration. Few, however, have been reproduced in their entirety, and none, to my knowledge, has ever been translated into English. Of the twenty documents presented in this book I have abbreviated or brought some minor modification to only two. With Document 11, the poem entitled "Chieu Hon Nuoc" (Appeal to the Soul of the Nation), in order to obtain the text I translated here I have collated two publications with moderately different versions of the poem and made up my own rendering. Second, I have omitted from the text I have thus established a number of verses I find repetitive and, at the same time, inferior in evocative value. As for Document 15, the original of Tran Huy Lieu's *Bag Full of Confidences* is a pamphlet of more than forty pages in length, so I had to select the passages that seem to me more representative of the mood of the time. In doing this, I have respected the outlines into which the pamphlet was divided: what I have done was to skip repetitions, intricate anecdotes, and overly elaborate arguments, some of which I have presented as citations in the introductory chapters. At some points I paraphrased short sections.

Although the documents can be completely understood and appreciated to the fullest extent by themselves and although each of them is totally independent from the others, after having familiarized myself with them, I felt that an introduction would be useful in allowing the reader to grasp their total value. I have, therefore, attached to the documents an introductory essay composed of three chapters. The first chapter attempts to describe in as much detail as I can muster the colonial administration the French established in Vietnam during the first three decades of the twentieth century. The end product consists of a text that is filled with minute details concerning complex institutions about which it was as difficult to establish the role as it was futile to try to comprehend the function. But what I wanted to get out of this first chapter is an impressionistic but, at the same time, precise and concise picture of the most basic structures of the colonial administration of the three countries of Vietnam so that, whenever a small detail is needed, one does not have to cast about thousands of pages in hundreds of different books before finding it. The chapter is, furthermore, indispensable if readers want to be able to visualize the institutions and practices Vietnamese patriots wrote about or fought against. I tried to make the chapter livelier by introducing vignettes of and anecdotes about the principal actors of the period.[1]

In chapter 2, I have tried to solve, albeit in a very small way, a problem that has preoccupied me for a great part of my life. As a person who has lived in a colonized country, I have personally experienced firsthand a number of situations that pointed unmistakably to a relationship between two unequal participants. At other times I happened to find myself in certain circumstances that compelled me to feel humiliated as a native of a colony and, therefore, alienated from my own country. On another plane I have heard time and again tales of horror arising from the unjust, brutal, cruel, inhumane way the colonizers treated the native people. Similarly, I have always wondered about the inferiority complex I have noticed everywhere in Vietnam, a complex that almost every Vietnamese person manifests vis-à-vis the French or any white person. Yet, ever since I started reading about the French colonial regime in Vietnam, I have not come upon any work that would depict systematically with realism and concrete examples the daily insult and humiliation that the Vietnamese people had to suffer at the hands of the French colonialists.

Obviously, studies abound that describe the political, economic, and social dislocation that has been wrought upon colonial societies. Books on colonial policies overflow the shelves of libraries, but not many, and none for Vietnam, to my knowledge, have dealt with what the colonial people experienced every day.[2] In selecting the texts to be presented in this book, I have read thousands and thousands of pages written by Vietnamese nationalists on colonialism. The only mentions of the colonial experience are to be found in two short passages in Document 9.[3] A recent book entitled *Revolution in the Village: Tradition and Transformation in North Vietnam, 1925–1988* devotes a major part of its content to relating the reminiscences of the author's informant of his momentous involvement in Vietnamese politics. Yet the informant recalled no souvenir of any concrete or painful colonial encounters.[4] Perhaps historians of colonial Vietnam judge the subject matter not important enough to merit their attention.[5] Maybe they think that the colonial experience will be best narrated by novelists.[6] In fact, even authors of early Vietnamese novels or short stories did not venture into reporting or mentioning "politically" tainted facts; they limited their narrative, rather, to problems of personal and professional ethics, to family relationships, mainly to the issue of free love versus parental choice, for men and for women as well. If they had any criticism for any social ills, it was directed toward the indigenous mandarinate, which they painted as corrupt and arrogant. Whenever they happened to refer to a French presence, it was done only in favorable terms. It is, therefore, not surprising to note that Ho Bieu Chanh, a well-known southern writer of the 1920s and 1930s, author of some sixty novels and short stories, and renown painter of Vietnamese society under French control, would have devoted only a few pages to relate a distasteful colonial engagement. On the other hand, he did not hesitate to attribute all success accomplished by his Vietnamese characters not to their talents or to their own entrepreneurial aptitude but to the intervention of some French benefactors.[7] Again in a selection of short stories published in the well-known magazine *Nam Phong,* from 1917 to 1934, I could glean only one fleeting allusion to the colonial situation of Vietnam. A young woman was abandoned in the middle of Hanoi by a crooked husband, who ran away with her jewelry, her money, all her worldly possessions contained in two suitcases. A man approached her to offer his help; she felt right away that she could have confidence in him "because he looks like someone who works for the French."[8]

We must wait for the next phase, after 1930, for Vietnamese novelists to embark upon the description of the unequal interaction between the French colonials and the common people of the colony. They would depict scenes of Vietnamese villagers selling their sons and daughters in order to raise enough money to pay taxes or, occasionally, allude to cases of brutal encounters between the colonizers and the colonized.[9] Daily experience of the colonial condition did not surface much anywhere in the written texts of pre-1930 Vietnam, except in newspapers and nonwritten documents. That is the reason why, in order to write this second chapter, I relied mainly on the direct evidence resulting from incidents, accidents, all daily happenings that are generally compiled under a general heading called "news items," or more appropriately qualified in French as "les faits divers." In addition, I surveyed the built environment of some urban agglomerations that were created on Vietnamese soil by the colonial authorities for the sole comfort and the exclusive enjoyment of the French colonizers. This chapter is conceived as a complement to the translated documents included in this work. It presents colonialism as it was lived and experienced by the common people in the streets, on the highways, in trains, in their own houses, in their places of work. Unlike the writers whose works I have translated here, they have not discoursed about colonialism or such lofty subjects, but the experience they had of colonialism was personal, existential, and difficult to erase from their memory.

The third chapter shows how the Vietnamese people defined and described the colonial reality. Besides the documents translated in this work, I used the oral tradition, the writings of other Vietnamese patriots, as well as pronouncements and opinions recorded in newspapers and magazines of the time.

The names used in this work can lead to confusion. As the readers may know, until 1945 the name *Vietnam* was not used at all but in very rare cases by the Vietnamese people, who referred to themselves as "nguoi Viet" or "nguoi Viet Nam" (Viet or Vietnamese people); more often, they called themselves "nguoi Annam" (Annamite people). This last name is the one that creates the confusion. It refers, principally in texts written in French, at the same time to the inhabitants of Annam, the central part of Vietnam, and/or to the Vietnamese people as a whole. In this book I use *Vietnamese* to translate the word *Annamites* every time I feel that that word designates the inhabitants of the entire Vietnam. I use the other names for the inhabitants of each of the divisions of Vietnam when they designate specifically the inhabitants of the particular regions of French Indochina, that is, Tonkinese for northern Vietnamese, Annamites for central Vietnamese, and Cochinchinese for southern Vietnamese.

Some readers might wonder about the vocabulary used by Vietnamese writers to express concepts such as nation, people, race, ideology, democracy, congress, etc. One should not forget that a few of our documents were written in Chinese principally in the early years, and written Chinese had by then benefited from a long period of adaptation and modernization under the aegis of Japan. As for the documents written in Vietnamese, their writers simply used the same Chinese words, transcribed into the Latin alphabet, or, on rare occasions, pure Vietnamese words. For example, *nation* and/or *country* are rendered as *quoc, quoc gia, nuoc nha;* people: *quoc dan* or *dan;* race: *chung~ loai, toc loai, giong noi;* Vietnam: *Viet Nam, Viet quoc, nga~ quoc, Dai Nam, Nam quoc;* Congress: *nghi vien;* Senate, or Higher Chamber, *thuong nghi vien;* Chamber of Representatives, or Lower Chamber, *ha nghi vien;* ideology: *chu nghia;* patriotism and/or nationalism: *ai quoc, yeu nuoc.*

Notes

1. I am fully aware of the fact that a great number of studies have been done on this subject; one of them was published no earlier than 1995 by P. Brocheux and D. Hemery, entitled *Indochine, la colonisation ambiguë* (1858–1954). This work can answer any questions we might have on the whole period of the French colonial regime in Indochina. The book is, however, bulky and not easy to use for two reasons: it does not have a detailed index, and it is in French.

2. The only work that most closely fits the model I have in mind is Syed Hussein Alatas, *The Myth of the Lazy Native: A Study of the Image of the Malays, Filipinos, and Javanese from the Sixteenth to the Twentieth Century and Its Function in the Ideology of Colonial Capitalism* (London, 1977).

3. See Document 9, in this volume: "It is the 'European prestige' that kills justice in the courtrooms; that prevents the judges from giving the same sentence to a Frenchman and a Vietnamese indicted with the same offense; that metes out very light sentences, sometimes even suspended ones, to Frenchmen who kill indigenous people. In Hanoi, a few days after the inauguration of the reconstructed Doumer bridge, the automobile of a certain David, employee at the Central Post Office, crushed a Vietnamese by the name of Do Van Ngoc. The owner of the automobile was fined one hundred francs—a suspended sentence—for homicide committed through 'imprudence.' The attenuating circumstance is based on the ill health or the fragility of the pancreas of the victim: that is a classic case." Again: "Phan Chu Trinh, when he was still in Annam, was locked up by a [French] customs agent with one of his students because

of a trifling point of etiquette: they did not remove their hats when they passed by that agent's house."

4. Hy Van Luong, *Revolution in the Village: Tradition and Transformation in North Vietnam, 1925–1988,* with the collaboration of Nguyen Dac Bang (Honolulu, 1992).

5. Ironically, there exists a book on the daily life of the French people in Cochinchina in the 1930s: Charles Meyer, *La vie quotidienne des Français en Indochine, 1860–1910* (Paris, 1985), 273: "All the time, people gripe about colonial brutalities and unjustifiable measures of repression. All that did exist."

6. It is of interest to report that, when asked about writings on the colonial experience, many of my informants answered by quoting titles of novels.

7. See Ho Bieu Chanh, *Ngon co gio dua* (Saigon, 1926) and *Me ghe con ghe* (Vinh hoi, 1946). See also Nguyen Khue, *Chan Dung Ho Bieu Chanh* (Saigon, 1974).

8. Pham Duy Ton, "Con nguoi so khanh," in Lai Van Hung and Nguyen Phuong Chi, *Truyen ngan Nam Phong (Tuyen)* (Hanoi, 1989), 133.

9. See Ngo Vinh Long, *Before the Revolution: Vietnamese Peasants under the French* (Cambridge, Mass., 1973).

CHAPTER 1

The Colonial
Administrative Reality

The beginning of the twentieth century ushered in a period of relative calm for the French colonial possession of Indochina. Governor-General Paul Doumer (1897–1905), the man of the hour, had been able to realize the dream of all empire builders, which was to balance the budget of the colony as well as extend the administrative and economic infrastructures needed to secure its exploitation. It was no insignificant task, and France manifested her deep gratitude by naming the longest bridge built in Indochina after him: the one spanning the Red River in the middle of the city of Hanoi, which was the capital city of the five countries comprising the French Indochinese Union.[1]

France tried to give some rationality to the administrative structure of Indochina.[2] The 1887 creation, on paper, of the French Indochinese Union, together with its actual implementation in 1897 by Governor-General Doumer, could not easily conceal the fact that Indochina was not one but five distinct units. Indeed, the gradual nature of France's expansion into Indochina had given rise, to a large extent, to the particular status of each of its parts. Southern Vietnam, or Cochinchina, the first casualty of the French policy of annexation in 1863, became a full-fledged colony four years later. To the west the king of Cambodia submitted the region to French protection in 1863. These two initial French possessions were at first governed by naval officers and depended administratively on the French navy until 1875, when they were attached to the Ministry of Colonies. France then sent out its first civilian governor, Le Myre de Vilers, to govern both possessions from Saigon. The protectorate of Tonkin, northern Vietnam, and that of Annam, central Vietnam, were added to the colonial territory in 1884 and placed under the control of the Ministry of Foreign Affairs. The protectorate of Laos did not join the empire until 1892. In 1900 the French government assigned a small French territory in southern China, situated on the shores of the Guang Zhou Wan bay, northeast of the Hai Nan island, to the authority of the governor-general of Indochina. Already by 1887, however, all the existing Indochinese possessions had been placed under the supervision of the Ministry of Colonies.

It is generally believed that, notwithstanding the differences in their legal status, colony and protectorates were ruled pretty much the same way. This view is undoubtedly correct but limited. All the Indochinese countries were indeed structured as dependencies of France, and Doumer, in order to seal up that principle of unity, was quick to establish special agencies that wielded authority in all five countries. Administratively speaking, each of the five components had its own makeup, and a common budget for the Indochinese Union was not established until 1897. The traditional monarchy of Vietnam— which extended its authority only over Annam and Tonkin—and the royal families of Cambodia and Laos preserved their symbolic prerogatives. The Vietnamese monarchy staffed its own central and regional government with indigenous civil servants called mandarins, who, as could be expected, had to defer most of their power and function to their French counterparts. The ultimate authority in each of the four protectorates was the locally based French superior resident. That situation, however, characterized only the four protectorates. There was to be no indigenous administration in the Cochinchina colony, which was placed under the direct and sole control of a French lieutenant-governor. Although called lieutenant-governor, this official was nevertheless the supreme authority in his domain. The humble qualifier in his title served to distinguish him from the governor-general, who usually resided in Hanoi but, nevertheless, maintained for his own use an awe-inspiring palace right in the middle of the Cochinchinese capital city. Beyond that vast bureaucratic machinery, one common feature predominated the entire system: French officials reserved for themselves all the highest positions, reducing the indigenous monarchs as well as the latters' henchmen to the role of ceremonial figureheads.

The Governor-General

Appointed by the French Council of Ministers and confirmed by the French Parliament, the governor-general served as the chief representative of the French Republic in the colony and, conversely, as the spokesman for the colony in its relations with the mother country. In other words, he was the means by which France instituted a conversation with itself. The governor-general was empowered to issue decrees and laws that regulated the conduct and behavior of all the peoples living in Indochina. He figured as the supreme overseer of the entire colonial administrative system as well as the head of all the services that were funded by the federal budget and that were common to the five parts of the Indochinese Union. These services covered fields of government activity, such as education, public works, hygiene, finances, tourism, mines, industry, labor, security, information, etc. Aside from that vast bureaucratic machinery, "representative" councils advised the governor-general in matters of general policy. The first such body to be created in 1887 was the Superior Council of Indochina, composed exclusively of French members appointed by the governor-general. In 1911 it was replaced by the Council of Government, which included all the top French officials in the colonial government and five indigenous members, chosen by the governor-general from among active or retired indigenous civil servants, presumably one for each country of Indochina. The governor-general was compelled to consult with this body on the federal as well as the five individual budgets. The council's opinion, which was only advisory, was also required in matters concerning state loans or the imposition of new indirect taxes. Members of the council, which met but once a year, could submit "nonpolitical" wishes— political desiderata were simply not allowed—to the council's executive committee no sooner than six months after the closing of a previous session.

In 1928 that consultative body was superseded by the Grand Council of Economic and Financial Interests. This assembly had twenty-eight French and twenty-three indigenous members, eleven of whom—six French and five indigenous—were appointed by the governor-general and the remainder elected by the various chambers of commerce and agriculture. This council advised the governor-general on all matters pertaining to the economic and financial situation of the country, and, as with the Council of Government, its input was obligatory in the formulation of the general budget of Indochina. A less important assembly was the Defense Council, which helped the governor-general map strategy to defend the colony as well as plan public works designed to aid in that defense.

It has been said that Indochina was really ruled from Paris because the tenure of the governors-general was so short that they hardly had any time to devise an adequate and sufficiently encompassing policy to cover their own terms let alone a longer period. In effect, during the thirty years under consideration here, from 1900 to 1930, eleven governors—not counting the interim ones—shared the responsibility of managing the affairs of the colony. Only four of them had long-lasting influence: Paul Doumer (1897–1902), Albert Sarraut (1911–13 and 1917–19), Alexandre Varenne (1925–28), and Pierre Pasquier (1928–34). Doumer, as previously noted, was extremely able and active. Sarraut was a popular administrator so far as the indigenous people were concerned.[3] In a speech to the students of the Colonial School in Paris, who will graduate to become administrators in the many French colonies, an influential Vietnamese writer, Pham Quynh, eulogized him in the following terms:

Governor General Sarraut inaugurated the third period in the history of French colonization of Vietnam, a period characterized by a reciprocal confidence and an intimate cooperation between the government and the

Vietnamese elite . . . And such was the magical power of his words, continued Pham Quynh, and such was the charisma of his personality that the crisis I referred to earlier dissipated as if by enchantment. Mr. Sarraut has conquered for ever the heart of the Vietnamese.[4]

Sarraut was the one who first spoke, in his eloquent addresses, to the possibility of emancipation for the Indochinese countries. Indeed, in a 1919 speech, Governor-General Sarraut did not mince his words:

> Indochina has attained her majority, but she still carries restraints of an infancy which, given to support her forward march, are now too confining and imprison her movements. These restraints were created in the mother country and it is there that one must go to break them.[5]

It was also Sarraut who presided over the change from the policy of assimilation, which aimed at turning the colonized peoples into Frenchmen and imposing French institutions and culture on their societies, to the policy of association, which considered that colonies and the colonized peoples are distinct entities with their own cultures and institutions, albeit ultimately convertible to "civilization" and to the high status enjoyed by France and the French.[6] These liberal ideas did not make the French colonial community applaud Sarraut's achievements. Instead, they lavished on him their more bitter humor:

> a golden age reigned in Indochina. The indigenous peoples finally delivered by Sarraut from the abject regime of the mandarinate, defended by the illustrious Governor General against the French colonial brutes, acclaimed French domination with enthusiasm, proclaimed Sarraut to be the 60th incarnation of Buddha . . . In brief from point Ca Mau [the southernmost point of Cochinchina] to Lao Cai [a city on the Sino-Vietnamese border, so the northernmost point of Tonkin], people as one chanted the praises of Prince Albert.[7]

Varenne's appointment in 1925 was also warmly received by the indigenous people of Indochina, who saw in him a liberal administrator. Because of his background as a member of the Socialist Party of France, they concluded that he would be more attentive to their aspirations and demands.

The day Varenne arrived in Saigon after a long voyage by boat from Europe, a delegation of Vietnamese handed him a "notebook" in which they had written out all of the reforms they wanted him to implement in their favor. That document came to be known as the "Wish List of the Vietnamese People."[8] The document made their desiderata known to Governor-General

Varenne in a more courteous way than that accorded his predecessor.[9] A Vietnamese patriot threw a bomb at Governor-General Merlin (1923–25) during a dinner reception held at the Victoria Hotel in the Shameen concession of Canton. The explosive spared the French high official but killed five persons in his entourage.[10]

True to his socialist reputation, Varenne set in motion a number of judicious changes, the most important of which was the opening of higher positions in the colonial administration to indigenous candidates, without, however, collapsing the enormous disparities existing between the two pay scales. But even this mild reform was already too much for the colonials, who, the minute Varenne ventured to mention the word *independence* in talking about the distant future of Indochina, directed their lobby in Paris to seek his immediate recall.[11]

Pierre Pasquier, who replaced Varenne, was the first governor-general whose entire career unfolded in Indochina.[12] He climbed the colonial administrative ladder to its zenith in 1928, just as the most tumultuous period in the history of the Indochinese colony materialized. It was during his tenure that the uprising of the Nationalist Party of Vietnam (Viet Nam Quoc Dan Dang, VNQDD) took place; that the Indochinese Communist Party (ICP) was founded, following a series of workers' strikes and peasants' demonstrations throughout the colony; that the Soviets in the provinces of Nghe An and Ha Tinh in Central Vietnam were created; that the devastating effects of the world economic depression struck. Pasquier was, indeed, the first governor-general to deal with communism in Indochina. At the end of 1931, in a speech given to the Council of Government, Pasquier boasted about several accomplishments, foremost being the repression of communism:

> A severe and methodical repression of the trouble makers was necessary so as to effect within a minimal time the destruction of local centers of communistic infection, while measures that I called last year "measures of political hygiene" served to prevent that infection from spreading. In fact, for several months now, there has been a complete truce throughout the country.[13]

The Administration of the Five Political Entities

As noted earlier, each part of the French Indochinese Union had a separate administrative apparatus serviced by its own officers. Appointed by the governor-general, the lieutenant-governor of Cochinchina and the residents superior in the protectorates retained all powers in their own hands except the power to legislate, which rested with the governor-general. These heads of states ruled their bureaucracies and received the advice of the states' appointive and elective bodies.

In Cochinchina the elective body was the Colonial Council, created in 1867. In the 1920s it was composed of twenty-four full and eleven substitute members divided into the following categories: four French full members chosen by the Chambers of Commerce and Agriculture; ten French full and six French substitute members to be elected by French residents of Cochinchina who were at least twenty-one years old; ten indigenous full and five indigenous substitute members elected by a restricted electorate composed of French subjects—that is, indigenous people living in Cochinchina—who were twenty-five years of age or older, and, at the same time, landowners, industrialists, or businessmen who paid at least twenty piasters in annual taxes or were in possession of an academic degree attesting to at least four years of a secondary-level education. The candidates had to be able to speak French fluently, for, if elected, they would have to take part in the deliberations of the council, which were conducted only in French. Otherwise, they were prepared to play the role of what the Vietnamese people sarcastically characterized as "nodding councilors" or "yes councilors": they never said anything meaningful and acquiesced to everything that was presented to them for their approval. This council's power was essentially of a consultative nature as far as the annual budget was concerned. Nevertheless, it was in the council that some Vietnamese members played a significant role in the politics of their region. Names such as Nguyen Phan Long, Bui Quang Chieu, and Truong Van Ben surfaced often in newspapers because of their active participation in this body, although, according to one of them, as late as 1925, their role was to "vote for the local budget, without the ability to modify even the smallest detail," and their rights were rather well delimited: "We are allowed to make wishes . . ."[14]

In Tonkin and Annam, the protectorates had separate institutions for French citizens and indigenous people. The Councils of French Economic and Financial Interests were composed of twenty French members elected by the French and naturalized French citizens. They essentially gave their opinion on the annual budget. For the indigenous populations there were the indigenous consultative assemblies, called Chambers of the People's Representatives of Tonkin and Annam, created in 1908 (originally as the Consultative Chamber of Tonkin) and 1925, respectively. One-quarter of its members were appointed by the residents superior, the other three-quarters were divided into two categories. Those who belonged to the first category assumed the title of people's representatives because they were elected by taxpayers who were at the same time "notables" or degree holders in the ratio of one representative for every forty thousand persons. The others—businesses representatives—were licensed indigenous merchants or businessmen chosen by their peers in the ratio of one member for every one thousand licensed merchants. The government was required to consult the chambers only for the annual budget; it could also submit to their examination any other matters deemed useful. As for the representatives, they were able to submit "wishes" concerning the well-being of the indigenous community, as long as they were "nonpolitical." This rule was clearly not heeded, as history records some very heavily political suggestions, such as those contained in the speech given by Huynh Thuc Khang, a member of the Chamber of the People's Representatives of Annam in its third session, in 1928.[15]

The people of Tonkin had a longer experience with this kind of representative institution, and some voiced their disappointment in the relative powerlessness of their council. To assuage their concerns, the influential monthly magazine *Nam Phong* argued that the people who put their council on the same footing as the Congress in other advanced countries made a gross mistake in not trying to understand the level of development of the Vietnamese people.

> Our people cannot be compared with the civilized peoples in other countries; our people are in fact incapable of participating in the political affairs of their country . . . Look at what recently happened in Russia and China. These two countries have had an unfortunate encounter with democracy. What a catastrophe! How many difficulties they had to face and yet they have not succeeded in putting law and order back into their affairs. In political matters, our people may be compared to a child who has never gone out of the house. How then can you expect people to entrust it with the management of the household?[16]

There were finally what the French called "elected corps," whose opinion the colonial governors were required to seek in cases concerning the budget or other financial and economic matters. These were the Chambers of Commerce and Agriculture. Three Chambers of Commerce existed in the Indochinese colony: one in Cochinchina, at Saigon; and two in Tonkin, at Hanoi and Haiphong. Each had sixteen French members elected by French merchants twenty-one years or older and four indigenous members chosen by indigenous merchants twenty-five years or older. Indochina counted two Chambers of Agriculture with the same composition as the Chambers of Commerce; one was located in Cochinchina and the other in Tonkin. In addition, there were two Joint Chambers of Commerce and Agriculture, both of them located in Annam: one at Tourane, with fourteen French and four indigenous members—eight French and two indigenous members for commerce and six French and two indigenous for agriculture. The other Joint Chamber was situated at Vinh—the capital city of the province of Nghe An, in Central Vietnam—with seven French and three indigenous members. These chambers were often invited to send delegates to the various representative institutions of the colony.

The French Local Administration

The units of the French dominion were divided into a varying number of provinces. Cochinchina had twenty-one, Annam sixteen, and Tonkin twenty-three provinces and four military territories. French authority was represented in each province by a French administrator of the civil services. In Cochinchina he wore the title of chief administrator of the province or simply administrator; in Annam and in Tonkin the title was that of administrator resident of France or simply resident. The military territories were naturally governed by a French military commander.

In the protectorates of Tonkin and Annam the French local administration stopped at this level; we shall see later how the court in Hue maintained, particularly for Annam, a Vietnamese parallel administration. In the colony of Cochinchina, as no parallel indigenous administration was available, each province was in turn divided into smaller units, called administrative delegations, entrusted to a French or indigenous administrator with the title of delegate of the chief of the province. The delegate was appointed by the lieutenant governor, and his power was defined for him by the chief administrator of the province. The provincial chief as well as his delegates were also invested with judicial prerogatives.

Saigon was the only municipality administered by an elected council presided over by an elected mayor chosen from among the members of the city council. Council members were eighteen in number: twelve French and six Vietnamese. There were also four French and two Vietnamese substitute members. The Vietnamese members were elected by a highly chosen indigenous electorate of fewer than four thousand voters from a population of approximately three and a half million. To elect their twelve representatives the French had just under three thousand voters. Here, as in other official agencies in Indochina, the Vietnamese members of this council might as well have been French, because in order to become eligible the Vietnamese candidates had to be naturalized French citizens and speak French fluently, since all deliberations were conducted in French.[17] Cities such as Hanoi, Haiphong, and Tourane-Da Nang were governed by a French administrator of the Civil Services appointed by the governor-general.

The Indigenous Administration

The two protectorates of Annam and Tonkin maintained a monarchical administration centered in Hue, the capital city of Annam, and headed by none other than the emperor and his government,[18] which operated on a somewhat parallel track to the French government. The indigenous government thus reflected the shadow of the monarchical system that existed in Vietnam before the arrival of the French, except that Cochinchina had been removed from its jurisdiction, because it had been declared a colony of France—that is, a French territory—and hence placed under the direct and sole authority of the French.

Tonkin, a protectorate, should have been fully dependent upon the monarchy of Hue, but the French removed it from imperial control in a two-stage maneuver: first, they forced the emperor to delegate his sovereignty over Tonkin to a Vietnamese viceroy in 1886. The first such representative of the monarchy was an old mandarin of the court who had collaborated with the French colonial army in its pacification of northern Vietnam. He bore with what he considered to be "great pride and honor" the infamous reputation of having been the first among the Vietnamese mandarins to rally to the French cause as early as 1882.[19] The old mandarin expressed his feelings about the French presence in Vietnam in speeches and in several books. The title of a chapter in one of his books is "On the wisdom for our country to rely on France."[20] The second stage took place in 1897. With the formation of the Indochinese Union the French authorities deemed that the Tonkin protectorate should be severed even from the indirect control of the Vietnamese monarchy. They unilaterally suppressed the position of viceroy and conferred its prerogatives on the French resident superior of Tonkin. Tonkin was thus detached from the Vietnamese imperial sway.

Annam constituted thereafter the only territory subject to the direct rule of the Nguyen Dynasty, which the French refrained from revoking when they conquered the northern and central parts of Vietnam. Yet, even in Annam, the French subsequently found the parallel Vietnamese administration inconvenient. At the death of emperor Khai Dinh in 1925, the colonial government, citing the youth of his successor, Bao Dai, who, in the event, had remained in France to finish up his studies, forced a new arrangement on the regents in which France reserved almost all administrative prerogatives to the French resident superior in Annam. Other than his ceremonial powers, the most important among which was that of conferring titles to the tutelary deities in the villages, the Vietnamese emperor was left only with license to head the powerless administration of Annam, whose mandarins were paid with subsidies granted to him by the French colonial government.[21]

The Imperial Court of Hue

The city of Hue is the traditional residence of the Vietnamese ruler and constitutes the seat of the imperial government. Directly under the emperor were his four pillars of the empire, with the title of "Great Scholars." In addition to occupying the top positions in the government, these four Great Scholars also stood at the apex of the mandarinal hierarchy. They held its first rank, first degree, in a scale of nine ranks, from nine up to one, each rank divided into two degrees. The imperial cabinet was composed of seven ministries: Rites, Civil Service, Finances, Public Works, Public Instruction, War, and Justice. The position of minister was generally held by mandarins of at least rank 2, degree 1. After 1925 the French colonial authorities appointed three high French civil servants to supervise the work of the ministries. The Council of Ministers, the Co Mat, was furthermore placed under the presidency of the French resident superior in Annam. The ministers, even during the 1930s, were men still deeply rooted in the Confucian educational system, men who had learned little about the modern world or about the French.[22] Emperor Bao Dai, after he came back from France to ascend the throne in 1932, introduced some younger and more Westernized elements into his cabinet. Though young and/or Westernized, however, the "mandarinal mentality," which included marked rigidity, unresponsiveness, aloofness, arrogance, pomposity, and also venality, sooner or later surged to alienate them from the people. And, if not the mandarinal mentality itself, French supervision made sure that they would not be able to carry out sustained effort for the benefit of the kingdom and its people.

In addition to the ministries, the central imperial government also included a number of agencies responsible for various administrative and specialized functions. There were, for example, the Council of Regency, in place to take care of the imperial government during the minority of Emperor Bao Dai, from 1925 to 1932; the Censorate, which supervised the civil service; the Imperial Family Office, which dealt with the affairs of members of the imperial family; the Astronomy Office, which established the calendar with dates for the annual agricultural cycle of activities; and the History Office, which compiled the imperial historical chronicles and preserved the national archives.

From 1900 to 1930, while eleven French governors-general took turns managing the affairs of Vietnam, only three emperors successively sat on the throne of Vietnam. Emperor Thanh Thai's reign (1889–1907) coincided partially with Governor-General Doumer's tenure. The latter forced the emperor to sign an ordinance recognizing the right of French citizens to own land in Annam, thereby opening up the entire region to the regime of land concessions to French settlers.[23] It was Doumer who removed from the imperial government its financial independence: after 1897 the colonial government collected the taxes the people of Annam owed to the emperor. The resident superior then transferred to the imperial treasury annually a sum of money sufficient for the maintenance of the imperial family, the imperial services, and the civil service. The French, in other words, put the imperial government on an allowance.[24] Relations between the emperor and the French administration thereafter became so tense and so vicious that, in order to get rid of their antagonist, the French administrators launched the rumor to the effect that the emperor was not in full control of his faculties and that he had been subjecting his entourage to sadistic actions.[25] In any event the French authorities removed the emperor from the throne in 1907, sent him to Vung Tau in southern Vietnam for a while, and then exiled him to the island of La Reunion, which was at the time a colony of France situated on the southeast end of Madagascar, in the Indian Ocean.

Duy Tan, his son, was nine years old when the French designated him to succeed his father (1907–16). Then World War I broke out, during which France was able to maintain full military control over Indochina and thereby disrupted Vietnamese society tremendously in requiring that more than 100,000 recruits be sent from the colony to help the metropole fight its war. Numerous anticolonial movements took on the French administration at this time. One of them, under the direction of the well-known scholar-writer Tran Cao Van, in 1916 succeeded in enlisting the participation of the young emperor, who was poised to issue an appeal to the people calling on them to fight the French. The plot was uncovered by the French Security Services before its proponents were able to act. Emperor Duy Tan was then helped out of the imperial citadel of Hue by his supporters into the surrounding mountainous regions, ready to lead a drive against the colonial power. The French arrested him two days later and sent him to join his father in exile on the island of La Reunion.[26]

Khai Dinh, the next emperor (1916–25), was a pallid figure, subservient in every sense to the colonial master. If he had distinguished himself, it was in three ways. First of all, his mausoleum, which without doubt reflected his state of mind, was built in the most complicated conception of Euro–East Asian rococo style imaginable. Clouds, dragons, flowers, leaves, animals, insects, all made up with multicolor shards cemented to ceilings and walls, overwhelm the visitors as they enter the main pavilion. After their eyes are accustomed to the dim light of the innermost part of the mausoleum, they find themselves in the place where the emperor is supposed to be interred, face to face with a bronze statue of the emperor, dressed in his official imperial apparel, sitting rigidly on his throne, under a huge cement awning. The entire edifice stands in stark contrast to the serenity, peace, and harmony so characteristic of the tombs of his forefathers of the same dynasty. A journalist who visited the mausoleum offered this description:

> I walked up more than a hundred steps; my legs were about to drop out of my body; so I sat down right on the ground; while panting, I looked in the four corners around me and could not prevent my tears from flowing, thinking about the wasteful architecture of this building, wasteful in human labor as well as in resources of the land. I then compared this mausoleum with the house where I spent last night in Quang Nam. The house had no doors; only two ramshackle bamboo beds, a few rags serving as blanket. The wife lay on one of the beds, sick and moaning, without

any medicine. The husband curled up on the earthen floor against the warm stove, allowing me, their guest, to have the second bed. I then said to myself: "Really the Creator is playing tricks on people."[27]

His second distinction consisted of his trip to France in 1922 to lend local color to the Marseille Colonial Exhibition. The trip so revolted the nationalist Phan Chu Trinh that he composed his famous condemnation of the monarchical system, in which he listed seven reasons why Khai Dinh ought to be bodily removed from the throne of Vietnam.[28] His third notable act was to die in 1925, while his son, whom he had left in France during his infamous 1922 trip in the care of a former French resident superior in Annam, was still in minority. These circumstances incited the French colonial government to force on the regents the 1925 convention mentioned earlier that robbed the monarchy of its last vestiges of authority.[29]

The Vietnamese Local Administration

The protectorates of Annam and Tonkin had a double local administration at the provincial level: the French resident had jurisdiction over Europeans or other non-Vietnamese citizens; he also supervised the work of the Vietnamese mandarins who managed the affairs of the Vietnamese people. The indigenous officials were appointed and compensated by the court in Hue.

The more important provinces had four Vietnamese administrators: a governor (*tong doc*); a vice governor (*tuan phu*); a treasurer (*bo chanh*), who attended to all regulatory matters of the province, particularly the perception of taxes; and a justice officer (*an sat*), who cared for all affairs of justice. Smaller provinces were generally placed under the control of the two last officers or, less often, a vice governor and a justice officer.

Provinces were divided into prefectures (*phu*) and districts (*huyen*) governed by their respective chiefs (*tri phu* or *tri huyen*). Districts were in their turn divided into villages, administered by notables chosen by their own people. These notables were not civil servants and, therefore, did not receive any salary from the government, although they were responsible to the colonial authorities for the amount of taxes to be levied in the territories under their jurisdiction. The idea was that they had to pay for the difference themselves if they could not levy the amount of taxes assigned to them.[30]

The Indochinese General Services

The governmental agencies responsible for the development of transportation and communication, the maintenance of law and order, the management of financial needs, the supervision of the educational program, the administration of the judicial system, as well as the regulation of the health services were called the Indochinese General Services. There were no set rules as to the ethnic composition of each of these services, although the general practice was that decision-making positions were strictly reserved for French citizens. Each service was divided into several bureaus, and it was expected that the chiefs of these bureaus would be French. They were called general services because their jurisdiction covered the entire colonial possession with branches in the five different parts of Indochina; their headquarters, however, were located in Hanoi and were placed under the direct supervision of the governor-general.

The Army and the Police

The armed forces stationed in Indochina were part of the French Colonial Army, which was divided into five groups. Group 1 was assigned to duty in Indochina, and the other four were stationed in the other French colonies. The Indochinese Group was placed under the command of a French officer of the rank of general, assisted by a colonel, a lieutenant-colonel, and four bureaus. The commanding general was appointed by the minister of colonies in consultation with the Ministry of Defense. He belonged to the governor-general's cabinet and was also a member of the Defense Council, which advised the latter on matters concerning the military situation in Indochina and also on projects of public works necessary for the defense of the colony. The armed forces in Indochina consisted of the infantry, artillery, air force (which the French called *aéronautique*), and navy. The air force was both minimal and recent;[31] it consisted of four escadrilles, with six to nine planes in each, under the command of a lieutenant-colonel. In spite of their small number, the planes played a very important role in the repression of the numerous rebellions of the 1930s.[32]

Ground troops were divided into four different sections: (1) the Annam-Tonkin section, composed of five European, one mixed, and eight indigenous battalions; (2) the Cochinchina-Cambodia section, with three European and five indigenous battalions, together with three mixed groups of artillery; and (3) the Mountain section, composed of two European and seven indigenous battalions. To all this was added one regiment of artillery, which constitutes the fourth section. The total number of men under arms present at any one time in Indochina would therefore reach about twenty-six thousand (presuming each battalion had one thousand men).[33] The proportion between European and indigenous troops was that for every one European soldier there were three indigenous ones, which puts the number of Europeans military at about eighty-seven hundred.[34] Notice the word used throughout this passage is *European* and not *French,* because few of the European troops were French. They were called European to distinguish them from the indigenous. In fact, many of them were not even European. They came from the other French colonies: Algerians, Moroccans, Tunisians, Senegalese, etc. A few were ethnically Europeans: the majority of them were Germans who belonged to the notorious terror-striking section of the French army, that is, its Foreign Legion, which was called upon whenever there was resistance to be crushed.

No cavalry came to Indochina. The navy's presence grew to be insignificant compared to the role it had played in the conquest of South Vietnam and Cambodia. The navy's entire mission was located in the naval yards of construction and repairs known as the Arsenal of Saigon. All ships anchored at the Port of Saigon when not on patrol duty along the coast. It is interesting to note that the Indochinese Communist Party recruited its first members in Cochinchina from among the workers in this arsenal. Ton Duc Thang, for example, who was to become the president of the Democratic Republic of Vietnam after Ho Chi Minh's death in 1969, was a worker there and had involved himself intimately in several of its strikes.[35]

The expenses of the armed forces stationed in Indochina were defrayed by the budget of the metropole; these expenses were, however, reimbursed by the general budget of Indochina under the disguise of "contributions" that were imposed by the French Ministry of War on the various colonies that received military protection from the mother country. The contributions from Indochina to the budget of France for military expenditures for the year 1931 amounted to eighty-three million French francs, which represented a tremendous increase over the year 1920, when that contribution was only fifty million. In turn, this figure equaled 10 percent of the general budget for all of Indochina.[36]

The French colonial army stationed in Indochina was supplemented by the militia, which consisted of a variety of indigenous troops placed naturally under the command of French officers. These were called Indochinese Riflemen, Indigenous Guard, Urban Guard, Partisans of Tonkin, Civil Guard of Cochinchina, etc. The Vietnamese referred to them as "soldiers in blue, red or yellow loin-cloth" according to the color of the piece of cloth they wore on top of their shorts. The "Yellows" were the imperial guards at the palace in Hue, charged with protecting the emperor and his family. The "Blues" and the "Reds" played a critical role in the early pacification campaigns along with French soldiers.

The "gendarmerie" may be viewed as a glamorized police force, hybrid between cavalry and police. It was authorized to arrest military men as well as civilians. Two detachments of gendarmerie were organized in the entire territory of Indochina, one at Hanoi and another at Saigon. Each was commanded by an officer with the rank of captain. The detachments were divided into "arrondissements" and further into posts. Tonkin had two arrondissements, located at Hanoi and Haiphong, with thirty-two posts. Cochinchina had also two arrondissements, at Saigon and Cantho, with forty-one posts. The Indochinese gendarmerie formed an integral part of the metropolitan gendarmerie and enjoyed the same privileges and advantages as their counterparts in France, unlike the army and other forces, which had a colonial status. The gendarmerie also possessed a contingent of "foot gendarmes," called the auxiliaries of the gendarmerie, a force of roughly twelve thousand men composed of indigenous people, recruited on the basis of voluntary enrollment.

The police and security forces were composed exclusively of indigenous people; it was extremely rare to encounter a French or nonindigenous policeman unless he was a station chief, or what was called a commissar of police.[37] There were police stations in every district of every province and in every provincial capital city; the heads of these posts were invariably French. The police, and particularly the security agents, inspired great fear in the hearts of the Vietnamese. Elders constantly reminded the less wise not to talk politics to anyone lest he be an "agent provocateur" working for the security services. The Saigon police station and security unit located on Catinat Street, not far from the Catholic cathedral, stood as a symbol of torture and death for generations of Vietnamese. Much later, after the building had been modified and converted into one of the ministries of the Republic of Vietnam's government, people still floated the rumor that, while walking next to its forbidding fences, on calm and dark nights, one could still hear the howls, bawls, wails, moans, and groans of the victims amid the yells and shouts of their interrogators.

The Judicial System

The judicial system reflected the complex nature of the apparatus of French control of Indochina, made up as it was of a colony and four protectorates.[38] Furthermore, one must distinguish between justice for the French, justice for the Vietnamese, and justice for both when they were parties to a common legal entanglement. French tribunals were competent to hear all cases concerning French citizens or those who were accorded the privilege of being considered French citizens or French subjects, that is, the inhabitants of French colonies and foreigners. Some of these tribunals had jurisdiction over more than one state in Indochina. For example, there were only two Courts of Appeals: one in Hanoi, covering the northern part of Indochina, Tonkin, northern Annam, and northern Laos; and the other in Saigon, for the remainder of the union. Crimes committed in these two same regions by French citizens or foreigners were judged by two separate Criminal Courts, established also in Hanoi and Saigon. Included in the list of French tribunals were special courts called Criminal Commissions. These special courts were established with the aim of ensuring a "rapid repression of crimes and derelicts committed against the security of the protectorate or against the advancement of French colonization by the indigenous people or those who were considered as such."[39]

A typical Criminal Commission was composed of a high-level French administrator who functioned as the president of the commission; he was assisted by the chief of the province in which the infraction occurred, a prosecutor (with the title of prosecutor of the republic) and a French officer with the rank of at least captain in the French army stationed in Indochina. Such commissions, in fact, were created in several provinces of Tonkin in the 1930s in order to cope with the many insurrections then sprouting.

In the colony of Cochinchina crimes or derelicts committed against the security of the colony together with any other common crimes perpetrated by Vietnamese or other Asians were heard by four French Criminal Courts located in Saigon, My Tho, Vinh Long, and Can Tho. No Vietnamese courts operated in Cochinchina. Regular tribunals of original jurisdiction existed in important urban centers. Justices of the peace held court in even less important places. It is not necessary to add that all judges, of whatever level of jurisdiction, were French citizens. The legal code used in the courts was simply the French penal code modified somewhat for use in Cochinchina. As for civil matters, the courts resorted to a number of Vietnamese traditional codes known as the Le Dynasty (1427–1791) code,[40] or the code of Gia Long promulgated during the reign of the emperor of that name (1802–20),[41] and also to customary law, and finally to the decrees and laws passed by the French colonial government of Indochina and, particularly, of Cochinchina.

In Annam Vietnamese were brought before the same officials who administered the protectorate in the name of the Vietnamese emperor. This means that, at the lowest level of jurisdiction, the *tri huyen* (district chief executive) or the *an sat* (district justice officer) were empowered to hear all legal cases brought to them, however serious or frivolous.[42] These courts used the Gia Long code, which indistinctly blended civil and penal matters. All sentences, however, had to be reviewed by the chiefs of the provinces in which the districts were situated: the *tuan phu* or *tong doc*. They then had to be approved by the French provincial residents and ultimately forwarded to the French resident superior in Hue. Only the more important cases were submitted to the emperor. When the courts in Annam applied the Gia Long code to cases involving revolutionary Vietnamese who had engaged in anti-French activities, an ambiguous situation obtained. An editorial in a Saigon newspaper even suggested that Vietnamese courts should not hear these cases, because the law was not calibrated to the transgression:

When the Vietnamese mandarins judge these cases, they have to apply the Vietnamese legal code. We do not know for sure what article of that code they are applying. Very probably they used the article pertaining to the "ten malicious crimes." For only that article provides for heavy sentences. We seem to remember that the "ten malicious crimes" article carries provisions similar to the case under consideration which includes "grave rebellion" or "treason against the country." These were probably the crimes the Court accused the people of committing. But the clause "grave rebellion" applies very clearly to the people who gather together with the aim of overthrowing the dynasty, or the people who raise armies to fight against the imperial court, while the clause "treason against the country" explicitly defines treason as a move against one's own country in favor of another. If indeed the people have acted in these ways, then they would have plainly transgressed against the "ten malicious crimes." What, in fact, did the Revolutionary Youth Association [the case under consideration] want to accomplish? Did they plot to overthrow the emperor or fight against the Court? No. Did they intend to betray their country, Vietnam? Of course not![43]

In Tonkin the judicial system was certainly no less cumbersome. Justice was assured by a special judiciary staff placed, as was all administrative personnel, under the control of the provincial residents and ultimately under the resident superior. At the lowest level of the system a tribunal of the first instance, presided over by the chief executive of the district, heard all simple police, civil, or commercial cases. At the provincial level were the tribunals of second instance, composed of the chief executive and the highest indigenous official in the province. Finally, in the capital city of Hanoi sat a Court of Appeal, in which was included a high indigenous mandarin of the rank of tong doc. The codes used in all these courts were composite, with the Gia Long code being the most important. By the 1920s, however, the colonial administration had completed and was introducing the use of a new civil code.[44]

The Financial Structure

The general budget of the Indochinese Union was supported by indirect taxes, and each of the five parts of the union had its own separate budgets financed by direct taxes. At least, that was the prevailing principle. Direct taxes consisted mainly of taxes on land, on certain incomes, and the poll, or "head," taxes. The last was imposed on all indigenous men between the ages of eighteen and forty-five.[45] Indirect taxes were revenues from customs and monopolies, from charges imposed on official documents and on commercial and industrial licenses. The colonial government derived a substantial amount of revenue from the monopolistic sale of opium, alcohol, and salt. Up to World War II a major part of the general budget of French Indochina was provided for by those three monopolies.[46] This meant that the government of Indochina retained the sole privilege and right to the production and distribution of those three commodities, while the people of Indochina had to ensure their consumption.

All opium available in Indochina was officially sold by the colonial government, which purchased it from wherever it could find it: Yunnan in China, Burma, India, Thailand. Opium poppies do not grow well on the Vietnamese plains, so the native population's contribution to the opium monopoly was, therefore, reduced only to the consumption of the goods. The government did not spare any effort to encourage that consumption, and it established a large number of opium dens, which were the only legal places where people could consume or purchase opium. It fixed the sale price before distributing it to the retailers. People addicted to the drug could buy it from these official outlets, which operated under license from the government. In addition to all the benefits derived from the sale of the drug, the government also collected the licensing fees.

The monopoly on alcohol involved a more complicated operation and assumed different patterns in the various regions of Indochina. On the whole the difference lay mainly in the fact that the alcohol was not imported but produced in the country and that the government did not directly handle the sale of the beverage, as was the case with opium. Instead, it farmed out first the distribution of the merchandise and later the distilling of the alcohol as well. These privileges went generally to French companies, which were allowed to fix the price as they saw fit. The alcohol monopoly did not produce revenues as significant as those generated by opium, because the distillers and dealers channeled a major part of the profit into their own coffers. To the indigenous people, the arrangement brought several disadvantages. First, it wiped out all competition: small businesses could no longer operate once manufacturing was contracted to designated distillers. Retailers had to be licensed by the government: only stores with the plaque RA (Régie Alcool [Alcohol Monopoly]) affixed to their facade could offer the commodity for sale that had to be handled according to the conditions spelled out very minutely by the dealers. Consequently, the consumers had no choice.

The third monopoly, that on salt, was no less burdensome to the consumers. At first production was left free as long as producers sold their output to the government. Then, as the government found out that it was not equipped to handle the necessary storage and transportation of the merchandise, it farmed out distribution to private firms, as long as they were owned and operated by French citizens. Then, as even these French firms could not efficiently deal with the venture, they turned distribution over to small retailers. The presence of intermediaries had the net result of driving up the price and also produced shortages, owing to its misdistribution. The consumers had to pay the price for their government's trial and error.

It has been said that the colonial administration often fixed quotas for the quantity of opium and alcohol that each province in the colony was to consume in a given period. The charge is difficult to substantiate, but it is fair to say that the profit from the monopolies, combined with those of Customs, supplied more than 83 percent of all the ordinary revenues from indirect taxes. In other words, the revenues from the monopolies represented more than three-fourths of the general budget for the entire Indochinese colony.[47]

The governor-general had the prerogative to float loans or bonds in order to install infrastructures that would serve the entire Indochinese Union rather than any particular region and benefit the general budget. The colonial government could also issue bonds on behalf and in favor of the French government, as it did during World War I so as to help the mother country prosecute its war against Germany.[48]

The direct taxes that financed the local budgets of the different units of the union, as noted earlier, came from taxes on the land. Beyond these basic taxes everything else under the sun seemed to the Vietnamese people to be taxed, even their persons. Although the head taxes represented an apparently small amount of money in itself, it was nonetheless common for the majority of the Vietnamese people—who were chronically short of cash—to go through untold hardship so as to come up with the levy. Furthermore, for every living Vietnamese it also symbolized a patently humiliating means by which the colonial authorities controlled and exploited the people. Every indigenous person, aged from eighteen to forty-five years old, had to pay the head taxes in order to obtain an identity card, which they had to carry at all times. A person without an identity card stood at great risk. The police could demand the piece of paper anytime, anywhere, from anyone; not having it could mean jail and fines.[49]

Another local imposition consisted of corvée labor. There were no fixed regulations with regard to this form of duty. It was exacted from the people of that village anytime the government undertook public projects in its vicinity. The people then had the choice of neglecting their own chores to work on the project or paying so that others replaced them.

The Educational System

Education, as everything else, was centralized with the formation of the Indochinese Union. Educational policies were taken up in the Consultative Council of Public Instruction, which was created in 1889. All of its members were appointed by the governor-general from among high officials of the government or persons in the education field. The council, however, did not bring about any innovation and on the whole reproduced for the entire union the structures set up twenty years earlier in the colony of Cochinchina, which started to operate soon after the annexation. The colonial authorities there had to train quickly an entire body of agents who would be capable of helping the French administrators as interpreters, since the latter did not know the local language. The French also needed a literate staff to work in the numerous new offices established by the new government. The need was aggravated by the fact that many Vietnamese mandarins chose to withhold their service to the colonial authorities by isolating themselves in their villages or by moving away from Cochinchina into yet unoccupied territories of Annam and Tonkin.

The first emphasis of the French educational enterprise in Vietnam was the teaching of the national romanized writing system, the *quoc ngu,* which simultaneously accomplished three goals for them. It was very easy to learn; it weaned the Vietnamese away from their traditional mentors, the Chinese; and it also estranged them from their monarchical government, since this government still clung to the official use of Chinese characters. French was also being taught in the first years of primary school. By the time of the conquest of the remaining parts of Vietnam, in 1884, more than eight hundred primary schools had been established in Cochinchina, many of them simple constructions sheltering one or two classrooms filled with a handful of pupils.[50]

It was Governor-General Paul Beau who gave education a big push forward, when, in 1905, he instituted a General Directorate of Public Instruction in Hanoi and an additional directorate in each of the regions of the union. The next year, he created the Commission for the Improvement of Public Instruction in Indochina and entrusted it with the mission of defining a program of studies for the schools in the colony.[51] The commission's report found that the Indochinese colonial educational system, which, in its general outlines, pretty much followed the French system, needed to be divided into three degrees: the elementary, comprising the first three years; the primary, the next three years; and the superior primary, the following four years.[52] Toward the end of his tenure as governor-general, Albert Sarraut got the opportunity to overhaul the educational structure, when, in 1919, the Vietnamese royal government terminated its traditional system of Confucian learning and mandarinal examinations, the medium of which was classical Chinese. With some modifications here and there the Sarraut reform lent the Indochinese education the general characteristics it was to retain for a long time. Sarraut devised completely separate and distinctive programs of instruction for French citizens and native peoples. The French system, as could be expected, was the simple replica of the one used in the metropole. The main feature of the indigenous system was its division into four levels. At the end of each level students had to pass a final examination or be prevented from pursuing further studies. In effect, as in France itself, education in Indochina became an extremely selective process. Its main purpose was to train a very tiny elite that could assist the government all the way up to an advanced level. Whether that was the avowed purpose of the plan or not, it so happened that the majority of children quit school after the six years of the primary cycle—or sometimes even after the elementary phase, which covered only the first three years of school—as a result of both the

French scheme and their own society's exigencies. In the agricultural society of Vietnam people could ill afford to allow an able-bodied youngster to while away his time on school benches: his rightful place was either in the rice fields, all the more so if he was not too successful in his academic endeavors, or behind a very small and lowly desk in a governmental office as soon as he acquired the necessary diploma. Within the existing context, then, the system was set up in such a way as to encourage its students to abandon their schooling.

The first level conferred an elementary degree following three years' schooling, during which the Vietnamese students learned how to read and write *quoc ngu* and were taught rudiments of civics, agriculture, hygiene, and "traditional" ethics. At the end of the third year they took an examination for the Certificate of Elementary Indigenous Studies; if they failed, they had to drop out of school. During the school year of 1929–30, 223,511 children were enrolled in the three classes of the elementary level. In the fourth year they entered the primary cycle, which also lasted three years, during which they were introduced intensively to the French language, with the aim that they be able to understand it well enough to study the other disciplines, which were taught in French during the last year of the cycle. At this stage the teachers, who were all Vietnamese, used a very simple French, which they mixed with a great deal of Vietnamese. In addition to basic introductions to geography and history, students also learned a few hundred Chinese characters. At the end of the sixth year students again sat for an examination in order to obtain the degree called the Certificate in Franco-Vietnamese Studies, which was given out selectively. For the year 1925, of 40,367 candidates to the examination, only 4,399 were successful, a little better than 1 in 9. After passing that examination, candidates still had to take a highly competitive entrance examination to enroll in one of the rare secondary schools in order to start the next level of education. Statistics show that for Cochinchina alone, in the session of 1928, of the 2,110 candidates, only 273 obtained admission into public secondary schools or teachers' colleges.[53] In the 1930s the entire territory of Indochina, which had a total of 20 million people, had fewer than ten public secondary schools, including those primarily reserved for the children of French citizens. Luckily, a few private institutions, managed mainly by missionaries, supplemented this figure. Because governmental regulations concerning the establishment of private schools were extremely rigid,[54] not many private schools, besides the religious ones, developed. Only the latter obtained governmental licenses with ease, for, in general, they were sponsored, first of all, by the Catholic Church, with their teaching staff composed almost uniquely of French citizens, and, second, they were so well financed that they could satisfy all the material conditions imposed by the authorities.

All classes at the secondary level were conducted in French. This level consisted of seven year of studies; it was a two-tiered affair. The first tier consisted of four years, during which, in addition to the usual disciplines, students continued to work on their own language, together with a thousand or so of Chinese characters that would allow them to "penetrate the complexities of the moral philosophies of the Far East." The administration, in effect, labeled this level of education "Classic Learning," or "Humanities of the Extreme-Orient." At the end of the fourth year students sat for an examination to qualify for the Diploma of Superior Franco-Indigenous Studies, known popularly as the Diploma. For 80 percent of the successful candidates, this examination represented the highest academic degree they would pursue. They now could choose among a vast array of possibilities. They could simply go to work, as both the public and private sectors were ready and even eager to employ them and paid rather good salaries. Diploma holders definitely belonged to the chosen few who stood in the upper stratum of indigenous society. Indeed, the Vietnamese gave that examination a name, *thanh chung,* that translates into something like "ultimate success." In addition to a good and prestigious position, the Diploma could also be used as the key into many rich families with daughters of marriageable age. Novels and short stories of the period are replete with stories of "gold-digging" adventures, of degree holders who tried to marry rich, that usually ended in tragedies.

As if these structures were not complicated enough, the French colonial government also established Teacher Training Schools, or Ecoles Normales, that ran parallel with the four first years of the secondary cycle. Students in these schools received scholarships from the government and were consequently selected through rigorous entrance examinations. Their program of study included everything taught in the regular secondary schools as well as courses in psychology, pedagogy, and teaching practice. The duration of their training was also four years. At the end of those four years students sat for the regular Diploma of Superior Franco-Indigenous Studies as well as another examination that granted them a teaching certificate.

Those who wanted to continue their studies could go to the University of Hanoi and gain admission into one of the professional schools that did not require students to have finished the secondary cycle, such as the School of Public Works, Commerce, Agriculture and Forestry, Post and Telegraph, Fine Arts, or Veterinary Medicine. After three or four years of studies students found easily employment in their chosen profession.

Students who remained in secondary schools—very few of them, indeed—had to study for three more years and, if they succeeded in two further examinations, would obtain the Brevet of Capacity of the Secondary Level of Public Instruction, better known as the Local Baccalaureate. Up to 1930 that degree could only lead to the University of Hanoi, where, without having to go through any entrance examination, students could register for either the School of Medicine and Pharmacy, the Superior School of Pedagogy, or the School of High Studies in Legal and Administrative Sciences, which later became the School of Law. After 1930, when the local baccalaureate was assimilated to the metropolitan baccalaureate, its holders could, if they so desired and if they could afford it, pursue their studies in a French University or in any institution of higher learning of any other French colony.

It was Governor-General Beau who laid the foundations for an institution of higher learning in Hanoi, which would constitute the fourth level of the system: the level of superior learning. The School of Medicine and Pharmacy was the first created to train native medical assistants. It was followed by the establishment of a School of Pedagogy to train teachers for the newly established secondary schools. Several other schools—the last being the School of Legal and Administrative Studies—were added. Together the schools, however, did not add up to a genuine university. Rather, they constituted an ensemble of technical and professional institutions. In any case, they taught only a handful of students: in 1930 there were 504 students in all the faculties and professional schools of the University of Hanoi.

Public Works

Public works were undertaken by the General Directorate of Public Works, an office of the government of the union, with branches called Directorates of Public Works, in each of the countries of Indochina. The directorates took care of the transportation infrastructure and also canal and irrigation networks.

In 1930 the railroads, started under Paul Doumer, reached the sum of some 2,500 kilometers laid tracks.[55] Running along the coast of Vietnam, the 1,225 kilometer-long Trans-Indochinese connected Hanoi to Saigon, except for the portion between Nha Trang and Da Nang (Tourane). Another line (859 km) connected Haiphong, the main port city of northern Vietnam, with the capital city of the province of Yunnan in southwestern China: Yunnanfu, via Hanoi and Lao Cai, in the mountains. This is the region of China that interested both France and Britain in the second half of the nineteenth century. It was to secure an exclusive passage into this so-called economically untapped part of China that France first wanted to control navigation on the Mekong River in 1863. On discovering that the Mekong was not wholly navigable, France then cast her eyes on the Red River of northern Vietnam in 1873 and in 1883. Britain for the same reason annexed the northern regions of Burma in 1883. With this Haiphong-Yunnanfu rail line the French finally realized their dream of serving as, and controlling, the bridge between the outside world and China, albeit its southwestern backwater areas. The French also planned to connect Haiphong and the province of Guangxi, another backwater Chinese province. By 1930 the line was yet incomplete. From Hanoi it went midway between Haiphong and Nanning, the capital city of Guangxi, and stopped at Na Cham. In south Vietnam the Trans-Indochinese continued toward the Mekong Delta with the extension of the Saigon-Mytho line, seventy kilometers long. Another line joined Phan Rang (Tour Cham) and Dalat, sixty-five kilometers, signaling the beginning of the colonial penetration into, and exploitation of, the mountain regions of south and central Vietnam. These kilometers of railroads were laid at the total cost of 162 million piasters.

Roads and bridges cost slightly more than railroads but covered a much longer distance. Up to the end of 1931, 24,493 kilometers of roadways had been built, of which 15,246 were paved at the cost of 175 million piasters. In the 1920s, 22,000 motor vehicles rolled on these roads and bridges, a ratio of more than one kilometer of road per vehicle. The layout of the railroads and roads compel the conclusion that they served not only economic needs but clearly military exigencies as well.

Besides transportation, the General Directorate of Public Works also took care of hydraulic works, such as the maintenance of the dykes along the Red River in north Vietnam, the laying out of an irrigation network principally in central Vietnam, the dredging of rivers in the Mekong Delta, the draining of marshes also in southern Vietnam, and the digging of canals to connect navigable rivers. By 1930 the colonial administration had dredged more than 180 million cubic meters of soil, which represented a larger volume than was involved in the piercing of the Suez Canal. It dug up 650 kilometers of principal canals—those which are at least 40 meters wide and 2.5 meters deep—and 2,500 kilometers of secondary canals. Thirty-five thousand hectares of land were reclaimed from the marshes, and almost 2 million hectares of fields were cleared and put into production. From 1917 to 1930 the government spent more than 19 million piasters on the maintenance and construction of the dykes. Irrigation lines capable of combating drought watered more than 162,000 hectares, mostly in central Vietnam. Other works were set up to irrigate an additional 340,000 hectares.

Colonial Vietnam

Although French occupation of Vietnam dated from the 1860s for Cochinchina and the 1880s for Annam and Tonkin, its impact did not start to show its imprint until the beginning of the twentieth century. The first three decades of the new century introduced into the three countries of Vietnam changes of a tremendous magnitude to every aspect of life. The presence of a few thousand foreigners occupying the highest levels of the administrative, social, economic, and cultural systems could not fail to signal to the indigenous peoples that, although the monarchical government was still functioning in Tonkin and Annam, their country had ceased to be isolated and detached from the rest of the world. The cycle of guided modernization and Westernization has hit Vietnam in every aspect of her traditional making, putting into question every article of her millenary faith. A new generation trained in the newly established Western school system or even in French universities took over from the Confucian scholar elite class the mission of maintaining the determination to do away with colonialism. Their means may be new, but the motivation springs from the same conditions: the humiliation, alienation, and inferiority complex that could only be cleansed through a cathartic struggle.

Notes

1. See Paul Doumer, *L'Indochine française, Souvenirs* (Paris, 1905) and *Situation de l'Indochine (1897–1901)* (Hanoi, 1902). This bridge, now called Long Bien, testifies to the statement made by some French geographers and historians that France brought the Indochinese colonies from the vegetal to the metal civilization.

2. This entire section on the French administration in Indochina is largely based on Jean de Galembert, *Les Administrations et les services publics indochinois, Gouvernement de l'Indochine (Office Indochinois de la Propagande),* 2d ed., rev. and enlarged by Erard, administrator of civil services in Indochina (Hanoi, 1931); on Sylvain Lévi, ed., *Indochine: Documents officiels,* Exposition coloniale internationale de Paris, Commissariat général (Paris, 1931); and on Eugène Teston and Maurice Percheron, *L'Indochine moderne. Encyclopédie administrative, touristique, artistique et économique* (Paris, 1931). Two old but by no means obsolete thorough descriptions and evaluations of the French colonial system in Indochina can be found in Virginia Thompson, *French Indochina* (New York, 1937); and Thomas Ennis, *French Policy and Development in Indochina* (Chicago, 1936). Joseph Buttinger gives a more recent assessment in his *The Dragon Embattled,* (2 vols., New York, 1964). An even more recent and detailed study is offered by D. Hemery and P. Brocheux in their copublication: *Indochine: la colonisation ambiguë (1858–1945)* (Paris, 1995).

3. See Albert Sarraut, *La Mise en valeur des colonies françaises* (Paris, 1923); and Phillip T. Thornton, "Albert Sarraut, a Metropolitan in the Colonies: Indochina, 1911–1919" (Ph.D. diss., History, University of Hawaii, Honolulu, 1980).

4. Pham Quynh, *L'Evolution intellectuelle et morale des Annamites depuis l'établissement du protectorat français* (Paris, 1922). Talk given at the Colonial School in Paris on Friday, 31 May 1922.

5. See Thornton, "Albert Sarraut," 201.

6. See Raymond F. Betts, *Assimilation and Association in French Colonial Theory, 1890–1914* (New York, 1961).

7. See *L'Opinion,* 12 July 1913 as quoted in Thornton, "Albert Sarraut," 201.

8. See Document 10, in this volume.

9. See William Frederick, "Alexandre Varenne and Politics in Indochina, 1925–1926," in Walter Vella, ed., *Aspects of Vietnamese Culture,* 96–159 (Honolulu, 1973).

10. See *La Presse Indochinoise,* 22 and 26 June 1924, which gave several ac-

counts of the assassination attempt on the person of Governor-General Merlin during a dinner reception held in the Hotel Victoria in Canton. Merlin wrote himself one of the accounts.

11. Later on, Varenne had a rather interesting way to explain Vietnamese anti-colonial feelings. In an interview published by a newspaper, *Le Petit Bleu,* of 6 June 1930, he said the following: "Recently I told a senator colleague of mine who asked me to explain to him what was happening in Indochina: Suppose one day France was conquered by Japan which will send you, my dear Senator and former Minister, to work as a third class clerk in some unknown administration! I am certain you will find it of the worst taste and you will turn communist with great enthusiasm! That, my dear, is the Indochinese drama. That is more or less like that if it were not exactly that" (ANSOM, Indochine, Nouveaux fonds, 325, 2631).

12. Pasquier was interested in studying the civilization and culture of his country of residence. He put all his knowledge about Indochina in a book he entitled *L'Annam d'autrefois* (Paris, 1930).

13. Speech given by Pierre Pasquier, governor-general, to the Council of Government of Indochina, December 1931, in Conseil de gouvernement de l'Indochine, *Discours prononcé par M. Pierre Pasquier, Gouverneur Général de l'Indochine, à l'ouverture de la session du Conseil de Gouvernement, le 8 décembre 1931* (Saigon, 1931).

14. A list of the elected French as well as Vietnamese councilors with the numbers of votes they respectively received is provided in *La Presse Indochinoise,* 17 Oct. 1925. See also *Than Chung,* 12 Oct. 1928; and *Nam Phong,* Oct. 1930. The words quoted here are from Councilor Nguyen Tan Duoc in *Discours prononcé au Conseil Colonial par Monsieur Nguyen Tan Duoc, Séance plénière du 24 Novembre 1925. Interventions de MM. Gallet et Monin, Conseillers Coloniaux, Carence du government* (Saigon, 1925), 1.

15. See Document 16, in this volume.

16. See "Hoi tu-van Bac ky," in *Nam Phong* 10, no. 59 (May 1922): 361–74.

17. *Than Chung,* 7 May 1929.

18. The ruler of Vietnam is usually referred to as emperor and not king. This practice may have derived from the title that Vietnamese rulers gave to themselves in documents written in Chinese or Vietnamese, which was *hoang de* (emperor), and not *vuong* (king). I simply follow that usage.

19. The name of the viceroy is Hoang Cao Khai. For more information about him, see Truong Buu Lam, "Patterns of," 26–27, in Tran Van Giap et al., *Luoc truyen cac tac gia Viet nam,* vol. 1 (Hanoi, 1971), 662; 484–86; and also André Brébion, *Dictionnaire de bio-bibliographie générale, ancienne et moderne de l'Indochine française,* Académie des Sciences Coloniales, vol. 8 (Paris, 1935). P. Doumer relates an amusing bit of conversation with Hoang Cao Khai in his souvenirs book (142). The two men apparently talked about the quality of the indigenous mandarinate, which is generally low and rife with disloyalty, incompetence, and corruption. Hoang Cao Khai then assured P. Doumer: "You will never have any reproach to make to me, except for what concerns my honesty," meaning that Doumer should not worry about his loyalty and competence. As for corruption, because of the heavy demands put on him in his official position, he

could not get rid of it. In reaction to that statement, Doumer said to himself that, if we could eradicate that evil practice, "not only would it make possible the increase in the collection of taxes that would flow freely into our coffers, but it would also give great relief to our taxpayers."

20. See Document 4, in this volume.

21. See Paul Mus, *Le Destin de l'Union française* (Paris, 1954), 313–20; and *l'Echo Annamite,* 20 Nov. 1925.

22. For more information about the Vietnamese modern mandarinate, see my book *New Lamps for Old: The Transformation of the Vietnamese Administrative Elite* (Singapore, 1982).

23. Paul Doumer, *Indochine française,* 296; and Virginia Thompson, *French Indochina* (New York, 1937), 78.

24. *Tieng Dan,* 27 Aug. 1928, gave the details concerning the budget of the Royal government for 1928. It looked quite simple:

Estimated Receipts:

From the French protectorate	1,700,000	piasters
Rent from special land in provinces	1,000	
Contribution from Laos	1,000	
Sale of brevets, medals, etc.	10,000	
Taxes on land and persons in citadel	1,000	
Sale of special paper to mandarins in North Vietnam	200	
Tuition for His Majesty's schools	20,000	
Taxes on vehicles in citadel	400	
Revenue from the Tinh Tam pond	200	
Extraordinary receipts	5,000	
Rent of good rice fields in Binh Thuan Province	20,000	
Total of estimated receipts	1,758,800	

Estimated Expenses:

Expenses for the citadel	102,807
Military	16,195.15
Royal family	102,058.68
Salaries for civilian and military mandarins	1,148,392.88
Religious ceremonies	47,489.10
Public works	142,000
Travel expenses for the mandarins	20,000
Miscellaneous expenses	38,120
For mandarinal promotions	17,000
Extraordinary expenses	20,420.45
Expenses for the good rice fields in Binh Thuan	20,000
Total of estimated expenses	1,674,483.26

25. See Doumer, *Souvenirs,* 165; and Roland Dorgeles, *On the Mandarin Road,* trans. Gertrude Emerson (New York and London, 1926), 142–48.

26. A report from the island of La Reunion published by *Nam Phong,* in May 1931, noted that Thanh Thai, Duy Tan, and a brother of Duy Tan lived together on the

island in a house provided by the French government. Duy Tan was married to a French woman and had two children. He worked as an electrician and a musician. Thanh Thai supplemented the "pension" paid to him by the French by raising racing horses. For more detail on the rebellion that resulted in the decapitation of Tran Cao Van, see Hoang Trong Thuoc, *Ho so Duy Tan* (Laguna Hills, Calif., 1984); and my book *Rebellion, Resistance*, 27. Later on, in 1945, Duy Tan offered his services to the French (see SLOT II, 6).

27. *Than Chung*, 29 Aug. 1929.

28. See Phan Chu Trinh, "That Dieu Tran," trans. Tran Huy Lieu, in *Nghien Cuu Lich Su* 66 (September 1964); 15–21 and 33; see also *Thu That Dieu cua Phan Chau Trinh goi vua Khai Dinh o Paris nam 1922* (Hue, 1958); "Thu ke toi Khai Dinh," in Thai Bach, *Thi Van Quoc Cam,* 432–55; Nguyen Quang Thang, *Phan Chu Trinh, cuoc doi va tac pham* (Hanoi, 1992), 127–28.

29. Ngo Duc Ke (1879–1929), a writer and political activist, a one-time prisoner in the Poulo Condore penitentiary, expressed his irritation against Khai Dinh in the following poem:

Questions for Gia Long, the founder of the dynasty

I

Whoever goes to Hell should ask of Gia Long
Whether this guy Khai Dinh was really his grandson?
He amused the kids in organizing festivities to celebrate his forty years'
  birthday!
He worsened the peasants' lot by consenting to an increase of 30 percent in
  their taxes.
Of late several disasters hit North Vietnam
Last year he went to France and dishonored our country
The Protectorate has carved a wooden statue
That is the king all right; but where is the country?

II

If there is no country, why have a king?
To have such a king amounts to not have one; he is, after all, of no use.
"While the people's head and land are taxed so heavily that rice fields are left
  uncultivated
I am proud to issue decrees and edicts from my vermilion palace."
How could you find any glory in receiving monthly subsidies [from the
  French?]
What a shame to steal your salary from the mandarins.
The longer you live, the greater is your humiliation
A coolie you were when you were young; now old, you still are a coolie.

In the third and fourth stanzas the author continues in the same tone his derogatory treatment of the emperor.

30. *L'Indochine Enchaînée*, no. 8, 1925–26.

31. According to Colonel Duboc, author of the book *L'Indochine contemporaine* (Paris-Limosges-Nancy, 1932), 167: the air force was installed in Indochina only in

1929. According to Duong Kinh Quoc, in *Viet Nam: nhung su kien lich su 1858–1945,* vol. 3; 1919–1935 (Hanoi, 1988), under the date of 14 February, military planes were introduced into Indochina earlier, in 1919.

32. The first village in Vietnamese history to receive aerial bombardment was Co Am, in which some rebels had sought refuge. In a single day in 1930 fifty-seven bombs of one hundred kilograms each rained down on that village. The planes strafed the villagers with machine-gun fire as well. Compared with what Vietnam was to receive in the way of ordinances later on in its American period, this quantity seems ridiculous. But we are now only in the beginning of the 1930s, when such an event still was shocking. See *Tieng Dan* and *Phu Nu Tan Van,* 20 Mar. 1930; and *Nam Phong* 26, no. 154 (Dec. 1930).

33. According to the *Encyclopédie Larousse,* a regiment has somewhere around 3,000 to 3,200 men and 80 to 100 officers. A regiment is then composed of 3 battalions, which have 4 companies each. Each company has more or less 250 men.

34. According to P. Bernard, *Le Problème économique indochinois* (Paris, 1934), 16, the estimate is 8,500 military French personnel. See also Colonel Duboc, *L'Indochine contemporaine,* 163–70.

35. Duong Kinh Quoc, *Viet Nam: nhung su kien,* under the date of 4 Aug. 1925. It is quite normal that it should be so, for the arsenal represented the first industrial establishment in Cochinchina that produced the real proletariat, in the Marxist sense.

36. See De Galembert, *Les Administrations,* in the chapter entitled "Services coloniaux." See also *Discours prononcé par Maurice Long, Governeur Général, à l'ouverture de la session ordinaire du Conseil de Gouvernement de l'Indochine tenue à Hanoi le 18 octobre, 1920* (Hanoi, 1920). The contributions for the years following the 1914–18 war were unusually high because they also had to take care of more than 150,000 Vietnamese "volunteers" known as the ONS (Ouvriers Non-Spécialisés), a French abbreviation meaning nonspecialized workers, who had been sent during the war years to bolster France's war efforts.

37. This is how the famous satiric poet Tu Xuong expressed his awe of the commissar of police, who had to be a Frenchman and who would be the equivalent of the chief of a police precinct nowadays:

In the province of Ha Nam, there is a Commissar
When you see him, you do not dare to cough
I can see through my roof but I [would] rather suffer the leaks [than to seek a
    building permit from him]
When the clock strikes eight, I must lie down, still [because of the curfew]
If you do not have your identity card on you, pray only to God,
The owners must pay the fine to him if their dogs run free in the streets,
And if he lays his hand on you while you are foolishly relieving yourself
"This, he would say, is certainly a big bite."

38. For more information, see Ha Van Vuong, *La réforme de l'organisation judiciaire en Annam* (Paris, 1934).

39. See ANSOM, Indochine, Nouveaux fonds, 647; and S. Lévi, *Indochine,* 41–42. For a summary list of all the sentences pronounced by the various Criminal Commissions from 1908 to 1929, see SLOT III, 2.

40. See Nguyen Ngoc Huy, *The Le Code: Law in Traditional Vietnam* (Athens, 1986).

41. See Phan Van Truong, *Essai sur le Code Gia Long* (Paris, 1922). The title page of this book bears the following dedication: "Dedicated to Marius Moutet, Attorney at the Court of Paris, in homage to his 'indigénophilie,' Paris, 9 juin 1922." It is this same Marius Moutet who will preside over the 1946–54 Franco-Vietnamese War as minister of colonies or of overseas France in successive governments.

42. Ha Van Vuong, *La réforme,* 11 and 109.

43. *Than Chung,* 8 Nov. 1929.

44. See *Code pénal modifié à l'usage des indigènes et asiatiques assimilés; décret du 31 décembre 1912 et textes modificatifs. Textes français et quoc ngu,* Bibliothèque juridique et administrative indochinoise (Hanoi-Haiphong, 1924); and Nguyen Van Dien, *Luoc khao ve bo luat moi Bac ky co phu mot ban Phap luat danh tu giai nghia* (Hanoi, 1923).

45. See *Extrême-Asie,* no. 8 (Feb. 1927), 265: For the year 1925, in parts of Cochinchina, the poll taxes on 200,193 registered men brought in 1,136,107.35, which came to approximately 5 piasters and 67 cents per head.

46. See Whitehouse, U.S. Embassy to Dept. of State, Paris, 12 Oct. 1927, in National Archives Microfilm Publication, Microcopy no. 560, *Records of the Dept of State Relating to Internal Affairs of France, 1910–1929,* roll 150, 851g: *French Indochina.*

Year	Total Budget	Opium Revenues
1914	44 million	13
1915	52	13
1916	56,500	20,687
1917	52	20
1918	62,500	21
1919	51	18
1920	57,344	13,321
1921	76,355	15,099
1922	83,500	17,862
1923	84,663	18,322
1924	79,667	14,933
1925	78,173	12,198

47. Following are data for the years 1926, 1927, and 1928. See S. Lévy, *Indochine. Documents officiels,* 51; and Teston and Percheron, *L'Indochine moderne,* 142–43.

Indeed, the monopolies had to contribute the major part of these figures as practically everything that was imported into Indochina came either from France or her other colonies, and all entered duty free.

	1926 Piasters	*1927 Piasters*	*1928 Piasters*
Customs and monopolies	61,929,482	74,156,713	74,855,343
Total of ordinary revenue	73,892,041	87,527,647	89,406,586

48. Many rumors circulated in Indochina pertaining to the forceful ways French administrators used to twist the arms of Vietnamese officials, businessmen, village headmen, etc., to get them to buy these bonds. On the other hand, newspapers and magazines were filled with slogans, poems, and drawings encouraging the Vietnamese people to buy the bonds. The most famous drawing was the one representing a dragon spitting fire in the form of Vietnamese currency to burn down German soldiers and their military equipment.

49. A newspaper's article reported a weird incident happening in the marketplace of a provincial capital city. A peasant was required to show his identity card to a policeman, who—for reasons that the article did not go into—put it in his mouth and started to swallow it! Terrified and oblivious of all deference he should have shown to the policeman, the peasant grasped the policeman's neck and choked him, preventing him from swallowing the card. In this fashion they walked to the police station. The article failed to give us the punch line! It is to be noted that a head tax was also imposed on the colored peoples in South Africa and the carrying of an identity card compulsory as well. Gandhi opposed that practice and urged people to burn their identity cards!

50. See Henri Gourdon, "L'Oeuvre sociale et intellectuelle," in Georges Maspero, *Un Empire colonial français: l'Indochine* (Paris, 1930), 2:90.

51. The full text of that document is found in *Bulletin de l'Ecole Française d'Extrême-Orient,* vol. 7 (1907), under the rubric *Chronicles.*

52. See John de Francis, *Colonialism and Language Policy in Vietnam* (Honolulu, 1977), 179.

53. See *Duoc Nha Nam,* 1 Oct. 1928.

54. See Document 16, in this volume, in which Huynh Thuc Khang, in his speech at the Chamber of the People's Representatives of Annam, expressed the wish to see the colonial government reduce the rigor of its regulations of private institutions of learning.

55. For more information about this section, see P. Bernard, *Le Problème,* 80–90; Teston and Percheron, *L'Indochine française,* 420–34; and Lévi, *L'Indochine,* 60–69.

CHAPTER 2

The Vietnamese Perception
of Colonialism

The question of whether there exists an objective outside world or whether every reality is simply a concept of the mind remains a controversial issue for thinkers concerned with metaphysics. For the historian it may be sufficient to describe as accurately as possible a set of data constituting an event, a phenomenon, or a situation. Yet what would be more essential and probably also more interesting is to establish how an event was perceived or experienced by the people who played a part in it. In effect, any happening, any event, would take on its genuine significance only as it became alive, interiorized in the mind of the people who experienced it. The colonial institution that existed in Vietnam is fully documented and was described in the preceding chapter. What is more important now is to uncover the imprint that the colonial situation has engraved in the minds of the people. In other words, what was the nature of the Vietnamese experience of colonialism? Before answering that question, however, we must find out how the Vietnamese people became aware of the colonial status of their country. It has been contended that, in a traditional society where the means of communication have not been properly developed and where the economy was principally based on subsistence, people seldom moved around; they rarely left the comfort of their community, the confines of their village. It is further argued that the establishment of a foreign administrative apparatus usually took place in the capital city and in urban agglomerations and that the implementation of colonial policies relied primarily on indigenous subordinates so that the rural people could remain uninformed for a long time about the change in the ruling circles of their country. While it is true that the colonial authorities governed almost exclusively through native collaborators, who functioned as tax collectors, police agents, and public works engineers, there were many other instances in which the villagers could experience firsthand their condition as a colonized people. The French and their colonial feats did reach them right in the middle of their habitat. And so, even if a villager never set foot beyond the bamboo hedge of his village, he still had ample opportunities to experience his colonial predicament existentially.

The Rural People and Vietnam's Colonial Condition

We often hear that peasants generally preferred to be left alone and that whatever disturbances that took place in any given country were routinely blamed on manipulations perpetrated by small groups of agitators, whether from the ranks of local troublemakers or from an outside band of rabble-rousers. The gist of that theory consists principally in the belief that peasants are not interested in or, even worse, they are not informed about political happenings other than those occurring within the boundaries of their communes. But mass movements did take place in the past, and in no country were rural rebellions rare events. And so, if peasants took part in mass movements, it is obvious that they did not want to be left alone. Nor, for that matter, were they totally ignorant of or indifferent about the political situation they shared with their compatriots. If peasants were willing to participate in popular movements, then how were they persuaded or motivated to join them? Many scholars have tried to find the answer to that question. Some have explained it by constructing a theory of the "moral economy" of the peasants; others speculated about the rational reaction they showed in times of crisis; still others referred to the traditional causes of rebellion, such as natural calamities, corruption, high taxes, religious fanaticism, or millenarian fascination.[1] Their answers, however, apply only to peasant rebellions, to movements usually referred to as *jacqueries*.

What I am interested in here are anticolonial movements. For people to respond positively to the call of an anticolonial movement, the usual appeals against oppression, high taxes, and mandarinal exactions would not suffice. Neither moral economy nor rational behavior could account for their willingness to embrace the abstract concept of freeing their country from foreign domination as opposed to fighting their oppressors or seeking an immediate relief from daily injustices and inequities. No religious zeal or millenarian appeal could move them to go against a powerful enemy they could see in front of them in exchange for some vague political and social advantage to be had in the distant future. Consequently, in order to motivate the villagers to rise against the colonial authorities, their leaders had to introduce a new component: they must attempt to strike an antiforeign chord; in addition to the traditional appeals against high taxes, mandarinal corruption, a xenophobic element was needed. The instigators of anticolonial uprisings had to demonstrate to the peasants that the people who oppressed them, who imposed heavy taxes on them, who demanded exactions from them, came from a different race; they did not speak the same language; they didn't have the same cultural tradition: they were, in a word, foreigners. Furthermore, they also must convince their followers of the necessity for their country to be liberated from the colonial bondage. They did not have much difficulty doing so, because the people were able to experience personally the harmful impact of the colonial system, and therefore many felt more than ready to remove the causes of their ordeal. It was indeed quite common for these demanding foreigners to manifest their presence right in the midst of the indigenous villages.

French Land Concessions in Indigenous Milieu

One of the chief means by which the French presence projected itself into the consciousness of Vietnamese villagers was the colonial plantation. Although the French administration concentrated its presence mainly in the urban centers, a significant number of French private citizens received small—as compared to companies' properties but still huge as compared to the indigenous average holdings—concessions of land and exploited them on an individual basis. They did it usually with Vietnamese help, and they treated their tenants harshly.[2] Generally, the colonial authorities took these pieces of land from newly developed areas or from properties belonging to the state. This, however, was not always the case. Sometimes these concessions consisted of lands that had belonged for generations to Vietnamese villagers but which for some reason had not been properly registered. Unfamiliar with legal procedures and unwilling to submit themselves to the obligation of going to a distant court and ultimately risking humiliation, the villagers oftentimes resigned themselves to their dispossession and simply moved away in search of other means of subsistence. Rarely did they choose to resist an eviction, and, if they chose to do so, the result was inevitably death or long-term imprisonment.[3]

If these cases of outright spoliation were rare, there existed on the other hand ample occasions in which the power of the Frenchmen was exhibited in the countryside for all to see. First of all, there were vast rubber, coffee, and tea plantations and other kinds of agricultural exploitations owned by French companies and managed by Frenchmen scattered all about the Vietnamese territory, generally in the more remote corners of the countryside. A comparison between two sets of numbers suffices to show the importance of these concessions: in 1932 the total surface of land conceded to "European" individuals or companies amounted to 872,000 hectares, while the total cultivated land in all of Indochina was substantially less than 5 million hectares. The proportion stands at about one-fifth, or 20 percent, which represents an enormous portion, considering the small number of French private citizens living in Vietnam.[4] These concessions were not an official part of the colonial administration, but their owners enjoyed privileges by simply appropriating them to themselves.

The workforce on these French plantations consisted entirely of indentured labor recruited from all regions of Vietnam, with the bulk coming from the poorer provinces of northern and central Vietnam.[5] The living and working conditions were scandalous. Even so, the workers might have endured them with some resignation if they could have perceived them as transitory. In other words, if the workers could have felt, for example, that after their contracts, which were usually for three to five years, had expired they would have saved enough to return home to their native village decently loaded with some "capital," they may have accepted the situation. But as it was, the owners of the plantations had designed their economics in such a way that workers could never accumulate savings.

Generally, workers came alone without any family and were gathered into dormitories, which they shared with other workers. Women were often mentioned among the workers transported to plantations in southern Vietnam or to other French colonies in the Pacific. Apparently, the recruiters enrolled them as workers in their own right and not as female companions or wives of male workers.[6] There was no kitchen in the dormitories, so the workers had to take all their meals in a canteen managed by the wives of the foremen. When they were allowed to cook their own meals, they still had to buy their provisions from the plantation store controlled by the same people who ran the canteen. The plantation store also carried all the other merchandise they needed. Meals and goods thus came to them at prices that were fixed by sellers free of any competition, as plantations were generally located far from commercial centers. It has been reported that some plantations were in such remote areas that food could not be sent in adequate quantity or on time, so that some workers died of exhaustion due to lack of food.[7] It was not unusual that a day's meals would cost as much as a half-day's wage.[8] In cases of sickness they were tended, if at all, by the people who ran the canteen and the store. Medicines, if they ever were available, were administered at astronomical cost. There was no sick leave, let alone vacation, and working hours were as long as the daylight lasted, usually eleven to twelve hours. Notwithstanding the scorching sun of noontime, workers were allowed only fifteen minutes' rest at midday.[9] Incidents of severe beatings—not infrequently leading to death—of workers by the French owners, the French supervisors, or the Vietnamese foremen, were reported regularly.[10] Victims sometimes succeeded in escaping from the plantation to find refuge in neighboring houses, where they would try to nurse their wounds. Escapes, however, only prodded the plantation owners and their henchmen to assert yet more control. Under their direction other workers were required to burn down the houses that dared give shelter to the refugee and rough up the occupants when they tried to flee the fire. Little need be said about the fate that awaited the wounded workers who had sought refuge in these houses. They might as well have accepted death by fire because a fate worse than that awaited them outside their burning refuge. If caught alive, they were sure to be humiliated, tortured, and most probably beaten to death anyway.[11]

Planters also dealt harshly with theft or burglary. The foreigners' residences and estates were supplied with the most tempting goods, highly sought-after items, such as timber, coffee, tea, and rice. The punishment meted out to Vietnamese suspected of stealing bore no relationship to the level of larceny involved and was certainly incommensurate with punishments for similar crimes perpetrated against a fellow Vietnamese or non-European victim.[12] European plantation owners rarely bothered to send the suspect to a court of law; they simply acted as plaintiff, police, and judge all at once.[13] The makeshift tribunal, however, meted out no jail term for convicted criminals, because, after all, what was the purpose of a jail term if not to serve as a deterrent? In these cases the culprits had already received all the deterrent they needed from the hands of the plantation owners. If they were killed by the planters, then there was no more to be said. But if they remained alive, the beating and humiliation they had received from the kangaroo court would keep them away from mischief for a long, long time.

It is not surprising that the common people were deeply affected by the conditions of life on the plantations. Sayings and songs circulated widely around the plantations to decry the degrading plight of the workers:

How healthy and beautiful are the rubber trees!
Under each one of them, a corpse of a worker is buried

The rubber trees enjoy much better conditions
When they are sick, they rest right away
Eastern doctors, Western doctors busily fuss around them
We can die of exhaustion and of sickness
No coffin will receive our dead bodies

Coolie Recruiting

Because of perpetual labor shortages, European plantations interfered indirectly but substantially in the separate life of the Vietnamese communes. The treatment of workers on the plantations created an endemic demand for manpower: workers died off or became incapacitated after accidents, beatings, or attempted escapes.[14] Even on the rare occasions when workers finished their terms in good health, they refused to renew their contracts.[15] For this reason French recruiters, known as "coolie recruiters," constantly roamed the countryside seeking new laborers. The people's resentment against these recruiters was such that violent encounters between them and villagers became common and sometimes resulted in murder. The most famous such incident happened in broad daylight in a residential quarter of Hanoi in February 1929. The assassin even left a note on the corpse of the victim, a certain René Bazin, who had been responsible for the recruitment of a great number of workers.[16]

Last, it is important to note that workers were recruited not only for plantations in Indochina, but were also contracted for service in other French colonies, such as New Caledonia and the New Hebrides.[17]

The recruitment process, therefore, brought the French into the center of village life. In the ensuing interaction the villagers could not fail to notice the superior demeanor of both the foreigners and their indigenous assistants, who treated them with contempt and considered them lower than their own domestic servants. Little needs to be said about their behavior toward the peasants, who were prepared to sign a work contract. Even before the ink was dry on their documents, the workers-to-be were already verbally abused by the recruiters and were subjected to severe manhandling; they were dealt with like cattle. Furthermore, they never received the full amount of the advance they were promised. A newspaper investigating the recruiting process reported:

> The recruiters are taking 800 workers. Each male worker was to receive an advance of $9 to $10, each woman worker $5 or $6 from the recruiting agent. That sum would have corresponded to 20 full working days' pay. Of the advance they were supposed to receive, the agent deducted $2.20 representing the cost of two sets of clothes made in cotton. They then bathed the workers and scrubbed them clean. The workers were later on led to the ship which was overly crowded. The food seemed to be adequate, although a small piece of dry fish would have been greatly welcomed by these peasants.[18]

For the recruits the notorious plantation life thus started the moment they set foot on the boat to take them to their place of work.

The Military Draft

Another direct imposition of the French presence at the village level, and no less traumatic for the villagers, were the visits of military recruiters. Every village of Vietnam had the duty to provide a specified number of draftees for the various sections of the Indochinese armed forces. There were never enough volunteers to fill the vacant slots, so the government had recourse to a lottery system. Once a year representatives of the army acting as recruiters came to the villages in order to ascertain the physical quality of the recruits and to make sure that all procedures were closely adhered to, particularly when substitution was involved. Frequently, well-to-do families would pay sizable amounts of money to poorer villagers for them to take the place of their sons, whose lottery number had assigned them to military service. One of the wishes presented to the Colonial Council of Cochinchina for the year 1920 was precisely to legalize that practice so that rich people be allowed to pay other people to assume their military obligations. According to the authors of the measure, that was one of the most cherished desires of the people of Cochinchina.[19] Recruiters were also expected to deal with the violence that often erupted during the recruiting sessions. The literature on Vietnamese village life uniformly notes the villagers' tenacious attachment to their village, which they rarely chose to leave, whatever its conditions. Recruiters, under these circumstances, provoked bitter hostility in the villages where they were sent to pick soldiers. The scope of the recruitment process, and therefore of the disruption wrought upon the villages, may be easily understood when one recalled the fact that, during World War I, more than 150,000 inhabitants of Indochina were sent to France to help the mother country fight her war in Europe.[20] Even in times of peace Vietnamese soldiers were sent to ensure order, under the divide-and-rule logic, in the diverse colonies or concessions of France in China, Syria, Senegal, North Africa, New Caledonia, and the New Hebrides.[21] In any case, the life of a military recruit in the French colonial army was not enviable, and among the popular songs and sayings many expressed a bitter resentment of the French imposition:

> The birds are flying toward the Son Tra mountain
> You were recruited into the army and you are so far away
>
> The French caused this separation
> Of the jade chopsticks from the golden tray
>
> While you join the French army
> Who will care for your wife and young children?

Many other exigencies brought French officials into the villages. Land surveyors, for example, appeared in the countryside at regular intervals of three to four years, first to establish and, subsequently, to update cadastral surveys. This presence was fairly neutral and did not interfere much with the life of the villagers. Although they could not understand the precise nature and significance of the Frenchmen's activities, villagers were nevertheless overwhelmed by their seemingly vast knowledge and, above all, by their power to assign ownership of land.

Sociology of the Road

The French passion for constructing a transportation network of roads and canals did much to reinforce the negative image of the colonial presence in the eyes of the Vietnamese villagers. The colonial administration generally boasted of the impressive number of kilometers of roads built and of canals dug in colonies as major achievements of its civilizing mission. Little did they realize that the road constituted a key factor in alienating the colonized from the colonizer.[22] While roads and canals certainly improved communication, facilitated travels, and multiplied the exchange of goods and ideas, the problem was that roads also introduced an untold number of strains and stresses upon the lives of the people in the countryside. First of all, roads or canals violated rice fields and, worse, ancestral burial sites. French engineers ran them through all the sacred spots revered by the communities, and, naturally, they totally ignored the people's geomantic beliefs. Painful expropriations triggering deep-seated resentments further exacerbated the execution of these public work projects. Then, too, the people in the countryside were forcefully impressed into the workforce for these projects, whether on the basis of famine wages or simply corvée duty.

A completed road did enable villagers to stroll in comfort from home to rice fields and other workplaces. Villagers readily used this modern means of communication and quickly crowded it with their buffaloes, horses, cows, chickens, wives, and children. They did it at their own risk, since the roads were built without anticipation of these impediments; they were, rather, constructed for the convenience of fast-moving, mechanized, four-wheeled vehicles. And who then owned and drove these infernal, life-threatening machines of speed and noise? In the early decades of the twentieth century only the affluent and the powerful could afford them. And they were almost exclusively European, high officials of the government, successful businessmen, prosperous professionals. In fact, popular sayings such as the following one quickly emerged:

> Automobiles belong to the French and the mandarins
> While bullock carts are for the Vietnamese.[23]

The two types of road users were bound to clash, and it was a foregone conclusion who would be the victims and who would have to yield. News reports coming from the remotest corners of the country frequently related automobile accidents in which, more often than not, farm animals paid the price of their slower pace. Peasants did not escape unscathed either. First, they were held accountable for the behavior of their animals. A physical punishment was generally meted out to them right on the spot, or, if the Frenchman was not too violent, too brutal, too much in a hurry, or if he succeeded in controlling his temper, they would be taken to the next seat of authority to be dealt with by the officers of the justice system. There they would be fined or even put in jail for a short time; their offense was to dare walk their animals on the main road.

Car accidents involving pedestrians also took their toll. This toll in our own day may have become an accepted price to pay for the convenience of our mechanized lives, but in the beginning of the twentieth century and in rural Vietnam it carried its full fearsome weight. Usually, the drivers who hit a pedestrian walking along the highway simply sped away from the scene of the accident. Or, if they stopped, due to curiosity or to check their car, they still left the victims to their own devices. Newspaper accounts routinely detailed such occurrences:

> At kilometer 143 in Quang Nam province, there was a car accident. A Vietnamese woman lay in the middle of the road, blood flowing all over the pavement. Her head was cracked, her chest punctured. The people around her said that a small red automobile in which there were a French man, a French woman and a Vietnamese woman, hit her and sped away!

> The accident occurred because the pedestrian walked on the wrong side of the road from Nha Trang to Ninh Hoa!

> The accident happened on the road from Saigon to Binh Chanh. Two Frenchmen hit an oxcart from behind and injured 2 riders on the oxcart. The Frenchmen got out of their car to inspect the damages done to their car, got back into it and drove away, after they were satisfied with the material condition of their vehicle![24]

Accidents aside, the road never proved inviting. It brought dust during the dry months, and, in the rainy season, mud thrown by a fast-moving car could ruin the one set of decent clothing the pedestrian might be wearing on the way to a celebration in the neighboring hamlet or village. To this day, if one drives on the main roads in Vietnam, it is possible to see peasants, their animals and agricultural implements close to their sides, treading very carefully—even in the absence of any heavy automobile traffic—along the edges of the thoroughfare, in that no-man's-land that lies between the familiar rice fields and the alien gash the French called a road. For peasants the road was not there to be walked on; it was a cut, an intrusion into their daily life.

The State Monopolies

The weight of colonialism was heavily felt through the state monopolies of opium, alcohol, and salt. The opium monopoly contributed a great deal financially to the official coffers, but in itself it did not disrupt the lives of those who were not addicted to it. In effect, the government could not force anyone to smoke opium, nor could it prevent anyone from buying it who wished to. And so the villagers were beyond the reach of the custom officers, unless they involved themselves in the illegal procurement of the commodity by smuggling it. Indeed, opium was not produced in Vietnam; it was imported by the colonial government, which resold it to the people at fixed prices. Significant smuggling could hardly thrive in small villages, and, consequently, the control of the monopoly authorities did not violate overwhelmingly the customary intimacy of the villages. The scourge of opium smoking nevertheless did not spare its inhabitants: in a normal-size village of two hundred able bodies, there could exist more than fifty opium smoking sets.[25]

The same could not be said of the monopolies of alcohol and salt. The enforcement of these two monopolies truly pitted the rural people against the French colonial authorities, for it allowed government customs officers to infiltrate, and interfere with, the lowest levels of the Vietnamese administrative structures. Under the pretext of looking for illegal distillers of alcohol or producers of salt, French customs officers and their Vietnamese staff would roam everywhere in the countryside, entering and searching at will any house at any time of the day or night. Moonshining tended to be quite widespread because of the monetary incentive: regulated alcohol was too expensive. But there was a more important consideration, and that was the quality of the alcohol. Vietnamese felt that the alcohol produced by the French was not pure enough for religious purposes and that, if presented on the altar as an offering to their ancestors, it would taste foreign. The ancestors needed alcohol that was produced according to the traditional methods transmitted from generation to generation. Nor did the living like the taste of the French-produced alcohol, even when it was made with the right kind of sticky rice, selected with the most rigorous criteria.[26] Thus, moonshiners were not a rare species in the countryside. They were assured of a rural clientele.

The salt regulation was at one time so cumbersome and its cost so exorbitant that the money produced by the monopoly could hardly cover the salaries of the customs agents involved.[27] And it was much more difficult to produce salt on the sly. Indeed, what the French customs officers prohibited was not only illegal production but principally illegal withholding. Under the law every ounce of salt produced had to be sold to the government or to the company designated by the government at the price specified by the government. It so happened that many Vietnamese small producers would withhold a small quantity of the product for their own use or to sell to a few users in the neighborhood. The people thought it unreasonable to sell a commodity at very low prices and then to buy back the same product at a later date from an official dealer for ten or twenty times the original price. Salt smuggling was pervasive among the people living along the coast. These were modest folk who made salt principally for their own consumption simply because the raw material was freely available to them. In a good year their production sometimes exceeded their need, so they put the surplus in baskets they balanced over their shoulders and went out to sell it. A number of tales are told about their encounters with customs officers and the humiliation the latter meted out. Sometimes these encounters resulted in tragedy: in order to escape from the officers, one young girl threw herself into the river and drowned because she could not swim.[28]

All such activities criminalized by the French attracted a constant horde of customs officers to the countryside in search of evidence, always with a Frenchman heading the groups. Search warrants were unheard of, and the house search was a deeply humiliating experience for its occupants. They were forcefully thrown out to sit in the yard while the inspection proceeded. The ordeal would stop there if the officials did not find evidence. In either event, much material damage would have taken place: the customs officers would have put everything in the house upside down; they would have opened up all that was closed, knocked down everything that was standing up. Neither religious altars nor humble but fragile peasant belongings counted for anything. And, of course, none would have understood that peasants also prized privacy.

An altogether more horrifying result obtained if the officers were able to find evidence of an illegal activity. They then would feel entitled to abuse the master of the household publicly and loudly and to insult members of his family. Even before any trial could start, let alone conviction be secured, the owner of the house would be arrested, put in irons, and led to the provincial or district capital city. Most of the time, evidence would be found, because officers generally operated on tips provided by neighbors. Too often, evidence would be found for the simple reason that a neighbor who hoped to receive credit from the authorities had planted it there or because the fellow villager had other incentives to want the suspect hauled away in irons in the presence of the entire village.[29]

These examples illustrate the several ways in which the rural people came directly in contact with the colonial administration. The knowledge they formed of the latter thus came by way of firsthand experiences, not hearsay; not rumor; not newspapers or books. The point here is that, even if the peasants had isolated themselves in their villages, the colonial lords would have sought them out to remind them of the subjugation of their country and their people to men who did not look like them, who obviously belonged to another race, who spoke another language, and who behaved in a very powerful and arrogant manner. Under the circumstances it appears useless to maintain that the rural people were apathetic toward events transpiring outside their own villages. There was no segregation of locales in the events that occurred in colonial Vietnam. No matter how secluded, how sheltered, the villagers were from the outside world, the political realities came looking for them, foisted themselves on their consciousness, and left them with no choice but to make decisions about their consequent responses.

The Colonial Reality as Experienced by the Urban People

For the average urban Vietnamese who lived in the many towns and administrative centers, colonial reality was even more obvious. There the superiority and power enjoyed by the French was plain to see.

Any Vietnamese residing in one of the numerous provincial capital cities could not fail to notice that French officials occupied all the high positions in all spheres of activity, whether governmental or economic, judicial, or social. In Cochinchina the chiefs of the provinces, and their deputies, were all French. Commissars of police were likely to be French, as were directors of the high school, if and when there was one: indeed, not all provincial capital cities had their own high school.[30] The chief medical doctor of the provincial hospital was French, and, if the hospital was large enough, he would be surrounded by a few other French doctors in charge of special departments. The director of the electric plant for the city was French; so was the supervisor of water management. If the city was important enough, it would have some important commercial outfits, the owners of which were French. The same state of affairs obtained in Tonkin and Annam, although there Vietnamese mandarins usually occupied the positions of chiefs of provinces. Placed clearly above them, however, were the French residents, who obviously disposed of much more power and authority. In the provincial capital cities French bureaucrats resided in palatial homes with spacious gardens, insulated and isolated from the Vietnamese world by high fences made of wrought iron. The gates were at all times guarded by Vietnamese soldiers. The only indigenous people one could see coming from and going into these citadels were either servants or prisoners, whose duty it was to maintain the grounds by weeding, watering, planting, and trimming.

In the Public Sector

Every important agency of the administration was headed by Frenchmen. In big train stations the masters were Frenchmen. Some trains even had French conductors who went back and forth checking tickets.[31] The people who sat behind the counters in the post offices might be indigenous, but the postmasters were Frenchmen. In the treasuries, which were governmental agencies set up to function as banks but handling only official financial transactions, the executive officers and important supervisors were French. In 1919 a newspaper article welcomed with great fanfare the appointment of a Vietnamese national—most likely with French citizenship—to such a position, which must have ranked quite high in the French civil service hierarchy. It was evidently a very rare happening. According to the article, there were no more than four or five such appointments—Vietnamese nationals to head a governmental agency—in the whole of Cochinchina. The article then went on to conclude: "But we must not complain. The high spheres tell us to be patient and that everything will come at its proper time!"[32]

If an indigenous person was unlucky enough to violate the law, the person arresting him might be an indigenous policeman. He would, however, probably be interrogated by the chief of the station or commissar of police, who was likely to be French.[33] After that, if his bad luck persisted, he would go to jail, where all the guards would be Vietnamese, except for two or three French soldiers charged with guarding and protecting the director of the prison, who was French.[34] After his detention he would have to appear in court. The judge or judges were French, as were the prosecutors and the lawyers, if any. In rare cases some lawyers looked Vietnamese, but that made no difference: they were obliged to speak French and therefore communicated, even with the indigenous accused person, through interpreters. The rationale for this was that the official language of the court was French, and Vietnamese lawyers, in order to be allowed to appear in court, had to have French citizenship and consequently to behave as if they were Frenchmen.[35] In criminal cases in which trials by juries had to be instituted, the juries were all French.[36]

The explanation behind the appointments of Frenchmen to all high positions in the administration seemed to derive from two principles. The first was that only Frenchmen should be assigned to the decision-making, managerial, and prestigious positions. The corollary was that no Frenchman should find himself under the direction or leadership of an indigenous person.[37] The two principles were bolstered by the policy that Frenchmen should earn a salary commensurate with their status in Indochinese society, which was naturally on top of the social scale. In the late 1910s Governor-General Albert Sarraut set out to reduce the number of French civil servants employed by the colonial administration. He did it for the sake of reducing the general budget of the Indochinese Union. At the same time, he also was pursuing the policy of safeguarding what he esteemed as French prestige. Sarraut found that too many Frenchmen held lowly positions in the colonial government and, consequent with the low salaries that came with these positions, they could not maintain a standard of living commensurate with the French "national prestige."[38] By 1930 there were in Indochina about five thousand French government officials to administer a country of fewer than twenty-five million inhabitants. The same number of Englishmen then administered India, a country ten times the size of Vietnam and more than ten times its population.[39]

In the Commercial Sector

The presence and power of the French were visible in nongovernmental spheres of activities as well. A walk around the docks of Haiphong or Saigon would show that almost all ships moored there came from France. Longshore-men unloaded cargoes of merchandise made in France. In the commercial quarters of the cities the more impressive retailing outlets were likely to belong to the French. In Saigon the Grands Magasins Charner and the Nouveautés Catinat, for example, captured the essence of what would be called luxurious, chic, elegant, and rich. These department stores occupied whole blocks and catered principally to a French clientele. If indigenous people dared venture beyond their monumental gates, they would witness many firsts: elevators, mannequins, modern appliances, toys, in short all that bespoke the high tech-nology and scientific realizations of French civilization. Outside the streets were filled with automobiles and other motor vehicles. They were, with few exceptions, made in France. In 1923 Indochina imported about one thousand cars from France, which represented an important number for that time.[40] These vehicles were mainly owned by Frenchmen or the very wealthy Viet-namese. An automobile would have cost a Vietnamese teacher in a primary school more than twenty years of his salary.[41] The great majority of these vehicles came from France because Vietnamese customers were persuaded that they were the best available on the market. The same situation obtained for bicycles.[42] The dream of every Vietnamese who was able to financially afford one was to own a Peugeot equipped with a pair of Michelin tires.[43]

In Saigon the most luxurious hotels were frequented, and owned, by the French: the Hotel Continental, situated in the middle of the city, and the Hotel Majestic, which sat on the bank of the Saigon River. A French company, the Compagnie des Grands Hotels, owned the Grand Hotel in Cap Saint Jacques, a sea resort about 105 kilometers east of Saigon; it also possessed the Langbiang Palace in Dalat, a mountain resort town 200 kilometers north of Saigon. The French also controlled the Hotel Morin in Hue and the Hotel Metropole in Hanoi, among many others.

In the Language

In the Vietnamese language the word *Tây* means "West" or anything associated with the West. It is interchangeably used also to designate anything French and ultimately has come, for good cause, to denote anything big, powerful, or out of the ordinary. The turkey, for example, which in the eyes of the Vietnamese is a big and powerful chicken, is called the "French chicken," without of course any derogatory connotation that either the word *chicken* or *turkey* have in the English language. The word *onion* in Vietnamese designates two different vegetables. The Vietnamese onion is that fragile, slender weakling: the long, green tube ending in a white bulb called in English scallion or green onion. The other, bigger, stronger, and juicier bulb, made of many layers that make its peeler cry, is called the "French onion." The adjective *Western,* or *French,* also tends to be synonymous with *better, stronger,* or *more durable;* it may also serve as the criterion for good-looking. In a store, should a customer hesitate about the quality of a product, it sufficed for the seller to certify that the product was "Western merchandise"; then all doubts concerning its value would disappear as if by enchantment. Vietnamese were not considered good-looking until people could say that their skin was as white or their nose as pointed (the Vietnamese say "high") as a Frenchman's or woman's. A man was not handsome until he could be said to be "as handsome as a Frenchman." A Vietnamese lady was not well dressed unless she was "as elegant as a French woman." It was often said that children went to sleep with a clothespin on their noses, in the hope of making them look less flat. Otherwise, they simply tried to pinch their nose as hard and as often as possible, wishing for the same result.[44] On the other hand, Vietnamese have derogatory expressions to label those indigenous people who pretend to look or act like the French: expressions such as "Rotten French," "Blind French," "Muddy French," or "Local French"; the last expression derives from the fact that, if, as we said earlier, everything coming from France is first-rate, then it implies that anything made "locally" could not be anything but of a lower quality.

In the Behavior

French people were automatically accorded better treatment by the indigenous people. Vietnamese became so conditioned to French superiority that the sight of a Frenchman crying disturbed them inordinately. An uncle of mine had married a French woman, so I had a cousin, who was thus half French. Whenever we played together, all my aunts, including my mother, gathered around us to gratify his minutest requirements. They rushed to him whenever he seemed about to hurt himself. They tenderly took him into their arms each time he was about to cry. The pure Vietnamese kids could have spent the rest of the day sobbing and whining: they could not get as much as one-tenth of the attention lavished on the Franco-Vietnamese boy. All that on the premise that the harm done to a Frenchman, or even to a Eurasian, since it is suffered by such powerful individuals, must be worse.

In the Schools

Big cities counted a couple of secondary schools where French was not only taught as a language but was also used as a medium. People walking by the classrooms could hear teachers speaking in French and students repeating their lesson in the same tongue. Some of these schools were supervised by a French director, and some of their teachers also were French.[45] In all schools Vietnamese children recited from history textbooks with great pride and innocence:

"Our ancestors, the Gauls . . ." Following are some of the questions asked at an examination in history and geography that was held in Saigon in 1919, right after the end of World War I. In history: "How were the two provinces of Alsace and Lorraine wrested from France? How did Germany deal with these two provinces? Describe your impressions concerning the cession of these two provinces back to France." In geography: "Indicate the regions of France where a lot of grapes are grown. What are the regions of France that give the most famous wines?"[46]

The official holidays that punctuated the monotony of the years for Vietnamese students and workers were the 14 July French National Day; 11 May for Saint Joan of Arc;[47] Easter Monday, Ascension, Pentecost, All Souls' Day, Christmas, and New Year's Day. A people deeply informed by Confucianism and Buddhism thus got to celebrate not a single holiday associated with these two main religious systems. The only concession the French colonial government made to the Vietnamese was to give them a day or two for the Vietnamese New Year. Interestingly, Joan of Arc Day, particularly the solemn and dignified ceremonies surrounding the celebration in 1929 of the five hundredth anniversary of her triumph at Orléans, provoked some Vietnamese to think of their own heroines, the Trung sisters, who, of course, had no day set aside in their honor.[48]

In the Streets

In any Vietnamese city, even the smallest, streets names reflected the domination of France. Because the names were all French, the native people, in using them, felt alienated from their own country, to say nothing of giving and receiving wrong directions because of unfamiliar sounds and syllables. A journalist described the situation as follows:

> If the streets of Saigon are not named after French generals who have served France well, then they are given names of those who have bravely risked their lives to conquer this very piece of land and made it into a French colony. One or two streets are given names of those Vietnamese who have been loyal to their core to the French mission in the Far East . . . In a capital city, where the Vietnamese population represents more than three times that of the French [the journalist did not know his arithmetic; he should have written more than one hundred times], up to 99 streets out of 100 have French names. How pitiful are the Vietnamese whenever they have to pronounce one of those names.[49]

The same journalist revisited this subject a few days later, this time with even more biting observations:

Franco-Vietnamese collaboration means that the two people are going to hold hands together; it also means that they will discard all suspicious sentiments they bear for one another, that they will reject all hostile feelings they maintain against one another so as to be able to go to work together . . . Why then invoke again and again the names [of the French conquerors of Indochina] at those street corners with such arrogance and such contempt . . . Of course, we are not asking to replace them with names such as Phan Boi Chau or Phan Chau Trinh [anti-French patriots].[50]

The cities of Vietnam, principally Saigon and Hanoi, enjoyed the reputation of being very graceful cities, at times called the Pearls of the Far East or the Paris of the Orient, because they were adorned with attractive villas, the majority of which were occupied by French or other Europeans. The streets in the European section of town were lined with tall and widespread trees. Their pavement was excellently maintained. Local people were not welcome to linger too long in front of the mansions strung along both sides of these streets; sooner or later dogs or guards would shoo them away.[51]

A stroll in the more attractive and dignified center of Saigon while paying special attention to its most impressive monuments would reveal numerous reminders that, although the weather was hot and muggy, the vegetation lush and luxuriant, this land was definitely not made for the Vietnamese. The most magnificent residence was located at the end of a large thoroughfare surrounded by high wrought-iron fences, in the middle of a huge park where the grass was greener than the leaves of the surrounding trees. This was the imposing residence of the supreme authority in the land, the governor-general of Indochina, a Frenchman. Its architecture betokened nothing of Vietnamese architecture. If the soldiers standing guard at the gate were not white Frenchmen, they belonged to some other ethnic groups, like Senegalese or Tunisian, that had no connection whatsoever with the soil of Vietnam. A stone's throw away was the palace of the number 2 authority in Indochina but number 1 in Cochinchina: the lieutenant-governor of Cochinchina, a Frenchman. Close by this magnificence rose a severe-looking building with a large solid iron gate and walls almost as high as the treetops, topped with broken glass. The residents of that building were almost all native Vietnamese, but the director and many of his assistants, as well as those on duty at the gate, were Frenchmen or people from other colonies or possessions of France. That building was the central prison of Saigon. Around the gate there were always throngs of Vietnamese women and children sitting or squatting on the sidewalk, at a respectful distance from the barricades set up along the sides of the gate, and loaded with containers of food and drink as they waited patiently to be allowed to catch a glimpse of their relatives and pass the food the prison authorities did not care to provide to him or her. Once in a while, as if to break up the monotony of the day, the French guards would vaguely and without much conviction aim a rifle armed with a bayonet at the crowd while proffering a long sentence that nobody understood. The people, nevertheless, as if on a cue, moved further away from the barricades, and the soldier returned to his duty of keeping an eye on the gate and on whomever or whatever approached it. Even from a distance it was easy to see who held power and who suffered the obligation of having repeatedly to renew the act of obeisance and the pledge of submission.

Turning left away from the prison, the next building encountered was rather unusual. It displayed all the enticements and entrapments of the vulgar and arrogant rococo colonial architecture that was totally out of place in this tropical land, but it was built there obviously with the aim of marking French power and glory. This was the City Hall of the Prefecture of Saigon. The mayor who worked in that building was a Frenchman. Beyond the City Hall two landmarks emerged, tame in comparison, although rife with the same implications: the overpowering presence of the French. In the Pagoda Restaurant and the terrace of the Continental Hotel's Café-Restaurant on Catinat Street, the customers were generally French or European; the managers French, the waiters and busboys Vietnamese. Except for the latter, few Vietnamese or Asian faces were to be seen. When they appeared, it was in the company of Frenchmen, and they most certainly spoke French. There were two long rows of rickshaws, their handles resting on the sidewalks that ran along Catinat Street. The rickshaw pullers gathered in groups of two or three, squatting next to their vehicles, smoking cigarettes, picking their teeth, or finishing a chew of betel. Others leaned lazily against the trees talking softly to one another. Still others, reclining against the wheels of their rickshaw, attempted to catch a brief nap, during which they surely dreamed about some good fares.

Catinat Street was the main gathering place for people who counted in Saigon, the Frenchmen. Here they came to exchange ideas, while sitting comfortably sipping an aperitif or a refreshing long drink on the restaurant terraces. It was also the best shopping area of the city, where all the French or modern stores were located. If instead of strolling in the direction of the shops, one went in the opposite direction, for just one block, one landed on the most notorious testimony of the French presence in Indochina: the building euphemistically called the "Catinat police station." In fact, the station sheltered a chamber where tortures were inflicted on violators of the law, particularly political ones. Catinat Street then ended in a very spacious square bordered on three sides by tall, dark-green, healthy-looking trees.[52] In the middle of that block stood the Notre Dame cathedral of the Roman Catholic Church. By no means an architectural jewel, the romanesque structure, marked by red bricks and two slender towers that rose 150 feet above the already elevated grounds, succeeded in communicating the superiority of the Christian faith as well as the supremacy of the French polity. In this capital city of a colony whose people followed Confucius or Buddha, no temple or pagoda could be seen for miles around.[53]

On the street directly behind the cathedral was what the French called a "Monument to the Dead," an obelisk erected to the memory of the heros who had fallen protecting France during the great war of 1914–18. The list included one or two Vietnamese names (naturalized French citizens), but the overwhelming majority were French or European names, men killed in action at battles unknown and insignificant to the people of Vietnam. The main inscription nevertheless reads: "To all those who fell for the protection of France, Cochinchina is profoundly grateful."[54]

The cathedral was interestingly situated midway between the "legitimate" power of France, the palace of the governor-general and its brute power, the Eleventh Regiment of Colonial Infantry. The regiment was housed behind forbidding iron fences, in neatly arranged rows of two- to three-storied brick buildings, ornamented with fancy black wrought-iron balconies. The soldiers billeted in these barracks bore the responsibility of protecting all French officials, including the governor-general, their neighbor on the other side of the cathedral. They also carried the mission of keeping law and order in the capital city or any other corner of the Indochinese colonial possession to which they might be sent in connection with similar forces stationed in other administrative units. The guards at the Saigon barracks were armed to the teeth and seemingly ready to strike on a second's notice at any target stirring too close to them. The native people considered it advisable to avoid the regiment side of the street. Stories abounded about pedestrians being manhandled by the military for no reason other than daring to look at them.

A tour of the city could not have neglected the statues that adorned the public places. The same principle that accounted for French street names motivated the existence of these statues. Besides all the statues that honored the French officers, administrators, and others who conquered and maintained the colony in peace, there was one erected in homage to a Vietnamese national: his name was Petrus Truong Vinh Ky, a man of many talents, including some spying skills, which he put essentially to the service of the French.[55]

Physical Superiority of the French

The conclusion of the city tour goes far to explain why the Vietnamese felt intensely alienated in their own country. They were strangers in their own land, powerless outsiders. The French were convinced of their own superiority— moral, intellectual, and physical—over the indigenous population. Their sense of physical superiority created a highly violent and brutal environment for the Vietnamese. The French recourse to brute force as needed, and even when not needed, followed a certain logic. Constantly confronted with a people of another culture, a culture the majority of them were not interested in and had learned nothing about or from, not even its language, they became frustrated.

> One day we passed by the corner of Taberd and McMahon streets, right in front of the central tribunal. We heard piercing screams: "Oh my God! Please do not beat me to death! Please help me!" My friend and I turned the corner to see what was happening. It was a very ordinary tragedy, because we can see it being played out every day. There was one French man beating one Vietnamese man because the French man was not satisfied with the Vietnamese man.[56]

And, since many of those who came to lord it over the indigenous people in the colonies did not generally issue from among highly educated Frenchmen,[57] they were not predisposed to fight with words that, in any event, would not have been understood by their interlocutors. Thus fists, feet, or weapons became the ready tools for resolving frustration.[58] A frequent bit of advice given to newly arrived French in the colony went something like this: "Do not scream. Just sock it to them in their faces."[59] Few French who committed violent acts against the Vietnamese needed to fear consequences, because if, by chance, they got hauled into court, the law bent in their favor and indulged their "venial" weaknesses. Tribunals regularly meted out, for murder or other extremely violent acts perpetrated against Vietnamese by Frenchmen, sentences of one, two, or three months in jail. But even these light sentences were generally suspended sentences. The heaviest actual punishments for such crimes consisted simply of fines.[60]

The two most frequent incidents in which Frenchmen were bound to lose their composure and temper were haggling over rickshaw fares and vehicular accidents. Indeed, the world would have seen fewer beatings and violent altercations had rickshaws been equipped with meters or some objective device for calculating fares other than the contest between the "demands" of the pullers and the "generosity" of the French riders. Everyday, everywhere in Indochina, French riders viciously quarreled with their rickshaw men. Though the scenarios varied, the contests shared a common happy ending for the French, who simply threw whatever they thought was fair to the puller and left, generally to disappear into a posh restaurant, a high-class store, or behind a heavily guarded gate. The rickshaw man's role was to pick up what was contemptuously thrown and assuage his anger with a few obscene swear words. Or, if the quarrel endured, it was generally and definitively sealed with a slap in the face or a punch to the body of the rickshaw man, which would send him to the ground. Even in cases where the riders simply ran away from the rickshaw men, the latter were hardly in any physical condition to chase after them, notwithstanding the fact that their profession was to run.[61] Vehicular accidents abounded not because traffic was dense but because it was largely unregulated.[62] Most of the time, violence exploded because there was an expectation on the part of the French that the streets belonged to them and that, if an accident occurred, the fault lay with the indigenous people. Some examples reported in the newspapers bear this out.

A Vietnamese office clerk rode home one evening in a rickshaw. From the opposite direction came another rickshaw with a French woman in it and next to it, a Frenchman, her husband obviously, on a bicycle, hanging on to the rickshaw so that he did not have to pedal. Nobody knew how, but the clerk's rickshaw collided with the Frenchman's bike, sending the latter to the ground with lacerations on his face and forearms and shattering one lens of his eye glasses. Both rickshaw pullers vanished. As for the clerk, he landed on his overturned rickshaw. The accident had knocked the wind out of him, so he sat there trying to recover his senses; the thought of fleeing did not even cross his mind. Before he realized what had happened, the Frenchman had picked him up by his hair and started to punch and kick him. No Vietnamese bystanders dared interfere, let alone stop the Frenchman from beating the clerk. It was the man's wife who finally pacified her husband. The Frenchman calmed down; they then loudly left the scene. A few minutes later the police arrived and led the clerk, who could hardly walk, to the nearest police station. They never found the two rickshaw pullers.[63]

In another incident two Frenchmen ran after a Vietnamese driver and beat him up badly because the latter had maneuvered his car in such a way that it obliged the French car to leap onto the sidewalk.[64] As for the unfortunate Mr. Xuan, who was taking a stroll on a sidewalk in Saigon, he was suddenly hit by a bicycle from behind; the shock threw him to the ground. The bicycle rider, a Frenchman, instead of apologizing, gave Mr. Xuan a beating he would not soon forget.[65]

Cases of violence committed on the persons or belongings of the indigenous people defied normal causal analysis. The explanation sprang from too deep a source: a presumed sense of superiority that the French esteemed natives should recognize and acknowledge at all times, added to which was the sense of total invulnerability and therefore absolute impunity. A Frenchman could traverse a market and "buy" whatever he wanted at prices he himself decided to give to the sellers. If the latter did not agree with him, he simply threw the merchandise away—for example, fish into the river, meat into the street, or vegetables onto the ground. Other examples abound. Two Vietnamese servants were quarreling over an unpaid debt. The creditor reported the matter to his French master, who sent him to the floor with a massive slap. "Where would you have got the money to lend him in the first place?" A French train conductor slapped the face of a young Vietnamese because he was slow in showing his ticket.[66] A Vietnamese man was drinking his coffee and smoking a cigarette at a table on a terrace. Two Frenchmen passed by on the sidewalk; one of them stopped in front of the Vietnamese and with his cane whacked the cigarette off his mouth, thundering "Impolite! Insolent! How come you don't salute Frenchmen?" On a train two Frenchmen walked down the aisle of a fourth-class car. As usual, the aisle of the fourth-class car was filled with all kinds of luggage, baskets, packages, and goods. The Frenchmen did not like it at all, so they simply picked up whatever hindered their walk and threw it out of the window. A Vietnamese secretary in an office went privately to visit his French boss one evening. The boss was unfortunately not home, so the secretary asked the servant, "When does he come home?" The next day the secretary was arrested and sent to the provincial capital's court of justice. The reason was that he dared use the common pronoun *he* when referring to his French boss, a usage that placed himself on an equal level with his superior. The newspaper article did not say what punishment awaited the secretary at the court.[67]

Finally, Frenchmen would slap the faces of the native people for no known reason at all. One day in My Tho, a town situated about seventy kilometers south of Saigon, the French commissar of police, for reasons not explained in the article, slapped the face of a certain Jacques Duc. He was ill advised in his behavior because it so happened that Mr. Jacques Duc was the son of a high mandarin in the royal Court of Annam and also a very rich and powerful personality in the region. The commissar, therefore, had to present his apologies to Mr. Duc's family and offer the excuse that he mistook Mr. Duc for a *nha que,* a peasant. The commissar obviously believed that he could slap the *nha que* casually and without compunction.[68]

Faced with this kind of humiliation and constant reminders of their subjugated situation, the Vietnamese saw few choices. Some of them tried to beat the system by attempting to join it. That involved emulating as much as possible the French model. They put on French clothes; they wore French shoes; they competed to enter French schools; they went to school in France; they spoke French; they even took on French citizenship. Still, they were not French, and so they endeavored to persuade the colonial government to implement reforms to reduce the difference in the social status between the French and the Vietnamese.[69]

Others chose the easiest and perhaps most painful path: total submission and complete dependence. The French were the lords; they were the slaves. The French were the masters; they were the servants. The French were the kings; they were the subjects. Others resolved to fight the system. They placed themselves outside the colonial law; they took up arms against the French; they poisoned French officers; they assassinated French officials; they mutinied; they exiled themselves in foreign countries; they founded political parties; they established "soviets." None of their activities in the 1900–1930 period under discussion met with success, and in the end the French remained the supreme masters of their land.

Notes

1. The literature about these theories is so vast that I would not dare give even the beginning of a bibliography. For Southeast Asia the names of researchers such as Erich Jacobi, Eric Wolfe, Hue Tam Ho Tai, Pham Cao Duong, Michael Adas, Samuel Popkin, Sartono Kartodirdjo, James Scott, Benedict T. Kerkvliet, and D. Sturtevant—and I am certain to have missed a few—come naturally to mind.

2. See *Than Chung,* 13 Apr. 1929. The French landlord did not allow his tenants to work for anyone else. The tenants, after paying him the rent, had to sell whatever surplus rice they had to him at prices he specified. Otherwise, he simply sent his truck and scooped the content of the tenants' rice reserves. See also *Tieng Dan,* 29 Feb. 1928.

3. See *Tieng Dan,* 29 Feb. 1928, in which an eviction in the province of Bac Lieu, South Vietnam, ended in three Vietnamese deaths and the wounding of a French commissar of police. In another case, also in the province of Bac Lieu, the dispossessed owner was so outraged that he died of a stroke. Through the services of a medium the family wanted him to indicate which of his children should avenge his death. Three times the medium pointed at his seventeen-year-old daughter. *Tieng Dan,* 24 Mar. 1928. For another case, see *Duoc Nha Nam,* 26 Sept. 1928, in which a French gendarme and four Vietnamese were killed. Sometimes the dispossessed peasants gathered together to demonstrate against the local authorities; see *Bua Liem,* 1 Nov. 1929.

4. See Ngo Vinh Long, *Before the Revolution* (Cambridge, 1973), 18, who cites figures from Paul Bernard, *Le problème économique indochinois* (Paris, 1934). See also *Tieng Dan,* 7 Sept. 1927, which cites a decree of 26 December 1913 conceding land in the province of Lam Vien; of nine names of persons receiving land eight were French. See *Journal Officiel de l'Indochine* (1898), under "Concessions": Of thirty-seven concessions of land thirty were given to Vietnamese and seven to French. The average size of the concessions to Vietnamese was about 50 acres, whereas the seven concessions to French were as follows: M. Favier: 665 hectares (ha.); the Society of Foreign Missions: 363 ha.; M. Blanchet: 2,435 ha.; M. Dussol: 234 ha.; M. Alzas: 300 ha.; M. Doctor Monseaux: 1,545 ha.

5. Mention of ships transporting workers from Haiphong to Saigon to work on these plantations surfaced regularly in newspapers of the time. See, for example, *Tieng Dan,* 16 Nov. and 3 Dec. 1927; 28 Mar., 7, 21, and 25 Apr., 4 July, 25 Aug., 16 Nov. 1928. See also *La Tribune Indigène,* 12 June 1919; *Than Chung,* 25 July 1929.

6. See *Tieng Dan,* 7 Apr. 1928; and *La Tribune Indigène,* 12 June 1918.

7. See *Tieng Dan,* 1 Oct. 1927.

8. *Tieng Dan,* 14 Apr. and 21 Nov. 1928.

9. See *Tieng Dan,* 14 Apr. 1828.

10. See Louis Roubaud's article in *Le Petit Parisien,* 31 May 1930, as cited by F. Challaye in *Le Malaise indochinois,* Comité National d'Etudes Sociales et Politiques (Paris, 1930), 6: "In one and the same day, I have witnessed the tribunal of Hanoi

sentence a young Vietnamese student, convicted of the crime of having composed a patriotic song, to three years in prison and a French foreman who had beaten with his boots a Vietnamese worker to death to three suspended months in prison." The young Vietnamese student in question here was Pham Tat Dac, author of the *Appeal to the National Soul* (see Document 13, in this vol.). See also *Tieng Dan,* 3 Dec. 1927 and 8 Aug. 1928.

11. For more detailed accounts of life on a plantation, read P. Monnet, *Les Jauniers* (Paris, 1931). The title of this book is already quite meaningful. It means something like the "Yellowers" or "dealers in yellow slaves," to parallel the accepted French word *Negriers* or *Negroers* to designate "dealers in Negroe slaves." See also Tran Tu Binh, *The Red Earth: A Vietnamese Memoir of Life on a Colonial Rubber Plantation,* trans. John Spragens Jr., ed. David G. Marr (Athens, Ohio, 1985). See also some articles on the general situation of workers on the plantations in *Tieng Dan,* 12 Nov. 1927; and *Than Chung,* 3 June and 6 Sept. 1929.

12. This seems to confirm the popular saying to the effect that if you steal from the Buddha, you pay back only ten times the value of the stolen item, but if you steal from Jesus Christ, then you pay back one thousand times.

13. See *Than Chung,* 14–15 Apr. 1929. On suspicion of burglary, the Frenchman organized a posse to catch the culprit; they tied him up and shot him dead. *Indochine Enchainée* (n.d.) reported that an Indian policeman at the service of the French commissar of police in the province of Bac Lieu in southern Vietnam attached a Vietnamese suspect to a tree and beat him to death. The newspaper added: "If France has asked the governors of its colonies to secure the attachment of indigenous peoples, it did not mean attachment by the feet."

14. See *Tieng Dan,* 1 Oct. 1927; 25 Mar. and 14 Apr. 1928: in an interview a worker complained that of his team of 100, only 8 remained alive. The article did not specify the time frame nor the proportion of dead to escapees. See also *Tieng Dan,* 25 July, 24 Oct., and 21 Nov. 1928: a complaint from a worker states that of eight hundred workers coming from the north with him, only one hundred were still present on the plantation. See also *Than Chung,* 8 June 1929: of the original 146 workers, after three years, there remained 82.

15. *Than Chung,* 8 June 1929, related an interesting anecdote concerning workers in a sugar cane plantation in the province of Baria, South Vietnam. A group of workers walked down to the tribunal in the provincial capital of Baria, complaining that their owner had not paid them their wages for the past few months. The judge told them there was not much he could do to help them but suggested that they go to work for another plantation, whose trucks were parked right in front of the tribunal ready to take them to their new place of work. The interesting detail was that some of the trucks were military trucks with soldiers in them. The workers, however, declined the offer, saying that they wanted to be sent back to their homes because they had completed their contracts.

16. See *Than Chung,* 18 Feb. 1929; and SLOT III, 39, and SLOT V, 18: Note for the Minister of Colonies, n.d. Ironically enough this assassination caused a Vietnamese worker living in France by the name of Dang Ba Lenh to be brought to a tribunal in Aix-en-Provence, accused of anarchistic propaganda. Dang Ba Lenh published an article in *Viet Nam Lao Dong,* a newspaper published by the Committee for the Defense of the

Vietnamese Workers headquartered in Marseilles. According to a letter of the prosecutor to the minister of justice (Aix, 20 Dec. 1929): "The article in question constitutes a veritable provocation to murder. After announcing that a certain person by the name of Bazin, whose profession was to recruit coolies, had been killed by a firearm shot and that a student, Le Van Sanh, had been arrested, the author added: this example given by student Le Van Sanh, we, workers, must we not emulate it? One Bazin dead is not enough, for there are many more other Bazins." On what basis the tribunal in Aix acquitted Dang Ba Lenh, we do not know. But the Court of Appeals reversed and sentenced him, in absentia, to two years of prison and a fine of five hundred French francs.

17. See *Nam Phong,* no. 149, Apr. 1930; and *Tieng Dan,* 4 Jan. 1928, in which it is mentioned that two Vietnamese medical doctors volunteered to go to the New Hebrides to take care of the health of Vietnamese workers. See also *Than Chung,* 29 Mar. 1925: five hundred workers were sent to New Caledonia; and 12 Apr. 1925: a commission was formed to investigate the working and living conditions of Vietnamese workers in the French possessions of the Pacific.

18. See *La Tribune Indigène,* 12 June 1919.

19. See *Echo Annamite,* 21 Oct. 1920. See also Colonel Duboc, *L' Indochine contemporaine* (Paris, Limosges, and Nancy, 1932), 87: in 1926 a rich landowner offered a medical doctor who was to examine his son for military service a sizable bribe to induce him to declare the son unfit for service.

20. See Duong Van Giao, *L'Indochine pendant la guerre de 1914–18* (Paris, 1925).

21. See *Dong Phap Thoi Bao,* 7 July 1923: the colonial government awarded some money to recruits who reenlisted in the army; fifteen dollars for four more years; thirty-five dollars for five more years; forty-two dollars for six more years. *Echo Annamite,* 29 June 1920: by orders from Paris two battalions were to embark from Haiphong for Syria. *Tieng Dan,* 15 Oct. 1927: Vietnamese militia were sent to Shanghai; and 7 Apr. 1928: recruitment of soldiers from Central Vietnam to be sent to foreign places. *Than Chung,* 2 May 1929: moving scene of wives and other people seeing their husbands and relatives off for military service.

22. Paul Mus saw this problem clearly when he wrote the most sensitive and illuminating passages about it in *Vietnam, Sociologie d'une guerre* (Paris, 1952), 124–37. Portions of this work have been freely paraphrased and translated in Paul Mus and John McAlister, *The Vietnamese and Their Revolution* (New York, 1970).

23. *Tieng Dan,* 15 Oct. 1927.

24. See *Tieng Dan,* 3 Sept. 1927; 21 Dec. 1927 and 15 Feb. 1928, respectively.

25. See *Nam Phong,* Apr. 1926. According to this article, most of the opium used in villages came from smugglers who bought it in Yunnan. Their opium was much cheaper than the monopoly's: the difference in price could reach the ratio of one to four.

26. In 1920 the main distillery that provided government alcohol circulated in the press an article comparing the Chinese and French methods of distilling alcohol. The article asserted that, in spite of the self-serving propaganda of the Chinese, the quality of the alcohol distilled by the Fontaine distillery was appreciated by people throughout Indochina, in Tonkin as well as in Cochinchina. It suffices to taste that alcohol but once,

the article claimed, to be convinced of its exquisite quality both in taste and in look. *L'Echo Annamite,* 20 Apr. 1921.

27. See *Indochine enchainée,* no. 3, 1925–26.

28. See *Tieng Dan,* 18 Jan. 1928.

29. See Vo Nguyen Giap and Truong Chinh, *The Peasant Question, 1937–1938,* trans. Christine White Pelzer (Ithaca, 1974); and ANSOM, *Indochine, Nouveaux Fonds,* 28 (2). In a letter dated 17 July 1911 the prosecutor-general in Indochina wrote to the governor-general about the abuses the agents of the monopolies committed against the people in the villages when they came to look for fraudulent operations: "We must not, under the pretext of detecting conspiracies, allow civil servants in search of favors and advancements, sow troubles to families and the entire country through unjustified house search and arrests. From time immemorial Vietnamese have always worn over their pants belts of different colors: blue, red, green, etc. . . . To see in them signs for conspiracies seems quite a risk to me."

30. Only three of twenty-one provincial capital cities of Cochinchina had their high schools: Gia Dinh, My Tho, and Can Tho. In Tonkin, Hanoi and Vinh and, in Annam, Hue and Qui Nhon were the only cities that had high schools.

31. See Hy Van Luong, *Revolution in the Village: Tradition and Transformation in North Vietnam, 1925–1988* (Honolulu, 1992), 81, in which a Vietnamese eyewitness narrated to the author the humiliation he had to endure from a French train conductor in the mid-1920s, while a Japanese companion slapped that same French conductor. "The Japanese dared to slap the French conductor in response to the insult because of the emergence of Japan as a power after her victory over Russia in 1905. The French had to treat the Japanese with some respect. As a Vietnamese, I was boiling with anger at being insulted and being unable to respond at all. What could a Vietnamese do, given the power of the French conquerors? I felt deeply humiliated."

32. *La Tribune Indigène,* 5 June 1919.

33. See *Tieng Dan,* 29 Feb. 1928; and *Than Chung,* 14–15 Apr. 1929.

34. In the 1916 uprising, for example, the rebels attacked the central prison of Saigon in order to liberate their leader by the name of Phan Xich Long. In the brawl they injured two French soldiers and a French sergeant. According to Nguyen Chanh Sat, *Am muu khoi loan* [in Chinese characters]. *Toa quan vu xu Nguyen Huu Tri va noi bon ve toi an cuop kham lon trong dem 14 rang ngay 15 thang Fevrier 1916* (Tan Dinh, 1916), the insurrection elicited two sessions of the Military Court. The first session was convened only six days after the event, with the following sentences: thirty-eight death sentences and two banishments (usually banishment means that the convict is to be deported to the Con Son penitentiary for an indefinite period.) The second session took place on 14 April of the same year, 1916, with the following sentences: thirteen death sentences, eighteen banishments, and seventeen acquittals. See also *ANSOM, Indochine, Nouveaux Fonds* 8, 28 (1) and (2).

35. Vietnamese lawyers were not allowed to appear in court. They could, however, offer legal consultation. They usually worked under the supervision of a French lawyer. See the advertisement in *Than Chung,* 24 July 1929: "Legal consultation office of Mr. Pham Van Gia, Master in Legal Studies. $10.00 for a legal consultation. If a lawyer is needed, Mr. Gallois Montbrun is available for $3 to $4,000.00."

36. *L'Echo Annamite,* 21 June 1927: article entitled "When Will We Have Composite Juries?"

37. See U.S. National Archives Microfilm Publication, microcopy no. 560, *Records of the Department of State Relating to Internal Affairs of France, 1910–1929,* roll 150, 851g: "French Indochina." L. Smith, consular agent to the State Department, Saigon, 13 Dec. 1922: "There are only 111 French physicians in Indochina. There is a necessity for the government to give the native doctors permission to treat Europeans. The political importance of that permission is immense and most displeasing to the French population as it places a European in the position of soliciting assistance from a native."

38. See Phillip T. Thornton, *Albert Sarraut,* 97; and Charles Meyer, *La Vie quotidienne des Français en Indochine, 1860–1910* (Paris, 1985), 201–3.

39. Paul Bernard, *Le Problème économique indochinois* (Paris, 1934), 16.

40. *La Presse Indochinoise,* 5 Apr. 1925.

41. *La Tribune Indigène,* 3 July 1918: the salary of a primary schoolteacher was thirty piasters a month, after thirty years of service.

42. A popular slogan of the time was "If you want to alleviate the Vietnamese burden / If you want to promote French factories / Abolish the taxes on bicycles" (in *Than Chung,* 28 Aug. 1929).

43. It seems that the infatuation with Peugeot bicycles has not subsided in Vietnam. In the novel *Nhung thien duong mu* by Duong Thu Huong, published in Hanoi in 1988 (translated into English by Penguin Books in 1994 under the title *Paradise of the Blind),* we read the following promise: "[If and when you pass the entrance examination] you are going to have to travel all that way to the university. I'll buy you a French Peugeot bicycle" (87).

44. In the early 1970s, when American scholars were allowed back into China, a friend of mine, an old China hand, returned from there and told us about his experiences. Among other things, he said that on the campuses that he visited Chinese students, male as well as female, would flock all around him to "exchange ideas" with him. What happened most frequently was that some more daring students would come closer to him, touch his arms, and confide: "We did not know that Westerners could be so good-looking."

45. See, for example, *Dong Phap Thoi Bao,* 14 Dec. 1923, in which it is said that the director of the Gia Dinh high school had a French director as well as several French teachers.

46. *La Tribune Indigène,* 5 June 1919.

47. Here is what a student newspaper, *Lien Hiep,* 5 May 1930, thought about the commemoration of Joan of Arc: "The French imperialists suck our blood; they shoot us to death; they bend our head down; they strangle us; they steal our money to celebrate the memory of Joan of Arc while forbidding us to commemorate our own ancestors. That's really cruel, uncivilized. That's a real shame for us. We must unite our efforts. We must stand up to protest against the irrational prodigality of the French imperialists. We must demand our liberties, the liberty to form associations, the liberty to commemorate those who have served well our poor and miserable people . . . Furthermore, we should definitely not participate in the festivities of 11 May, showing plainly that we can no longer tolerate our shame."

48. See *Than Chung,* 14 May 1929; see also *Dong Phap Thoi Bao,* 14 May 1924.

49. See *Than Chung,* 16 May 1929.

50. *Than Chung,* 20 May 1929.

51. It is interesting to read the following passages from Marguerite Duras's novel *Un Barrage contre le Pacifique* (Paris, 1958), 143: "As in all colonial cities, there were two cities in that city: the white and the other. The white quarters of all the colonial cities in the world were always, in these years, spotlessly clean. It was not only true of the cities. The white people were also clean . . . The streets and the sidewalks in the white quarters were immense. And on the avenues glided their automobiles rubbered, suspended, in an impressive silence. All that was alphalted, wide, bordered by sidewalks which were planted with rare trees and separated by flower beds. But the real sanctuary was the center of the white quarter. There, under the shade of the tamarind trees, unfolded the long terraces of their coffee shops. There, in the evening, they met with themselves. Only the waiters were indigenous." See also F. Fanon, *The Wretched of the Earth* (New York, 1968), 38: "The colonial world is a world cut in two . . . The zone where the natives live is not complementary to the zone inhabited by the settlers . . . The settlers' town is a srongly built town; the streets are covered with asphalt . . . The settlers' town is a town of white people, of foreigners."

52. Interestingly enough, this square much later on was baptized the John F. Kennedy Square.

53. The Xa Loi Pagoda, which became so famous for its antigovernmental activities in the 1960s, was a much later addition to Saigon.

54. It is interesting to follow the erection of this monument from its conception. It was to be a private endeavor without any subsidies from the government. The campaign to raise funds was to be done entirely through private means. Yet there was a commission composed of forty members, all appointed by the lieutenant-governor of Cochinchina. It included the general commander of the French troops in Cochinchina; the Apostolic vicar; the Protestant pastor; the consuls of Great Britain, of the United States of America, of Portugal, of Italy, and of Japan; delegates of the government of Cochinchina; delegates from the Colonial Council, the Chamber of Commerce, and the Chamber of Agriculture; the directors of the Bank of Indochina, the Chinese Bank of Industry, the Hong Kong and Shanghai Bank, and the Bank of Australia and China; representatives from various military groups. There were apparently no Vietnamese representatives, but, for some unknown reason, both the Colonial Council and the government of Cochinchina selected two Vietnamese each to send to the commission. In any case the commission very quickly reached the consensus that this monument was to be a monument erected in honor of only French soldiers. Then, possibly out of decency, since more than 100,000 Vietnamese had been sent to bolster the French war effort and some of these Vietnamese had fought and fallen alongside the French, the members of the commission suggested that, after this French monument was completed, then they would reconvene to raise funds to build what they called very ambitiously a "Vietnamese Pantheon," similar to the one in the Fifth District in the city of Paris. Needless to say, the plan for the Vietnamese Pantheon remained at the level of a good intention. See issues of *Echo Annamite,* from 6 Mar. 1919 on.

55. I was quite surprised to read in a popular almanac recently published in

Vietnam entitled *Van Hoa Viet Nam, Tong Hop* (Culture of Vietnam. Generalities) (Hanoi, 1989), 226, no. 39, the listing of a pamphlet written by Truong Vinh Ky among the one hundred most remarkable works of Vietnamese literature. That pamphlet is entitled *Chuyen di tham Bac Ky nam At Hoi* (Voyage to Tonkin in the Year At Hoi) (Saigon, 1876), in which, according to the authors of the almanac, "Truong Vinh Ky records his experiences gained during a three-month trip in North Vietnam in 1876. This is a rare work written in Vietnamese in the early period of formation of prose, a genre for which South Vietnam was more in advance because of its special historical and cultural circumstances." It was precisely during this trip that Truong Vinh Ky reported to the French colonial authorities in Cochinchina whatever he thought was useful to them, in their preparation to invade the rest of Vietnam. See "Le Tonkin en 1876; Rapport de Truong Vinh Ky, adressé le 28 avril 1877 à l'Amiral Dupré, Gouverneur de la Cochinchine," in *Indochine,* no. 60, 20 Oct. 1941, 4–8, in which we can read sentences such as the following: "The King [King Tu Duc] has not heeded the advice of the reformers. Utter misery, therefore, reigns among the people; from all quarters, we hear demands for changes and hopes for an administration [i.e., French administration] that will be capable of maintaining order, of giving to the people a stable future, of guaranteeing their property rights, of granting industrialists and traders the security and the dynamism they sorely need: in one word, to remove from their pit of hunger a people that smells the coming of death . . . The people here are docile, very easy to lead, hard working . . . they are not too loyal to their leaders, who, most of the time, cannot defend them. They have the impression that only a firm power, a just authority that, at the same time, is also honest and well established, can put an end to their sufferings . . . Consequently it is with coveting eyes that they compare their fate with that of the inhabitants of Lower Cochinchina [who were living under French control]."

56. See *Tieng Dan,* 28 Mar. 1928.

57. In this the French obviously pay no heed to the advice Rudyard Kipling gave to Theodore Roosevelt:

Take up the White Man's burden,
Send forth the best ye breed,
Go bind your sons to exile,
To serve your captives' needs."

Alexandre Varenne, governor-general of Indochina from 1925 to 1928, declared in a speech in 1926: "There are, among our compatriots residing in Indochina, certainly some less interesting individuals who do not understand nor do they observe towards the local people the basic elements of civility which, for a people such as ours, should not be too difficult to practice" (in *Discours prononcé le 20 Septembre 1926 par A. Varenne, Gouverneur Général de l'Indochine* [Saigon, 1926]).

58. In a particular rubber plantation workers nicknamed two French supervisors after the way they mistreated them. One was called "Mr. French-Thrower" because, upon any slight mistake of any worker placed under his supervision, he would throw whatever lethal or nonlethal weapon was at his disposal there and then in the direction of

the guilty worker. The other supervisor was called "Mr. French-Snatcher." Fortunately, the article did not tell us what this latter's specialty was. See *Than Chung,* 27 Aug. 1929.

59. See *Indochine Enchaînée,* no. 5, 1925. "Ne crie pas. Fous leur sur la gueule!"

60. See *Tieng Dan,* 24 Oct. 1928: a French foreman severely beat up a pregnant native woman, stripped her naked, and threw her out of the factory into the street. He received the suspended sentence of eight days in prison. He only paid a fine of sixteen French francs. See also *La Tribune Indigène,* 4 Apr. 1918: a justice of the peace was accused of violent behavior toward his prisoners. He was sentenced to four months in prison. His sentence was subsequently suspended, and he was fined two hundred French francs.

61. See *Tieng Dan,* 8 Aug. 1928.

62. See the article in *Argus Indochinois,* 15 Apr. 1922, which complained that cars usually sped through the city of Vinh, causing quite a few accidents, and yet no driver had ever been bothered by any law enforcement agency.

63. See *Tieng Dan,* 5 Oct. 1927.

64. See *Tieng Dan,* 17 Mar. 1928.

65. See *Tieng Dan,* 15 July 1928.

66. See *Than Chung,* 22 Sept. 1929.

67. See *Than Chung,* 25–26 Aug. and 28 Sept. 1929; *Tieng Dan,* 21 Sept., 22 Oct., and 7 Dec. 1927.

68. *Van Minh,* 9 Mar. 1927.

69. Here is what a Frenchman thought of the Vietnamese who acted like Frenchmen: "I have a real contempt for those so-called emancipated people who represent nothing more than a caricature of themselves in their attitude as much as in their clothes or in the tangible or intangible states of their soul. They do not embody in any way or to any degree the normal and harmonious blending of an extreme oriental essence with a coat of culture of the West . . . Hybrid products, rotten fruits, no particle of the Vietnamese soul could be found in them." A. Barthouet, *Variétés Indochinoises* (Hanoi, 1933), 259.

CHAPTER 3

The Vietnamese Description
of Colonialism

The colonial situation was a reality the Vietnamese people had to reckon with no matter who they were, what they did, and where they lived. It hit each and every one of them at some juncture in their life, leaving an indelible mark on their minds and a searing shock from which their hearts seldom recovered. After the awe-inspiring encounter with colonialism under one form or another, the majority of the Vietnamese people would continue to live their existence as if that engagement was nothing out of the ordinary. They readily concluded that there was nothing they could do to alter that condition. If worse came to worst, they could always try to avoid any further encounter with the unfair, unjust, and unethical system. They could conduct their lives in such a way that they would never again be confronted with it. They would probably be lucky enough to succeed in doing just that. But, if that was not at all feasible, then they could at least attempt to render the encounter as painless as possible. Some others tried to reconcile themselves with the colonial state by persuading themselves, and sometimes others, that it was a good, beneficial situation for their country. They formulated an apology for colonialism and thereby constructed a myth through which they justified the presence of the foreign lord in their own land. These people were generally well-off, thanks to the colonial government. They played an active role in the colonial administration or in the royal administration sponsored by the colonial power. They indeed derived a comfortable living out of the colonial society.

A few others went to war against the colonial master. They denounced it and refused to have any part of it. They described the colonial reality in grisly detail in the hope of convincing their compatriots of the humiliating situation their country found itself in. Through their writings they tried to arouse in their fellow citizens the feeling of hatred that would motivate them to take up arms against an unjust and unjustifiable state of affairs. Although their description of colonialism may not be 100 percent accurate, it was the message the people in Vietnam received, and that's what was important. In effect, it was not what the colonial situation was actually like that played a crucial role in the minds of the people and in their daily lives; rather, what mattered was what its critics said about it.

The Meaning of Colonialism

Following are some of the assessments of the colonial situation as seen through the lenses of its critics as well as those of its apologists.

> Colonialism is nothing but an international plunder built up into a legal institution to serve the cupidity of the Europeans.[1]

It is a form of slavery:

> People pay to be served; colonized peoples pay to serve; they pay to be enslaved.

The last statement was printed in big characters on the masthead of the newspaper *La Cloche Fêlée;* it reminded its readers everyday of their colonial and, consequently, pitiable condition.[2] Colonization, according to another journalist, is the subjugation of a country and its people for an indefinite time by an army of foreign exploiters in such a way that the indigenous people no longer have any control over the public affairs of their country and are robbed of all liberties that alone can ensure to modern men the ability to attain their freedom and their individual development.[3] However colonization is defined, it is a political regime that is rotten to its core, and the men and women who implement it wield absolutely no power over its nature, nor do they exercise any impact on it, because

> the evil is colonization itself. It constitutes the cause of all our sufferings. To demand that this colonial official be replaced or that colonial administrator be transferred elsewhere will not be enough. It would then mean that we, the indigenous people, have accepted the regime that is imposed on us, without our consent.[4]

In any case, what colonization did to the countries it affected is certainly not to be wished on anyone:

> Vietnam was an empire, an independent state; France reduced it to slavery by making it a colony. The Vietnamese were a free people with pure customs; France has turned them into a horde of traitors and slaves. Vietnam had no secret police; today, the French colonial administration snoops constantly on the people through a multitude of squealers who

thrive within and without the country. The Vietnamese had the liberty to educate themselves; at present, the French colonial government detains the monopoly of education and takes advantage of that power to hinder the evolution of the Vietnamese people through a very smart system of obscurantism. Vietnam could have elevated itself to the level of other newly modernized countries of the region but instead France has reduced it to the status of the most ignorant and the most backward land in all of Asia. There is no freedom of the press. There are, on the contrary, the state monopolies of alcohol and opium. The Vietnamese people are oppressed by the heavy weight of taxation and contributions while French civil servants gobble up each year 80 percent of the budget's revenues. Vietnam had no standing army, so there existed no military conscription; today, French imperialism compels the Vietnamese, who no longer have anything to protect to serve in the army for 4 years while French citizens are conscripted only for 18 months.[5]

Fundamentally, colonialism meant exploitation of the colony by the colonizer. There was not to be any redeeming value for colonialism, because all talks about the civilizing mission of colonial powers were just that, talks. Nguyen An Ninh, a French-trained lawyer who became a famous political activist in the 1920s, wrote the following penetrating remark:

It was not to perform a sentimental deed that France came to Indochina, after covering a distance of 15,000 kilometers. Vietnamese who, over the last few years, talked about humanitarian motives on the part of the French with the sole aim of humoring the colonialists, are as naive as those Europeans who still believe in the civilizing mission of Europe.[6]

If some indigenous peoples persisted in seeing some virtues in colonialism, it was because they stood to profit from the colonial situation. For the workers and peasants *colonialism* is synonymous with words like *pilfer, steal,* and *squash,* as in an article written by one of theirs that was published in the underground newspaper *Lao Nong* (Workers and Peasants):

To this day, some naive people still think that France came to "civilize" the Vietnamese. Those people live in tall houses with wide gates; they occupy important jobs and powerful positions; they never open their eyes to see how the imperialists are pilfering our resources and how they squash our compatriots. Right now, imperialist France uses all of its exploiting power to steal from its colonies in order to support its own economy. That's why, in Indochina, they are busily laying down railroad tracks, clearing wild forests, confiscating ricefields and land, taking advantage of our cheap labor.[7]

Furthermore, colonialism creates a big artificial gap between the colonizers and the colonized. And that wide disparity was caused by an erroneous conception of "European prestige," which is

> based neither on the moral nor the intellectual superiority of the Europeans over the Asians. It is based on the color of the skin. In Indochina, it adds on the "prestige of the conqueror." It is also based on the conceit and the ego of the slave who becomes the master through brute force. It is nurtured by the colonial government because it is the only moral strength that sustains that government.
>
> It is the "European prestige" that accepts that a European, as idiotic as he can be, could be a boss over a Vietnamese. The reverse situation is unacceptable. It is the "European prestige" added to the "prestige of the conqueror" that explains the advantages and privileges granted to Frenchmen: high salaries, innumerable scholarships given to European children for schools in the colony or in the metropole while at most one or two Vietnamese can obtain a grant to finish their studies in France; the right to receive free and scandalously immense concessions of land: a thousand acres for a European and forty for a Vietnamese, etc. . . . etc. . . .[8]

Nguyen Ai Quoc agrees that colonization carries a civilizing mission; it does bring a very special kind of civilization to its colonies, the "bourgeois civilization of the scaffold, the prison, and exile." In an article written in response to the question of whether the communist regime could be introduced to Asia in general and to Indochina in particular, he wrote in *La Revue Communiste* in 1921: "We can answer that question by the affirmative . . . Indochina, exploited by French capitalists, benefits only a few sharks." He went on to say:

> The Indochinese people are assassinated in the imperialist butchery so as to protect one wonders what! They are poisoned with alcohol and opium. They are kept in illiteracy: there is one school for one thousand official opium dens. Conspiracies are invented so that the Indochinese can be introduced to the bourgeois civilization of the scaffold, the prison, and exile. 75,000 square kilometers, 20 million inhabitants, the prey of a few cruel colonial bandits, that's present-day Indochina.[9]

Colonialism as a Necessary Evil

For the proponents of colonialism nothing is simpler than to explain it away by invoking the superiority of French arms and ammunition, French science and technology, French knowledge and dexterity—in other words, French civilization. Because of that superiority, so the argument goes, the Vietnamese people should feel happy to live under the protection of a country that will place in their hands the power of arms, reveal to them the mysteries of science, and confer upon them the full benefit of knowledge. The French will civilize Vietnam if they are given the chance, which means that the Vietnamese people should accept their colonial status and welcome the protection of France. Furthermore, they should commit themselves to not interfering with the French colonial government and, of course, to not disturbing the regime of law and order that the colonial power has established with no small effort over the native population. Hoang Cao Khai, the representative of the emperor of Vietnam in Tonkin, gave the Vietnamese people friendly advice to the effect that they should not think—let alone do anything—about expelling the French from their country—and that for two reasons. First, the Vietnamese should not compare the French with the Chinese. If, in the past, the Vietnamese had been able to oust the Chinese several times from their country to regain their independence, it was primarily due to the difficulties in communication on land between China and Vietnam, notwithstanding the fact that the two countries were not very distant from each other. In the present day, although France is thousands of miles away from Vietnam and separated by large and wide oceans, the means of transportation have made such progress that France can send military reinforcements to any place situated on the Indochinese peninsula in a matter of days in order to quell any attempt at revolt. Second, to wage war one needs a lot of money, and the Vietnamese have next to nothing compared to what France and her allies can muster. The Vietnamese, Hoang Cao Khai continued, should, therefore, not infer from the Japanese victory over Russia that any small country could from now on hold its head high against an international power. Furthermore, in case Vietnam wanted to seek help from Japan, which is supposed to belong to the same race and share the same traditional culture, it needs to do nothing more than look at what Japan has done over the last few years in and to Korea![10] In the final analysis Hoang Cao Khai was convinced that there existed only one easy way toward total independence, and that way was through education. In order to become educated, the Vietnamese had only one thing to do: that was to accept France as their teacher.[11]

The French teacher will undeniably conduct Vietnam toward freedom. Over the last decades, declared an editorial of a Hanoi newspaper, France, indeed, has not spared any effort to reveal to the Vietnamese all the mysteries surrounding the benefit that comes with freedom. They have built all kinds of schools: trade schools, technical schools, agricultural schools; they have dug canals and widened rivers; they have split mountains; they have installed sewers; they have constructed bridges. They have laid for us, the editorial continued, practically all the material foundations of freedom. It is now up to us to take advantage of the benefits brought about by freedom. We must, indeed, study hard and follow the examples of our teacher. After we have graduated, then our teacher will hand over to us the freedom machine. But as long as we find ourselves in this apprentice stage, we should not play with that machine lest we botch it up; it would then be much more difficult to put it back into shape.[12] Anyway, the Vietnamese people and the French administration are in the same boat, which the French help steer away from every obstacle toward a safe haven: the only thing the Vietnamese have to do is just row the boat.[13]

This was a rather common conception of the role France played in the colony; we can, indeed, read in *Huu Thanh,* a prestigious magazine published in Hanoi and for which Nguyen Khac Hieu, a well-known writer and poet, served as the editor-in-chief, the following declaration of purpose:

> we take fraternity as our ideology. Our purpose is to promote fraternity among our compatriots so that they will love one another as brothers and sisters. We can then rely on France to get us on the road heading toward civilization.[14]

The Vietnamese cannot compare themselves with the civilized peoples of the world, "so they should not claim any part in the government of their own country," wrote a commentator of another magazine, *Nam Phong,* also published in Hanoi, in 1922.

> In politics, the article continues, the Vietnamese people are like children who have never left the gate of their own house. How then can they be entrusted with the public affairs of their country?[15]

Ten years later the person who wrote the previous comments has not substantially altered his position. In an open petition addressed to the French minister of colonies, who came to Indochina to take its pulse after a long series of disastrous upheavals directed against French colonialism, its author asserted that the Vietnamese people did not at all complain about their fate, which—they are fully aware of—is being indissolubly associated with that of France, nor did they even ask the question about whether that fate could have been different or more promising than what it was! The protection that France extended to Vietnam was, assured the writer, in the opinion of the majority of the Vietnamese, simultaneously beneficial and useful.

> In half a century—Pham Quynh,[16] indeed it was he who is the author of both preceding comments, reasoned—we have made immense progress in all domains. Principally, France has brought us peace and order and,

owing to the security that resulted from it, our mind has opened up, our conscience became more resolute and our personality has flourished under the refreshing breeze of liberal ideas blowing from the West.[17]

Franco-Vietnamese Harmony

In the meantime, in the midst of World War I, the governor-general of Indochina, Albert Sarraut, instituted a new colonial policy he labeled "Franco-Vietnamese Harmony," or "Franco-Vietnamese Collaboration" (Phap Viet De Hue), which, he hoped, would rally the support of the Vietnamese masses in face of the intense anti-French propaganda orchestrated by German agents among the Vietnamese emigrants in China and in France.[18] Although this policy did not entail any notable improvements upon the usual colonial practice, nor were its details ever clearly spelled out, France received a strong endorsement from unexpected quarters. It is likely that Phan Boi Chau, who dominated the anti-French scene during the first twenty-five years of the twentieth century, wrote, sometime before the end of World War I, a short pamphlet he entitled *Political Thought on Franco-Vietnamese Harmony.*[19] It looks as if Phan Boi Chau fell for that revamped colonial policy, and, in order to make it work, he formulated advice for both the French and Vietnamese. Considering the diplomatic successes and territorial acquisitions Japan garnered before and during the war years, mainly at the expense of China, Phan Boi Chau made a prophetic prediction about the role that, according to him, Japan would play in Asia and the Pacific. The next conflagration, he foresaw, would oppose Japan to other Western countries. In that case he had "one worry and one fear" for both peoples. For the French he worried that, in the event that Vietnam was conquered by Japan, there would be nowhere for them to stand in the vast region of East Asia. For the Vietnamese, once their country fell under the control of the Japanese, then for thousands of generations and for thousands of future lives Vietnam would never be able to rise up from the dead in order to throw the Japanese colonialists out of Vietnam in order ultimately to reach independence. What had to be done then for both the French and the Vietnamese was to change their attitude vis-à-vis each other so as to attain Franco-Vietnamese Harmony.

> I advise the Vietnamese not to consider the French as their enemies, because I fear that the next enemy who will come will be a hundred times more cruel than the French are now. I advise the Vietnamese to look at the French from now on as competent teachers and good friends. I advise the French not to treat the Vietnamese as buffaloes and horses, because I fear that after the years [of war] in Europe, those buffaloes and horses will belong forever to others."[20]

In his memoirs Phan Boi Chau explained his conciliatory attitude toward the French administration by saying that he was fooled by a follower of his who had convinced him of the sincere desire of the French authorities to apply a new colonial policy that would foster a genuine collaboration between the colonial government and the people of Vietnam.[21] In writing such an essay, Phan Boi Chau had probably hoped that the French authorities would negotiate with him the terms for his return to Vietnam in order to assist the colonial government to implement such a policy, with the ultimate goal of giving independence to Vietnam. As it was, the French authorities did indeed send an emissary to Hangzhou to show Phan Boi Chau what the French colonial authorities considered the ways and means toward a Franco-Vietnamese Harmony. It was for the Vietnamese leader, first of all, to write a declaration to be made public in Vietnam wherein he would renounce to all revolutionary designs; second, to return to Vietnam or to go into exile in a third country, situated not too far from some French possession. On its side the French government would appoint Phan, if he chose to come home, to a high position in the Vietnamese royal government, with a very special salary. In case Phan Boi Chau preferred to reside in a foreign country, France would grant him a pension covering all personal needs. Phan Boi Chau, as expected, did not accept those conditions and wrote a letter to the governor-general in which he detailed his ideas about what he considered to be a genuine policy of Franco-Vietnamese Harmony. That document is lost, but it would have shown, as Phan Boi Chau lamented in another piece of writing of his, that between the French ideas about a Franco-Vietnamese Harmony and his own, there was an unbridgeable gap.[22]

In any case, Nguyen An Ninh, among others, disagreed fundamentally over what Phan Boi Chau esteemed as an appropriate cause for a rapprochement with the French colonial authorities: "The threat of Japan is not sufficient to persuade the Vietnamese to give up their freedom!"[23] Tran Huy Lieu, a well-known radical journalist, did not proffer as harsh a criticism against Phan Boi Chau's advocacy of such a policy because, in his opinion, Phan did it at a time when the threat of Japan was real and also because the Japanese barbarous colonial policy as it was applied over many years in Korea would have been intolerable for the Vietnamese. Furthermore, he agreed with Phan Boi Chau that the Vietnamese people would never be able to shake off the Japanese yoke, once the harness was allowed to be put on. Tran Huy Lieu continued his argument by making a scathing presentation of Japanese colonial policy as it had been implemented in Korea. He seemed surprisingly well informed on that particular topic. He indeed mentioned with great authority, for example, the interdiction for the Korean people to speak the Korean language. Indeed, they were obliged to learn Japanese in schools, to speak it only among themselves, and even to exchange their Korean names for Japanese ones. In other respects the Japanese colonial government encouraged mixed marriages between

Koreans and Japanese so that, according to Tran Huy Lieu, future generations of Japanese-Koreans would have no feelings whatsoever toward the Korean nation or the Korean race. He concluded by ridiculing those Vietnamese—the most prominent among them, in fact, was Phan Boi Chau himself, whom Tran Huy Lieu set out to defend in the first place—who, after the Japanese victory over Russia in 1905, sought assistance from Japan against France to the point of glorifying Japan, as in the following popular song:

> The independence flag was raised first
> By Japan, a country with the same writing system
> Modernization has reached Asia
> The Japanese emperor has no equal in enlightened rule![24]

Ironically enough, however, the Franco-Vietnamese Harmony policy, continued Tran Huy Lieu, enjoyed a formidable fad ever since Phan Boi Chau was arrested in China and brought back to stand trial in Vietnam in 1925. All public speeches, all newspaper editorials, drummed up support for that policy.

> The rickshaw man, his body covered only with a tattered pair of shorts, his stomach empty, his two hands clutched to the two arms of his vehicle while a fat Frenchman uncovering his big tummy and sprawling all over the cushion of the carriage: both of them shout the slogan Franco-Vietnamese Harmony. A Vietnamese girl, her face a flower, her skin a repository of cosmetics, her body so frail, her bones tiny, her arms locked in with those of a Westerner endowed with curly hair, a protruding nose, an oversized stomach and a pair of yellow eyes: they both also shout Franco-Vietnamese Harmony. From cities to rural areas, everyone seems to have forgotten their own buffalo and dog existence so as to think that they were already able to harmonize with "them."[25]

For the communists the question is easily disposed of:

> To put one's faith in the policy of harmony, the policy of collaboration with the capitalist class is no different from offering one's body for them to swallow . . . raw.[26]

Association or Assimilation?

But suppose Sarraut was sincerely committed to promoting a genuine policy of harmony;[27] his ingenuous efforts were most probably to be thwarted anyway by the next governor-general in Hanoi or the next minister of colonies in Paris; in fact, as late as 1927, Phan Van Truong, who published the newspaper *L'Annam,* defined French colonial policy in Indochina in the following way:

The policy of association, which is another name for the policy of collaboration [Franco-Vietnamese Harmony], is a policy in which the Vietnamese play the role of buffaloes in order to feed their exploiters.[28]

In 1930 it seems as if France, even at this late hour, had not yet decided on
a course of action to pursue in Indochina. The colonial authorities still vacil-
lated between the old worn-out concepts of assimilation or association, to the
point that their own staunch supporter, Pham Quynh, had to deplore:

> The question is to know what policy France intends to implement here in
> this country; a policy with the aim of turning Vietnam into an integral part
> of France, on the same footing as Algeria and other old French colonies,
> or a policy that strives to create an autonomous Vietnamese nation within
> the confines of the French Empire.[29]

He then went on to define what he would like to see included in the policy.
Assimilation must consist of

> helping us acquire the frame of mind of the Europeans with its most
> subtle, energetic and noble features; with what resides in it that makes the
> passion of the scientist or of the explorer, the courage of the combatant,
> the abnegation of the missionary, the entrepreneurial zeal of the business-
> men, the honor and virtue of the citizen, the predisposition for order, for
> style, for foresightedness, for frugality, of the most humble worker. As we
> see it, assimilation must start from the top and not from the bottom. It will
> be realized only by a selected elite trained in such a way that they will be
> able to gain the best and most original traits of the spirit of the West. There
> are thus assimilation and assimilation. If assimilation were to make us into
> artificial Frenchmen, to de-assimilate us from our race, from our culture,
> then assimilation would be dangerous; it would be treacherous. But if, on
> the contrary, assimilation aims at improving our mind, at endowing our
> personality with a few qualities inherent in the European intellect in
> general and in the French intellect in particular, then assimilation is good
> and we shall undoubtedly benefit from it. We can accept it with confi-
> dence, without fear or worries.[30]

The reason for accepting French domination because it represented the
lesser of many evils seemed to be quite widespread in the early 1920s. In an
editorial for its issue of 16 June 1924 the newspaper *La Cloche Fêlée,* which
was known as a rather radically anticolonial newspaper, asked the question: "Is
a Revolution Possible in Vietnam?" The answer came in a resounding "no" that
was based, according to the journalist, on several grounds. First of all, we

Vietnamese are still too self-centered, too opportunistic. Furthermore, we lack confidence in our compatriots. Finally, France did very well in buying the friendship of all of Vietnam's neighbors. Cambodian and Laotian soldiers would not hesitate to fight against us, while China, Japan, and Siam are good friends of France. Under these circumstances, continued the author,

> even if we succeeded in expelling the French from our frontiers, other colonialists will come, and it will be necessary to make the revolution again. Should we try to gain our independence with the help of another power? No, for Siam, China, and Japan all would think more of swallowing us than developing our country. Providence has willed that France settles down in our country; let us try to live peacefully with the French because, ultimately, the French will still be the ones who can give us and assure to us our independence.[31]

The last idea expressed here, in 1924, will have a long history. Indeed, the conception that only France could guarantee Vietnam's freedom and independence was reasserted again six years later:

> In the present situation, a Vietnamese nation can subsist and prosper only within the powerful institution of a French federation. It is in our interest to wish that institution be as strong as possible for it is the guardian and the guarantor of our national existence.[32]

The colonial powers like to cultivate this idea—that they are unique and indispensable to the colony—and the colonial subjects seem readily and naively to accept it, whether they be Vietnamese, Indonesians, or Indians!

The Loss of the Country

For all the propagandists who tried to convey to the common people of Vietnam the meaning of colonialism, the theme that recurred again and again was the loss of the country.[33] Here is how Phan Boi Chau defined that rather abstract and confusing concept in a manual he entitled *Questions to Young Adolescents*. It is a book written in the form of questions and answers, in the same direct style as in the catechism of the Catholic Church. In fact, Phan Boi Chau enjoined his Vietnamese fellows to revere and respect that small book as Catholics would do their catechism. He wrote in the preface:

> If a Christian wants to do faithfully his duties as a Christian so as to enjoy eternity in Heaven, then he must penetrate the teaching of the *Catechism*. Similarly, if a Vietnamese citizen wants to discharge faithfully of his

duties as a Vietnamese so as to enjoy future benefits accruing to his country, then he must penetrate the meaning of this book, *The Questions*.
Question: Today, is our country still there or is it already lost?
Answer: We have already lost it!
Question: How strange! The land is there! The people are there! Why do you say we have lost our country?
Answer: In order to have a country, you must have three elements: first, of course, is the land; second, the people; and third, the self-determination (meaning that we are masters of our destinies). Self-determination is, however, the most important ingredient. In fact, if the territory is there, but we do not have the right of self-determination, then the territory belongs to others, not to us. You should think about it. Does our country have an ounce of self-determination?
Question: What are we to do?
Answer: We should try to get self-determination.
Question: Do you know how we lost our self-determination?
Answer: Because the French came to establish their protectorate over us, thereby ending our self-determination.
Question: So can we ask the French to give us back some self-determination?
Answer: No! Probably not possible! Definitely not possible!
Question: So what are we to do?
Answer: When the twenty-five million of our compatriots are united, then we can talk about that![34]

The loss of the country has ultimately the meaning that the people who are born in this country of Vietnam or those who have made it their home are no longer in control of it, and men of another race retain all the powers in their hands, including the power of life and death. Again, Phan Boi Chau had some sharp, bitter, and sarcastic words concerning the surrendering of all powers to a foreign authority. In a funeral oration in honor of Tran Qui Cap, who was decapitated by the French because of his alleged involvement in the peasant rebellion of 1908 in the central provinces of Vietnam, Phan Boi Chau wrote the following lines:

Only as citizens of a lost country can we know that
To be a good and virtuous man means a transgression against some
    legitimate authorities
To search for the truth is equal to committing a crime in the eyes of
    some judicial establishment.
Were we not citizens of a lost country, we would be forever ignorant
    of these things.

How pitiful is Dr. Tran Qui Cap!
In 1908, he was condemned to death by the French protectorate for a
 "crime that does not have a name."
The 15th of August, they decapitated him in the middle of the market
 place.
Everyone knew it was a miscarriage of justice.
But it was not so.
Because when you belong to a lost country and are governed by a
 despotic government
To be condemned to death without a reason is a common occurrence
 . . .
So why was he decapitated?
Simply because he committed the crime of belonging to a lost
 country.[35]

Nguyen Thuong Hien, who followed Phan Boi Chau into exile in south
China, discussed with a Korean friend of his what it meant to belong to a lost
country:

Within the four corners of the universe, when does it happen that the wild
tiger refrain from eating human flesh? When is it that the young bird can
keep its feathers and skin intact after it has been caught by a hawk? In my
country my compatriots' bones are piling up as high as the Huong mountain; their blood flows as dense as the water of the Red River. Have you
not heard of all that?[36]

The Korean man took good notes of the exploitation wrought upon Vietnam by colonialist France and compared it with what imperial Japan was doing
to Korea and concluded:

Our two countries differ from one another as to their language, their
clothing, and yet they have received the same name: they are both called
"lost countries."[37]

The Loss of Freedom

The loss of the country means ultimately and quite obviously the loss of
freedom. Two journalists put it very convincingly in the following editorials:

—Vietnamese people, are you free?
—No, we are not free as soon as we have a government in which we do
not have any part!

—Well spoken! You are strangers to the government, which is a government of strangers! You are restricted to your role of being exploited. They exploit you in all manners, and they even succeed in persuading you they are doing that just for your own good. Better yet. They'd tell you they came to your country to bring you Western civilization, the motto of which is: Liberty, Equality, and Fraternity. Yes, it is in the name of Liberty that they remove from you your freedom, including the most basic forms of it. Yes, it is in the name of Equality that they came here to grasp the lion's share of everything. Finally, it is in the name of Fraternity that they kill you without being branded as assassins and dispossess you of your land without being considered bandits.[38]

Indeed, when a country is lost, it is no longer a country; it has instead turned itself into a prison:

Today is the commemoration of the seizure of the Bastille. It is of course a good occasion for the French people to celebrate. On the contrary, it is a day of sadness and of serious meditation for the Vietnamese, whose country is but a huge Bastille.[39]

The "Bai ca A-te-A" (Asian Ballad) expressed the same state of affairs in two short verses:

The mountains and rivers lie in shame looking at our nation
The king is but a wooden sculpture, the people but buffaloes.[40]

Along the same lines Tran Huu Do, a young writer and political philosopher, wondered in one of his publications, entitled *A Declaration about the Loss of Freedom,* how France, who holds so high the principles of Liberty, Equality, and Fraternity and who gives herself the mission of "civilizing" the Vietnamese people and protecting their interests, could snuff out their liberty during the last seventy years.[41] But what really amazed Tran Huu Do was that the Vietnamese people as a people were able to survive the loss of their freedom. For, he asked, does liberty not mean the vital essence of human beings, or do Westerners not repeat again and again "liberty or death"? So how come the Vietnamese, who had lost their liberty long ago, are still alive? That, for the least, is really very strange! In these circumstances is it surprising to see printed almost every day in daily newspapers exhortations such as this one:

Vietnamese, let us get out of our country. Let us run to foreign countries. Under other skies, we can enjoy more freedom than in our own land, for which our ancestors have paid a high price.[42]

The Loss of Human Rights

Not only did the notion of loss of the country translate for these people into the inability to participate in the government of their own country; it also encompassed the loss of dignity, simple human dignity, or the right to be treated as human beings:

> According to the people who came to protect us, we have no right to be treated as human beings . . . That is why they can afford to crush our human dignity under their feet, on every opportunity and without any reason whatsoever, by beating us up or by insulting us, as if we were pack animals immune to shame and devoid of honor.[43]

Before sailing from France toward Saigon to assume the office of governor-general, Alexandre Varenne, a former socialist congressman, received a petition signed by more than eight hundred French and Vietnamese intellectuals, the concluding remarks of which read as follows:

> It would be manifestly contrary to the principles of '89 [1789: the French Revolution] that in the twentieth century, the Indochinese, whose millenary past speaks clearly in their favor, be deprived of the most basic rights of Man and of the Citizen.[44]

So it is clear that French colonization removed from the Vietnamese all rights, human and otherwise. The freedom of religion or of conscience constituted one of these rights. In the 1920s, when Caodaism was founded, the French authorities became suspicious right away of that reformed Buddhist movement. A journalist asked why and tried to answer his own question:

> Some vicious people claim that Caodaism mixes religion and politics in the shadow of the altar, behind the curtain of a legitimate religion. Is it possible for a government endowed with soldiers and cannons to be afraid of a few thousands of bigots and crazy worshipers of the Buddha? Oh, no! What a joke! And yet the Caodaists, according to public rumor, would figure all in a blacklist of suspects and classified with great care as revolutionaries to be hanged at the first opportunity. We demand with energy and in a loud voice in favor of the mass of our compatriots the right to serve either "the Supreme Being or the Devil," as we see fit. Where would we be, o my Lord, if they came to remove the last right that is left to us, a vanquished people: the liberty of conscience and of opinion.[45]

Similarly, in 1927 two prominent journalists, Tran Huy Lieu and Nguyen An Ninh, protested in a letter addressed to the lieutenant governor of

Cochinchina that they had been arrested in violation of the freedom of religion: they were commemorating the second anniversary of the death of Phan Chu Trinh.[46]

Cultural and Racial Genocide

Colonialism may entail cultural and racial genocide. Phan Boi Chau, for example, wrote one of the most impassioned books of his life, entitled *The History of the Loss of the Vietnamese Country.* The main part of this work consists of a long list of French attempts at weakening the Vietnamese physical as well as intellectual and mental resistance to colonialism.[47] In the same spirit the author of the "Asian Ballad" expressed with some poignancy his concerns about the future of his country and its people:

> The word genocide evokes at the same time compassion and apprehension
> Will our race be able to survive?[48]

A newspaper editorial even blamed the collusion of some god for the terrible feat of genocide:

> Here it is: two words can summarize all the progress made under the guidance of our protectors: no schools although everywhere you can see opium dens and alcohol distributors; soon there will even be some gambling casinos. No intellectuals, but as many pimps and opium addicts as possible. If such a spectacle does not open the eyes of the Vietnamese, that is because some mean god has blinded them so as to exterminate their race.[49]

The inhabitants of a colony were naturally held in utter contempt by their masters. Phan Chu Trinh wrote about all this very astutely in his letter to the governor-general of Indochina in 1906:

> In Vietnam today, the opinion of the common people, whether they be intelligent or stupid, is that the Protecting Power mistreats the Vietnamese; that it does not consider them as human beings. When the people observe that the indigenous mandarins, instead of acting in the interest of their own folk, are rather harming them, the Vietnamese would again say that it is precisely the Protecting Power that unleashes these mandarins on them so that the Vietnamese would destroy one another in such a way that they will quickly exterminate their race. For the Vietnamese people, that represents the designs of colonialism. Over the last few years, the thinking

of our scholars and the songs of our villagers, all proclaim the same theme, from North to South.[50]

The unknown author of a pamphlet entitled *A Song of National Restoration* succinctly described the ravages of French colonialism in the following verses:

Looking at my country, my heart aches,
For sixty years now, the country of Nam Viet has suffered
What a pity to see the country lost and families scattered
Blood flows in the river, bones are strewn across the plains
Slaves, we serve the French
When shall we be free from cold and hunger
O look at my fatherland Viet Nam,
The people are numerous, the country vast, but its resources are
    exhausted
The working poor are hungry in the morning and frozen at night
Taxes are already burdensome but further burdened by corrupt officials
The oppressive authorities follow their barbaric manners
They take away all our gold and silver
While we kill ourselves working, they leisurely reap huge profits.[51]

Luong Ngoc Quyen, or Luong Lap Nham, son of Luong Van Can, who was the prime mover behind the Dong Kinh Nghia Thuc movement, was arrested by the British police in Hong Kong on his return trip from several years of study in Japan under the guidance of Phan Boi Chau. He was transferred to French security agents in Hong Kong who interrogated him during their voyage from there to Hanoi and ultimately to Thai Nguyen, where he incited the indigenous guards to mutiny against the officers of the penitentiary.[52] Luong Lap Nham explained to the French officers why he had joined the revolutionary movement:

I am a Vietnamese revolutionary. All real Vietnamese are anxious to liberate their country from French domination. The French authorities do not allow Vietnamese citizens to read foreign newspapers, nor do they permit them to study foreign languages. Vietnamese from North Vietnam cannot go to Saigon without a passport. We are forced to smoke opium and to pay a high tax to the government for opium. The country is strewn with opium dens. We are obliged to consume cheap alcohol and to pay a high tax on it. Access to education is very limited. For the Vietnamese, there are no universities nor specialized superior schools. Vietnamese soldiers cannot be promoted to high officer ranks. The main goal of the revolutionaries is to educate our people and to claim for a certain degree of freedom. Our conviction is that every country should be governed by its own people.[53]

The Loss of the Nation's Soul

At times colonialism has been equated with the loss of the nation's soul: *quoc hon,* which, when combined with the nation's essence, *quoc tuy,* represents the most sacred and most essential constitutive elements of a nation. Indeed, as with the loss of the country, the absence of a national soul leads to the same results:

> Although our homes and our country are all here
> Yet our country is lost and our homes have all but disappeared!
> [Without the national soul,] people go astray; their bodies deteriorate;
>   their insides disintegrate.
> At night, they never cease weeping; daytime, they don't stop moaning
> Some are ready to shed their blood in the mountains and forests
> Others go into exile in faraway lands
> Some desert their families, their homes
> Still others are so filled with worries that their hair early turns white as
>   snow.
> But there are also those who are willing to be buffaloes and horses;
> Those who have become servants, even slaves
> And those who sell out their country, their race.[54]

The common people compare the loss of the national soul to quite a few very practical shortages, as this popular song indicates:

> Not enough cash to buy a scarf
> That's why my head is shaved
> Not enough money to buy material
> That's why my shirt is short
> The nation's soul is gone! Gone where?
> Japan? Nagasaki?
> Siam? Bangkok?
> O soul of the nation, if you are really sacred
> Please protect our people.[55]

The condition of the country elicited more than concerns and worries:

> The soul went astray, the body fully emaciated, only a weak breathing remains; our country's illness is indeed life-threatening.[56]

Saigon, City Hall. (Photo by Carl Hefner.)

Saigon, the Notre Dame
Catholic Cathedral. (Photo by
Carl Hefner.)

Hanoi, the Paul Doumer Bridge, renamed Long Bien Bridge after Independence. (Photo by Carl Hefner.)

Hanoi, a house in the former French Quarter. (Photo by Carl Hefner.)

Hanoi, a street in the former French Quarter. (Photo by Carl Hefner.)

Hue, steps leading to the mausoleum of Emperor Khai Dinh. (Photo by Carl Hefner.)

Hue, bronze statue of Emperor Khai Dinh sitting on his throne under a cement awning. (Photo by Carl Hefner.)

Hanoi, Central Prison, also known as the Hao Lo Prison or the Hanoi Hilton. (Photo by Ann Minzer.)

Tan An, Cochinchina, residence of the French chief-administrator of the province

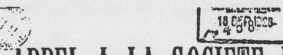

APPEL A LA SOCIETE DES NATIONS

A quoi in 2

Pour le droit du peuple annamite à disposer de lui-même

Les graves événements dont l'Indochine française fut dernièrement le théâtre, et dont l'écho troublant a retenti dans la métropole, n'avaient eu d'autre cause que l'oppression nationale et l'exploitation sociale dont souffre un peuple de 20 millions d'âmes, livré depuis un demi-siècle à la merci des colons et de l'administration.

Notre situation Politique

Nous n'avons pas la liberté de penser, d'écrire, d'enseigner, de voyager et d'émigrer, de nous associer et de nous réunir. Une juridiction exceptionnelle est réservée aux autochtones. Ils ne peuvent exercer un contrôle effectif sur le budget de leur pays. La plupart de nos écoles ont été détruites, très peu en ont été remplacées. Enfin, le préjugé de race nous écrase.

Lors de l'arrivée de M. Varenne à Saïgon, le 27 novembre 1925, 700 Annamites représentant toutes les classes sociales et pleins de confiance dans la politique de « collaboration » proclamée par leur nouveau gouverneur, ont présenté à M. Varenne un cahier des vœux annamites ; malheureusement M. Varenne n'a pas donné satisfaction aux représentants de notre pays.

Notre situation Sociale

Nous sommes assujettis aux capitations, aux corvées, à la gabelle. Aucune loi ne protège nos ouvriers et dont en fait pourtant que des enfants de deux sexes, âgés de moins de 12 ans sont employés dans les manufactures de caoutchouc et dans les mines de charbon.

L'administration force nos plus humbles villages à acheter en gros l'opium et l'alcool.

Le budget de l'Indochine étant consacré pour les 7/8 à l'entretien des fonctionnaires, les travaux publics de première utilité sont négligés. Ainsi le transindochinois n'est même pas achevé. Ainsi nos digues n'ont jamais fait l'objet d'une préoccupation de l'État, à tel point que, chaque année la population rurale du Tonkin voit sa récolte, ses maisons, son bétail, ravagés par l'inondation.

Telle est, grosso modo, la situation actuelle de notre peuple.

Comparaison avec nos voisins et notre passé national

Tout autre est celle de nos voisins, restés indépendants. Le Siam, par exemple, possède une armée de 400.000 hommes, un gouvernement stable, un réseau ferré qui s'étend tout le long de son territoire. Et pourtant les Siamois n'étaient pas plus avancés que les Annamites, il y a cinquante ans.

Songez, d'autre part, à ce qu'était l'Annam avant la conquête française. C'était un pays indépendant qui savait se faire respecter de ses voisins, tout en méprisant la guerre et le service militaire, tout en se bornant, pour assurer sa « défense nationale » à l'emploi de la milice. C'était une démocratie qui, sous l'apparence d'une monarchie absolue, jouissait de l'autonomie des communes, de la liberté et de la gratuité à tous les degrés, de l'enseignement, et qui avait banni de son sein la féodalité et le clergé. C'était une nation constituée sur l'unité de langue, de religion, de race, de mœurs. Enfin, de l'aveu même des, pé..... alités françaises, les Annamites possédaient, depuis des temps immémoriaux une haute civilisation morale.

Où en sommes-nous aujourd'hui, avec la tutelle française ? Vous l'avez vu. Où en serions-nous, sans elle ? Vous le devinez. En tout cas, nous vous affirmons que la situation actuelle de notre peuple est grosse de conséquences désastreuses.

Vers la guerre du Pacifique ? Vers la guerre de l'Indochine ?

Étant donnée la tournure déjà si grave que prirent les derniers événements de l'Indochine, il n'est pas chimérique de prévoir, dans un avenir prochain, un soulèvement général des indigènes. C'est vous dire, dans cette hypothèse, que la France qui a déjà sur les bras deux guerres coloniales et la crise financière, qui ne possède qu'une flotte de second ordre, serait obligée d'entreprendre une troisième guerre, par surcroît.

Et qui sait même si la guerre en Indochine ne sera pas l'étincelle qui déclenchera la conflagration du Pacifique et livrera l'univers à un cataclysme sans précédent !

Nos Revendications

Au nom de l'amitié véritable entre le peuple français et le peuple annamite, au nom de leur intérêt bien entendu, à tous les deux, au nom de la paix de l'Extrême-Orient et du monde, au nom du principe sacré du droit des peuples à disposer d'eux-mêmes que les puissances alliées, dont la France, ont proclamé au lendemain de la grande guerre, nous réclamons devant la Société des Nations, l'indépendance totale et immédiate du peuple annamite, sous réserve que notre pays, redevenu libre :

1° S'engage à payer, — en espèces ou en nature, en un nombre d'annuités à débattre, une partie à déterminer, — des dettes de guerre que la France a contractées envers l'Amérique et l'Angleterre ;

2° Conclut un traité d'alliance politique et commerciale avec la France ;

3° Élabore une constitution politique et sociale, inspirée des principes de la souveraineté du peuple, du respect des minorités ethniques, du respect du travail, et servant de base à l'instauration d'une République fédérative indochinoise ;

4° Crée une armée nationale, basée sur notre ancien système de la milice, et chargée de maintenir l'ordre à l'intérieur et la sécurité à l'extérieur ;

5° Envoie une délégation à la Société des Nations au même titre que le Siam et la Chine.

Hanoï, le 25 juillet 1926.

Le « Phuc-Viêt »
ou Parti annamite de l'indépendance nationale

Membres d'honneur :
Phan-boï-Châu et Phan-Châu-Trinh
anciens condamnés à mort

Membre délégué à Paris :
Nguyên-van-Ngoc, 22, rue Sommerard, Paris (5°)

Paris, le 30 août 1926.

Le « Viêt-Nam-Hôn »
ou l'âme annamite
Tribune libre des étudiants
et des travailleurs annamites

Fondateur : Nguyên-aï-Quôc

Administration : 7, rue Galleron, Paris (20°)

Imprimerie Française, Maison J. Dangon, 188, rue Montmartre, 188, Paris VI°, Georges Dangon imprimeur.

Appeal to the League of Nations for the Right of Self-Determination of the Vietnamese People

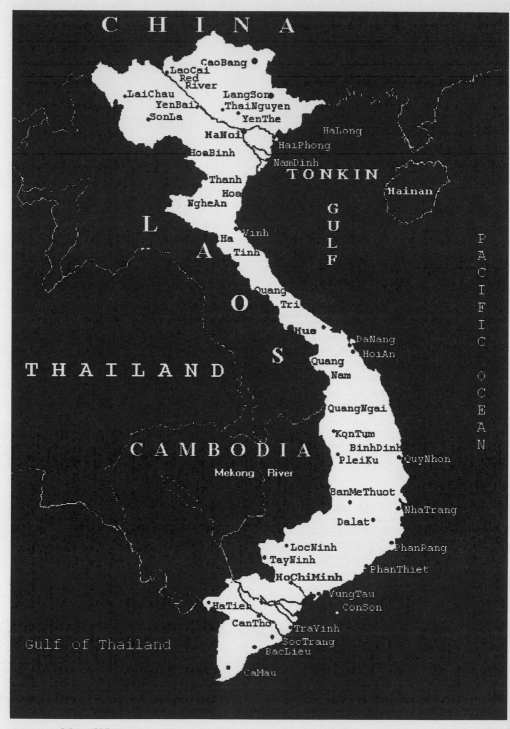

Map of Vietnam

That is why people who care about the future of the country naturally try to summon back the national soul:

> After your return, soul, people will wake up
> No longer will they be stupid and idiots as in the past
> They will no longer have to labor from early morning till afternoon
> No longer will they have to be exposed to sun and rain.
> You shall eradicate the greedy and the cruel
> You shall destroy those who harm their fellow compatriots
> Those who lined their pockets with the people's silver and gold.[57]

Most of the time, however, the summons is of no use because, as Tran Tu Xuong and Ngo Duc Ke said in two very concise sets of verses:

> The soul of a four thousand year old country has not awakened
> Twenty five million people are still stupefied with sleep.

> The yellow race must still suffer a great disaster, Heaven has not
>   changed its fate
> The soul of this ancient land has gone far away; it is not easy to
>   summon it back.[58]

Taxes and Corvées

Colonialism has consisted in more exorbitant and more varied kinds of taxes. It is a well-known fact that the impressive program of public works undertaken under the administration of Governor-General Paul Doumer (1897–1905) could not be materialized without hiking the tax rates on the native population of Indochina.[59]

But what really boggles the minds of the Vietnamese was not so much the exorbitant amount of taxes they had to pay as the confusing variety of taxes the French imposed on practically every activity the people were involved in. The following verses are extracted from *The Asian Ballad* (The Chant to Raise the Consciousness of the People), composed around the years 1905–6, the author of which is yet undetermined:[60]

> All the varieties of taxes,
> They increase them endlessly
> The land tax is hardly paid
> When the tax on buffaloes and cows is due,
> Tax on dogs; tax on pigs
> Tax on matches; tax on alcohol; tax on ferries; tax on cars

Tax on markets; tax on tea; tax on tobacco
Tax on licenses; tax on water; tax on lamps
Tax on houses; tax on pagodas and temples
Tax on timber from forests; tax on commercial junks
Tax even on cosmetic products and on city streets
Tax on emaciated people addicted to drugs
Tax on hillocks; tax on beaches; tax on dunes
Tax on dignitaries; tax on actors and musicians
Tax on oil, honey; tax on paints everywhere
Tax on rice, vegetable; tax on paddy; tax on cotton
Tax on silk; tax on iron; tax on bronze
Tax on birds; tax on fish throughout the three regions
Nobody can enumerate all the various kinds of taxes
The most stunning tax is on defecation
It is too painful to talk about all those things
Shame descends on fathers and sons
Separation comes between husbands and wives
At times, we are filled with grudge and anger
We want to scream to tear off the sky
We want to draw out our swords.

Another ballad says practically the same thing, although in a more elaborate way and also in a more popular form:

Some trade in junks, some in store,
They pay taxes on the rivers, on the streets
Some trade in the plains, others in the mountains
They pay taxes on military posts, on frontier passes . . .
Even the old fisherman must pay taxes for the use of the vast sea . . .

There are three pieces of vacant land
They declared them as good rice fields,
The tax is two piasters and a half per hectare
Plus twenty cents for fees,
Plus ten cents for fees . . .
Then there are taxes on the communal houses, on the inns
Taxes on doors, on houses,
Taxes on leaves, on flowers,
Taxes on venison, on sea food
Including venison and sea food . . .

Taxes on salines as well as on salt

So that the people have become bland and dry . . .
Taxes on the agricultural parks and plantations
Taxes on the roads, on the barges
Taxes on the civil servants, on the mandarins
Taxes on the buffaloes, the cows, the dogs, and the pigs
Taxes on oil, on salty dishes
Taxes on clothes, on cotton
Also taxes on iron, on bronze
Taxes on tobacco, on alcohol . . .

All three regions must pay
Taxes are imposed everywhere
Oh, earth! Oh, sky!
Our country of Vietnam is too miserable
The North, the Center and the South are all miserable.

The people of the old imperial capital city of Hue were convinced, however, that they were more heavily imposed upon by the colonial authorities. A well-known popular song on taxes and corvée labor originated from there; the two first verses serve to give the geographical location of the narrator:

When I take a look at the Perfume River, the water is as green as the
  leaves,
When I look in the direction of the stone dam, houses and buildings
  are all impressive,
But ever since the arrival of the French
I never cease paying taxes, doing corvée labor, and building roads.

Economic Exploitation

For everyone in the colony economic exploitation first of all took the form of slavery on the plantations or of hard labor in the factories or in the mines:

At this time, there are more than 40,000 workers on rubber plantations. On these plantations, countless number of people are dying everyday. Among 659 workers on the An Vieng plantation, 123 people died, and 242 were hospitalized, only during the month of November. From 1,000 coolies in Budop, 474 died. In the various mines, among the 15,900 workers, not one survived to be sixty! We simply must compare the wages, the standard of living of each of our workers with the benefits obtained by the imperialist enterprises, then we can clearly see how they "civilized" our people! Workers become more miserable, while peasants suffer more and more from poverty and hunger with every passing day; only those who betray their fatherland sing the praise of the "civilizing mission" of the mother country![61]

Colonial exploitation assumes many forms, but to Marxist evaluators, economic exploitation constituted the most obvious, and more condemnable, pattern of abuse. The newsletter *Lao Nong* (Workers and Peasants)— which inscribes next to its title two well-known calls of Karl Marx, "Proletarians of the world unite" and "Only the workers can liberate themselves," and under it the slogans "Destroy Imperialism!" and "Overthrow Capitalism!"—analyzes with facts and figures the extent of the exploitation of Vietnamese resources by French colonialists. It demonstrates with a great deal of conviction how the French used Vietnamese wealth to enrich the economy of their own country. That is why in Indochina now they are laying rails for their trains, clearing forests, occupying land, and taking advantage of the cheap labor.

The An Loc Company, which has 1,657 hectares of land, realized in 1927 a profit of 6,710,067 francs. The Rubber Company of Indochina with its 10,000 hectares brought in 27,965,420 francs in 1926. The 30,000 hectares of Bien Hoa Industry and Forest made in 1926 a profit of 2,058,000 francs. At the end of 1926, Indochina exported more than 9,000 tons of rubber.

In the northern part of our country, the French concentrate their efforts in exploiting our mineral resources. The Charcoal Company of Tonkin occupies 22,000 hectares of land and realized a profit of 55 million francs in 1926. At the end of 1926, the Dong Trieu Company of Charcoal produced more than 1,290,259 tons of charcoal for a revenue of over 161 million francs. All in all during the years 1926–27, 103 plantations occupied 297,526 hectares of land, 326 agricultural estates 223,070 hectares, 43 mineral companies 189,350 hectares, and that is to cite only the more important companies.

At the present time, there are more than 40,000 workers employed in rubber plantations. Close to 30,000 workers have been sent to New Caledonia and the New Hebrides. The number of deaths among the workers on the plantations cannot be reliably calculated![62]

If rails have been laid and trains roll on them, all that was of course not done for the benefit of the indigenous people. Phan Boi Chau evaluated the new means of transportation the French have introduced for the Vietnamese people in the following terms:

Look at the East Asian country of Japan
Trains and automobiles welcome the passengers
Who are treated with extreme courtesy
Whether they choose to sit or stand up;
In the place they take their meals or
In the bed they lie to sleep.
If they are sick, people take good care of them.
Human beings, they are treated with humanity.
The French of course do not belong to the same race.
Look at how they treat our people.
Their automobiles carry but putrid trash and rotten garbage.
In their trains, our people have to sit in dirty and tiny corners,
The sun shines directly on them, and rain falls on their head.
If they become sick, they are left to their own devices.
The [French controllers], furthermore, lavish on us contempt,
   humiliation,
Making the most out of their authority:
If you are too slow to show your ticket or pay your fare
Their feet start kicking and their hands whipping.[63]

The Cultural Exploitation

Education was a very important issue for the people, who assessed the nature and value of colonialism in Vietnam. They attributed to Confucianism one of the main causes of Vietnam's loss of independence; they naturally had many grievances against the traditional Confucian educational system, which, in their opinion, accounted for so many weaknesses in Vietnamese society. They, nevertheless, did not much like the new system established by the colonial government in its place.

The National School is named the Franco-Vietnamese School
Where Vietnamese people are taught the French language
As for the hundreds of other interesting disciplines
Such as military affairs, mechanics, electricity, chemistry
There are naturally no teachers available
Even in agriculture, there still are so many things we do not know
Let alone in industry and commerce.[64]

The demand for a scientific education, at times, was doubled with the demand for a "complementary education" that would be well adapted to local conditions and aimed at meeting the needs of a middle class, which became more and more numerous by the day, and also for a professional education equally tailored to satisfy local needs.[65]

But what the Vietnamese reproached the French most for was a policy they called "obscurantism," which was also defined as the policy of the "dropper." The Vietnamese student who is eager to acquire as much Western knowledge as possible is compared to a traveler in the desert, who is dying of thirst and to whom the French savior, although in possession of whole buckets filled with fresh and pure water, would give it only drop by drop to the thirsty traveler, through a dropper! Is it surprising, then, that some Vietnamese advocate the seizure of these buckets by force? For these Vietnamese, Vietnam, which has been in the past one of the more literate countries, has lagged behind other Asian countries and constitutes one of the most ignorant people of the region, although the Vietnamese people are endowed with no less intelligence than any other people![66] In practical terms there are simply not enough schools for the majority of the children of school age. Of a total of more than 2 million of them, there were only 200,000 seats in public primary schools in 1924, so that only 1 out of 10 children was able to attend school.[67] The same situation obtains through another set of statistics: in 1928 in Cochinchina 2,110 students graduated from primary schools, having passed the examination called the Certificate of Primary Franco-Vietnamese Studies. Of that number only 273 found entrance into the various high schools that existed at the time in southern Vietnam.[68] For that reason we quite often hear calls for the colonial government to relax its legislation regulating the establishment of private institutions of learning.[69] After a careful survey of the development of national consciousness in various countries of Asia, the newspaper *L'Annam* concluded that Vietnam lacked any and all of the manifestations of a nationalist movement, and that was because of the fact that the French denied the people of Vietnam a rudimentary education, let alone a civic or patriotic education. That resulted in the fact that

> there are naive Tonkinese and Cochinchinese who think they are strangers to one another! The weird Franco-Vietnamese system of education teaches everything; it even gives lessons on loyalism—or more exactly on servilism—but one never hears about lessons in patriotism or simply on civic virtues. In brief, the colonial government makes certain that Vietnamese children are never taught to know their country, to love it and, if necessary, to shed their blood to defend it![70]

That kind of curriculum allowed *La Cloche Fêlée* to come to the conclusion that Vietnamese nationalism does not exist! It is that simple! The evidence? Any Vietnamese nowadays would look with total indifference at a fellow compatriot being beaten up by a foreigner.[71] Anyway, as the lieutenant governor of Cochinchina made very clear to Nguyen An Ninh in the course of an interview cum interrogation:

This country should not have any intellectuals! This country is too simple. If you want to make intellectuals, go to Moscow. Remember that the grain you want to sow in this country will never germinate and grow.[72]

Those words echoed perfectly the educational policy implemented earlier by Governor General Long, who wanted to pursue what he called a "horizontal" rather than a "vertical" plan. These geometrical terms simply meant that the colonial government devoted its efforts and resources to expand the lower echelons of education without paying much attention to the middle or higher levels.

Vietnamese who graduated from primary schools were relegated to secondary positions reserved for them in the administration. Those who received a higher degree of education or who are trained in technical schools which constitute what they pompously call the University of Indochina occupied positions within the "lateral branches" created especially for them.[73]

Nguyen Ai Quoc had an interesting explanation about why the French were not willing to educate the Vietnamese, and that was because they are afraid that once the Vietnamese people are educated they would read those many books that deal with various political ideologies and with the history of revolutions.[74] This charge is not too different from the one leveled against the colonial regime by the editorialist of *L'Annam.* According to him, Indochina, officially a colony of exploitation for France, belongs neither to the colonialists residing in Indochina nor to the French people in France. It belongs, rather, to a very exclusive group of bankers and industrialists. To initiate the indigenous peoples into enjoying their liberties would be tantamount to losing a great part of the profits these sharks derived from Indochina.[75]

Another grievance expounded by Vietnamese anticolonialist writers lay in the obligation for high school students to follow a curriculum in use in France; this gave rise to ridiculous phrases such as "Our fatherland is France. Our ancestors are the Gauls," which Vietnamese students had to learn by heart! Furthermore, all subjects on the intermediate level of high schools were taught in French so that the French language had to be introduced to Vietnamese students already in the higher classes in the primary cycle. Why was the medium French? Because, replied a newspaper editorial, the goal of education "was to train a few workers or administrators of secondary rank in the French colonial government."[76]

Finally, a journalist instills some humor into this whole question of cultural imperialism. He came to a village and saw brand-new French flags unfurled over some thatched huts marked very prominently with two big letters,

RA. He said to himself: "We must have reached independence, because RA would stand for 'République Annamite': Vietnamese Republic." He was soon to be disappointed to find that RA means rather "Régie Alcool": state monopoly of alcohol, and not at all République Annamite. So he concluded:

> You see: our mother country takes real good care of us. We are thirsty for education. She quenches it with alcohol![77]

> In two words, here is the progress brought to us by the protecting nation! No schools, but everywhere alcohol retail shops, opium dens, and soon there will be official casinos. No intellectuals but a lot of card dealers, gamblers, and opium addicts.[78]

> If Vietnam had the same number of schools as the outlets for alcohol and opium, the Vietnamese people would be the most educated of all the peoples on this earth.[79]

> The French try to keep the indigenous people in illiteracy. There are ten schools for every one thousand outlets for opium![80]

But in spite of all these reproaches and grievances, the new Western system of education exerted a great deal of attraction on the young generations of Vietnamese. In effect, that new system offered to its followers unprecedented opportunities for employment in the modern sectors of the economy or in the colonial civil service with all of its privileges, which made the old Confucian learning look like a very poor avenue to the good life. The satirist-poet Tran Te Xuong, also known as Tu Xuong, expressed that dichotomy with a great deal of conviction using concrete images:

> Let us face it, what good are the Confucian letters
> Even with a doctorate or a master, you still will stay curled in bed
> Nothing can equal the learning to become a colonial clerk
> We drink champagne in the evening and cow's milk in the morning.[81]

The Unjust System of Justice

In no other domain are the injustices inflicted upon the indigenous peoples more patent than in the colonial justice system. First of all, the courts have been presided over exclusively by French judges, who cannot understand the local language. As late as 1926, even with the unusually liberal reforms of Governor-General Varenne, the editors of the French-supported magazine *Nam Phong* were still complaining that Vietnamese did not yet have access to the higher ranks of the judiciary.[82] As a result of this policy, those Vietnamese citizens who had obtained a high degree in law from French universities were still prevented from practicing law, that is, from appearing in person in court; in other words, they were not allowed to serve as counsel to a party in a legal suit. Toward the end of the 1920s, after a certain number of students had come back from France with their law degrees, we began to read advertisements such as the following one in Vietnamese newspapers:

> Legal consultation office of Mr. Pham Van Gia, Master in Legal Studies. Ten Vietnamese piasters for a legal consultation. Should you need a lawyer [for the court], we have Mr. Gallois Montbrun. He will cost you 3,000 to 4,000 Vietnamese piasters.[83]

At court, when the accused were interrogated, even though they could speak French, they were not permitted to speak it if they were not French or at least French citizens. They had to answer or speak through an interpreter. For example, Nguyen An Ninh, who got his Master in Legal Studies degree from a university in France and who was, therefore, fluent in French, was not authorized to use the French language when he appeared at the Appeal Court of Saigon in 1929. "You are a Vietnamese; you are not allowed to speak French," the judge told him.[84] On the other hand, as Nguyen An Ninh appeared in court dressed in a Vietnamese-styled pair of white cotton pajamas, his feet ensconced comfortably in wooden clogs, a white towel hanging from his right arm, the general prosecutor scolded him, saying that he was playing the role of a comedian and that he looked like a waiter in a second-class restaurant.[85]

In Cochinchina the justice system applied the French code of law, whereas in Tonkin and Annam the courts used a code of law that was completely outmoded and outdated, in which the judges could not even find the proper definition of most of the offenses. Anyway, in the minds of the indigenous people, the court in Indochina was not meant to mete out justice but simply to distribute sentences that put away Vietnamese citizens who happened to look undesirable to the colonial establishment.

The court also applied different standards to Frenchmen and indigenous people:

> Justice in the colonies is frequently used to cover up many revolting injustices. It is well-known that, since the time of conquest, the killing of indigenous people by Europeans has always gone unpunished. When the material evidence is too overwhelming, then doctors must be found to certify that the death of the victims had nothing to do with an accident. They were, rather, due to the congenital weakness of their spleen! But when the victims are too numerous, or when their necks are severed from

the rest of their body, or when their bodies are riddled with bullets, as it had happened at Thai Nguyen recently, then the criminal court condemns the assassins to a light fine! On the other hand, when a European is killed, the police never fail to come up with the killers, because the method consists of rounding up as many suspects as possible, and the criminal court will then pronounce a few capital sentences. That's why, among the indigenous people, there is the belief that, whenever the real culprits cannot be found, suspects are arrested and even sentenced, for the sake of preserving the prestige of the white folk.[86]

Even a French journalist could not refrain from writing the following observation:

In one and the same day, I saw the tribunal of Hanoi condemn a young Vietnamese student who has committed the crime of writing a patriotic song to three years in confinement and a French foreman who has killed, for a trifle, a worker of his by kicking him with his boots with a suspended sentence of three months in prison.[87]

A worse case occurred in Thai Nguyen. On 30 August 1917 a rebellion broke out in the town's penitentiary plotted by some noncommissioned officers and enlisted men from the indigenous guard, enticed by the prisoners who could no longer tolerate the cruel, brutal, and ruthless treatment dealt to them by the French chief administrator of the province by the name of Darles. After the insurrection the French colonial authorities established a special tribunal called the Criminal Commission of Thai Nguyen, to try the people involved in the rebellion. Apart from a few summary executions performed in the heat of the repression itself, the Criminal Commission met three times: on 18 and 22 December 1917 and on 27 May 1918. The three trials resulted in the following condemnations: ten death sentences, ten forced labor for life, eight exiles, sixty sentences running from four months to eighteen years in prison. As for the principal cause of the rebellion, who was a high-placed French civil servant, Mr. Darles, after being carefully investigated for violent and brutal treatment of subordinates, he was sentenced in March 1919 by the Court of Appeals of Hanoi to a fine of two hundred French francs.[88] There were other abuses, too: the newspaper *La Tribune Indochinoise,* for example, voiced its complaint against a justice system that gives itself the liberty of arresting and incarcerating the indigenous people for as long a time as it wants to, even if it ultimately frees them because they are innocent.

Of the twenty-five people who have been detained for more than four months, only one has been indicted. The prestige of the government will be seriously damaged by the outcome of this pathetic comedy.[89]

As one could easily surmise, this case was not unique or even rare. In 1929 a nationalist leader of some reputation was arrested in Ben Luc, some twenty-five miles south of Saigon. According to a newspaper reporter, hundreds of people living in the vicinity were also arrested and detained, suffering untold humiliations and indignities, to the point that there was no one left to harvest the rice crops in the fields and to water the vegetables in the patches. All the houses had their doors shut tight, and inside the children wept, waiting for their fathers, the wives for their husbands.[90]

There is no more dramatic and gloomier assessment of the colonial justice system than the remark made by a French lawyer during the trial of a Vietnamese writer, Tran Huu Do, who was accused of harming the security of the colony with his treatises on imperialism, on the loss of freedom, on independence, and on patriotism—all titles of his books:

There is no justice in politics. Here we condemn Vietnamese patriots in the name of French patriotism. It is to be noticed that of all the subversive activities that have taken place in this country, none was provoked by a newspaper or a book.[91]

Self-Reliance Versus Foreign Intervention

Two editorials summarize very accurately the mood of the people of Vietnam toward the questions of independence and colonization at the end of the 1920s. The writings represent the two streams of thinking that have polarized, during the entire French colonial period and even much beyond, the Vietnamese people into proponents of self-reliance and those who favored foreign intervention. The first editorial is taken from an issue of the daily newspaper *L'Annam:*

Colonization offers the spectacle of a wide field open to the most dubious appetites abandoned to a boundless exploitation. The most scandalous means are used to balance the budget: alcohol, salt, opium, and a heavily burdensome taxes asset . . . What has France done so as to earn our gratitude? A road network, a few sections of railroad, a couple of ports, a couple of shipyards, a certain material comfort that only our civilizers can enjoy without restrictions! No industry worthy of the name!

We must try to take back the possession of our land, reclaim the title of first occupants, a title our ancestors acquired in the past at the price of a continuous struggle and of untold sufferings. No, let no one be permitted to oppress us and to deprive us of our daily rice while advising us to work hard in order to regain our independence! No, no, and no, we reply to them. Before all else, we want our independence! We need air in our dried-up lungs, room for our expansion! Only a radical solution can bring about happier effects than the so-called policy of association, which, notwithstanding all the eloquent speeches, remains a bloodless reality![92]

The following *Nam Phong* article, entitled "Nation and Nationalism," was published in its December 1930 issue, following a series of anticolonial activities.

Our literary life has barely started; our agriculture has not been modernized; our industry is lagging behind in many ways; we have no entrepreneurs in the realm of commerce and trade; so why are we captivated by the extremist doctrine of communism, which will with certitude impede our progress in the future. Woe! The blood that has been shed does not flow from strangers' veins! The dead corpses are not carcasses of buffaloes or horses! How come our compatriots have not yet awakened to realities? Instead, they continue keeping their eyes shut and behave in irrational ways, causing so much pain and anguish in so many of us! The Great French Nation has come to bring civilization to our country; it has committed itself to enlighten our people with humanity and charity, and yet recently it was forced to treat the Vietnamese people with long swords, short shotguns, with bombs and planes. That certainly was a difficult course of action for her to take! In summary, if we find ourselves today in such quandaries, that is because we lack patriotism. If indeed we really love our country, then how come we do not love our families? How come we do not know how to love one another? Why are we so insensitive to the consequences of our actions? If we sincerely love our country, then we ought to wish that the recent events would be eradicated once and for all. If we are endowed with genuine patriotism, then France not only would not prevent us from having such sentiments; she would, rather, encourage us so that she would be empowered to help us exploit this country. A reminder, though: genuine patriotism entails sincerity, and if one wishes to help one's country, one must know the way! What do our people think about that? If the national soul is still wandering in our mountains and rivers, it should come back among us so as to enlighten us all![93]

Notes

1. *L'Annam,* 11 Oct. 1926.
2. *La Cloche Fêlée,* 26 Nov. 1925.

3. *L'Annam,* 27 Mar. 1927.

4. *L'Annam,* 30 May 1927.

5. *La Cloche Fêlée,* 24 Dec. 1925.

6. See Document 9, in this volume. Nguyen An Ninh, *France in Indochina.*

7. *Lao Nong,* n.d. [1927], n.p. It is a one-page "newspaper," handwritten and reproduced in a rather rudimentary form, through the "Jell-O" system. It is supposed to be an organ of propaganda issued by the Vietnamese political refugees living in southern China or in the mountainous regions of northern Vietnam. Copies of this newspaper are to be found in SLOT V, 40.

8. See Document 9, in this volume: Nguyen An Ninh, "France in Indochina."

9. In *La Revue Communiste,* 2, no. 15 (May 1921): 204–6.

10. As we shall see later, this constituted undoubtedly a very powerful argument against those Vietnamese who, after the Japanese victory over Russia in 1905, were seeking Japanese assistance to fight French colonialism. Phan Boi Chau, an ardent supporter of Japan, received that "friendly" advice quite a few times.

11. Hoang Cao Khai, *En Annam* (Hanoi, 1910), 41–47; the French translation was done by J. Roux.

12. *Thuc Nghiep Dan Bao,* 12 Aug. 1922.

13. *Thuc Nghiep Dan Bao,* 19 Sept. 1922.

14. *Huu Thanh,* 1 Feb. 1922.

15. See the article, entitled "Hoi Tu Van Bac Ky," in *Nam Phong* 10, no. 59 (May 1922): 361–74.

16. Pham Quynh had a very brilliant career as a politician and also as a writer. He was educated both in the traditional educational system and in the French colonial schools. He started his career as a researcher for the famous French School of the Far East (Ecole Française d'Extrême Orient). In 1917 he received financial aid from the colonial government to found a political and literary magazine called *Nam Phong,* the purpose of which was "to implement the civilizing mission of the state by publishing essays written in Vietnamese, Chinese and French so as to help elevate the intellect and safeguard the moral values of the people; propagate the knowledge of European sciences, principally the many philosophies of Great France; to preserve the essence of Vietnamese culture and to champion the economic interests of the French and Vietnamese peoples. *Nam Phong* will also pay particular attention to the development of the *quoc ngu* system of writing into a national literature." *Nam Phong* 1, no. 1 (July 1917): 5. Later on, when Emperor Bao Dai came back from his studies in France to assume the throne of Vietnam, Pham Quynh was chosen to serve in his cabinet in various capacities from minister of education to minister of the interior. To many Vietnamese intellectuals Pham Quynh was simply a "cultural valet" in the service of the French colonial administration; to others his contribution to the advancement of the Vietnamese language made him into a prominent literary figure of Vietnam.

17. See document 20, in this volume. See also Harry Benda and John Larkin, *The World of Southeast Asia* (New York, 1967), 179–81, which gives the translation of many more excerpts culled from this same document.

18. In 1913, as the supreme leader of the Vietnam Quang Phuc Hoi (Association for the Restoration of Vietnam), Cuong De, went to Europe on the invitation of the

ambassador of Germany in China. (See Document 7, in this vol.). As for Phan Chau Trinh (see Document 2, in this vol.), who was in exile in France, he was put in prison together with Phan Van Truong, a Vietnamese nationalist activist, for several months in 1915 on the suspicion that they entertained relations with Germany that were harmful to the security of France. The poems Phan Chu Trinh composed while confined in jail have been compiled by Le Am and published under the title *Tay Ho va Sante thi tap* (Tay Ho [Phan Chu Trinh's pen name]) and the poems of the Santé (name of the French prison in Paris) (Saigon, 1961).

19. See Phan Boi Chau, *Phap-Viet de hue chinh kien thu,* trans. Nguyen Khac Hanh (Hanoi, 1926). The translator provided this edition with a preface in which he tried to explain the new accommodating position advocated by the old revolutionary: "Franco-Vietnamese Harmony is now a doctrine approved both by the Government and the people who want to see it implemented. Even Mr. Phan Boi Chau, who in the past was ardently opposed to that idea, has recently come around, after a careful examination of the situation, to accept the harmony ideology. That shows that it is a very timely ideology indeed. Mr. Phan Boi Chau wrote this essay when the European war had not ended yet. Although the situation is now slightly different from what it was then, that ideology still fits appropriately the present state of affairs in our country. We, therefore, did not hesitate to translate this pamphlet in order to show to our people how much the ideas of the Vietnamese revolutionary leader have changed in recent years!" (3). See also "Phap Viet de hue luan," in *Phan Boi Chau Toan Tap,* vol. 3, ed. Chuong Thau, trans. Nguyen Khac Hanh (Hue, 1990), 452–63, which constitutes a simple reproduction of the 1926 Tan Dan Thu Quan's edition. For the original version of this text, which was written in Chinese characters, see *Nam Phong* 17, no. 101 (Nov. 1925): 61–68.

20. Although the first edition of this work appeared, as seen here, in 1926, this essay was composed apparently sometime earlier. Phan Boi Chau himself claimed that he had composed the text of this essay toward the end of World War I. See "Letter Sent to the French Minister of Colonies, Paul Reynaud, in Mission in Hue, October 1931," in *Phan Boi Chau Toan Tap,* 4:234–41: "Shortly before I came back to Vietnam [1925], I wrote a small booklet entitled *Political Thought on Franco-Vietnamese Harmony* in which I ardently wished that the French and Vietnamese who lived together on this land would become like brothers in the same family. Those ideas came from the bottom of my heart, not just words to please." See also "Tra loi phong van cua bao *L'Annam* ve 'Phap Viet de hue' [A reply to the interview given to the daily *L'Annam* on the subject of Franco-Vietnamese Harmony], in *Phan Boi Chau Toan Tap* (Hue, 1990), 4:31, in which Phan Boi Chau elaborated further on the political concept: "Franco-Vietnamese Harmony must be based on an absolute equality between the two peoples. No equality, no harmony. If they consider us as friends, we shall see them as our elder brothers. But if, on the contrary, they consider us as buffaloes and horses, then we look at them as our enemies, as invaders." See also the interview Phan Boi Chau gave to a reporter from the newspaper *Trang An,* on 23 August 1938: "The 'Franco-Vietnamese Harmony' doctrine must be implemented," *ibid.,* 365–67. The reporter asked Phan Boi Chau about the Sino-Japanese conflict and its impact on Indochina. Here is Phan Boi Chau's response: "The Japanese are going to win; that's certain. Their strength is formidable! After the

European Great War, I had anticipated that danger and tried to persuade our compatriots to wake up and collaborate with the French, the sooner the better."

21. This follower was Phan Ba Ngoc, grandson of Phan Dinh Phung, who had resisted the French intrusion into north Vietnam for many years toward the end of the nineteenth century. It is very possible that Phan Ba Ngoc was the double agent who had persuaded Phan Boi Chau to write the infamous pamphlet. According to a letter from the consul of France in Shanghai to the governor-general of Indochina, ANSOM, Indochine, Anciens fonds, 28, 3, dated 3 Mar. 1918: "Four Vietnamese revolutionaries were arrested in Shanghai among whom were Mai Lao Bang and Pham [*sic*] Ba Ngoc. While May (Mai) Lao Bang had nothing to say, the letter continued, Pham (Phan) Ba Ngoc was on the contrary extremely intelligent and interesting; he seemed to be the only one who would have some influence on Phan Boi Chau." The consul then suggested that Phan Ba Ngoc might be used to persuade Phan Boi Chau to submit himself to the French authorities. The same letter also mentioned an interesting reply made by Phan Ba Ngoc. When reminded that he had been earlier condemned to death in absentia, Phan replied: "I have faith in the clemency of Mr Sarraut [the governor-general of Indochina]; otherwise I would have committed suicide."

22. Voir G. Boudarel, "Mémoires de Phan Boi Chau," in *France-Asie,* 194–95 (fall 1968): 178–81.

23. See Nguyen An Ninh, *France in Indochina,* Document 9, in this volume.

24. See Tran Huy Lieu, *Mot bau tam su* (Saigon, 1927), 27–28, excerpts in Document 15, in this volume.

25. Ibid.

26. *Co Do* 1, no. 8, (15 Sept. 1930).

27. Sarraut seems to have well established in his mind what could constitute the crux of that policy, as he wrote in one of his letters: "I have kept during the years 1917–1918 in peace and tranquillity 20 million indigenous people with only 2,000 European rifles . . . What about that active and anti-French [Vietnamese] youth? There is a tendency in them not to suffer any longer a certain sloppiness inherent in our compatriots, sloppiness which makes them [our compatriots] confuse a rickshaw puller with a mandarin, over-utilize the derogatory pronoun *tu* [you], affect rude and brusque manners, those gestures showing physical strength which remind them [the Vietnamese youth] too much of the idea or the souvenir of [our military] conquest" (ANSOM, Indochine, Anciens fonds, Sarraut).

28. *L'Annam,* 13 Jan. 1927.

29. Pham Quynh, *Le Vietnam: problèmes culturels et politiques (Essais, 1922–1932)* (N.p., 1985), 253.

30. *France-Indochine,* 29 May 1931.

31. *La Cloche Fêlée,* 16 Jan. 1924.

32. Pham Quynh, *Le Vietnam,* 297.

33. See David Marr, *Vietnamese Anti-Colonialism, 1885–1925* (Berkeley, 1971). For pages numbers, check the index under the word *mat nuoc.*

34. Phan Boi Chau, *Loi hoi . . . ? cac anh em thanh nien,* ed. and trans. Le Phuoc Thanh alias Le Van Thinh, 2d ed. (Saigon, 1928).

35. See "Van khoc cu Nghe Tran Qui Cap," in Thai Bach, *Thi van quoc cam . . .* , 389–92.

36. See Document 6, in this volume: "Tearful Conversation over the Mulberry Fields and the Sea."

37. Ibid.

38. The article is entitled "Vietnamese Questions: Freedom" and signed by Nguyen Pho. It appeared in *Indochine Enchaînée,* no. 11, 1925. For further detail on Nguyen Pho, see Hue Tam Ho Tai, *Radicalism and the Origins,* 132, 138, and 150.

39. *L'Annam,* 14 July 1927.

40. "Bai ca A-Te-A" (The Asian ballad), in *TVYNVCM,* 692. Also in Nguyen Van Xuan, *Phong trao duy tan* (Saigon, 1960), 301.

41. Tran Huu Do, *To co mat quyen tu do* (Saigon, 1926).

42. *La Cloche Fêlée,* 28 Jan. 1924.

43. *L'Annam,* 31 May 1926.

44. Bui Quang Chieu, *France d'Asie* (Toulouse, 1926), 18.

45. *L'Ere Nouvelle,* 23 May 1927.

46. *Phap Viet Nhut Gia,* 2 Apr. 1927. See also *L'Annam,* 4 July 1927, which mentioned the decree of 24 June 1927 forbidding all ceremonies to be held in Cochinchina in commemoration of Luong Van Can's death.

47. The full text of this document, which was originally written in Chinese, and its translation into Vietnamese are to be found in Ta Thuc Khai, trans., "Viet Nam vong quoc su," in *Dai Hoc Van Khoa* 2 (1961): 3–51. Another translation of the same document can also be found in Dang Thai Mai, *Van tho Phan Boi Chau* (Hanoi, 1958). The translation of excerpts are found in *TVYNVCM,* 47–59.

48. "Bai Ca A-Te-A," in *TVYNVCM,* 693.

49. *La Cloche Fêlée,* 18 Mar. 1926.

50. See Document 2 in this volume: "Letter to Governor-General Paul Beau."

51. *TVYNVCM,* 799.

52. See Document 8, in this volume: "Proclamation of the Thai Nguyen Uprising."

53. ANSOM, Indochine, Anciens fonds, Albert Sarraut, letter of Consul of France in Hong Kong to Governor-General of Indochina, Hong Kong 13 Jan. 1915.

54. See Document 11, in this volume: Pham Tat Dac, "Appeal to the Soul of the Nation."

55. According to *VTCM,* 49, these verses constitute parts of a long popular song originating in the two provinces of Quang Nam and Quang Ngai in Central Vietnam.

56. Tran Huy Lieu, *Mot bau tam su* (Saigon, 1927), 40.

57. See Document 11, in this volume: Pham Tat Dac, "Appeal to the Soul of the Nation."

58. *TVVN,* 2:203.

59. See Ngo Vinh Long, *Before the Revolution* (Cambridge, Mass., 1973), 61–81.

60. The full text of this ballad can be found in *TVYNVCM,* 687–95; excerpts are to found in Nguyen Van Xuan, *Phong trao Duy Tan* (Saigon, 1960), 301–6.

61. See *Lao Nong,* n.d. [1927]. Copies of this newspaper can be found in SLOT V, 40.

62. See *Lao Nong,* n.d., but probably end of 1927, in SLOT V, 40.

63. Phan Boi Chau, *Hai ngoai huyet thu,* as cited in *TVYNVCM,* 62.

64. Ibid., 65.

65. *Le Progrès Annamite,* 13 Aug. 1927.

66. *La Cloche Fêlée,* 8 Mar. 1926.

67. *La Cloche Fêlée,* 28 Dec. 1925.

68. *Duoc Nha Nam,* 1 Oct. 1928. For a comparison with Indonesia, see Georg McT. Kahin, *Nationalism and Revolution in Indonesia* (Ithaca, 1970), 1–36.

69. See Huynh Thuc Khang's speech at the Chamber of Representatives of Annam, Document 16, in this volume: and Nguyen Tan Duoc, "Discours prononcé au Conseil Colonial, Séance plénière du 24 Nov. 1925" (Saigon, 1925). See also Document 10: "The Wish List of the Vietnamese People."

70. *L'Annam,* 25 July 1927.

71. *La Cloche Fêlée,* 2 June 1924.

72. Nguyen An Ninh, "L'idéal de la jeunesse annamite," in *La Cloche Fêlée,* 26 and 30 Nov. 1925; Phuong Lan Bui The My, *Than the va su nghiep nha cach mang Nguyen An Ninh* (Saigon, 1970); also in *TVVN,* vol. 5, bk. 1, 349–66.

73. Nguyen An Ninh, "France in Indochina," Document 9, in this volume. Under fierce protest from the Vietnamese who have graduated from the Western system of education with high academic degrees, Governor-General Varenne created a supplementary branch of the Indochinese civil service called the "lateral branch," which accommodated the new Vietnamese elite. The lateral branch ranks below the European branch but above the native branch.

74. See Nguyen Ai Quoc, "Duong Kach Menh," in *Ho Chi Minh Toan Tap, 1925–1930* (Hanoi, 1981), 172–254.

75. *L'Annam,* 3 Mar. 1927.

76. *L'Annam,* 4 Oct. 1926.

77. *La Cloche Fêlée,* 21 Jan. 1924.

78. *La Cloche Fêlée,* 18 Mar. 1926.

79. René Vanlande, *L'Indochine sous la menace communiste* (Paris, 1930), 22. The author here quotes a tract issued by the Constitutionalist Party.

80. Nguyen Ai Quoc, "Le Mouvement communiste international—Indochine," *La Revue Communiste* 15 (1921): 204–6.

81. Tran Te Xuong, "Nho Tan" (The end of Confucian education), *Van Dan Bao Giam* (Los Alamitos, Calif., n.d.), 77.

82. *Nam Phong,* Jan. 1926.

83. *Than Chung,* 24 July 1929.

84. *Tieng Dan,* 13 July 1930.

85. Ibid. This interdiction reminds us of Gandhi, who was not allowed to plead a case in South Africa dressed as an Indian with a turban.

86. *L'Annam,* 5 July 1926.

87. *Le Petit Parisien,* 31 May 1930. The newspaper clipping can be found in ANSOM, Indochine, Nouveaux fonds, 325, dossier 2633.

88. SLOT III, 55.

89. *La Tribune Indochinoise,* 27 Oct. 1927. Clipping to be found in SLOT V, 14.

90. *Than Chung,* 26 Apr. 1929.

91. *La Tribune Indochinoise,* 27 and 28 Sept. and 3 Oct. 1927. In a previous session of the same tribunal, the judge asked Tran Huu Do whether he will continue to write books after he has served out his sentence. The reply was: "Why not? I shall still be writing! I shall always write! Your Honor, that is my profession. I am a poor man. I live of my work and of my pen."

92. *L'Annam,* 28 Apr. 1927.

93. *Nam Phong,* Dec. 1930.

DOCUMENT 1

Phan Boi Chau (1867–1940)

The New Vietnam
(1907)

*Phan Boi Chau, more than anyone else in the history of the first quarter of twentieth-century Vietnam, personifies the struggle against French colonialism. He was trained in the traditional Confucian system of education and earned the equivalent of an M.A. degree (*cu nhan*) in 1900. The Dong Du, or Going East (Japan), movement, organized in 1904, was the first important anticolonial movement that Phan Boi Chau actively and directly promoted. Subsequently, he was involved in numerous campaigns, all aiming at gaining independence for his country. What, however, contributed mainly to Phan Boi Chau's greatness was that from abroad he inundated his people with countless pamphlets dealing with all kinds of subjects, ranging from the pains of losing one's own country to the joy and comforts attained with independence. All, however, to no avail. In 1925 the French colonial authorities arrested, tried, and condemned Phan Boi Chau to death for subversion. The sentence was, however, commuted, and Phan Boi Chau spent the next fifteen years of his life under close surveillance in Hue. A memorandum preserved in his personal file at the French Colonial Archives defines quite well the complex and contradictory nature of his confined life. A French officer wrote that Phan Boi Chau, in exchange for a commutation of his death sentence, had promised to behave with loyalty toward the French colonial government. Another official, also French, appended the following comment, naturally, on the same memorandum: "He hasn't given any value to his words."[1]*

In the following document, Tan Viet Nam *(New Vietnam), Phan Boi Chau describes to his compatriots how life would look and feel after Vietnam has been modernized and consequently regained her independence from France. This document somewhat constitutes the platform for the new movement Phan Boi Chau founded about this time, the Duy Tan Hoi, or Modernization Association.[2]*

After a thousand kilometers of railroads have been laid, merchandise to be exchanged would reach its destination in hours; sprawling cities and large villages would promptly communicate with one another, then even if we were to relax in a sculpted house or if we were just to sit on a flowered mat, it would still feel as though we have scaled mountains and crossed rivers. What a wonderful sensation that will be! But to attain that goal we must first go through worries and pains. How come, when we talk about difficulties, we just cross our arms and remain silent? That's simply because we do not know how marvelous we will feel after the railroad laying has been completed.

After a building a thousand meters high has been erected, we shall be able to hold in our hands the stars in the sky and the moon in the sea. Fresh air and wind will flow through our feet. Then, even if we were to relax sitting on a stone bench or if we were just to remain enclosed within four walls, we would still be able to see hundreds of islands in the five continents. What a wonderful feeling that will be! To attain that goal we must first make plans and estimate costs. How come, when we talk about great tasks such as these, we bow our heads and lose the color on our faces? Because we simply don't know how marvelous we will feel after the high-rise has been built.

To know that, in the future, our pleasure will be endless may encourage us to bear today's difficulties, which will bring us that pleasure to come. To know that, in the future, our joy will be endless may encourage us to bear today's pains, which will bring us that joy to come. To know that in the future the profit will be immense may encourage us to bear today's costs, which will bring us that profit to come.

Now I would like to tell you this, my compatriots. If we wanted a New Vietnam, we must bear the difficulties, the pains, and the costs involved. If our compatriots are unwilling to bear the difficulties, the pains, and the costs involved, it is because they simply do not know that Vietnam, after her modernization, will bring them sheer pleasure, joy, and profit.

The Ten Pleasant Conditions

Now I would like to tell you, my compatriots, about the ten pleasant conditions resulting from modernization. They are:

1. No protecting power.
2. No obnoxious mandarins.
3. No dissatisfied citizens.
4. No soldier without glory.
5. No unequal taxes or forced labor.
6. No unjust law.
7. No imperfect education system.
8. No unexploited mineral resources.

9. No neglected industry.
10. No losing commercial ventures.

1. No Protecting Power

Our country has an area of 250,000 square miles: that is not a small country. Our population amounts to more than fifty million inhabitants: that is not a negligible number.[3] Our soil is fertile, our mountains and rivers beautiful. Compared with other powers in the five continents, our country is inferior only to a few. Why, then, do we suffer French protection? Alas, that is simply because of our deep-rooted slave mentality; it is because of our inveterate habit of depending on others for over two thousand years. We gladly accepted the colonization of the Han, the Tang, the Song, the Yuan, the Ming. As slaves, we served them; we lacked human dignity. Today our enemy the French are very ingenious. They despise us, claiming that we are weak; they lie to us, because they consider us stupid. While our guardian, the lion, is in deep sleep, they act like bandits, oppressing the masters of the house. They trample over our people; they hold our fathers and brothers in contempt; they treat us like buffaloes and horses; they suck the sweat and blood from our people; and yet they dare broadcast loudly to the rest of the world that France is here to protect the Indochinese country. Oh! Compatriots, the country is ours; the people are ours. What interest does France have here for her to come and protect our country?

Ever since France came to protect us, Frenchmen hold every lever of power; they hold the power of life and death over everyone. The life of thousands of Vietnamese people is not worth that of a French dog; the moral prestige of hundreds of our officials does not prevail over that of a French woman. Look at those men with blue eyes and yellow beard. They are not our fathers, nor are they our brothers. How can they squat here, defecating on our heads? Are the men from Vietnam not ashamed of that situation? As long as our bodies remain able, we should try to flatten the crest of the open ocean; we should be determined to kill the enemy in order to raise the energy of the yellow race of ours.

After modernization we shall determine the domestic as well as foreign affairs of our country. The work of civilization will go on, day after day, and our country's status in the world will be heightened. We shall have three million infantrymen, as fierce as tigers, looking into the four corners of the universe. Five hundred thousand of our navy men, as terrifying as crocodiles, will swim freely in the boundless ocean. We shall send ambassadors into every country of Europe, America, Japan, the United States, Germany, England. These countries will make ours their first ally. Siam, India, and other countries of the South Seas will look up to our land as an enlightened example. Even the big countries of Asia, such as China, will be brother countries to ours. The enemy, France, will be afraid of us; she will listen to us, ask us for protection. Our flag will fly over the city of Paris, and our colors will brighten the entire globe. At that time the only fear we shall have is that we won't have enough time to protect other countries. All the shame and humiliation we have suffered previously, which resulted from being protected by others, will have become potent medicine to help us build up this feat of modernization. Commemorative monuments will be erected; a thousand torches will illuminate the entire world. The wind of freedom will blow fiercely, refreshing in one single sweep the entire five continents. Such will be the victory of our race. How pleasant that will be!

2. No Obnoxious Mandarins

The poison of absolutism coming from those people who have oppressed others for thousands of years spread from China into our country so thoroughly that a single individual surrounded by a few thousand mediocre men was able to treat our people like fish and meat. And yet our people are so naive and stupid that they do not know how to wrest back their democratic rights, how to preserve their country's destiny. Day and night, they simply think of how best to provide the ruler and his cohorts with their own blood for beverage and their own flesh for food. Alas! How pitiful that is!

After modernization the people's mind will be open, their energy increased, their sense of rights developed. Our country's destiny will be in the hands of our people. In the middle of our capital city we shall build a large Congress Hall. All political matters will be decided by the public. The Higher Assembly will wait for the consent of the Middle Congress; the Middle Congress will wait for the consent of the Lower Congress before any decision can be put into action. The Lower Congress is where the majority of the public can debate decisions taken by the Middle and Higher Congresses. Our people, however noble or humble, however rich or poor, however old or young, will have the right to vote. Whether to preserve or to do away with the monarchy, whether to promote or demote the mandarins: our people will have the ultimate right to make those decisions. The mismanagement done by the ruler or the abuses perpetrated by the mandarins, all behavior that is not in conformity with the public good, can be reprimanded or punished by our people in their deliberations in Congress. At that time those mandarins, of however high or low ranks, who are obnoxious to the people, will no longer have the right to live on our land. At that time our people will experience only joy and happiness. They will have their mouth full while pleasantly stroking their belly. When they lift their head, they can see the sky. The mountains will echo a thousand peals of laughter. Applause will strike like thunders, singing the praises of the government for a thousand years to come. We shall be that glorious and prosperous! How pleasant that will be!

3. No Dissatisfied Citizens

The French stole our country. They gagged our mouths. They tied up our limbs. They blinded our eyes. They plugged our ears. The publication of books and newspapers, the deliberations, the meetings no matter whether during daytime or night, no matter how many or how few participants, no matter whether young or old people, the French strictly forbade them all. We still have to obey their order, even when, in anger, they demanded that we look at our fathers as our enemies. When it pleases them to require us to respect a dog as a king, we still have to acquiesce to their request. Even the king and the mandarins, the rich and the talented people, would not dare go one step away from their houses without asking for special permission from the French. If your taxes are not paid in full to the French, you are regarded as burglars in your own homes. Here are French dogs, French horses, French women, servants of the French: all are free to insult whomever they choose to insult. Seeing them next to our people, it is like paradise on their side and hell on ours. Such iniquity, such inequality, where in the world can one find a more unjust situation? Are we going to sit back and relax instead of rising up to ring the bell of freedom? One who never loses never wins either; we should be determined to break this vicious circle of oppression.

After modernization we shall wield power in our country. We shall keep our own way of life. Civilization will reign through liberty everywhere. Newspapers will appear on sidewalks, and new books abound. Petitions and lawsuits, verbal and written polemics, will flourish. Domestic and foreign affairs will be discussed in every detail. Writers will be encouraged to create. Every hidden feeling of the rickshaw puller or of the horse attendant, of the mother-widow or of the lone orphan, will reach the leaders' ears. Then the people of our country will be drunk with happiness, a happiness as immense as the ocean, the limits of which the eyes cannot fathom, or as high as the sky the contours of which the arms are unable to grasp. Such freedom, how pleasant that will be!

4. No Soldiers Without Glory

Before modernization our people had barbarian customs that were deeply rooted, while their desire for progress remained very shallow. They venerated empty pictographs like gods and saints while despising practical professions like grass or thrash. From king to subjects, all looked down upon military officers as servile creatures to be trampled on; they considered soldiers as draft buffaloes or horses: just a bunch of wiggling creatures. Our people, being not highly educated, could not see very far. When the villagers saw the contempt expressed by those in higher positions for the soldiers, they filled themselves with disdain. They knew that soldiers, while living, always walked in front of their horses, and therefore they were being killed on the front line. And after their deaths they simply became wandering spirits along the roadside, leaving their corpses in deserted plains. Being a soldier is definitely very hard and also very lowly. In addition to all that, the soldiers also received all the mistreatment. The villagers quickly realized how pitiful the soldiers' fate was. And also how discouraging all those diverse feelings were. Under these conditions who would still want to become a soldier? And if no one wants to become a soldier, then who will protect our homes? After our country is lost, who then will be to blame? The country's destiny is, indeed, in the hands of the soldiers. The soldier is our country. If the soldier is so abused, how is the country to be preserved? Now that the country has been lost, it is as if a car in front of us had overturned. Let's look at it as a warning. We should keep in mind that the rights and duties of the soldiers are intimately tied to the destiny of the country. We should try to strengthen our country. That is the soldiers' responsibility. That responsibility is also ours. The soldiers should see how their fate will be in the future.

After modernization military officers, king, and people—all are united. The soldiers will protect the country. They will be respected. All our compatriots will know then that the country belongs to each one of us. Every one of us has the responsibility to protect our country; every one of us has the duty to become a soldier; every one of us will be willing to respect the soldiers. While living, the soldiers will constitute our national militia; they will show their pride for the whole wide world to see. After their death they form the national soul; their spirits will survive with our mountains and rivers. The people in the country will not spare their wealth to honor their soldiers. The king of our country will walk up the ritual platform to offer sacrifices in honor of our soldiers. In Japan there is a monument in Tokyo called the Yasukuni Jinja wherein sacrifices are offered to soldiers killed in battle. Twice a year the emperor comes to offer sacrifices at that monument.

After modernization we shall follow that example. The nation as well as the society have the duty to take care of the families of the soldiers killed in battle. The nation should build statues in bronze, erect stone stelae to commemorate the soldiers killed in battle. Soldiers! O soldiers! No one in the country can lay claims to the same glory as yours. The honor you earn will not be surpassed. At that time our compatriots will see how vast our country is and how glorious it is to take honor in the obligation of running ahead of the horses. When they look back at their villages, they would pity themselves, for they will realize how boring it is simply to die in their own homes. What a joy that will be! How pleasant that will be!

5. *No Unequal Taxes or Forced Labor*

Under the previous dynasties that reigned over our country, taxes the rulers levied from the people were not heavy, although their collection could not avoid the following barbarous abuses: (1) the corruption of the mandarins; (2) the greed of the powerful gentry; and (3) the mismanagement of the village notables. There were hundreds of ways to oppress the people, who, consequently, suffered a great deal. But that treatment was still somewhat humane. Today the French consider us no better than animals, buffaloes or horses to be traded in exchange. May I ask a question of our fathers, uncles, brothers, and nephews? The French levy every year from our people a head tax of two, three, four, or five piasters. Compared to the price put on a buffalo, a horse, or a chicken, what would be the difference? Alas! Our people have used up their sweat and blood to provide the Frenchmen, their women, their horses, and their dogs each year with so many hundreds, thousands, millions, billions . . . And yet taxes are levied on everything: on things essential to our survival, on places necessary to our production. Even our bodies, which are created by Heaven and Earth and raised up by our parents with so much pain and care, they also have to be taxed by the French enemy four or five piasters every year. What is the meaning of that? Alas, our bodies are worth less than a buffalo, a horse, or a chicken. How pitiful that is! How pitiful that is! Mistreated in that fashion by the French, how come we have not risen up yet? Taxes, head taxes—that is a form of taxes no other country in the world has, except our own country. Our people are not made of wood, stone, mud, or ashes: how can we accept being despised to that extent? An animal that is cornered knows how to attack and bite in order to escape; we are human beings, and yet we do not know how to get out of our quandaries. Even a caterpillar knows how to wish that the pine needle would become longer and longer, what then about us? When shall we be able to be proud of ourselves?

After modernization, first, we have to get rid of all the wretched old practices that have existed through many dynasties. Second, we shall reform all the inhuman institutions set up by the French. Taxes, corvées, head taxes— none of these will remain after independence. All taxes will be decided upon by Congress. Taxes on this or that commodity have to be agreed upon by our people, and the proceeds must be spent on useful enterprises for the public good. The government can only start implementing its tax policies after the people have given their consent. Our people will not pay even one piaster or one grain of rice, if it is not out of their own will and with enthusiasm. Their patriotism leads them to pay their taxes willingly. No more of the barbarous coercive tactics of yesteryear. Then we shall be as happy as the sky is high and the ocean deep. The day will be warm, the wind harmonious, everybody at peace. How pleasant that will be!

6. No Unjust Law

In the old days our penal codes involved cangues and cuffs. Our bodies were oppressed; we could not move around; our bodies were numbed. We could not speak; our mouth would simply shut tight. The culprit, while sleeping or eating, is no different from cows, buffaloes, chickens, or pigs. Alas! Are our compatriots not all our relatives? Are they not made of the same bones and the same flesh? How can we treat them in such a wretched manner because they have committed some crimes? After we have built up our country together, how do we have the heart to treat one another like that? O my compatriots! O my compatriots! Please take a look at our penal code after modernization.

After modernization, within our country, no one will lack patriotism; all will serve the common good, loving one another, obeying the laws of the country, pursuing the benefits of civilization. Under such conditions what do we need the cruelties of a penal code for? If by misfortune, however, some of us happen to commit some crime, then we shall have a few civilized articles in the penal code to deal with such cases. Our civilized penal code will take its inspiration from those of Japan and Europe. At the capital city we shall establish a Reeducation Center, presided over by a judge appointed by the Supreme National University. The people who have committed crimes will be sent to a school that will bring out and nurture the good side of their heart. That would give them back their civic dignity. We should also set up a workshop to teach them some craft with which they will be able to earn a living. That will prevent them from committing crimes again out of joblessness. We shall also place in that school a fair supervisor, a competent teacher, who every day would come to explain to the prisoners the good and the bad so that they can repent for their errors. After their terms of confinement they will be regarded as innocent people; all their civic rights will be restored to them; they will be equal to other citizens. While in jail, the prisoners are like children receiving education. After their sentences have been purged, they will be able to contribute to the affairs of state according to their ability. It is like the spring breeze blowing on everything. All sicknesses and infirmities will be cured. At that time our people will experience only peace and will not know what criminal law means. All sufferings, sicknesses, and infirmities will have been cured with effective medicines. Aggressiveness like that of the tiger, the panther, the peacock, and the owl will all fade away as if melted by sacred water. We shall live in such happiness. How pleasant that will be!

7. No Imperfect Educational System

Education is the mold that shapes human beings. Mandarins, officers, and soldiers all come out of it. Education is also the basis on which politics are built. Taxes, criminal law, everything is determined by education. We won't have anything to say about our premodernization system of education, which is so old-fashioned and conservative. It is as if one broke one's arm nine times before one finds a way to prevent it from happening again. After modernization our education will be perfect. I should not say more. But since some of us are still in the dark about this problem, allow me to address myself to it.

After modernization both the royal court and the society will devote all their efforts to education, moral as well as physical. We shall learn from Japan, China, Europe; we shall learn everything. Day care centers, kindergartens, primary and secondary schools, universities, will be created everywhere, from the cities to the countryside. Right after modernization we shall invite teachers from Japan, Europe, and America. After a while some of the teachers will still be foreigners, but some of them will be recruited from among our own people. Then, after complete modernization, our own people will know more than the people from Europe or America, so that we won't have to invite any foreigner anymore. How to establish schools, how to organize the curricula, how to teach, how to find jobs for our graduates—everything will be copied from the good model of Japan and Europe. We shall study philosophy, literature, history, politics, economics, military science, geometry. We shall study industry, commerce, agriculture, home economics, medicine, forestry. For all the disciplines we need to study, we shall employ enough professors. We shall open up enough schools so that our people, whether they be rich or poor, noble or humble, male or female, as soon as they reach five years of age, can receive a kindergarten education in kindergartens; as soon as they reach eight years of age, they can receive a primary education in primary schools; as soon as they reach fourteen years, they can receive a secondary education in secondary schools. When they reach the age of eighteen, their knowledge is already vast enough for them to be admitted into superior schools in order to receive a specialized higher education. All the expenses related to education will be supported by the court or society. If a citizen is too poor to contribute anything toward his schooling fees, then the court and society should come to his aid, so that no citizen shall be denied at least a primary education. Furthermore, before entering primary schools, everyone should already know *quoc ngu*,[4] be able to read newspapers, and learn about interesting news or about useful commentaries. Their minds will therefore be open more widely. After entering primary school, students should diligently study so as to build up the dignity of a citizen. Moreover, textbooks used in primary and secondary schools, as well as in universities, shall be prepared by the Ministry of Education, which will add all the comments and remarks resulting from discussions in Congress. All the textbooks will aim at encouraging patriotism in the people, cultivating their mutual trust and love, opening up their minds, promoting democratic rights so that everyone can advance a thousand steps a day.

With regard to education, that of the military and women is the most important. The soldier has indeed the duty to help the peasant, the trader; to open up new land so as to facilitate immigration; to strengthen the position of the country and improve its power. If his education is not thorough, how then is a soldier to die for the country, for the love of his compatriots, for the prosperity of the fatherland? Once our country has been modernized, the soldiers will receive an education at home while at home, in their garrisons while they are in garrisons. The soldiers who belong to the artillery, cavalry, or logistical corps will be initiated into the methods of artillery, cavalry, and logistics. The sailors, the infantrymen, and their officers will receive an education geared to their branch of service. There will be no place, no moment, where and when education is not dispensed to the soldiers to train them not to fear death, to increase the courage of the commanding officers, so that our country will be the most powerful of the five continents. That is the result of the education of the soldiers.

Women will become good mothers, loving wives, knowledgeable in literature and poetry, well trained in commerce; they also are expert educators of our children and efficient assistants to our soldiers. A good mother will have nice children; she will be a virtuous wife to a perfect husband. Moreover, in politics women will possess many rights. Only with education will one know how to neglect one's private interests in order to take care of the public good, so as to make one's country accumulate its riches and increase its strength. A country that has no patriotic women is bound to be subjugated by another country. In the modernization scheme of countries women's education plays an important role. Textbooks to be used by women must be selected from among the best. The schools that are reserved for women should have better teachers. In all matters related to finance, in industrial schools, in convalescence homes, in trading outlets, in banks, in post offices, in buses, in trains, it is best to employ well-educated women. They will strive to serve the country as much as men. Their pride and dignity will be equal to men's. The government and society will join in their praises. Every woman in the country should of course endeavor to become a good mother, a virtuous wife, but also a talented woman. They will leave their names in stone stelae and in bronze statues. Women shall not be inferior to men. That's the aim of women's education.

In political institutions justice and humanity will prevail over all other notions. People of the country will be like members of the same family.

Our national territory extends in the south to the province of Hatien and in the north to that of Langson. That's our common home. We are born and raised in that home, protected by Heaven and Earth. We are compatriots, standing on the same land, and after our death, buried under the same mound. We are of the same blood transmitted by our ancestors through thousands of years. We have the same name, no matter who does the calling. We are unlike the people of Hu, Han, Qin, Yueh.[5] How can anybody say that we do not belong to the same family? In our sufferings, in our affections, we share the same relationship of flesh and blood. We help one another without ever getting angry at one another. Everything looks much like the fresh ocean and the calm spring.

After the modernization of our country no one should be jobless. We should create charity houses, reeducation institutes, so as to reform those who have committed crimes and, therefore, have to be confined. Schools should be open to teach the blind, the mute, the deaf, the infirm. Orphanages should be established as well as resthouses for the aged and also maternity wards. Schools for the poor should be staffed by experienced teachers, who will treat their pupils with devotion and humanity so that our people may enjoy peace and happiness. Then, nothing will be missing in our system of education. It is as if trees and grass will grow with rain; fish and prawns will dance in a peaceful ocean. If that's so, how pleasant that will be!

8. No Unexploited Mineral Resources

Our national territory extends in the west to Siam; in the north to the province of Yunnan; in the east to the China Sea; in the south to the island of Poulo Condore. In the middle, next to the province of Nghe An, there are four marches: Tran Ninh, Tran Dinh, Tran Bien, and Tran Tinh. The northern part of our country includes ten *châu*.[6] The province of Quang Tri has two Cam regions: Cam Lo and Cam Linh. The south touches two countries: Water Haven and Fire Haven.[7] Our soil is fertile: we can raise cattle in our forests. The flanks of our mountains can be cultivated. Our country has several plains fit for agriculture for a long time. And yet our country is still a semicivilized, semi-barbarian one, because the mind of our people is not fully open yet. Our men of talent are few. We rely on human labor and not on machines. The yield of our field is still very low. When a flood or a draught occurs, we simply endure them as unavoidable natural calamities. Our people are unable to save even one, let alone one hundred, kilograms of paddy, and yet thousands of acres of land remain unexploited. Although the monarchy is all-powerful, it does not know how to develop the economy. Our country counts many entrepreneurs, who, unfortunately, do not know how to nurture their talents. The country becomes poorer and poorer. The people encounter more and more hardships. How pitiful that is!

After modernization agriculture will be developed. It will prosper. If human labor does not suffice, there will be machines to help. If rain and sun are not propitious, technology will remedy the situation. If one man does not dispose of enough resources to exploit a plot of land, society will contribute money to complete the work. If the people cannot finish a job, the court will dispatch mandarins to help. The high officials of the Ministry of Agriculture will be people experienced in agricultural sciences. The peasants will receive all necessary information from all quarters. Rice will abound; riches will pile up sky-high. We shall neglect no resources from the forests. In our villages money will be plentiful. Then, more and more land will be opened up for people to settle in. Our strength will be greater than all the neighboring countries combined. We shall be rich. Our fame will spread to the entire world. If we shall be that rich, how pleasant that will be!

9. No Neglected Industry

Compared to those of other countries in Asia, our people are probably more intelligent and more capable. And yet all the merchandises, all the goods, are imported from foreign countries. Foreigners rake in all the profits. Food such as tobacco, tea, alcohol; textiles such as brocade, velvet, cotton, silk, if they are not made in France, then they are sold by the Chinese; if they do not come from France, then they come from China. We are so stupid to spend all our money on these foreign imports. We feed the resources given to us by Heaven and Earth to the foreigners. Today we buy French merchandise; tomorrow we purchase Chinese goods. This man uses French material; that one wears Chinese clothes. Our people are intelligent and clever. Our country has silver and gold mines, factories, manufactures. Why, then, are we so stupid as to waste our resources and to subject ourselves to hard work, day and night? That's simply because the court does not know how to encourage the workers and promote the professions and because our society has no will to fight for its own good. While the French accumulate all the profits, they consider us stupid, incapable. Everyday they try to relegate us into obscurantism in the hope that we will become oblivious of everything.

After modernization our people will open up their eyes and ears. Their intelligence will expand. Technical schools will mushroom everywhere in the country. There will be engineers to prospect for mines, to smelt gold, to manufacture arms, to invent machines, to produce trading goods, to forge agricultural implements. Our draftsmen will be accurate, our tailors experienced. For every trade we shall have experts. Our technical schools will employ good teachers from Europe and Japan. Little by little, our mineral prospections will spread wider and wider; the profits derived from mineral exploitations higher and higher. The more resources we get out of our soil, the stronger will our country be. Our mountains and rivers will look like satin and brocade; our countryside will appear like big cities. Then, our people will acquire so much cleverness that nobody can surpass them. They will know everything pertaining to profession. Even Europe and America will not equal us. How pleasant that will be!

10. No Losing Commercial Activities

If the merchants are stronger than the tiger and the crocodile, then there is no country in the world they cannot swallow. If the traders hold in their hands rifles or swords, then there are no people in the world they cannot kill. How pitiful are the weak countries! Our country has been weak; its commerce has stagnated. So far, our resources have acted like oil and grease: they have simply melted away, without any hope of recuperation. The poor people would have been enterprising had they possessed the resources. On the other hand, those who dispose of enough means lack determination. Without resources or determination, how can one survive in this competitive world? In the final analysis, if the situation is that bad, it is because our people do not have mutual trust, mutual sympathy. They also lack the desire for progress and the sense of adventure. Without trust and sympathy the poor who have the mental abilities refuse to cooperate with the rich, while the rich who possess the means are unwilling to help the poor. It results in the destruction of our society, the decrease in our resources. Without trying to find ways to unite their efforts or combine their riches, how can they expect to do business? Without the desire for progress or the sense of adventure, they won't be able to invest a penny, let alone millions. They don't dare take one step away from their homes, let alone go across the ocean. The string tight on their purse, their money buried, devoid of any sense of adventure, lacking important investments, how do they expect to run sound businesses?

After modernization our people's mind will be wide open. They will learn more about business. Our people will have sympathy for one another; they will trust one another, gathering the resources of thousands and millions of individuals into a common fund, putting the know-how of thousands and millions of individuals into a common pool of knowledge, thereby developing a common enterprise. Our people will venture into faraway lands. The court will respect anyone who has a true profession; society will revere those who are experienced in business. Trade will be developed. Our people will cooperate with one another, combining their resources so as to compete with the foreigners in commercial ventures. Rice, tea, timber, and many other products will be exported to other countries. Our merchandise will top the list in the world. Commercial companies in the capital cities of France: Paris; Germany: Berlin; Great Britain: London; and America: Washington, as well as those at various port cities will agree that our trade constitutes the most prosperous. More than a thousand ships will enter or leave our ports every day. Millions in foreign currencies will be added to our treasury every day. At that time we shall use our riches as citadels that no enemy artillery in the world could penetrate. We shall line up our ships as shields so that threats from countries of Europe and America will be just like passing ocean waves. Our country will be that rich and strong. How pleasant that will be!

If the cultivator knows how pleasant it will be to harvest his crop, then he will not mind the hardships of rains and winds that he must go through at this time. If the builder knows that reunion means joy, then he will not find it annoying to carry stones to build roads. It is the same with the modernization of our country. How pleasant that will be! Who among our people will not agree with it? Who would not applaud it? But after the initial excitement people begin to doubt. For they have no clear ideas about the ways and means to build up a New Vietnam or about the investments necessary to foster a New Vietnam. I, Boi Chau, although my knowledge is limited, am nevertheless a beloved son of our country; I would respectfully like to present my humble perception of it so that our notables, colleagues, and friends can make their choice.

The Six Desirable Situations

There are six highly desirable situations:

1. Our people should desire progress and adventure.
2. Our people should love and trust one another.
3. Our people should be concerned about the civilizing process.
4. Our people should have true patriotism.
5. Our people should be truly virtuous.
6. Our people should endeavor to acquire fame and profit.

1. Desire for Progress and Adventure

Our people do not lack finesse in their thinking, intelligence in their mind, and heroism in their behavior. Then, how come that, within our country, the one who proclaims himself king can abuse our people at will while he is the servant of a foreign country? From the Chinese Han, Tang, Yuan, and Ming Dynasties to the French today, the skill of being slave has rather been well fine-tuned by our people. Why is that so? Because none of us has the desire for progress, the longing for adventure; because all of us bask in our stupidity and our weakness, finding that the best way to deal with the world is to indulge ourselves in good food and in sex plays. Our garden and our kitchen represent for us the wide universe. Other people can defecate on our head; still we stand there idle and console ourselves by saying, "I only want my peace." Foreigners may swallow our race and yet we meekly say, "I shall wait for my time." Alas, in this competitive world, where people's dispositions are as poisonous as snakes, where vultures pursue sparrows, the otter swimming after the fish, where can we find someone like the Buddha? If you don't want to progress, people will kill you. Who will care about you if you do not have the sense of adventure?

Even under these circumstances, is our country really incapable of rising up? Please, my dear compatriots, open your eyes in order to wash out the shame inflicted onto our mountains and rivers. All other people behave like heroes; why are we so cowardly and weak-hearted? Other people are all in commanding positions; why are we satisfied with being merely slaves? If all of us have one mind, then we can reach independence. If our desire for progress is firm, our longing for adventure strong, then we shall be able to capture lions and tigers with our bare hands, to catch whales and sharks in the vast ocean. If the strength of one man is not sufficient, then we shall have the strength of ten men. If the strength of ten men is still not enough, then we shall have the strength of one hundred, one thousand, ten thousand men so as to accomplish the task. If everybody in the country is brave to that extent, then the French will not know a single day of peace. This is the first pleasant situation resulting from modernization.

2. Love and Trust

Our population is not small; our territory not tiny; our resources not limited, as I have stated above. According to the head tax registers established by the French, our country counts twenty-five million taxpayers; the whole population, therefore, should amount to no less than fifty millions. That is not a negligible number. The area of our territory covers up to 250,000 English square miles. Five kinds of gold, five kinds of rice, are found here, and the soil is fertile. The rice of Saigon,[8] the goods of northern Vietnam, are sufficient to overfeed the Chinese, Indians, Malays, Siamese, French men, women, their dogs, and their horses. The servants and the cooks of the French masters indulge in wasting food and the rest. That serves as evidence to the vast amount of our resources. An important population, a vast territory, with plenty of resources, what can we not accomplish with all that? Why, then are our people still slaves, our resources shrinking away, our business always resulting in bankruptcy, our agriculture in losses, our crafts in shoddy trinkets?

It is true that Heaven has not been kind to us. That is because our people have no mutual love or trust. They treat one another as people from Qin and Yueh. Although of the same race, they regard one another as enemies. Walls and hedges are erected between houses, moats and ponds dug out in front of every door. A piaster[9] given to a brother is as heavy as five kilograms. Close friends are yet separated by a thousand miles, carrying in their mind contradictory thoughts. In time of sickness no help is ever available. People sing in my house without any regards whatsoever for you, who are crying in yours. The people in the eastern hamlet, eat and drink to satiety without any worries for the people in the western hamlet who are hungry and thirsty. Alas! After our mountains and rivers have been reduced to ashes, only our combined strength can save them. How do we have the heart to pursue our individual reputation, our private interests, enjoying our own virtue, our own dispositions. Our life is suspended by a single thread; how do we dare lift our arms to fight one against another? Catastrophe is threatening three generations of ours; why do we still fight among ourselves behind the fences, with so much hatred and rivalry? Alas! No strength can subsist without unity, no achievement without coopera- tion. For a game, a banquet, one needs at least a few dozen people. For an undertaking that will bring profit to ten thousand generations, which will leave its mark on the mountains and rivers, how can a handful people hope to complete the task? So now, what about getting all of us together, combining our intelligence, pooling our resources, renouncing all rivalry and hatred among ourselves, uniting ourselves in life as in death, throwing the riches of tens of thousands of people into a common fund, capitalizing on the strength of tens of thousands of people to build up a common force. You wear my shirt, while I eat your rice. When you fall sick, I'll bring you the medicine. If my house is dark, I light it up with your lamp. If thousands of people were to join their shoulders, what weight can they not carry? If thousands of people were to lend a hand, what task can they not accomplish? When the people of our country have reached such a mutual trust and mutual affection, will our eyes still see any French gentleman around? That's the second pleasant situation resulting from modernization.

3. The Civilizing Process

Soon our people will see automobiles and electric trains. They will hear French rifles and firecrackers. They will know all about French culture and French technology. But right now they are still like blind, deaf, and a bit drunk or benumbed. Why is that so? That's because we refuse to change. How our ancestors did it, we now do it exactly in the same way. We do not want to devise new methods. Disciplines like optics, chemistry, physics, are said to be too difficult to learn and impossible to imitate. The older people with experience are disappearing every day; the younger ones have family obligations with wives and children. Things related to automobiles and electric trains remain entirely in the hands of the French. What importance does it have that we serve the French as dogs and horses? Let the French make French rifles, French firecrackers. What importance does it have that, as their servants, we slave for the French? We do not have the same culture as the French. Our doctoral and master's degree holders do not have the same scientific knowledge as the

French. They are merely good enough to become interpreters in the offices of the governor-general or clerks in their residencies. Their knowledge being so limited, how would they understand anything about civilization? But expertly manufactured products do not spring out spontaneously from the earth. Without education how will one be able to achieve any feat of civilization? Other people have machines; we should try to learn how to make them. People have modernized their ways; why do we have to cling to the old ones? The professional training as practiced in England, Japan, Germany, and America takes at least two years to complete. We should not see it as too difficult. The military, agricultural, technical, and commercial training require at least five years; we should not consider it too long. In order to learn from other countries, we should first familiarize ourselves with their languages, their writing systems, for one or two years. If one has determination, that should not be too hard. And this is simply to get on the bandwagon of civilization. To follow in other countries' footsteps one should visit all their cities, be confronted with the high cost of living, spend a great deal of money. But if one has determination, one would not consider it too expensive. That is simply to build up the defense of civilization. If other people have taken one month to reach their goal, we should try to attain it in one or two weeks. If other people have the talent to make steps a thousand miles long, we should try to make steps of ten thousand miles. At first we learn from them. After that they will learn from us. The Japan of today is similar to the Vietnam of tomorrow. That is the third pleasant situation resulting from modernization.

4. True Patriotism

If the waves are rough, then the coast must be steep. If the rain is heavy, then the sky must be shaken by lightning and thunder. That should wake everyone up who has a soul. Our people have talked at leisure of patriotism, sounding like bells. But talking without doing is like no talking at all. To have knowledge without applying it is like being without knowledge. Our mountains and rivers, for fifty years now, have been moaning and groaning. Now they are like dead and drunk. As long as our bodies can still move, we should try to increase our will and energy. We should try to follow our time. In order to survive our compatriots will need to do two things. They are (1) to shed their blood so as to wipe out the horde of disloyal slaves; and (2) to shed their sweat in order to acquire a good future and to contribute their money so as to accomplish the great task.

I have always been ashamed of myself because I have not been able to accomplish anything significant. But you, my compatriots, why would you be unable to achieve something? With ten Xie Cheng, a hundred Jing Ke, there is no enmity that cannot be revenged. With one Zi Feng, two Lu Su, there are no mountains that cannot be propped up or even moved.[10] That is the fourth pleasant situation resulting from modernization.

5. *True Virtue*

In the marketplaces, in the villages, everywhere people talk about civic virtues; even women and children know how to discourse about them. May I ask our compatriots: nowadays, who among us would not be able to accomplish a great deed? In the final analysis one should not talk about the lance in the East as opposed to the shield in the West, or of the pearls of Qin as against the emerald of Qao. One should ponder over the fact that, if the bow from Qu is lost, then someone from Qu would have found it; nothing therefore is privately and individually owned. From one man to the whole population of the country, if everyone is of one will, what can we not accomplish? O my dear compatriots. If you have realized how important the civic virtues are, then try to act accordingly. If someone makes a mistake, his brother will bear the consequences. If someone has talents, his brother should benefit from them. Even lives can be exchanged, let alone money, belongings, resources. Everything should be held in common. The country is common to all of us who should reckon that fact. Everyone should care about the country; everyone should try to help. If you fall sick, I should worry about you as if we shared the same body. Why should we hesitate because we walk in the same direction, on the same road, toward the same goal ahead? After unity has been achieved among the whole population of our country against a small community of Frenchmen, will they still dare sit on our heads and ride on our backs? That is the fifth pleasant situation resulting from modernization.

6. *Fame and Profit*

When one talks about moral virtue, one should not think of fame. When one talks about heroism, one should not mention profit. Indeed, fame and profit have no common measure with moral virtue and heroism. Without reality, fame will quickly disappear. And if it is not genuine, fame will look like defamation for thousands of generations to come. If one pursues only one's own profit, in the volatile conditions of the world today, one will ultimately face a limitless catastrophe. On the other hand, if one has real fame, nobody will dare utter a word against it. People like Washington and Saigo Takamori do indeed have real fame; that is why the capital city of America now holds high the example of the former and the capital city of Japan erected a tall bronze statue in memory of the latter. The search for fame of these two men has certainly been well rewarded. Let our compatriots seek fame in these fashions. If profit is genuine, then not only one can accumulate that profit for oneself, but the rest of the people may have an equal share of it. It is like the opening of Africa or the digging of the Suez Canal. These two endeavors require the spending of vast amounts of money. Both aim at profit. But to spend money during more than ten years and subsequently be able to open up an entire immense continent for people to settle or to spend more than a thousand million and end up by reaping profit from the Eastern seas to the Western ocean, the search for profit in such a fashion is also well rewarded. Let our compatriots seek profit in the same way. But of the fame of one day and the one lasting for ten thousand generations, which fame is better? In life one must accept every hardship, including death. In wealth one spends thousands of ounces of gold in order to reach fame and reap profit. In the same manner the rights of the country should be fought for with bones and blood; we should utilize all available resources in order to seize the benefits of civilization. If our people are all determined to seek fame and profit, how then could our country not become rich and strong? That is the sixth pleasant situation resulting from modernization.

Only when the six desirable situations are realized shall we attain the ten pleasant conditions. After we have realized the six desirable situations, power will reside in our hands. We shall mold it in whatever shape we like. Our country will be rich and strong only when its people have one will, one determination. Then we shall be able to shake the sky and move the earth. Will our people hesitate to accomplish that feat of gathering the energy of all to build up an impregnable citadel and of uniting the intelligence of thousands of individuals to flatten the waves of the ocean?

Allow me to bow my head in wishing long life to the New Vietnam.[11]

Notes

1. SLOT III, 55.
2. This is how the prosecutor general, chief of the Judiciary Service in Indochina, expressed his opinion about this document, which was naturally banned by the colonial authorities. In a note sent to the governor-general of Indochina dated 28 April 1909, he wrote: "The document *The New Vietnam* contains trashy statements, defamatory remarks toward France as well as calls for massacre. It deals with laws and regulations to be enacted by the future government of independent Vietnam. The author assumes that the goal of independence has been attained and, from now on, one should plan the economic reconstruction, the political proportional representation, the responsibility of the ruler, the penal regime. Nothing has been left out of that draft of a new constitution and the chapter which spells out the promises for the future is one of the most elaborate in this document. Unjust taxes and the burdensome and tyrannical bureaucracy of the French are considered past realities! One should take good notice of this book for Phan Boi Chau and his devotees are all convinced of the success of their criminal project. Nevertheless, while reading the *New Vietnam,* one cannot fail to be

impressed by the ardent faith that moves its author" (ANSOM, Indochine, Nouveaux fonds 28 [2]).

Phan Boi Chau wrote in his autobiography (Apr. or May 1907) while in Hong Kong: "At this point having a few decades of free time, I wrote *Tan Viet Nam* (The New Vietnam). This book could be broadly divided into two parts: the first part deals with the ten deep satisfactions (*Thap dai khoai*) and the second with the ten earnest aspirations (*thap dai nguyen*). The book was printed in a thousand copies" (in G. Boudarel, *Mémoires,* 83).

3. Phan Boi Chau exaggerated the size of the Vietnamese territory, which covers approximately an area of 127,243 square miles, or 329,560 square kilometers, and its population did not exceed fifteen million at that time.

4. Romanized system of reproducing the Vietnamese spoken language.

5. Names of various ethnic groups in China.

6. Administrative subdivisions for ethnic minorities

7. For more information about all the names of areas bordering on Vietnamese territory that Vietnam traditionally considered as tributary countries, see Ta Quang Phat, *Nhu Vien trong Dai Nam Hoi Dien Su Le,* 2 vols. (Saigon, 1965–66).

8. Saigon here (in Chinese "Xi Gong") designates the whole of Cochinchina or southern Vietnam rather than Saigon itself.

9. A unit of French Indochina's currency.

10. The four personal names mentioned here refer to well-known Chinese historical figures who have accomplished the deeds alluded to in the sentence—that is, revenge enmity, prop up or move mountains.

11. I am indebted to Professor Chuong Thau of the History Institute in Hanoi for providing me with the photographic reproduction of a manuscript copy of the original text of this document that was written in Chinese. Its translation into Vietnamese can be found in Chuong Thau, "Tac Pham Tan Viet Nam cua Phan Boi Chau," in *Nghien Cuu Lich Su* 78 (Sept. 1965): 31–39. The same version of this text can also be found in Chuong Thau, ed., *Phan Boi Chau Toan Tap,* 10 vols. (Hanoi, 1990), 2:250–77. Professor Chuong Thau must have used the copy in Chinese to do his translation. The original text is preserved in the National Archives in Hanoi.

Phan Chau Trinh (1872–1926)

Letter to Governor-General Paul Beau
(1907)

Phan Chau Trinh or Phan Chu Trinh was one of the two prominent nationalist leaders in the first quarter of the twentieth century. The other one was Phan Boi Chau. Phan Chu Trinh passed the doctoral examination in the old Confucian educational system in 1901, when he was thirty years old. In 1906 he resigned from his position as an official in the Vietnamese royal administration and, together with Phan Boi Chau, went to Japan to seek help for the Dong Du movement. There the two men discovered that they basically disagreed on two counts. First of all, Phan Chu Trinh did not believe Japan could lend assistance to the Vietnamese independence movement without being tempted to dominate it once the French had vacated the colony. Second, unlike Phan Boi Chau, Phan Chu Trinh intended firmly to put an end to French colonialism at the same time as he would also terminate the monarchical regime in a new independent Vietnam.¹

Upon his return from abroad Phan Chu Trinh wrote the following letter addressed to the governor-general of Indochina. In 1907 he helped found a private institution of learning called the Dong Kinh Nghia Thuc (Tonkin Free School).² In 1908 he was implicated in a peasant uprising protesting against high taxes. The Vietnamese royal administration condemned him to death, a sentence that was subsequently commuted to forced labor for life to be purged in the infamous penitentiary located on the Con Son island, better known as Poulo Condore, off the coast of south Vietnam. Three years later, in 1911, the French League for Human Rights obtained his freedom in exchange for a voluntary exile in France.

During World War I Phan Chu Trinh was arrested by the French government and confined for a short while in the Santé Jail in Paris. He was finally permitted to leave France to return to Vietnam in 1925. He died in Saigon on 24 March 1926.

A note written by a French Security agent whose mission was to spy on him and Nguyen Ai Quoc reports that he and Nguyen Ai Quoc were the "two

*most influential members of the Vietnamese community in France." Here is
how the editorialist of the* Co Vo San, *a publication of the Vietnamese communists, evaluated him at the time of his death: "he has never been a revolutionary. He never dared to conceive of an armed conflict against the imperialists.
He did not know that in order to liberate Indochina, blood must be shed."³*

*In this open letter Phan Chu Trinh describes in frank and candid terms the
shortcomings of the French colonial policy as it was implemented in Vietnam.
As Phan Chu Trinh sees it, the imperfection derives from three causes: (1) "The
first one resides in the fact that the Protecting Power gave too great a liberty to
the Vietnamese mandarins." (2) "The second cause resides in the fact that the
Protectorate has always regarded with contempt the people of Vietnam, resulting in a segregation syndrome." (3) "The third cause stems from the advantage
that the Vietnamese mandarins take of the segregation policy so as to maltreat
their own people." This document gives Phan Chu Trinh the deserved reputation of being less concerned about French colonialism than about the abuses of
the Vietnamese mandarins.*

I, Phan Chu Trinh, former mandarin, am writing to you to describe the critical
situation of the Vietnamese country.

Since Vietnam was placed under their protection, the French have built
roads and bridges; they have improved communication through the construction of railroads and steamships; they have established post offices and telegraph lines: all these works are indeed very useful to Vietnam, and anybody
with ears and eyes can hear and see them. There are, however, a few features I
cannot fail to mention to you: they are the abuses perpetrated by the mandarinate, the sufferings accumulated by the people, and the decay of our customs.
The French have not only shut their eyes to all these evils that are undermining
the future of our nation; they have, furthermore, allowed these evils to spread
their evil influence without even bothering to make an inquiry into their
destructive effects.

In recent decades the high officials of the Royal Court were content to
relax in their comfortable palaces, devoting their time to contemplating the
futilities of the past. In doing so, they thought they had properly fulfilled their
duty. As for the mandarins of the provincial administration, they ruled with
arrogance over our villages while sharpening their talent in flatteries toward
their superiors. Their ploy has become a daily occurrence. The dignity of the
scholars has all but vanished. Their exactions increase with every passing day,
so that the masses have no escape. Because of all this, public affairs have been
neglected, and the rural population has started to move out of the countryside.
The customs are in decay; ritual and propriety have all but disappeared. Thus, a
country that expands to more than 400,000 square kilometers and that counts
more than twenty million inhabitants is regressing from semicivilization into

complete barbarism. Maybe educated persons are not lacking who, in the deepest of their hearts, feel distressed over the ruin of their fatherland; to witness the disappearance of their race indeed fills them with anxiety. Everyone realizes the urgency of a solution. Among them those who are more courageous leave for overseas, and, once far away, they weep profusely and never think of a return. The less courageous people bury themselves in the corners of their villages and remain silent. No one dares appear before the Great Dignitary of the Protecting Power [the French governor-general] to denounce, with guts and blood, the inequities committed by the mandarinate and to speak up loudly about the people's sufferings over the past several decades. Nothing has reached the ears of the Great Dignitary of the Protecting Power so that today Vietnam has become a dying country, without hope for any cure. This is obviously the fault of the educated people, but that state of affairs also derives from the misunderstanding of the masses, who are convinced that the policy of the Protecting Power consisted mainly in mistreating the Vietnamese people.

It has been several years now since I resigned from the mandarinate. I have traveled extensively throughout the country, from north to south. My ears have been made attentive to what people say, and I have seen with my own eyes the abuses perpetrated by the mandarins. On the other hand, I have made a detailed inquiry into the feelings and opinions that Vietnamese and Frenchmen entertained toward one another. Today, without fear, I have come to describe the situation to you, Great Dignitary of the Protecting Power, in the hope that, upon hearing my testimony, you would sympathize with the situation I describe and not disapprove of my behavior.

Except for those who are in the mandarinate, in Vietnam today the opinion of the common people, whether they be intelligent or stupid, is that the Protecting Power mistreats the Vietnamese, that it does not consider them to be human beings. When the people observe that the indigenous mandarins, instead of acting in the interest of their own folk, are harming them instead, the Vietnamese would again say that it is precisely the Protecting Power that unleashes these mandarins upon them so that the Vietnamese would destroy one another in such a way that they would quickly exterminate their race. For the Vietnamese people that represents the designs of colonialism. Over the last few years the thinking of our scholars and the songs of our villagers all proclaim the same theme, from north to south. And since they realized that their own intelligence will not be enough to allow them to survive and their strength insufficient to preserve their autonomy, our people look up to I do not know what foreign power to save them.

Alas, how pitiful is a population of so many millions who count among them so many thousands of educated men and yet are so blind and so weak, so confused and so lost, as not to know how to help one another, to unite with one another, to live with one another, and to shoulder one another's efforts. In this world where might is right they only have complaints without any plan; they live as in drunkenness or in dreams. Isn't such a mentality profoundly pathetic?

In the past decades, of all the people in this country, whether intelligent or stupid, rich or poor, no one escapes from the tutelage of the Protecting Power, yet how is it that they all have reached the lowest level of their subsistence, that they are about to witness the destruction of their race? What are the causes of this predicament? I urge you, Great Dignitary of the Protecting Power, to scrutinize them thoroughly so as to understand them fully.

The causes are three in number. The first one, as I see it, resides in the fact that the Protecting Power gave too great a liberty to the Vietnamese mandarins. Up to now the Protecting Power has been satisfied with placing in the protected country two or three of its great officials, who, together with the Vietnamese royal government, governed the state. The provincial government, on the other hand, had only a few officers of the Protecting Power within its ranks; it obviously cannot function without the service of indigenous administrators to manage the affairs of state and control the people in the countryside. Whether the country is governed or not; whether the people are pacified or not, it all depends on the quality of these indigenous administrators. It makes a great difference whether these mandarins are capable men or incompetent ones, whether they have talents or are devoid of all faculties.

In the past forty years the decay of Vietnam has been evident. The higher as well as the lower classes are only interested in pleasure. The laws are not respected. Men of talents no longer exist. The high officials simply wait for time to be promoted to higher ranks. The lower-ranked mandarins resort to intrigues and briberies to obtain their advancement. The scholar-students follow their example and have made that kind of behavior into a habit. Those who desire a mandarinal title spend their time begging in front of the higher officials' residences. Those mandarins who live in the countryside take advantage of their official position and behave with unforgiveable arrogance in their villages. Others, beside their festivities and sexual adventures, hardly know anything else. The peasants, the artisans, the merchants, indulge as well in pleasure. Anywhere one turns one witnesses the same scenes. In cities, as in the countryside, those who have power behave as treacherously as the hare, while the weaklings act as stupidly as the pigs. Ignorant and greedy, they don't back off from any wrongdoing. Being victims of exactions and beatings, they do not dare show their anger. The entire country is intimidated into cowardice. *Human dignity* becomes an empty word. Those conditions can be seen clearly everywhere. I am not exaggerating, nor do I dare tell lies about the entire people of the whole country.

When the people of a country have reached such a low level of decadence, no matter whether they be mandarins, scholars, or commoners, only a clear definition of punishments can turn them away from crimes and induce them to live within the law. Only then can they be led onto the path of progress, with the hope that they might be able to help themselves find peace and improvement. The Protecting Authorities have been established here long enough for them not to be aware of that state of affairs. They also know that the customs of Vietnam could not be changed suddenly, and, since the Vietnamese were not capable of governing themselves, the Protecting Authorities have taken into their own hands the administration of the country in the name of the Vietnamese. But, ironically enough, they preserved the Vietnamese royal government; they kept the Vietnamese mandarinate intact while giving them only enough power to transmit orders and levy taxes. As for the affairs of state and interests of the people, the Protecting Authorities never bothered to know anything more. They simply proclaimed that they governed Vietnam with the assistance of the Vietnamese. Naturally, from time to time, they promoted one or two high dignitaries, dismissed one or two mandarins. But if the ones who got dismissed were incapable, the new recruits were not necessarily more competent. If the dismissed officials were rudely greedy, the new appointees have not necessarily kept themselves clean of corruption. Moreover, some who are dismissed one day can find themselves promoted the next day. Removed from this region, they are sent to another. Bad reputation and corrupt practices have accumulated. How pitiful all this is!

Knowing, for some time, that the Protecting Power favors and never punishes them, the Vietnamese mandarins grow accustomed to that treatment. Those who are greedy become more so, counting on their corruption to climb up the hierarchical ladder. Those who are lazy become even lazier, counting only on their apathy to remain in their position. What they are principally interested in is to show ostentatiously their gowns and their hats; they ride noisily in their carriages or on their horses. When asked about their mandarinal titles, they readily reply that they are the great dignitaries of the Vietnamese government or the high mandarins of the provincial administration. Besides their regular meetings and their routine court appearances, if asked about the strong and weak points of their country or of their province, they would not have a single idea. If one asked the same questions of the prefecture or district mandarins, they would say that they are indeed the chief executives of this prefecture or of that district, but, besides the collection of taxes or the reception of higher officials on visits, they would know nothing concerning the affairs of their constituencies. All officials, whether of high or low rank, considered corruption and exaction the outright privileges of the mandarinate. They paid no attention whatsoever to the people's complaints. Alas, if it had been true that the Vietnamese people are so corrupt and their mind so shut up and if they had lived in similar conditions for the past several centuries, then their race would have been annihilated long ago. How was Vietnam able to stand as an independent country for more than a thousand years, and how was it able to become an important nation in the Southeast Asian region? How could its people develop into an important race today? If France treated all the protectorates and colonies she has in the five continents in like manner, how would any of them accept with grace to follow her guidance? Alas, although Vietnamese law is known to be unjust, some articles would nonetheless exist to rein in the mandarinate. But the most stringent rules are now applied to oppress the common people, while the regulations are so lax toward the mandarins. It is as if the dyke had been broken and water has flooded the four corners of the land; no end seems in sight. All this evil results from the great liberty that the Protectorate has given the indigenous mandarinate, thus allowing it to become so rotten.

The second cause resides in the fact that the Protectorate has always regarded with contempt the people of Vietnam, resulting in a segregation syndrome. Great France and Vietnam have lived together for a long while now. Seeing that our mandarins are corrupt, our people unintelligent, our customs in decay, the French despise our people, who, in their judgment, have no national dignity. Therefore, in their newspapers, books, conversations, or discussions, they usually express the contemptuous opinion that the Vietnamese are barbarians and comparatively not much different from pigs. Not only do the French refuse to treat the Vietnamese as equals; they even are afraid that if the Vietnamese come too close to them, they might somehow be soiled. Over the last decades, whenever the French officials are angry, Vietnamese mandarins, scholars, or common people, whether they have committed any crime or not, are all humiliated. As for the poor people who sell their labor or the villagers who discharge simply of their corvée duty, many have died, having been kicked and beaten by the French. People from north to south relay that message to one another, and all those who still have some feelings are outraged by the thought that the French are treating us like animals, looking at us like wood and stone. Anger fills their heart, but they dare not speak up. The ignorant people in the villages fear the French like gods from Heaven; they are terrified by the French as they would be by lightning and thunder, running away from them as far as they can. Those scholars who have any conscience left consider a career in the mandarinate as an unenviable outcome. Only those who crave for mandarinal titles or those who are compelled by familial conditions would suffer that humiliation; they subsequently try to forget it, hoping that circumstances and conditions will change. Sometimes on clear nights, they attempt to awaken their consciences, uttering to themselves a few words of shame and anger. Quickly, however, they convince themselves that they are powerless, simply involved in some vicious cycle. Little by little, they grow accustomed to the situation and soon enough reach their peace of mind. It is, therefore, not true that all of them have lost their conscience or that all rejoice in their shame.

Up to the present day no Vietnamese official, whether of high or low rank, would not be terrified, all his hair standing on ends, whenever he meets a French administrator, lest his words or deeds should displease and anger the Frenchman. As for the simple folk in the villages, whether they be mandarins or belong to the scholar-gentry class, whenever they venture a few steps beyond their gates, if they chance upon a French official, a French soldier, or a French merchant, they all bow their heads, drop their ears, hasten their pace to proceed quickly through the encounter. They merely want to avoid being humiliated or beaten up. It is amazing that people of two countries living together on the same territory could have such diametrically opposed behaviors and feelings. It is, therefore, not surprising that only those who desire to become mandarins would sit day after day at the doorsteps of the Protectorate High Officials' residences. As for the scholars who still possess some sense of dignity, none would dare approach your courtyard. Those who bring their suit to court for one reason or another could hope to see the face of the [French] administrator; at any rate, the complaints and grievances of the common people never reach his ears.

Alas, it is undeniable that corruption and shamelessness charges can be lodged against the Vietnamese. But in a country this big, among a population of so many millions, are there not one or two persons with whom you could reasonably discuss the advantages and disadvantages to the country? Why, then, does the Protectorate maltreat all the people without exception? I am afraid that the longer the two people live together, the further they will move apart from each other. Given this sort of feeling toward one another, to hope for any kind of solidarity between them is difficult to imagine.

Recently I read in the *Dai Viet Tan Bao* newspaper that there are presently about twenty Vietnamese living in Japan. Among those twenty there certainly are one or two who would be somewhat aware of the hopelessness of the situation of Vietnam. These people used to live no further than a hundred miles from you or from the provincial chief. And yet they, who for thousands of years have never gone beyond their gates, have resolved to abandon their families and relatives to cross vast oceans to go to a foreign country that for thousands of years they had never heard of. There they lament with moving voices about all the grievances that trouble their soul. They have resolved not to come to your office or to the provincial chief's office to give vent to their sufferings. That kind of situation results directly from the policy of segregation practiced by the Protectorate, which consists in treating the Vietnamese people with contempt.

The third cause stems from the advantage that the Vietnamese mandarins take of the segregation policy so as to maltreat their own people. The isolation of the Protectorate from the people, the divergence of views with regard to the advantages and disadvantages to the country and the corruption of the mandarinate, have already been discussed earlier. Nevertheless, were it not for that segregation policy, maybe one day, because the French will have lived long enough to understand the situation or maybe because the Vietnamese people will no longer be able to contain their sufferings and will try to disclose their grievances, then East and West might be one; the two sides might understand each other, and the mandarinate would have no room to show its wickedness. I am afraid that such an idea is so seductive that the mandarinate would want to suppress it, and that is why its officials endeavor to sow the seeds of segregation. They also know that what the administrators of the Protectorate like or care for is the collection of all the taxes and the impression of all the corvée labors; what they dislike are obstacles put in the way of the implementation of official business and conspiratorial assemblies. Therefore, what the Protectorate officials like or care for the mandarins put it in their heart and their feet, eager to satisfy them, even if they have to skin the people alive, suck their blood, or carve out their bones. Nothing will stop them. When the mandarins are sent out to administer a province, a prefecture, a district, they use their position to threaten the people; they exercise their power to oppress the scholars. Then, fearing the possible reaction of the people and the scholars, the mandarins quickly implicate them in activities they know the Protectorate dislikes: if the mandarins do not accuse them of taking advantage of their wealth to prevent the administrators from doing their duties, then they accuse them of rallying the scholar-gentry for illegal purposes. All these denunciations are, of course, false and groundless, but, being unaware, the Protectorate believes them. That is why some people are falsely accused and are even indicted. Sometimes the Protectorate recognizes the groundlessness of the accusations, but still it would not punish the mandarins, under the pretext that they were but doing their administrative duties. It all results in the people being further alienated from the administration, the scholars' morale sinking to a lower level, and the mandarins' power becoming more consolidated.

The prefecture and district mandarins simply choose the domain in which they want to exercise their corruption. When it comes to lawsuits concerning robberies or homicides, the mandarins can always use some pretext to extort bribes; this, naturally, ends in hundreds of abuses. With regard to the number of schools (in any given province), the culture of silkworms (those who desire to raise them are given the breeding larvae for free), the cultivation of rice (the cultivators who harvest the best rice are allowed to auction them), to the annual registration of manpower and rice fields, the general census of population, the inspection tours of the Protectorate officials, the smallpox vaccination tours by medical doctors, the transportation of merchandise—none of these matters, in the eyes of the Protectorate officials, should be a burden to the common people. To the Vietnamese mandarins, however, they are important social activities or urgent businesses to be pressed upon them. So they scatter to the four corners to sow untold misery among the people and to put forth exacting demands on them. The money collected from welcoming or farewell parties, from the legalization of official deeds or contracts, from the fines imposed by the notables of the village and other officials of the administration, pile up as high as mountains. For the past several decades, when the grievances of the people have reached the ears of the mandarins, they are considered gratifying opportunities to make money. Whether it pertains to important or trivial matters, whether it is urgent or not, as soon as the mandarins receive a piece of paper from the Protectorate officials, it is as if they had laid their hands on a precious pearl. They would treasure it as a protective talisman, happy that it would make them into prosperous mandarins. As for the small clerks, the cantonal notables, all oppressors of the people, seeing this, they all become so highly envious that they carry gold and silver to the capital city or to the provincial cities in order to buy a low-rank mandarinal title in the hope that even a bit of left over would be enough to make themselves and their families prosperous. Such are the sufferings of the poor people that can be seen only in their general outlines. Under so many layers of power and authority nobody, understandably enough, dare speak up. A few scholars, being aware of this kind of situation but feeling that they belong on the outside and fearing that they would be held in suspicion, are unwilling to be concerned with the problem. The grand mandarins, although conscious of it, prefer to let that situation slip by as if they had not heard of anything, because of their own corrupt practices. As for the officials of the Protectorate, perhaps because of a lack of communication or because of their isolation from reality, they do not know anything.

Today the people are ruined; poor as rich are suffering; many are lying dead from starvation in the streets; robberies and banditry crop up everywhere; reproach and grievances are heard all over: the situation has indeed reached some degree of urgency. The scholars in the country advocate the study of the West, the abolition of the mandarinal examinations, and the foundation of trading corporations; all that, if successful, will relieve the situation maybe by one or two percentage points only. Even so, the mandarins still view these activities as directed against them. If they do not consider them as unsound enterprises, they see them as conspiracies. These false and segregationist accusations must have reached your ears not once every day but many times over. Alas, even if Vietnam is a barbarian or semicivilized country, it has, for thousands of years, transmitted its writing from generation to generation. Its poetry and its books are still extant. Is it not a well-known fact that to serve the people deserves praise and to mistreat them constitutes a crime? How can the mandarins, who are familiar with books and writings, see their offices as marketplaces, the common folk as fish and meat, those who are concerned about the well-being of the people as mad persons, those who think about the people's interest as rebels, so that nowadays black is no longer distinguishable from white, right is confused with wrong. They act evil, and they speak evil.

Nothing is sacred to them anymore. This stems from the fact that the mandarins exploit the distance separating the French from the Vietnamese people to alienate them completely from each other.

Of the three wrongs mentioned here I have presented only one or two examples. As for the clever flattery of the mandarins and their strange cruelty, even the most imaginative scholar of Europe in his hundred cogitations would not be able to understand them. How the common people suffer from cold and starvation, how they endure their hardships, the most talented painter of Europe in his hundreds of sketches would not be able to reproduce them. If the situation is so desperate, it is simply because the Protectorate favors the mandarinate, maltreats the people, and lets the mandarins abuse the people. That's all.

The policy of the Protectorate in its management of the affairs of Vietnam lends itself to some comments. These comments concern the Protectorate's refusal to teach the people efficient ways to earn their living, to familiarize them with new methods to make profit, while taxes have all been increased and corvée required from the people in a hundred different schemes—so much so that now, out of ten poor people, five or six reach the stage of misery through the corruption of the mandarins, three or four through corvée and taxes. For thousands of years Vietnam was an agricultural country; people also raised cattle and silkworms. Specializations did not prevail yet, and industry and commerce were still lacking; that state of affairs does not invite any remark. Recently, however, people from every walk of life, high and low, every one, are only in search of pleasure, interested merely in finding their own peace. The court is incapable of renovating anything, while the people happily indulge in their laziness. Money stagnates, the ways leading toward profit are without issue; that is why among hundreds of taxes none is sufficient. Whenever a bad crop occurs, the peasant relies on charity. The ignorant people, not knowing what to do, sit noisily around, waiting for food to come: they thus sit unto death. Today people start to migrate from their land and scatter into the four corners of the country. Governmental efficiency breaks down; the people's customs deteriorate: this indeed has not resulted from only one day's evolution.

From the time Vietnam became a protectorate of France, bridges, sewers, and roads have been built and repaired; military posts and stations have been erected; salaries and indemnities for the mandarins have accumulated into the millions. And yet, beside the taxes, principally those imposed on land and per head, and not counting the customs duties, the government does not know where to go in order to improve its finances. Given the present situation, there is indeed no other way out. But if the government had secured the collaboration of two or three high mandarins with some technical knowledge and some human feelings and the assistance of a few hundred officials with talent and honesty, if it had treated them with sincerity, delegated some power to them, the government would have been able to discuss with them ways and means to raise profits and decrease expenses, to change this or modify that, to plan improvements in economic fields, to devise new methods for earning a good living, and after all that and only then, slowly, it could increase the taxes. In this way benefit would accrue to the state, and no harm would befall the people. It is, therefore, not true to assert that there is no way out.

But now, claiming that the mandarins are incompetent and the village people deceitful, the Protectorate applies its own policy. No matter whether the lands are large or small, with good or bad soil, the manpower is big or small in number, rich or poor, they are equally taxed. This year taxes have been increased by 1 percent; next year it will be another 1 percent. This year an item is added to the tax assets, next year another one. That is the Protectorate's financial policy, which is enforced with utmost energy. The mandarins, seeing it as a way toward promotion, suck all the blood of the people in order to reach the quota. All of them see in that fiscal policy the easiest way to get as much money as possible. It is only to be feared that, once the fish is caught and the pond empty, the policy cannot be applied over a very long period. The Finance Department of the Protectorate knows its mathematics well. I don't question its figures. For any given province all it has to do is to calculate the surface of its fields, its other resources, the number of its inhabitants, the cost for their food and clothing, their other expenses, the amount of taxes paid . . . It would immediately see whether the resources of that province were abundant or scarce, whether the standard of living of its people was high or low; everything would be so clear. To all the expenditures one should add the bribes paid to the corrupt mandarins, the energy spent in forced labor, the resources lost through natural calamities—all this is in fact difficult if not impossible to compute. Finally, one should also take into consideration the alms donated to the homeless, the wealth lost to burglars and bandits. In these conditions is it realistic to wish that people would not die of hardships?

What to say now of the abuses pertaining to forced labor. Every able body, each year, has to give fourteen days of forced labor: four days for public works and ten days of corvée. In addition to these fourteen days the people have to pay for every other public work done by the state in the interest of their community. All this, in fact, does not represent too great a burden. But it does elicit, in the villages, a great deal of disturbance: some people leave; others return; there is a constant movement on the road to and fro; not a single day is peaceful. In addition, the mandarins take advantage of the situation to exercise their arbitrariness: they set this villager free from his obligations but draft the other; they replace this name by another name; they take everything into their own hands, consulting no one else. It should be the mandarins who put out the money to hire the people, but it turns out to be the people who put out the money to hire the mandarins. How many poor people came out of this quandary losing their jobs or ruining themselves completely? As for the money the government should receive for their hired labor or from other transactions, the clerks in public offices retain most of it. The poor people, all year round, run from place to place offering their labor, carrying their products, and yet only one- or two-tenths of the wages due them reach their pockets. In these miserable circumstances it is difficult to ask the people not to leave everything and become vagabonds.

The fate of the Vietnamese people today is indeed miserable and insecure, indeed not different from that of buffaloes and horses. People can tie them up, whip them at will. They have a mouth but dare not speak. They are about to die without being allowed a lament. Weighing down on them is the power of the Protectorate government compounded by the cruelty of the Vietnamese mandarinate. What can one not get out of them through whipping? I am afraid that soon the rich people will be ruined, the poor ones resourceless; the mild people will become beggars and the tough ones robbers and bandits. A few more years from now villages will be deserted, old and young people will have died, if not of hunger, then of imprisonment or exile; if not from drifting along the highways, then from the oppression of the mandarins. The day will come when rice fields will have no one to tend them; corvée will no longer be honored; taxes no longer paid. Even if you peel their skin or carve their bones, the only good that it will do is to send the Vietnamese people onto the same path as the Red Indians of America. That's all.

Alas, the French emperor Napoléon as an envoy from Heaven spread around him the flowers of freedom, so that until today the European people have not ceased singing his praises. As for the saying "consider your enemy as friend," it is a principle regularly professed by French women and children. Today, as this old country of many thousand years in Asia has come under the protection of the French flag, it has become so wretched and oppressed that it can no longer stand on its own. I am sure that you must be deeply moved and troubled by that situation and that, day and night, you are pondering a remedy that would not let that misery linger at the expense of French honor and with the unfavorable criticism of other nations. Because of the abuses of the mandarins, because of the burden of taxes and corvée, the sufferings of the people have reached alarming proportions, and yet the Protectorate continues to ignore their supplication: wouldn't it be now too late?

Recently, people in the North and South have been entertained by the rumor that the Protectorate is going to change its policy within the government of Vietnam: it will modify its treatment of the Vietnamese people; it will regard the French and Vietnamese in the same way so as to conquer the hearts and minds of the people. I presume all that is to be seen as long-range policy goals. I have read many newspaper articles coming from Hanoi and have learned that the governor-general of Indochina, in speeches delivered in Hanoi, talked of improving the treatment of the Vietnamese, of civilizing the Vietnamese. Many matters are mentioned over and over again—things like reform of the penal code, renovation of the educational system. But with regard to the abuses of the mandarinate, the exactions of taxes and corvée, not a single word has been uttered. The French editor of the newspaper *Le Courrier d'Haiphong* has written thousands of words commenting on the policies implemented in Indochina. He is not at a loss for words when it comes to criticizing the taxes and the corvée systems. But, concerning the Vietnamese mandarinate, his argument is that if this old institution of Vietnam is not preserved, the Vietnamese people cannot be governed. That kind of interpretation is indeed frightful. After all, the Protectorate's use of the indigenous mandarins to oppress the Vietnamese people is not a new phenomenon. The fact that the mandarinate relies on the authority of the Protectorate to oppress the people provokes the resentment of the people against the Protectorate: that sentiment is quite deep and widespread. Now if one wants to pursue the good while not, at first, eradicating the evil, or, in similar fashion, if one wants to govern the people without first selecting good mandarins, I doubt that one can attain any success. At the present time the Vietnamese people are awaiting their imminent death, while the mandarins do not know anything else besides carrying out orders and running errands. If you force them to apply your new policy, I am sure you don't want it to be only in words. The mandarins, however, will not cooperate. What they want is to remain silent and abuse the people, that's all. To paint a mural in five colors on a wall of mud or to garnish with eight most delicious dishes a dusty table is not only a useless act; it is an uncouth masquerade. Can one call that attitude generosity toward the Vietnamese people? Is it what civilization means? It is in fact not different from giving a cake to a child who makes a nuisance of himself or to offer gold and silver to the people lest they revolt because of starvation. Alas! What all that does is to increase the doubt in people's minds: what is left for them to do is to await death. I cannot see in it any gain to the Protectorate's civilizing policy toward Vietnam at all.

When one examines the Protectorate's policy closely, one has the impression that the Protectorate is afraid that the scholars and people will conspire to resist it. The Protectorate, therefore, uses the mandarins to spy on them; it relies on punishments to oppress them. Encouraging the mandarins to indulge in abuses would simply result in dulling the spirit of the scholars and people. That should, of course, be avoided. To love freedom, to conspire for independence, to be ashamed of being slaves to others, all that can be suspected of peoples of Europe. But to suspect the Vietnamese people of these sentiments is no different from suspecting a weakling of climbing a wall to commit a burglary or a three-year-old child of burning houses to kill people. That's being oversuspicious.

In the past years education has not been too well developed in Vietnam;

the customs have deteriorated, intelligence has decreased, and honesty has all but disappeared. Within the confines of a village or a hamlet people consider one another as fish and meat; those who belong to the same family and share the same blood cannot help but see one another as the enemy. Even if they had any rebellious design, they would not have had any land to retreat to, no arms and ammunition to use, nor any resources to count on. But, if by some weird circumstances, the Protectorate were to lend them a few thousand rifles along with the territory of a few provinces for them to keep as their own without asking any further questions, I am sure that after a few years, if they don't take revenge on one another, then they will become rivals; if they don't steal money from one another, then they would fight against one another over rank and position; they would kill one another to the last one. It is certain that they cannot survive one single day in the present world. What to say about rebellion against anyone else?

The scholars and people of Vietnam are powerless; therefore, there is nothing to worry about as far as they are concerned. But to say that they are of one heart and one aim together with the Protectorate, that they have no suspicion whatsoever, that they trust the Protectorate unto death, that's certainly not the case either. Over the past several decades the abuses of the mandarins have been more than severe; the resentment accumulated by the poor people runs deep enough. In addition, the tax burden, the natural calamities of drought and flood, the impossibility of acquiring the means of subsistence, the threat of death and perdition, sufferings piling upon sufferings—all this seem to have no end.

Now the resentment has become momentous; the people's feelings are at a boiling point; their complaints echo mournfully to faraway places. If they did not stand up to fight against the mandarins, that's simply because they have not had any opportunities. Should some day a strong neighbor come to sow trouble [in Indochina] and should France and that troublesome neighbor come to fighting against each other, then surely the people will rise up. The greedy will plunder in order to appropriate wealth, the strong will kill to settle old scores, while the mandarins will side with the stronger party. The great order having been shattered, the fastest will then occupy whatever territory they can lay their hands on. If people were allowed to choose their masters and their owners, they would not hesitate to do so. These are the deep feelings of the Vietnamese people today. If you say that it is the duty of the Vietnamese people to fight to their death on behalf of the Protectorate against the invaders, I am afraid that within the borders of this country there are quite a few people who disagree with that assertion of yours. Naturally, if the Vietnamese people have pushed themselves into these quandaries, it is simply because of the hardships they have endured from bad government, because of the oppression they have suffered from an unreasonable power, and not because the Vietnamese people have any special predilection for rebellions, calamities, or catastrophes.

If France is really interested in changing her policy, she should employ only those mandarins who have talent; give them authority and power; treat them with propriety; show them sincerity; deliberate with them over the best means to promote the good and eradicate the evil; open up new ways for the people to earn their living; provide the scholar-students with the freedom of discussion; widen the freedom of the press so as to know the people's sentiments; put an end to the abuses of the mandarinate by resorting to just punishments and fair rewards. Furthermore, if, little by little, the legal system is improved, the mandarinal examinations abolished, the educational system renovated, libraries built, teachers trained, commercial and industrial knowledge encouraged, the taxes and corvée systems ameliorated, then the people will quietly devote their efforts to do their work well. The scholar-students will discharge their duties with joy. At that time people will only fear that France will abandon Vietnam. Who would and could see her as an enemy?

Alas, the Vietnamese people are in full decay, their intelligence totally blackened. Compared to other countries of Europe and Asia, the distance is great. The only way for us to keep our territory and to allow our race to survive on this globe is to have a capable teacher to educate us and regard us as his pupils; to find a good mother who would treat us like her own children, raise us and take good care of us, with confidence and with affection. From East to West, from North to South, wherever one goes, everything points to dependence. If there must be dependence, then to talk about the glory of depending on X or the shame of depending on Y, all that is sheer nonsense.

If out of untold sufferings, by throwing away thousands of those ignorant heads, discarding thousands of liters of dirty and colorless blood; by tossing out a thousand corpses whose blood flies and gnats would not dare suck, whose flesh foxes or raccoons would not dare nibble, the people gain in exchange a slave condition for hundreds of generations to come, do you expect them to be fully satisfied? I don't think the Vietnamese people are that stupidly mad. If this time I am not more outspoken, it is simply because I would like to see what designs the Protectorate has in the way it intends to treat the Vietnamese people. That's all.

It is with a sad and resentful mood, not knowing where to vent my frustrations, that I took up my pen courageously to write to you these frank remarks. I also set aside everything about rite and ritual. If you sincerely have any regard for the Vietnamese people, then you will generously examine my intention, receive with goodwill my suggestions. You will allow me to come to your doorstep. Without haste you will ask me questions. I will then open to you my heart, discuss with you the good and the evil, in the hope that the people of my country will have a chance to come back to life. That is my deepest aspiration. But, on the contrary, if the unique policy of the government of the Protectorate is to mistreat the Vietnamese people; if it has resolved to abandon 460,000 square miles of national territory and sacrifice more than twenty million people; if it is determined not to allow the scholars and people of Vietnam to raise their head in dignity, then accuse me of treason, indict me with slander and libel, put me in handcuffs and shackles, then throw me into a cauldron of boiling oil, so that those scholars within the country who are endowed with some intelligence and talent will have their legs paralyzed and their mouths shut. They will then know how to behave properly, how not to follow in my footsteps, and how not to speak up improperly so as to be implicated in crimes similar to mine. That would be the misfortune of Vietnam, and that also is my warning.

I await the instructions and orders of Your Excellency the Great Dignitary of the Protecting Power.[4]

Notes

1. According to Phan Boi Chau's biographers, Kiem Dat and Phan Ba Can, in *Phan Boi Chau* (Sepulveda, Calif., 1981), 23, Phan Chu Trinh would have explained the difference between the two of them in the following way: "The entire country is in a deep sleep, their snore sounds like thunder. Far from the outside, you appeal to their patriotism, you scream your lungs out, but to no avail! What you really need is some one in the country who would knock people's head, twist their ears so as to wake them up! I'll go back home and play the role of Mazzini while, outside, you will be Garibaldi."

2. See Document 3, in this volume.

3. SLOT III, 52.

4. The Chinese version of this letter was published in *Nam Phong* 103 (March 1926): 25–34. Several Vietnamese translations can be found in The Nguyen, *Phan Chu Trinh* (1872–1926) (Saigon, 1956), 81–100; Thai Bach, *Thi van quoc cam thoi Phap thuoc* (Saigon, 1960), 349–66, in *TVYNVCM,* 179–97; *TVVN* vol. 2, bk. 1, 63–72, and in *Nghien cuu lich su* 66 (September 1964): 8–14. The French version is in *Bulletin de l'Ecole Française d'Extrême-Orient,* Chronicles, 7 (1907): 166–75.

DOCUMENT 3

Anonymous

A New Method to Study Civilization
(1907)

This is a text used in the private institution of learning Dong Kinh Nghia Thuc, set up in 1907 by a group of scholars under the leadership of Luong Ngoc Can, or Luong Van Can. Luong Van Can held the degree of cu nhan, one level below the doctorate, in the traditional educational system. He was later implicated in the affair of the bombing at the coffee terrace of the Hanoi Hotel in 1913, for which he was banned from Vietnam to Cambodia for ten years.

The Dong Kinh Nghia Thuc had a short life span—less than a year—but its impact on the Vietnamese people was enormous. It was a school without tuition, putting an emphasis on technical disciplines more than on literary ones. It published classical Vietnamese texts at the same time as it introduced from China philosophical and/or political works written by Western scholars such as Voltaire, Locke, Hobbes, and Montesquieu. It organized public lectures attracting throngs of people so that it put the French colonial administration ill at ease. And so the French government of Indochina moved quickly to close down the school.

In our judgment *civilization* is a beautiful word. Its beauty is not made up by its brilliance or its glamour. Studies about civilization are, indeed, happy undertakings; one cannot acquire them in one morning or one evening. In order to gain them one has to rely on a great ideology. What ideology? The ideology of opening up the people's mind.

Among the countries of this globe, some are uncivilized, some semi-civilized, and others civilized. The difference between them stems from the state of their people's mind: whether it is open or closed; whether it is adequate or deficient; whether it is fast or slow.

There is this saying pronounced by a Western scholar: "One cannot buy civilization with a price; one must acquire it with sufferings." What is the price? It is the thinking. What are the sufferings? They are the competition. The more people think, the more they compete. And the more the people compete, the more they think. From that [competition and thinking], disciplines such as acoustics, optics, physics, electricity, mineralogy, hydrology, meteorology, chemistry, geography, astrology, mathematics, and engineering will develop like brush fires. That's why one should try to reach the highest level of civilization.

Civilization and people's mind are in a cause-and-effect relationship. But in order to open up the people's mind, one has to first determine where it is being blocked and from where the development can originate before one can know where to begin. Otherwise, the only thing one might be able to do is to stare at the immensity of the ocean and let out a big sigh.

If we carefully examined the past, we would notice that the sages of remote antiquity have already invented all the things we are using now in our everyday life; they also have provided mankind with convenient tools. Scientific notions can be found scattered in books such as the *Zhou Guan,* the *Guan Zi,* or *Mo Zi.*[1] Asia has always stood at the source of all civilizations. Our country, Dai Nam, is a big and civilized country. It is situated between the tropical and temperate zones. The soil is fertile, the climate balanced, and there is an abundance of rice and silkworms. Our resources in forest products and our marine riches exceed those of other countries in the world. Our people earn their living without difficulties. Through the many dynasties the sainted emperors and their loyal subjects have made this country more prosperous, more prestigious, and more extensive. Our country's fame as a civilized country spread far and wide, within and without our frontiers. The books *Lao Shi Qing Zi* and *Feng Er Cong Bian*[2] both have registered the fact that other countries have often praised the reputation of our country and its scholars. That is an accepted fact.

But what about today? We can no longer enjoy the precious products of our mountains and forests. We can no longer hold on to the benefits derived from hundreds of commodities. The brocade, velvet, wool, cotton, silk, shoes, sandals, handkerchiefs, eye glasses, umbrellas, petrol, porcelain, china, watches, barometers, thermometers, telephones, microscopes, cameras, stationery, ink, vermilion ink, needles, thread, buttons, dyes, soap, cigarettes, tea, etc., if we don't buy them from the Northerners [Chinese], we purchase them from the Westerners [French]. Just take a look at the statistics concerning the annual imports and exports of our country. We should soon realize that once our gold is brought to be dumped outside, there won't be any hope that the pearls will ever return to our shores. Is it not a real pity to squander our national resources in such a manner?

Agriculture has its opportunities: people are busily competing in agriculture. As for us, we still cling to the past. Do we have any tractor to help in plowing our fields, electricity to improve the quality of our rice plants, new methods to save our crops from drought, from parasites?

Trade has its structures: people are actively competing in trade too. As for us, we still cling to our past. Do we have a fleet to protect our trade, a market to absorb our products, a big company created by our government with shares subscribed by our people?

Industry has its factories: people are really competing there too. As for us, we still cling to our past. Do we have anyone who would show his talent, demonstrate his knowledge, so that each day would bring about a new invention, each month a sensational device; a person in the caliber of a Watt or an Edison? How terrific it would be to possess such talents among our people.

Look at those who indulge in mellow music, billiard, cards, chess, riddles, word games, physiognomy, geomancy, magic. Everyday they devote all their effort into something completely useless; they live drunk and die dreaming; we shouldn't talk about them. But what about those who are a bit more concerned, who have got some academic degrees? As soon as they have acquired some reputation, they contemptuously declare right away that they are the elders; they attribute to themselves the title of keepers of the world's way. Everyday they boast about their nice prose. Sitting tightly, they preserve all the conservative theories, while despising the entire new learning about civilization. Those who find themselves on a lower echelon will not hear anything other than promotion into higher ranks or the number of people to be promoted: they absolutely close their mind to any other query. There was some high mandarin who wrote the following to his juniors: "If you want to climb to higher ranks one day, you should keep away from reading new books or new periodicals." Alas, if you have never heard anything about new books or periodicals, then it would have been understandable. But after you have heard about them, and then to hide them, to cover them up as if you have never heard anything about them, as if you have not seen anything so that you can continue to cultivate a slave mentality, is such human nature not a lamentable one?

Upon reflection we can honestly say that our civilization has always been static; the Western civilization is full with dynamism. That is a well-known fact. But why was it so? It was so because of a "contradictory influence" and an "original cause." Let us explain these concepts one by one.

What is meant by "contradictory influence"? In European countries, on top there is Congress to preserve the national good; below, there is the press to express the people's will. Among their great books are Rousseau's *Social Contract,* Spencer's *Theories on Progress,* and Montesquieu's *Discourse on Human Rights.* By and large every speech, every poem, every song, aims at increasing the people's patriotism and their devotion to their race. What are we doing in our country? An author when he writes is only afraid of using unintentionally taboo words;[3] when a poet offers his poetry to a superior, he is afraid of being accused of aiming too high. Only these two points would already set our country apart from those that do not forbid their people from deliberating. What we end up with, then, is nothing more than mere myths, legendary stories, a number of poetry books, volumes of prose, all brilliant literature, but nothing that would open our people's mind. That is what we have that is contrary to other people with respect to thinking.

The Europeans divide their educational system into three degrees: elementary, secondary, and higher education; each degree requires about four years of study. When the children start school, the principal subject matters are their own national language, Latin, literature, foreign languages, mathematics, geography. After they graduate from the first degree, they still have to climb up the ladder to higher degrees. At the top they will study whatever discipline is most suitable to their talent: law, astrology, military science, medicine, natural sciences, etc. After they have completed their studies, they will be employed. After they have served with efficiency, they will be promoted. Do things happen this way in our country? Whatever we study and retain comes from Chinese books; the texts we annotate are utterings of the dead people; the material we are tested on consists of the explanation of the classics, the five-syllable or four- and six-syllable poetry.[4] That is what sets us apart from other peoples in the field of education.

The Europeans organize their political regime through a constitution that may adopt a monarchical or a republican model. A predetermined number of people may elect a representative. Whenever there is a question to be debated, they convene a meeting. There, while one person is speaking, the others listen, and then together they discuss. If they reach a formula in the morning, they are free to modify it the same evening. The important thing is that their decision conform to the truth or to the prevailing situation. Is it so in our country? Concerning the administrative system, it is forbidden to change or even to modify it. When we recruit our personnel, we value them mostly for their silence, their obedience. We apply the ancient customs, but they have never been well codified. We do create new laws; the people, however, cannot read them. That is where we differ from other countries with regard to the management of public affairs.

The Europeans consider that between the nation and its people a very intimate relationship exists. Thus, they have the republican regime wherein the national good is also the familial good. They have the tradition of chivalry wherein the national soul is also the familial soul. They have the habit of contracting public loans wherein the national wealth is also the familial wealth. They have a way of shouldering responsibilities wherein the national affairs are also the familial affairs. They have a party standing for freedom wherein the national power is also the familial power. Is it the same in our country?

Besides literature, nothing else can be precious. Besides oppression, there is no other ideal. Besides obedience, there is no other thought. That is where we differ from others in the realm of character.

The Europeans value travel; they are not scared of danger or difficulties. It took Moses forty years to reach Canaan. Christopher Columbus drifted disoriented for decades in the Atlantic. Matteo Ricci spent nineteen eventful years in China. In addition to all that, in Europe explorations into the Arctic sea or voyages around the world were quite often heard of as adventures. Is it so with our country? We have never heard of studies about colonization. We have never ventured out in search of markets to absorb our products. A few hundred kilometers away from our house, we already feel ill at ease as if it rained yellow flowers. A few years spent in a foreign country would make us unhappy and would make our hair turn white. We won't talk about Siam, Burma, Laos, or Cambodia, which, indeed, are remote and undeveloped countries: it is understandable that nobody wants to go to any of these countries. But what of China, which belongs to the same race, which has the same religion, the same rites, the same culture, including the rules of personal behavior, where everything is similar to what we have in our own country? And yet, while the Chinese people are so conspicuous by their presence in our cities and in our towns, not a single individual of our people has ever set foot even in Wu Yang, the capital city of Guangdong. That is where we differ from others with respect to customs.

Now, what is meant by "original cause"? First, it all originates from the tendency of highly valuing one's own achievements while denigrating as barbarian everything that comes from the outside. We never inquire about the technical and scientific capabilities of other countries. Second, it originates from our worship of the "kingly way" while despising the way of the vassals, never bothering to learn how other nations have reached wealth and power. Third, it originates from our habit of thinking that everything that is old must be right and good while everything new must be wrong; we never take the pain to examine the learning and the thinking of modern men. Fourth, it originates from our attitude of revering the mandarins while slighting the people; we never pay any attention to the real situation prevailing in our villages.

These four points constitute the four causes of the contradictory influences, the "limitations" or "differences" from other countries we have just talked about, and the five limitations are naturally the direct consequences of these four points. That explains why for the last several thousands years our civilization has had a permanently static character; it has never had any enduring dynamism. That is really a sad thing we should lament upon.

Thus, living in this world, if one wants to attain civilization, one cannot avoid developing people's mind. The fact that people have intelligence is a divine law. Our yellow people have nothing less than the white men. The only problem is that, if the eyes have not seen through, then they cannot perceive where development lies. If people have not experienced many models, then they do not know what to imitate. If there is no capital, they can do nothing to increase it. Therefore, if we have no guide to open up our mind, there will be no way that we can aspire to attain any good result. Today, after having looked up and down, after having thought thoroughly about the possibility of opening up the people's mind, amid thousands of difficulties, we can only distinguish six ways.

1. The Use of Our National Script

In the world, writing systems have been devised by three men: Qu Lu, Ce Zong, and Shang Xie.[5] The writing system of the countries that share the same language as ours is the one that writes from top to bottom. Writing systems are invented to transcribe spoken languages. Thus, the In Ban and Qu Cao chapters in the *Shu Jing* reproduced in their entirety the spoken sounds; the fifteen Guo Feng chapters are full of the local dialects spoken by the Chinese people. Other countries in the world do the same. For example, Siam and Laos have their own system of writing that is to reproduce the sounds of their language, and they write from left to right. Recently, Japan also invented its own script. Up to the present day we have none yet. That's a very strange point. Maybe in ancient times we did have some writing system that simply got lost through the generations.

Recently, Portuguese missionaries invented the *quoc ngu,* the national language or national script. They used the twenty-six letters of the Latin alphabet, to which they added six diacritic marks and eleven vowels. Then they combined the letters to transcribe the sounds of our spoken language. It is quite easy and fast to learn. We should at once adopt it. The people in our country, when they go to school, should first learn the *quoc ngu* so that within a period of a few months they may become literate. We should use the *quoc ngu* to record events from the past, to write down happenings of the present. We may also use it in our correspondence so that we communicate our ideas in an elegant manner. That is the first step in our mission to develop our intelligence.

2. The Revision of Books

Up to now writers have been quite numerous in our country. Books like the *Kham Dinh Viet Su Thong Giam Cuong Muc,* the *Thuc Luc, Liet Truyen, Nhat Thong Chi, Lich Trieu Chi, Van Dai Loai Ngu, Cong Ha Ky Van, Du Dia Chi, Gia Dinh Chi, Nghe An Phong Tho Thoai, Do Ban Thanh Ky, Hung Hoa Thap Luc Chau Ky, Phu Man Tap Luc,*[6] etc., give us enough information concerning our mountains and rivers, our customs, our personalities, our institutions, and also serve as mirrors for later generations to adjust their behavior. And yet our people, once in school, have immediate recourse to Chinese books. They don't even give one look at our own publications. How regrettable to be like "Ji Dan who has forgotten all about his ancestors."[7]

After all, Chinese books record Chinese history; they have nothing much concerning us. Even those works that have been labeled by the wise men of the Song or Ming Dynasties as reflecting the substance of the classics and written by the sages, such as the *Qian Shuo, Cun I, Ding I, Shang Xin, Meng Yin, Jing An,* including the *Shi Jie* and *She Luo,*[8] even though they contain plenty of commentaries uttered by the great philosophers, they do not differ from the works of those who wield their lance in the privacy of their room or those who needlessly criticize one another. They are similar to those who out of nowhere invent cryptic questions to which they devise smart answers. The aim of these books is simply to confuse their readers and plug up the memory of students.

Let us take the example of the following phrase: "the first month of spring." Some scholars assert that that first month was calculated according to the Xia calendar; others countered that it was based on the Zhou calendar.[9] They mouthed noisily their arguments to no end, and now, hundreds and thousands of years later, their discussion has not yet come to any definite conclusion. Ma Yuan's bronze pillars are but vestiges of the past.[10] And yet some people say they are to be found in Jin Zhou; others place them in Lin Zhou; still others put them south of Lin Yi.[11] After spending thousands of words in useless discussion, they haven't even started to see the beginning of a solution. Then they manufactured the following conjecture: maybe, after so many years, these pillars have been washed out to the sea. Alas, even if we were able to call the sages and the wise back from the other world, it would not be too useful after all; what to say then about our vain efforts to seek answers to these questions? If the classics and history books are like that, what, then, of the other books?

In this world how many people can live a hundred years and yet devote their useful mind to these useless piles of books, enough to fill chariots up to their roofs. There are so many responsibilities to fulfill in the lives of men, and yet half of their intelligence is given away to these masses of paper nibbled by worms, eaten by insects. So, are these not good enough reasons to revise all these books? We think that a publishing house should be established to determine what sets of books should or should not be read. Those that should be read will be worked into a schedule with different phases so that they will be all studied one after the other. Books like *The Classic of Filial Piety, The Classic of Loyalty, The Annotated Collection of Primary Education,* etc., as well as the good words and the exemplary behavior of old thinkers both from the East and the West, anything that could be useful to the people's mind and the conduct of world affairs—all these should be summarized in their broad outlines, gathered in one volume, translated into Vietnamese. That book should then be used as reading material in classes for beginners. From the classics only their original text should be kept. From books of history we should only retain what pertains to the rise and fall of the successive dynasties, their modes of formation and their institutions; we shall translate it into Vietnamese. We shall consider Vietnamese history as the principal subject matter. To that material we shall add a number of maps with drawings of our villages, our country, roads, rice fields. From Chinese history we shall retain only its general outlines. As for Western history, we already have books such as the *Description of Five Continents, Summary of Ten Thousands Countries, History of Modern Institutions, Research on Western Studies,* etc. We only need to streamline these publications so as to make them more easily accessible.

3. Change Our Examinations System

The meaning of the classics is very profound, and yet is it fair to verify whether they are properly understood by using superficial literature? There is no limit to the speculations of the hundreds of philosophers, and yet is it reasonable to verify whether there is true talent through the memorization capability of the candidates? Thus, even after we have revised our books, if we still cling to the old examination system, that will not be good enough.

Consider this: interpretation of the classics, rhyming prose, poetry, edicts, decrees, dissertation, policy discussion, all these have constituted the subject matters of our examinations. Of what practical use, may we ask, are the styles called introductory, continuing, starting, concluding, clear, regulatory, parallelist? May we ask whether there is someone, among the old scholars or among the younger laureates of our examination system, who would know what the five continents are or in what century we live now?

In the way the compositions were to be written there existed, furthermore, so many restrictions. The candidates were to avoid taboo words pertaining to personal names of the royal family members, of the mandarins; they were to abide by the regulations concerning rhythm and rhymes; they were not to make any mistake or omission in copying down the text of the topic that was given out; they were not to write anything around the authentication seals; they must, by all means, avoid erasures, omission, confusion, or alteration of any character in the text. What more can we say about all these rules? All this aims at simply reducing the people's freedom, diminishing their intellectual enthusiasm, and obliging them to devote all their attention to a useless kind of scholarship. We read in the magazine *The Laughter of the World* an article that contends that examinations are like poison; they are, in any way, a rotten institution. There indeed is no exaggeration in these words.

Alas, from the camp of "seven resemblances"[12] and from the section of "selling your name,"[13] some remarkable men may have come out, but that is pure chance. Today, while we are still unable to establish specialized disciplines as in the West, and while we still must rely on literature to select people, at least we should provisionally use only dissertation and policy discussion. That would at least make some sense. Even China, from the 1900 session of the examinations onward, has given up the eight-line stanza poem to have only a policy discussion and a dissertation. Maybe we should only use these two fields to test our students. Our examination questions should be taken from the classics, the Five Books, and the three histories (Chinese, Vietnamese, and Western). We should allow our students to comment liberally on and answer freely to our questions without any constraints imposed on their ideas or any rules pertaining to their style. We should add to this a few questions in mathematics, in our national language, so that what the students study and what they are tested on are not contradictory to the work they will be asked to perform in real life. That will at least be correct for now.

4. How to Encourage Talents

In the preface to the book *Jiang Xue Hui*[14] it is written, "If one wants to open up the people's mind, one must first open up the scholar-gentry's mind." This is a very correct observation, which addresses itself to the roots of the problem. For the people always imitate the scholars; the later generations like to emulate the earlier ones; the ears and the eyes usually entertain some relationship between themselves. Now that books have been revised, rules of examination modified, our hope is pinned on the thousands of secretaries, clerks, future mandarins, directors, and deputy-directors of education, doctors, licentiates, bachelors, students. If these are unable to develop new ideas from what they hear, open up new avenues to their mind, so that everything becomes new, then we are going to see a conflict between the old and new generations. The [Quoc Tu] Giam[15] school is a place to groom talents, but what they teach and study there all belongs to the literature of the old time without any relationship whatsoever with today's practical matters. The Quoc Hoc school, established eight or nine years ago, has indeed trained a number of bright talents in diplomacy, but they are not called upon to do anything else. If there are no jobs after graduation, who will want to continue studying? School officials should, therefore, look around for students who have graduated and appoint them into the ministries and various offices. Let them translate official letters and let them join in negotiations when these come up so that they won't have to worry about the possibility of one Qin man teaching a crowd of screaming Ji or that those who are already well trained would worry lest Ji talents would be utilized only in Qin.[16] As for those who cannot learn the Western languages, we should establish an Institute for Scholars into which we shall send books on Public Law, on the History of Western Law, on Institutions, Maps, and Mathematics, etc., We shall devise a program of study and stipulate on its precise duration. We shall ask these students to teach one another and learn from one another. There will be a test each year; those who pass it will be recruited to fill in vacancies. In this fashion, within a few years the old faction will slowly yield its place to the new faction.

5. How to Develop Industry

We often read in the *Treatise on Rituals*,[17] composed during the Le Dynasty, an article that says: "Ceramics imported from China are to be used only by mandarins who have a seal." After reading this, we cannot help but wonder how old-fashioned those who managed our country's affairs were. In ancient China at first Xia An alone wore a robe of soft silk, but then all the mandarins at the royal court liked it, and so soft silk was produced in great quantity. As one can see, fashion evolves rapidly. In Western countries, whenever there is a newly invented product, people imitate it, no matter what difficulties or expenses are involved in the research. To study under a master does therefore represent some advantage. On the other hand, if the supervisor chooses the best [foreign] products to use, how can the subordinates be ordered to do otherwise? To know that there are people who do things better than oneself without trying to do things better than them, how can one hope to be useful to one's country? It results that the best way to restrict one's expenses is to allow one's resources to flow freely.

In addition to a few objects inlaid with mother-of-pearl that are well-known in the world, we can also manufacture hats, conic hats, rattan furniture, multicolored mats, objects in lacquer, gold, wood, stone, ceramics, porcelain, satin, crepon, cotton, silk, etc. Whatever the Chinese can manufacture, we also can manufacture it, perhaps better. But, compared to the Chinese goods, ours look clearly less refined. That's because we do not know how to improve our crafts. It has been rumored recently that in Tonkin people have found new methods to grow mulberry trees and raise silkworms. The fact was published in the newspapers. In the capital city an Agriculture Service and a Polytechnic School have been recently established. That is a very good idea and an efficient method. Our people should be encouraged to imitate in the most useful ways. But the court has been neglecting them, and consequently the scholar-gentry class has not been very active. All the craft schools are frequented only by coolies, and students in agricultural stations are but tree growers. That is because we do not know how to develop industry.

Industry is a very essential element to our country. If we are not better than other people, then they will drop us. There is nothing more detrimental to our economy than to spend money in foreign countries. We dare suggest that good teachers be recruited, good products be bought to use as models. We should select people who are clever with their hands and quick in their intelligence to be sent to schools. The court then should closely follow their educational progress. It should decree that in the country, whoever learns of new methods, whoever invents new products, will be, as in Europe, granted diplomas of congratulations, given honorific mandarinal titles in appreciation, provided salaries as encouragement, and their inventions protected with patents. Those who are good in natural sciences, chemistry, physics, should be granted higher honors than those who pass the highest levels of Confucian examinations. In such circumstances it would be incomprehensible if our students should not rival in talents and compete in know-how.

6. Publish a Newspaper

In other countries the press has a great variety: dailies, monthlies, weeklies, biweeklies. Their content ranges from politics, news, current affairs, advertisements, etc. Domestic news, foreign news, inventions, and commercial activities are all published, and lawyers, doctors, cultivators, workers, and businessmen all have their own newspapers. France counts more than 1,230 news publishing houses, Germany more than 2,300, England more than 2,180, Russia more than 430, America more than 1,150, and in Japan there is no district that does not bring out its own newspaper. China has recently established many news publishing houses. Owing to all this, the people's mind will be opened up. As for our country, only Saigon and Haiphong have newspapers written in French; few can read them. There is only one single newspaper written in Chinese, and that is the [Dai Nam] *Dong Van Nhut Bao.*

In the case of the *London Times,* for example, the editor-in-chief is a former prime minister, so the newspaper's comments and criticisms are very fair and correct. We think that our capital city should found a newspaper publishing house, at the head of which we shall select a high-level mandarin along with a number of scholars. Half of the newspaper will be written in our language (*quoc ngu*) and the other half in Chinese. In that newspaper we shall print everything concerning effective institutions, stimulating ideas, unusual professions, beautiful artifacts of Europe and America; we shall write about all the statements and events found in books that we would like to use as examples; we shall reproduce interesting examination papers or books on current affairs; we shall talk about extraordinary men among talented ones or about new techniques discovered by professionals, techniques that could be useful to our country so that everyone of our compatriots may know about all of this. The price of subscription to our newspaper will be maintained at a low level, and on specified days we shall send free copies to all the mandarins, high or low, whether at the court or in the provinces, as well as to every hamlet and every village. Prizes will be given to private citizens who subscribe on their own. Those who are in charge of delivery will be punished if the delivery comes late. The revenue will balance the expenses. The newspaper will put an end to the tendencies toward obstinacy and ignorance.

In the past students devoted many years to study a foreign language [Chinese], and still they could not show much result; now they would not spend more than six months, and yet would know their own language [*quoc ngu*] very well. It is, therefore, clear that we cannot not study our own language. In the past the educational system so emphasized the complexities of literature, forcing students to memorize chapter after chapter, and in the final stage they still came up with an empty mind; now students will concentrate on simple, clear, and essential matters, and yet they will acquire real knowledge. So we cannot afford not to revise books, not to modify the rules of the examination, and not to encourage talent. That is understandable enough.

Once the contempt for industry has set in, then gold, silver, timber, stones, all become raw materials for foreigners. But if industry is encouraged, then water, fire, wind, electricity will contribute to satisfy the daily needs of our people. It is, therefore, a natural attitude to encourage industry.

To sit tight in the lost corners of a remote village is no match to letting our spirit escape into the outside world so that the entire universe becomes our familiar playground. How can a laborious study of a pile of old papers equal the reading of one newspaper, both the paper and the ink of which belong to the genial spirit? That's why we cannot refrain from founding a newspaper.

Some people would say: the mountains and the rivers of Vietnam have been drawn in the celestial book; its civilization dates from a long time past; the six ways to write the characters having been fully assimilated—why do we need a new writing system? Our laws and institutions are sufficient to administer our country—what do we need new regulations for? If we brought in all these reforms, does it not mean that we simply want to alter all the foundations of our traditional culture in pursuit of new elements?

Alas! If that criticism were true, then our people's mind is definitely closed and forever lost; it will never open up to receive anything good. Suppose that the "isolationist" policy does not move into the "electricity, technical" phase; then what we have said earlier about the four points and the five limitations will forever linger on in the thinking of our philosophers and politicians. Whenever they find some defect, they will try to mend it, to straighten it out, to make it look better: that for them will be enough to be called civilization. But, unfortunately, that will not do. Just like a string in a violin: if it does not harmonize with the rest of the strings, then it has to be taken off, and the violin must be sent to be repaired. Just like a house, if it has been lived in for thousands of years then it will have to be torn down in order to be rebuilt anew so as to become livable again (according to Liang Qi Zhao). If such are the data, such should be the solution. Have you not heard of the case of Japan? In the past thirty years, it has assimilated the European civilization; now it has reached its goal. Have you heard of the Siamese story? A few decades ago Siam entered into relations with Europe; it sent its students to be trained overseas. Now its political status has improved tremendously; the situation looks very promising. Furthermore, have you heard of the story of China? China remains an old country, and yet, since external threats and internal upheavals stimulated them, the Chinese have awakened; their leaders slowly realize that European methods are worth adopting, while the people also understand that European science is worth acquiring. Today China has factories established according to models imported from Europe; it also has universities. The Chinese are in the process of substituting their old obstinate ways for a modernized spirit; the progress they are making is difficult to gauge.

Alas! Other people have awakened, while we are still deep in sleep. While people have crossed the river, we are still anchored in the middle of it. How shall we be able to survive in this arena of civilization and progress? Furthermore, because the movement has no end, the progress also has no end. A society qualified yesterday as civilized has become semicivilized today. A society qualified as semicivilized yesterday is a barbarian one today.

There is a saying: "To reach a dead end is to change. To change is to let things flow through. To let things flow through is to endure." Also another saying: "To evolve with modifications is to change. To reflect upon what is to be done is to let things flow through." How rational are the words of the sages.

Are the present times not the times to change and let things flow through? The Europeans, having accumulated all their experiences, have created their civilization, which spreads out continuously and slowly expands into Asian countries. That constitutes a shining light in the midst of darkness. That's an opening made by Heaven; we cannot close it up. If every day we cling to our pleasure of dancing and singing the praise of our lakes and our mountains without any worries, and after that we watch our mountains and rivers change without expressing any regrets, is it to be wondered what will happen to twenty-five million of our compatriots? Is it to be wondered how the people of tomorrow will see the people of today and in what position the people of today will place us when they judge the people of yesteryear?

There is nothing more to say if we don't want to open the people's mind. But if we do, then we cannot not seek out the causes that made our civilization so static. The causes derive from the five limitations mentioned earlier. Furthermore, we cannot fail to examine the causes so as to see from where come the obstacles to the development of our civilization. What are the obstacles? They are the four points we described earlier. We cannot fail to hold onto the old ideology in order to go forward into civilization. What ideology? That is the six reform areas mentioned earlier.

Oh! We found it. We checked it. We held on to it. So let us bring out our biggest hammers, our sharpest knives, to destroy the old fortifications. Let us hang red banners, pink flags, on the new arena. Let us throw ourselves into the mainstream of the world so as to maintain our zeal. Let us grasp the moving times so as to stimulate the dynamism in our civilization, in such a way that our people become competitive because of their thinking or become thoughtful because of their competitive spirit. Then and only then can studies of civilization be acquired. Once the efficiency has been grasped, everything will work smoothly—exactly in the same manner as an alarm clock, which only has to be wound up for its mechanism to function harmoniously. Once the result is attained, everything will be like a thermometer whose mercury fluctuates without error up and down according to the prevailing weather. Inasmuch as the people's mind is extolled into higher spheres, the expansive power of civilization becomes greater, and, consequently, the foundations for culture will endure for a long time to come.[18]

Notes

1. All titles of Chinese classical books; one of them, the *Zhou Guan,* is supposed to have been composed during the Zhou Dynasty (1123–221 B.C.E.).

2. All titles of Chinese books.

3. The Vietnamese have the habit of avoiding pronouncing or spelling the names of persons they respect or of their superiors. Students, for example, when they wrote their examination papers, had to modify all the words that spelled the names of the members of the entire royal family. Should they fail to do so, they would be accused of having "violated a tabooed name" (*pham huy*) and were liable to be prosecuted or at least to fail the examination. Examples: Emperor Tu Duc's given name is Thi, so everybody must say or write *thoi* instead of *thi;* Emperor Thieu Tri's name is Ton, so that every *ton* should be said or written *tong;* Emperor Gia Long's name is Anh; that must be changed to *yen.* In my village the name of the richest man and therefore also a big landlord was Truong; so the word *truong,* which also means "school," is changed into *trang.*

4. Confucius's writings have been generally divided into two sections: the four books and the five classics, although all his writings may be referred to as the "classics." The five-, four-, and six-syllable poetry are books to teach children the basic Chinese characters written in simple verses for the sake of memorization.

5. The authors of this pamphlet must have made an error when they attributed the invention of writing systems to the three names mentioned here. According to the Chinese tradition—from which the authors of this pamphlet obviously derived their information—the three inventors of the various writing systems are the following: the first one is Pali (Phan), who invented the system whereby one writes from left to right. The second person was Qu Lu (Khu Lu), or Qu Lou (Khu Lau), who created the system that writes from right to left. Both of them lived in India. The third one was a historian who served the semi-legendary Chinese Yellow Emperor. His name was Shang Xie

(Thuong Hiet), and he is the author of the system whereby one writes from upside downward and also, of course, from right to left.

6. The titles mentioned here are all of Vietnamese books written in classical Chinese but deal with either the official or private history, general or local geography, political and social institutions, of Vietnam. Most of them date from the eighteenth or nineteenth century. See R. B. Smith, "Sino-Vietnamese Sources for the Nguyen period: An Introduction," *Bulletin of the School of Oriental and African Studies* 30, pt. 3 (1967): 600–621.

7. Ji Dan: a scholar of the Jin Dynasty who could not answer questions related to his ancestry and the institutions of his own country.

8. All titles of books written in the Song and Ming Dynasties, which consist primarily of commentaries on the Confucian classics.

9. Xia and Zhou are names of two dynasties of China. Xia (2205–1766 B.C.E.); Zhou (1123–221 B.C.E.).

10. This allusion refers to the campaign of repression conducted by General Ma Yuan of the Han Dynasty of China in 43 C.E against the famous rebellion of the two Vietnamese Trung sisters. It is said that Ma Yuan planted bronze pillars along the borders between China and the colony of Vietnam, called at that time Giao Chi or Giao Chau. These pillars wore the following inscription: "Should these pillars be uprooted, Giao Chi will be destroyed." According to the Vietnamese tradition, these pillars did not wash out to sea, as said here, but they were buried under piles of rocks and gravel, for the Vietnamese, who saw them as symbols of their subjugation by China, threw rocks at the base of the pillars while spitting at them. Over the years those pillars came to be buried under the pile of rocks. The pillars were therefore not uprooted, and Giao Chi, or Vietnam, continued to thrive.

11. One of the many names of Champa, a fragmented kingdom that was founded in the second century C.E. and was annexed into the Vietnamese territory in the fifteenth century. It was situated along the central coastal plains of Vietnam, stretching from north of Hue to south of Phan Rang.

12. This allusion refers to the story of Wang Zi An in Po Song Lin's book *Liao Zhai Zhi Yi*. Students who take the mandarinal examinations are compared to seven phenomena: (1) Before entering the examination camp, they clumsily hang on all their equipment, looking, therefore, like beggars. (2) When their name is called, the examiners and guards yell at them as if they were their prisoners. (3) Alone in their examination tent, they suffer from cold as much as a frozen bee. (4) When the examination ends, they emerge from the camp as lost as birds coming out of their cage. (5) When waiting for the results of the examination, they are as agitated as monkeys at the end of a leash. (6) When they do not hear their name called because they have failed the examination, they are as depressed as poisoned flies. (7) After a while, as the bitterness slowly sinks in, they want to take the examination again, and they are then as resilient as those birds whose nests have been destroyed and yet continue to carry sticks and leaves in order to build new ones.

13. It was not rare that students took the examinations in place of others, and that phenomenon is known under the expression "to sell one's name." Another way to sell one's name is to cheat at the examination.

14. Name of the school established in Beijing during the one hundred–day reform under the Guang Zi reign, with the collaboration of Kang Yu Wei (1858–1927).

15. Usually called the National University of Vietnam. This was a special school established at the capital city—in the Temple of Literature in Hanoi and in the Imperial Palace in Hue—for the princes, the mandarins' children, and talented commoners.

16. The expression alludes to the difficulties teachers had when they taught a foreign language; the students scream loudly while repeating the foreign words after the teacher.

17. This treatise—Le Nghi Chi—constitutes a part of Phan Huy Chu's nineteenth-century *Lich Trieu Hien Chuong Loai Chi* (The institutions of past dynasties recorded by categories). See the second edition of the translation into Vietnamese of this work published in three volumes in Hanoi in 1992.

18. The original version of this text, which was written in classical Chinese, is preserved in the Sino-Vietnamese Institute in Hanoi. The translation into Vietnamese can be found in *TVYNVCM,* 631–51; and *VTCM,* 161–82.

DOCUMENT 4

Hoang Cao Khai (1850–1933)

On the Wisdom of Our Country to Rely on France
(1910)

Hoang Cao Khai was the first Vietnamese high official to rally to the French cause when they invaded North Vietnam in 1883. He participated actively in the French efforts to pacify the country in subsequent years. His loyal service to the French earned him the position of Kinh Luoc, *representative of the emperor, or viceroy, in Tonkin, from 1888 to 1897, when the French colonial government abolished that function and made the French resident superior of Tonkin the official delegate of the Vietnamese ruler in Tonkin.*

In this excerpt from his book En Annam *Hoang Cao Khai tried to persuade his compatriots to stop resisting French domination because it would be far better to collaborate with France in order to study and become eventually an intelligent race. Once the Vietnamese become intelligent, he reasoned, France would surely give them autonomy in everything except foreign affairs.*

From the time France came to govern our country, all of us, kings, mandarins, and common people, have received benefits from the protector. And yet it seems impossible for the protector to satisfy everyone. Unhappy are those people who have not received their mandarinal appointment, even though they had successfully passed their examinations. There are others who have resigned from their mandarinal positions and have not been reappointed. Still others remained hostile to France simply because their ancestors or parents found themselves on the wrong side vis-à-vis France. All the people I just mentioned generally belong to the middle class.

In fact, from the time the French arrived in Gia dinh [1863] until their conquest of northern Vietnam [1883], with the exception of rebels and bandits, the opponents of the colonial administration were, on the whole, well-educated people. Among them were none other than Doctor Nguyen Huu Huan in Gia Dinh, Doctor Hien in central Vietnam, and Dr. [Phan Dinh] Phung in the North. They did what they did, guided only by their patriotism; they were neither concerned about the circumstances nor the conditions of their struggle against the French, so that they ended up being absolutely useless to their country and even dangerous to their people. They may serve as examples to us today; there is no mistake about that.

Five years ago, because our people knew about the Japanese victory over Russia, they concluded that small countries could fight against big ones, weaker races could rise up against stronger ones. That's why they started founding parties and associations; they began to agitate in our country; they even went plotting against the French in foreign lands.

Those who agitated within our borders probably gave the following argument: "Our country counts a surface area of more than 336,000 square kilometers and a population of more than 15 million souls. There is no reason why it cannot regain its autonomy." "In the past," they continued to reason, "China dominated our country twice. The first time [939], Ngo Quyen won his war on the River Bach Dang and successfully expelled the southern Han. The second time [1427] Le Loi fought his battle at Chi Lang and chased away the Ming. Are these not clear precedents? Why today can we not regain our autonomy?"

What these people are not aware of is this: in the past China and our country shared the same educational system and the same level of technology. Moreover, although China is situated near our country, communications between the two countries have always been very inconvenient. Let us take a look at Li Su's memorial, in which he wrote that "Chinese troops departed from the Yuan and Yu districts in the direction of Ri Nan [name of one of the districts of Vietnam when it was ruled by China] at nine thousand leagues away. Yet, it took them three hundred days to cover that distance. The expenses were high because the troops had to bring their food and supplies with them." We understand now why China had such difficulties in governing our country.

France obviously is separated from our country by a long distance by land. And yet within fifteen days a single telegram could bring colonial troops from India or even from the African continent to our country. Furthermore, technical progress occurs every day. Within the last ten years we went from the steamship to the submarine, from the train on the ground to the aircraft in the sky, from the telegraphy with wires to the wireless one. While these technical advances occur every day elsewhere, how can we, with our outmoded technology, expect to fight against these modern techniques?

In modern warfare, however, technology is not the only important factor; we must also take into consideration the financial side of things. Within the last ten years Transvaal in South Africa fought against England for more than two years [1899–1900]; England spent more than three hundred million pounds. And yet the war is still going on. In the end Transvaal was made a protectorate of England. Six years ago [1904] Japan fought against Russia, spending more than one million yen a day on military supplies alone. Although Japan is a poor and frugal country, it still had to accept such high expenditures. Finally, it exhausted its financial resources and had to accept the conditions for peace without imposing any war reparations upon Russia. Under these circumstances how can we expect to win if we, a poor country, fight against a rich country like France?

All this demonstrates the uselessness of any agitation to be organized within our borders.

As for those who venture into foreign countries to agitate against France, they must reason in the following way: "The French and our people do not belong to the same race; we do not share the same writing system, so France cannot protect us. We should, therefore, seek help from those who belong to the same race and share with us the same writing system so as to gain our autonomy."

These people are, indeed, not aware of the difference between colonization in the past and colonization in the present. In the past China colonized us, along with Korea and Burma, so as to oblige us to send tribute to China. It then could boast about having so many subordinate countries. Colonization in the present day is no longer anything close to that. In the present system colonial countries simply settle their people in their colonies and bring in their manufactured goods to be sold. Therefore, the closer the colonial countries are to ours, the faster the people can arrive in our country and the more numerous the goods. Our country will then be at a full disadvantage. Look at the Chinese who emigrated to our country. They simply came to settle down here; they did not enjoy any advantageous position, and yet they captured all the commercial businesses from our people. Again take a look at Japan. It has colonized Korea only for five or six years, and already Korea has encountered untold difficulties. What, then, can we expect of the people who belong to the same race or who share with us the same writing system? Of what use will they be? We know that France is a powerful country. It has already spent a great amount of money in our country, so that, no matter what happens, it will never readily agree to grant autonomy to our country. Every powerful country on this earth must entertain foreign relations. France allied herself with Russia in the past; now she lines up with England just for the sake of preserving Indochina. If France is that powerful and her foreign relations so strictly maintained, no matter what kind of agitation against the French we organize in foreign countries, certainly nothing will come out of it.

But, then, is our country capable of autonomy? Let us consider for a moment that proposition. Our country has had three opportunities to gain autonomy. All three depended on the help of France. The first opportunity occurred under the reign of Emperor Gia Long (1802–20). At the time, we started entertaining relations with France. Had we followed the example of France in reforming our educational system, we would have transformed our country into a very powerful one, ahead of all the other countries of Asia, not unlike Japan at the present time.

The second opportunity took place during the reign of Emperor Tu Duc [1847–83]. At that time France had already arrived in our country. Had France's arrival incited us to change our educational system, our country would have gained autonomy, not unlike Siam in the same period. These two opportunities belong to the past. There is not much we can expect of them now. But the third opportunity concerns the future. We may expect something out of it. It means that, from now on, we ought to rely on France so as to introduce modifications into our educational system. Then, after our intelligence has opened up, probably France will grant us our autonomy in internal affairs. In foreign relations she still will be our protector. Then we shall become like Canada, Australia, all colonies of England. We should also note that autonomy may be obtained only because we deal with France; there is no such possibility with other colonial powers.

The first reason results from the fact that all colonial countries nowadays are interested in settling their own people in their colonies. France behaves differently. Look at England and Germany; the people they send to their colonies are the very poor ones, and poor people, once settled in the colonies, never nurture the hope of one day returning back to their country. As for France, her people are prosperous; they are used to their bourgeois way of life. In fact, ever since Napoléon the First, French laws guarantee equal shares in inheritance, so that sons and daughters receive equal parts; they all can afford to live in comfort, even in affluence. Precisely because of the comfort and affluence of their way of life, even [French] farmers and businessmen, let alone civil servants, will return to their country after a stay of about three to four years [in the colony]. This shows us that the French, in acquiring their colonies, simply wanted a place to vacation and not at all an area for permanent settlement.

The second reason goes like this: in the present situation, of all the countries that surround us, some have become powerful; some are on the way to becoming powerful, so that in order to defend Indochina we need a greater number of troops, which will require a greater amount of money. Ever since France conquered our country, it has already spent approximately seven hundred million francs. The benefits it reaps from our country do not amount to that much. Therefore, if France wanted to bring in more troops and therefore spend more money in our country, her people will not agree to it. That's why, in the past few years, the great dignitaries of the government have all declared that France needs to apply a policy of association with our people. That policy aims at satisfying our people so as to enlist our support for the defense of our own country.

For these two reasons we may find that it was indeed the good fortune of our country to be protected by France.

But now, if we do want to become autonomous, what should we do?

To have autonomy we must study. In order to study well we must make France our teacher. And we cannot rush our study either. In fact, if you want to build a house, you must first raise the foundation; on the other hand, if you want to grow a tree, first you must plant a seed; that's the foundation for independence and the seed to grow into civilization. Upon the foundation we can erect a big house; from the seed we can expect a tall tree. But once our education progresses, there comes competition, a peaceful and nonviolent competition. Those who are highly intelligent and who have acquired specialized knowledge can expect the government to recruit them: that's competition in the mandarinal career. Those who are endowed with an ordinary intelligence and who are skillful in their craft can expect to be employed: that's competition in the professions. Although the French are the bosses, both in the mandarinate and in the professions, our people constitute the rank and file. Everywhere we hold the majority; the French are but a mere minority. Such competition does not lead to any loss of blood or falling of heads; it naturally provides rights and benefits. If our people follow that path, sooner or later, say within fifty or one hundred years, we will become the same as the French—that is, an intelligent race. It is relatively easy for an intelligent race to govern over a stupid one, but it will be difficult even for an intelligent race to dominate another intelligent race. At that time France will give us back our autonomy, and she will only protect us in foreign affairs.[1]

Note

1. The text translated here constitutes the third chapter, pp. 42–66, in Hoang Cao Khai's book published in Hanoi in 1910, both in French and Vietnamese. The two texts are on opposite pages. The French title of the book is *En Annam,* and the Vietnamese title is *Guong Su Nam* (Models in Vietnamese History). The original text is in Vietnamese, and its French translation was done by Jules Roux.

DOCUMENT 5

Hoang Trong Mau (1874–1916)

Proclamation of the Association for the Restoration
of Vietnam
(1912)

We do not know much about the author of this proclamation except the fact that he came from the same province as Phan Boi Chau, whom he followed to southern China, and he was his student. In 1912, after the success of the Chinese revolution, Phan Boi Chau and his supporters revised their program of action for an independent Vietnam: they consequently abandoned the hope of reestablishing the monarchical system and adopted the republican regime: they put an end to the Viet Nam Duy Tan Hoi (Association for the Moderniza-tion of Vietnam) and founded in its place the Viet Nam Quang Phuc Hoi (Association for the Restoration of Vietnam). Hoang Trong Mau was then charged with writing the manifesto of the new association . . . in verses.

Our entire people amount to fifty million
The country of Vietnam constitutes our inheritance
Its land and the privileges attached to it
Belong to all of us and not to any one family in particular
Whether we hold onto our land or lose it, we do it all together
But if we really wish to keep it, we must devise good plans
We all have the same flesh, the same bones, and the same blood flows
    in our veins
It is to all the people that we owe our mountains, our rivers, our land,
    our homes
That is the plain truth
And everyone of you, brothers and sisters, will agree
Our mountains and rivers are now shedding their red blood
We must see to it that we overcome all our difficulties.

Remember the past, when we lived under an absolute monarchy

They ate out of the people's hands, and yet they tormented those same
   people
Only they themselves were sages, deities
They looked down upon everyone else as horses and buffaloes
For so long a time that people became so stupid
As not to care anymore for their own country
In peace they levied all sorts of taxes
When the invaders arrived, the court alone determined
The destiny of the whole country, its life, its death
Of what use were they, anyway, those parasites of the people
After all, why did we lose our country? Obviously, because of the
   kings
Now our association, after considering the past and contemplating the
   future
Looking at the situation of our country over many years
Has come to the conclusion that, among our neighbors, we should
   imitate the Chinese
From far away, the Americans, the Westerners ought to be our teachers
And if by chance we should one day regain our independence
We owe it to the collective effort of our people
If we want to benefit our country and enrich our families
The only way left for us is to adopt a Democratic Republic.
We must unite all the people in the country
According to the directives that have been well defined
Compatriots do listen carefully
To the exhortations given to you from the bottom of our hearts
We must continue to seek revenge as before
At the same time, we must also build up and preserve the republic
That will be for our brothers, for our race
We must combine all our resources
Unite all our efforts, pool our riches together
From North to South, there will be only One Community
We shall paint our mountains and our rivers red with our blood
For a thousand years the children of Lac Hong[1]
Will have only One Will, that is to take care of their own affairs
From their dream we shall wake them up with a loud scream
Brothers and sisters, get up and look at life
In this stormy world the wind blows violently
Thunders break the earth, the waves shake the people's mind
Every one of us has our own responsibility
The affairs of the state will be cared for by a large number of people
We should lend our shoulders to bear our responsibilities in this world

Exchanging our past positions for New Horizons in the sky
If, by chance, our goal can be attained
Our Five Star Flag will fly over our celebrations
That's what we call Glory; that's what we call Fame
We shall one day meet each other around an exhilarating drink
We offer that Wish to our compatriots of the entire country
We should stand next to one another
Clapping our hands, we stand up fast
The heroes come few and far between
We must therefore seize the opportunity.[2]

Notes

1. Lac Hong: *Lac* refers to the name of the tribe from which supposedly came the Vietnamese people; the full name of the tribe is Lac Viet. *Hong* refers to the first dynasty that reigned over Vietnam in the legendary period of its history; the dynasty's full name is Hong Bang (2879–258 B.C.E.)

2. The original of this short poem must have been written in Chinese. Its translation into Vietnamese can be found in *VTCM*, 329–31. My translation is based on the Vietnamese text.

Nguyen Thuong Hien (1868–1925)

Tearful Conversation over the Mulberry Fields and the Sea
(1912 or 1913)

Holder of a doctoral degree, Nguyen Thuong Hien did not want to engage in a mandarinal career and followed Phan Boi Chau to Japan and from there to China.[1] He was one of the founding members of the Viet Nam Quang Phuc Hoi (Association for the Restoration of Vietnam), created in 1912 in Canton, the platform of which did away with the monarchical regime for an independent Vietnam.[2] Phan Boi Chau, another founding member of the association, wrote: "Disappointed by the uselessness of all his action against colonialism, Nguyen Thuong Hien entered a Buddhist monastery in southern China, where he died in 1925." Nguyen Thuong Hien is well-known for a number of other writings.

In this text Nguyen Thuong Hien pretended to describe to a Korean friend of his the inhumane and brutal treatment the French had dealt out to the Vietnamese people over the thirty years that French control had been established over Vietnam. Reading this document, one has the impression that the author has witnessed personally some of the infamous events he relates here in a moving, vivid, and realistic style.

I come from the country of Giao Chau [an old name for Vietnam]. I left my country six years ago. Of the hundred missions I was supposed to carry out, I was unable to accomplish a single one. My body is emaciated, my mind in agitation. I ask the sky above the reason; the sky has no answer. I complain to the earth below; the earth remains silent. In the immense space I feel so lonely, worried about a thousand things. I wander everywhere in search of someone who has experienced the same emotions so that we could, together, vent our frustrations. Finally, I met a friend from Korea, by the name of Man. On a certain day of a certain year, on the crest of a mountain situated near a seaport, sitting on tree branches, drinking blood instead of alcohol, sampling bile instead of appetizers, our swords driven into the ground, we poured our hearts out to one another.

My friend Man started the conversation: "Our two countries differ from each other as to their languages, their clothings, and yet they have received the same name: they are both called "lost countries." Oh! Brother Nguyen! The shame that visits upon my lost country is similar to yours, although my country Korea must have a much tougher time with those 'dwarfs.'[3] The two countries—Korea and Japan—are uncomfortably located near each other. That fact resulted in an untenable situation, similar to that of a sick man living next to the bandits. These may come at any time of their choice to squeeze out of his sick body all his possessions or stab and hack him to death. As for your country, I hear that it has suffered under the French. But, in my opinion, France is far away and a rich country. Its exactions, therefore, cannot be that bad."

I replied: "Do you really think our country is that lucky? I am sorry to say that if you do not know the real situation of my country, it is simply because you have never been there. Within the four corners of the universe, when does it happen that the wild tigers refrain from eating human beings? When can the young bird keep its feathers and skin intact after it has been caught by a hawk? In my country my compatriots' bones are piling up as high as the Huong mountain; their blood flows as dense as the water of the Red River. Have you not heard of all that?"

My friend Man confessed: "Nobody has told me about the cruelties committed by the French over the Vietnamese. If now you want to tell me all the details, I am ready to listen carefully to you."

Boiling with anger, I then told him everything at length, and, afterward, I consigned these stories to writing to record my rancor. I don't care whether my readers like me, despise me, or laugh at me for such a piece of writing.

The surface area of my country counts more than twenty-seven thousand square *li;* its population amounts to more than twenty-five million. Its soil is fertile, and the resources drawn from its forests and its seas are abundant. It has been a country with some standing in the world. For hundreds of years in the past it has known many invasions, but because its kings and its people were always ready to fight to death against the intruders, each time the country was saved. Fifty years ago the European invasion started; life was changing. The leaders of my country at that time were ignorant and arrogant; they clung to their policy of "closed doors," not knowing that foreign relations had become an urgency, while opening the people's mind was an absolute necessity. The French were able to take advantage of these shortcomings. They first used the pretext of propagating their Christian religion to snoop on us; then they resorted to trade in order to settle themselves right down in our backyard. Finally, they declared war and imposed their treaties on us so that the land of our thirty-six provinces passed entirely into their hands. They are very proud of their achievement. They simply eliminate those who oppose their action. They treat our mandarins as servants, our people as animals. They implement all their brutal policies aiming at tying the people's hands while they are sucking their blood. These predicaments have lasted for no less than twenty-six years.

Their evil policies can be summarized in four main points.

1. Mete out very harsh punishments.
2. Levy very high taxes.
3. Dry up all means of subsistence for the people.
4. Restrain the people's intellectual development.

Furthermore, they impose on our people so many other hardships that I cannot begin to enumerate them to you. In one word, the French want to exterminate our race!

The twenty-third day of the fifth month of the year of the Chicken (1885) is the anniversary of the loss of our country and also of our ruler. Earlier on, because they knew they could not fight back successfully against the invader, the commander of the Royal Troops [of North Vietnam], General Nguyen Tri Phuong, and the provincial governor [of Hanoi], Hoang Dieu, had committed suicide. Twice the southern and northern parts of our country had been lost. The French then brought the main corps of their troops to besiege the capital city, forcing our government to sign a new peace treaty with them. The high general commander of the Palatial Militia, Marquis Nguyen Thuyet [also known as Ton That Thuyet], who had always been siding with the resistance faction, flew into an unprecedented rage. During the night he led a surprise attack against the French, who were, ironically enough, not taken by surprise at all. Instead, they launched their forces into a murderous counterattack. In the morning the citadel was seized. Thuyet accompanied the fleeing emperor to Cam Lo; the French were unable to catch them. They immediately arrested Thuyet's father and exiled him to a deserted island. He was an old man of eighty years, physically in bad health, intellectually exhausted. He had paid practically no attention to politics, and yet the French sentenced him to a faraway exile in an unhealthy environment. It sure is weird that the French, who boast about being civilized, should resort to sentences of collective responsibility such as this one.

The general of the Left Wing, Tran Xuan Soan, raised an army in the province of Thanh Hoa and set up his headquarters at Ba Dinh. Several times the French attempted to overrun his encampment, but to no avail. They then excavated the tomb of the general's father, took out the bones, and exposed them in the middle of the street. They sent messengers to the general: "If you do not surrender, we shall crush all these bones." As no answer came out of the general's headquarters, the French threw the bones into the river. Does that look like one way the civilized people treat their enemy?

The inspector of military affairs, Phan Dinh Phung, controlled the mountainous regions of the province of Nghe An for more than ten years. The French, with all the means at their disposal, attempted many times to destroy him, without any success. They then excavated the tomb of Phan's father, threw all the bones into the river. Soon after, Inspector Phan died in his military headquarters, at which time his supporters scattered all around. The French invaded the place anyway, burned Phan's remains to ashes, and spread them over the water. How pitiful that was! They treated human beings in contravention of all norms of justice and decency. They killed many innocent people with swords and knifes. They buried countless righteous citizens in streams and rivers. People's corpses scattered on the ground like grass; they floated on water like duckweed. By myself, I would be inadequate to narrate or write down all these tragic happenings. Nonetheless, I would tell a few of them in testimony to my sufferings.

In the spring of the year of the Pig (1887) the resistance movement in the province of Thanh Hoa had already disbanded, but the French still continued to look for its members all over the place. They arrested all the people who ran on the highway or hid in the mountains. Back in their barracks, they interrogated these prisoners. If any of them were found to be former resisters, they were then taken to the northern side of the city to be executed. Inhabitants of the Tho Bac village [native village of Tran Xuan Soan, leader of a resistance movement, mentioned earlier], including the old and the weak, were handcuffed and led out to the southern part of the citadel, there to be sequestered on the bridge over the Bo Ve River. At each end of the bridge soldiers kept watch. Every evening French officers came by, barking out orders to toss the prisoners one by one into the river. If the prisoners sank in the water, they all applauded, laughing to one another. Whenever a prisoner bobbed up and down refusing to sink smoothly, they finished him up by firing their rifles at him. They repeated that macabre game for three to four months. The water of the Bo Ve River became as red as pure blood. Ever since, no one dared pass by that bridge.

The viceroy of North Vietnam, Nguyen Thien Thuat, gathered righteous troops from the province of Hai Duong. Together they held a strategic point in one of the districts so as to slow down the French advance. The French wanted to recruit some inhabitants of that district to use them as spies. Since no one volunteered, they attacked the district with the bulk of their troops and executed all of its inhabitants. Afterward they marched to the native village of the viceroy. There, in the communal house, they assembled all the villagers, including the old and the children. They ordered the village chief to show them the burial grounds of the viceroy's family. Upon hearing him answer that he did not know, right away they decapitated him. Then they tied up a young boy of sixteen, pointing their sword in his face while asking him the same question. The boy spoke no words; they simply drove the sword into his face. Blood gushed out and flowed along his body down to his feet. Angry, the boy shouted out: "You dirty bandits. The viceroy is a genuine patriot who gives his life to the country. I have only one regret that I could not follow him. Far from me the desire to help you commit a crime." The French burst with rage: they bound up his body with rags, doused it in petrol, and set him on fire. Well into his death, the boy heaped insults and abuses upon the French. Until this day no survivor, whether a villager or a resister, could relate this tragic event without shedding tears over the young martyr and crying out curses against the French bandits.

In the year of the Monkey (1896) the French assembled several battalions of their troops to comb the two provinces of Ha Tinh and Nghe An. They posted proclamations of total amnesty on the gates of their headquarters for those who surrendered. Yet, wherever they went, their troops destroyed and burned everything in their way, killing everyone they encountered, whether these people had surrendered or not—to the point that around the commanders' headquarters blood soaked acres of land. After they had declared victory and withdrawn, in the regions that cover hundreds of square *li* between the mountain Hong and the River Lam there remained no shadows of any human beings.

In the past our government taxed us in the following manner: rice fields, which were divided into three categories, were taxed but very lightly. Whenever there was a bad harvest, the tax rate was reduced according to each category. Sometimes the people were exempted from taxes altogether. Ever since the French began governing us, the tax burden has increased a hundredfold. In the beginning, they taxed the third-category rice fields with the second category's rate and the second-category rice fields with the first category's rate. Afterward, whether the rice fields were fertile or not, they were all taxed as if they were of the best kind. Moreover, the French inflated the surface area. Where in the past fields measured only one thousand acres they are now said to be two thousand. Where in the past there were only ten thousand acres, there are now twenty thousand The peasants could no longer bear that situation. They complained to the authorities, requesting that they verify the data in the registers or make new measurements of the field. The authorities refused to listen to their complaints or to heed their request. They ordered the peasants to continue to work their fields and pay their taxes according to what the registers recorded, no matter how burdensome the taxes were. And, of course, they were not to complain anymore. Furthermore, even when there was a bad harvest, the French still collected the full amount due them. To the village that did not pay its full share, they sent a regiment of their terrifying troops with rifles and swords. They killed pigs, cows, chickens, and ducks to feed themselves. Then they tied the elders and threw them in jail, while they put the children on leashes or in iron locks. The moans and cries of the villagers were so heartrending. The poor peasants had to sell their wives and children to raise enough funds to pay their taxes. Or they simply drowned themselves in rivers in order to escape paying the high levies. The French, on their side, insisted upon collecting the full amount. They never mentioned the word *reduction.*

In terms of head taxes, every male of eighteen years has to pay three piasters. In exchange for that sum the French issued him a piece of paper called "head tax paper." Whoever was caught without that document was classified as a "smuggled being." The punishment for that is very harsh. The French employ the cruelest people in their police force; they position them at every crossroad in town to check on all the passersby for their head tax paper. Those who are without it are immediately thrown in jail; and, after these prisoners have served their term, they still have to pay the fines, which are double the amount of the head taxes that were due in the first place. As for the policemen, they are severely punished if, in the course of a week, for example, they have not come up with some violations, resulting in the fact that these policemen do whatever they can to catch the people at fault. Once, in a certain province, there was a policeman who, after checking the tax card of a peddler, tore it into small shreds and put the pieces into his mouth. Before he could swallow them, the peddler seized him by the throat. As the policeman refused to spit out the shreds of paper, the peddler, naturally, was not ready to let go of the policeman's neck. After a while, the latter died of suffocation. The affair went to court, where the peddler just told the whole truth. The judge ordered an autopsy of the policeman's corpse. Upon finding in his throat all the pieces of the tax card, the judge acquitted the peddler. Finding himself in dire straights such as these and yet still ready to fight for survival, this peddler must be a very rare exception indeed; most of the people would have accepted their fate: although innocent, they would have endured untold miseries.

The common people had to pay this poll tax once every year, while the mandarins were exempt from it. Upon hearing this, you may think that the French knew how to appreciate the degree holders, our scholars. That's not the case, however. Every three years people who had reached the mandarinal ranks must show their official appointment diplomas to the French administrators and pay fifteen piasters. That money is called "patriotic contribution." For sure, *contribution* sounds better than *imposition,* but, in terms of cash, they disbursed about three times the amount paid by the common people. Who would have thought that Mr. Shu's trick of giving three fruits in the morning and four in the evening, which worked so well on the monkey, has migrated all the way [from China] to Europe and has, moreover, become so fashionable there.[4]

Those who live in cities, in addition to the head tax, must pay two piasters a year as a "coming and going" tax. One may come and go freely in the city's streets only after one has paid that tax. After the two piasters are paid the French authorities issue to the taxpayer a card bearing his photograph. The police compares the likeness of the photograph to the bearer before allowing him to go free. Consequently, it is not possible to pass a card around among several people. Outsiders who come into the cities for any kind of business that keeps them there for more than three days have to pay that tax; failing that, they would be subjected to heavy fines. For those who live in the cities everything in the household is taxed—the food, the clothes, the utensils used in everyday life. They even have to pay sixty cents a month for urinating and defecating. Must we say anything more?

The French don't only impose taxes on human beings; they also tax dogs. In the cities, if you raise a dog, you must pay one piaster in tax every year to receive a tag you attach to the dog's neck. If the dog runs into the street without that tag, its owner will be fined right away. The government does not collect the taxes on cattle, buffaloes, and cows because that right belongs to a private company that specializes in raising cattle. Any household that owns a buffalo or a cow must pay two piasters for insurance. If a beast falls sick or dies, the company will pay its value to the owner. Yet, whenever there is an outbreak of a disease that kills many cattle heads, their owners put the claim to the company, which then replies in the following terms: "We shall first proceed to an autopsy, and then we'll pay." But nobody, naturally, will come to give any attention to the dead cattle, autopsy or not. In the entire country there are millions of heads of cattle; the premium of insurance paid to the company must amount to a very big sum. When it comes to settle the claims, however, no owner has as yet been paid a penny. People are not stupid enough to waste their money in that kind of scheme, but it is the French government that stands behind the company and benefits from it. When the claims are not paid up, the owner can do nothing else but accept the loss. To insist forcefully on the claims is not only useless; under the French system it may also become a risky proposition.

In the countryside the market fees are very high, even on the most inexpensive merchandise. It often happens that peddlers who sell vegetables in the market see their produce assessed a fee higher than its selling price. If they do not pay up the fines, the tax collector invents all kinds of difficulties for them. In order to escape the hassle the merchants often have to throw their vegetables into the garbage can. Even then the collector still runs after them to pin a fine on them. They have to make a quick escape. Once there was a poor man who went to the market to sell the pig he had raised himself. Because of low offers on the animal, he had to return twice to the market. When he succeeded in selling his pig, the price was just enough to settle the market fees. The poor man thus not only lost his pig but also the three days' labor he had put into going and coming to and from the market.

In brief, on this earth a blade of grass, a tree trunk, a piece of broken tile, a chip of stone, if any of these had any use for the people, it is inscribed in the French tax register. For the dwellings taxes are levied on land and houses separately, and the license fees increase every year. On the road taxes are imposed every day on buses, horses, baskets, and carrying poles. As for the fees on ferries, these must be the most lucrative ones because streams and rivers crisscross our country in all its regions, like threads on a loom. People living on either side of the riverbanks, if they want to exchange merchandise, must cross to the other side using ferries. That's why every year the fees collected from ferries must amount to very big sums.

Besides ferry fees, the taxes imposed on alcohol are even heavier and more bizarre. Since our country is situated within the tropics, people don't consume too much alcohol. Thus, its price has always remained very low. About ten years ago some French businessmen asked their government for permission to establish an alcohol company and to levy taxes on its production. From then on people were forbidden to distill alcohol privately; it could only be produced by the French company, which, therefore, possessed the monopoly of distilling alcohol. The company sells its alcohol at very high prices, and furthermore, it contains some poisonous ingredients: after three cups of it the consumer may already feel dizzy or come down with a headache; those who are addicted to it and therefore drink a lot of it may fall sick and even die after six months. People subsequently pass the word around not to drink that kind of alcohol. The company, unable to sell its products, requests that the government set a quota according to the population register: each registered citizen must buy three liters of alcohol each month. It does not matter whether the villagers drink it or not so long as they pay up the price. Delays in payments are seldom tolerated. This quota system has just begun in a few provinces; it has not yet been applied to the entire country. But if the enemy insists on obliging our people to drink all that alcohol, what then shall become of our people's health?

Assured of the protection given by the government, the alcohol company shows no inhibitions, not anymore. They send their guards every day into every corner of every village. These guards even penetrate into the private rooms of the villagers' houses; they follow every passerby; all year round they behave as if they were pursuing rebels. Whenever they find a moonshiner, even for a small pot of alcohol, the fines can reach three hundred to four hundred piasters. If that poor person is not able to pay the fines, his relatives must do it for him; if the relatives are unable to do it, then the neighbors and fellow villagers must. They also throw people in jail, most of the time innocent people. Some families have to desert their homes and take to hiding elsewhere. Those who are arrested and unable to pay the fines have to do hard labor in the daytime and spend their nights in jail cells for six months or even one whole year. The sufferings are indescribable. When they are set free, their health may have been ruined, their household devastated. Some of them end up committing suicide. In the district of Quang Xuong, Thanh Hoa Province, a hamlet of about one hundred houses counts more than one hundred persons implicated in moonshining. The reason is that the hamlet by tradition specialized in producing alcohol. The French resident [the chief administrator of a province] ordered the district chief to impose the fines on the moonshiners and their fellow villagers altogether. They took turns going to jail but still were unable to meet the payment of fines. The inhabitants of the hamlet finally requested that they be allowed to sell all their rice fields in payment of their fines and that the authorities stop all the arrests and imprisonments. The district chief presented the proposal to the French resident, who then put these rice fields up for sale and sent all the proceeds to the company. As a result, after the sale, that particular hamlet had only people but no more rice fields. And yet the people did not dare go elsewhere because they still owed some fine money to the government. I myself witnessed that situation. I wouldn't be surprised if, in the ensuing years, the entire population of that hamlet ended their lives by throwing themselves into rivers and streams.

Our country has a long coastal line and many salt fields. In the past our government let the people make salt for personal consumption. Their salt was clean; it tasted good, and its price was very reasonable. Ever since the French created the Monopoly of Salt, they forbade the people from making salt or selling it; they held the monopoly on salt. Their salt is full with sand; its price very high. The poor people can hardly buy it, and when they can they value it as much as they do rice. The famous verse of the poet Du Fu, "It is not that I am so absorbed in listening to the music that I cannot smell the meat's flavor; it is simply because for three months, I haven't tasted any salt," resounds often in our people's mind.[5]

The French people must think that it's easy to do lucrative business in our country. That's why they follow one another to come to our country. Besides the monopolies of alcohol and salt, they also establish plantations; they seize land, hire people to raise cattle, take care of the rice fields. Wherever they settle themselves down, they count on their privileges to permit them to transgress the law; they steal good fields from our peasants and declare them theirs. Our people dare not fight against them, and so the French reap all the benefits from these fields. The land they exploit for themselves does not represent five- or six-tenths of the whole acreage they own, whereas the fields they steal amount to more than three- or four-tenths of it. Moreover, they recruit their employees among the hoodlums. They falsely accuse the good people, sowing difficulties in all areas. Should they lose a chicken or a dog, they descend on the seat of the district or subdistrict government to claim for damages. The mandarins are intimidated by the plantation owners as they are by the French resident. The people, therefore, are pressed from all sides and dare not confront them.

In Quang Nam, a small province south of the capital city of our country [which was Hue at the time], the people were taxed so heavily that they marched to the residence of the French administrator, requesting that he rescind the latest tax increase. Not only did the administrator refuse to listen to them; he ordered his guards to chase the people out, pushing a great number of them into the river: three persons drowned. In great anger the people placed the three corpses at the gate of the residence of the French official; then several thousand of them in white clothes and white turbans [the color of mourning] squatted around the corpses, crying loudly for more than a full week. Others simply laid down on the streets of the town. The French resident reported the incident to the French resident superior, who came and asked them, "Why are you rebelling?" The people replied: "We don't even have a blade of iron in our hands, why do you call us rebels? We came simply to complain about the taxes, which are so heavy that we simply cannot pay them." The resident superior said: "You are so poor that you are not able to pay your taxes? Better die then." With these words he ordered the soldiers to open fire on the crowd: a few hundred were killed. Blood gathered into pools, and then the people dispersed. In this event, besides the number of people killed here, the former judge Le Khiet and the doctor Tran Qui Cap have also been executed by the French. Mr. Le has for a long time been infuriated with the evil policy of the French, while Dr. Tran, upon hearing of this demonstration, wrote down the following seven words: "Our people did this? Wonderful! Wonderful! Wonderful!" The French heard of this and accused him of inappropriate and seditious behavior. So they executed him. O! People gather to present their requests, without any weapon in their hands, and they are shot to death. Others simply utter courageous words, and they are decapitated. The lives of my people are not worth more than grass or trash.

A few years ago a railroad line was launched in the frontier area of our country going all the way to the province of Yunnan in China. As the local people could not do the job alone, so the French recruited poor peasants from all the other provinces. That region being well-known for its unhealthy climate, they promised the workers high wages. They did not keep their promise. In addition to long hours of hard labor, the workers did not receive even one decent meal per day. They quickly fell sick, and the corpses of the dead piled up in the caves of the mountains. Passersby who witnessed that tragic spectacle and who were still endowed with some conscience could not help but declare that it was many times worse than yesteryear's battlefields. Of the tens of thousands of workers on this railroad only a few made it back home. But because they had suffered so much from cold and starvation they became weak both physically and mentally. Back home for no more than two or three months, they either died out or became paralyzed and therefore useless members of society. That's why the winding road that meanders through the corners of three provinces of Vietnam all the way to the Sipsongpanna region of Yunnan, which the white men call the railroad, is known to the people of my country as the blood road.

They have stolen our country for no more than thirty years, and within that short period they have changed our emperors four times; two emperors were dethroned and exiled to a distant place, and one emperor was killed by poison. They hated these rulers because they were enlightened or because they could not bear the colonial situation and dared rise up in opposition to the French, who got mad and then got rid of them. The one emperor who succeeded to the throne is now only seven or eight years old. The French put him there in order to use him to control the people in the country in his name. Whenever they killed honest people, they'd say they are "following the emperor's orders." If they increased taxes, it was to "obey the emperor's will." Although he sits on the throne, the emperor is no more than a figurehead, and the French consider him a tool in their hands. Where, then, is the fun in being emperor? I give it ten more years until the present emperor wises up. He may then be victim of an accident!

As for the mandarins, the French not only consider them their servants; they treat them no better than their dogs. They beat them up like buffaloes so that the mandarins' sense of compassion and their desire for integrity cannot develop. Naturally, these mandarins are not to be pitied because those who today travel in cars or ride on horses, those who today exhibit medals, were all servants not long ago, whereas those who have any feelings, those who refuse to be servile, suffer in poverty. Those who have any propriety, if they are not killed, are exiled. The French cannot obtain their collaboration with the lure of privileges, nor can they subjugate them with the threat of punishments.

In the past people living in the various provinces of the north or the south of our country could come and go freely. Without any constraints they could trade or exchange the merchandise they needed. Two or three years ago the French suddenly issued orders strictly forbidding the people from southern Vietnam to go to central Vietnam and the people from central Vietnam to go to northern Vietnam. Merchandise, therefore, can no longer circulate, and it has become difficult for the Vietnamese people to do business. When a bad crop occurs and relief cannot arrive from elsewhere, people have no other recourse than to cross their arms over their knees and wait for death to come and take them away. I wonder what happened to the oppressive policy that England applied in India and America in the Philippines? A country is like a human body. If the throat is squeezed in such a way that it is unable to communicate with the intestines and the stomach, if the hands are nailed so that they cannot touch the legs, if up and down, right and left, are to be totally separated from each other, then how is the body to breathe or to remain alive? The French really use all the means at their disposal to block all the ways out for our people.

Recently, as the influence of America and Europe spread over all of Asia, everybody realizes that to cling to the old ways is to remain in mediocrity and to refuse survival. It means that every passing day more and more of our compatriots go overseas to study. In the country itself the people's mind is slowly opening up; everywhere schools have been established as trading companies have mushroomed. With the new knowledge and the priority put on practicality, everything points toward progress. Seeing that, the French tried to stop and to destroy everything, while frowning and gnawing their teeth. First of all, they made peace with the strong countries in the region. After that, they removed an enlightened emperor from the throne of our country. This emperor was training an army and painstakingly following the path of new knowledge. The French forced him to change all the articles of the convention, and, upon his refusal, they dethroned him. They subsequently issued orders to arrest all the people who belonged to new political parties. They executed some, exiled some, confiscated all the possessions of some others—all that according to their fantasy of the moment. Those who had gone abroad were given six months to return to the country. Otherwise, the government would punish the absentees' parents, their wives and children, their relatives. They forbade people from reading books about the new knowledge, discussing affairs of foreign countries, or establishing commercial ventures. They also employed hundreds of thousands of intelligence agents, who all looked like ghosts and devils. These agents also changed their appearance at every moment. They came and handcuffed people who were simply sitting in their cars; they threw innocent passersby in jail. These victims could only suffer and cry while wondering what wrong they had committed. Really, the thinking people of my country feel like they are sitting on thorns or on an open fire. They cannot do anything but suffer or burn with anger in silence. Yet the French are still not satisfied: the taxes keep on increasing, hard labor keeps on coming, prisons keep on being built. Alas! The sad situation of my country is not different from that of your own country [Korea]. The evil policy of the French becomes harsher and harsher day by day. What they want to do to us is to make us follow the same path as the Red race of America.

But it is in the nature of things that, when they have reached the extreme bottom, then they tend to bounce back. The more one is bitter, the more durable one's desire is for revenge. The more life-threatening is the danger, the stronger the will for survival. America obtained her independence and Germany rose up in arms simply because they were oppressed, humiliated. Would it be inaccurate to say that, in history, there was no country that stayed strong forever, without going through a period of decline, nor was there any country that remained weak forever, without an era of restoration? My body has not died; my will is still here. I swear to you all, aunts and uncles, brothers and sisters, that I shall continue to engrave deeply into my mind the idea of revenge and nurture in my body the strong desire to do away with all humiliation. I shall keep the determination and the enthusiasm to accomplish our divine mission.

The first man falls down, the second one advances to take his place; the old folks disappear, the younger generation continues the task—to fight with courage and energy; to help with good strategy; to increase the efficiency with the new knowledge; to maintain the energy and the will, in dire straights or in eminent danger, all according to the dictum "To be thrashed but not diminished." Then one day the cruel tiger will encounter its master, the lion; the poisonous snake, the eagle. In that way and seizing upon every opportunity, we shall take the hot stream of blood from hundreds of thousands of our compatriots to clean up our rivers and our mountains. There won't be any difficulty in pushing away all the enemies and restoring the old territory of the Hong Bang Dynasty [the legendary first dynasty in Vietnam's history] founded four thousand years ago.[6]

Notes

1. The mulberry fields and the sea in the title of this text are images that suggest very slow but drastic changes. The sea rolls now where the mulberry fields had been, or the mulberry fields spread now where the sea had been.

2. See Document 5, in this volume.

3. In the popular mind and in the writings of scholars from neighboring countries, the Japanese people are generally referred to as dwarfs.

4. A certain Mr. Shu, of the Song Dynasty in China, was quite well-known for raising more than a few monkeys in his house. As these almost depleted the fruit supply of the surrounding forest, a rationing system became indispensable. Lest hungry monkeys be troublesome, Mr. Shu gathered them in a meeting to explain to them the situation. He then concluded: "From now on, I can give you only four fruits in the morning and three in the evening. Is it all right with you?" The monkeys were highly upset. Mr. Shu then corrected himself: "Well, then, I shall give you three fruits in the morning and four in the evening. Does that sound better?" The monkeys were all satisfied! Thus, people likened Mr. Shu's trick on the monkeys to that played by the intelligent people on stupid ones. In this case the mandarins were happy to pay the taxes so long as they were called "contribution" and not "taxes," although the amount of money exacted from them was the same.

5. This allusion refers to Du Fu (712–770), the famous Chinese poet of the Tang Dynasty. With this verse the poet intended to blame the Song emperor for levying such heavy taxes on salt that he could not afford to buy salt for three months.

6. The Chinese version of this text is excerpted from a manuscript preserved at the Sino-Vietnamese Institute in Hanoi, under the title *Nam Chi Tap, Quyen Ha, Viet Nam Ha Noi Nguyen Thuong Hien, Tang Hai Le Dam,* 1a–14b. The Vietnamese translation of this document is to be found in *TVYNVCM,* 264–79; and in "Giot Le Be Dau cua Nguyen Thuong Hien," in *Van Su Dia* 43 (Aug. 1958): 80–88, trans. Trinh Dinh Ru; and also in Le Thuoc et al., ed. and trans., *Tho Van Nguyen Thuong Hien* (Hanoi, 1959), 135–46.

Cuong De (1882–1951)

Letter to Governor-General Albert Sarraut
(1 December 1913)

Cuong De was a descendant of Emperor Gia Long, the founder of the last dynasty of Vietnam, the Nguyen (1802–1945). Issued from a line that has not provided any monarch associated with the French, he was judged untainted and, therefore, worthy enough to become the ruler of a future independent Vietnam.[1] That was why Phan Boi Chau brought him to Japan to head the Viet Nam Duy Tan Hoi (Association for the Modernization of Vietnam). After the success of the Chinese Revolution, in 1911, republican principles of government reached Vietnamese nationalist leaders in China, who formed the Viet Nam Quang Phuc Hoi (Association for the Restoration of Vietnam), whose aim was to establish a republican regime for Vietnam (see Document 5).

Although Cuong De—probably because of his royal blood—did not follow the rest of the Vietnamese community that was expelled from Japan in 1908 and continued to reside in Tokyo, that association nonetheless reserved for him the title of president of the republic. It was in this capacity that in 1913, apparently at the invitation of a German diplomat in China, Cuong De went to Europe. The trip resulted in nothing spectacular, and he returned to live in Japan. One no longer heard anything about him after the arrest of Phan Boi Chau in 1925, until 1945, when the Japanese government brought him back to Hong Kong, probably with the intention of using him to set up a Vietnamese government after Japanese occupational troops would have confined all French personnel present in Indochina through the coup they effected on 9 March 1945. For some reason the Japanese government did not carry out the Cuong De plan—if indeed it had such a plan—and Cuong De went back to Japan, where he died shortly thereafter.[2]

During his trip to Europe Cuong De wrote this letter to Albert Sarraut, then governor-general of Indochina, advising him to adopt a more compassionate policy toward the Vietnamese people if France wanted a less rebellious colony. The interesting point is that Cuong De was extremely well informed

about the colonial situation of the world and extolled knowingly the virtues of
the policy Britain implemented in her dominions of Canada and Australia.

1 December 1913

To His Excellency Albert Sarraut,
Governor-General of Indochina,
In May of last year I received a letter from one of my supporters by the name of
Am Vo. That letter introduced you in the most glorious terms, as a hero of the
period, as an unequaled genius. Furthermore, the author of the letter wrote that,
as the head of the party of freedom, you kept close to your heart the virtue of
humanity. When you came to govern Indochina, you found the Vietnamese
people unhappy, under the total control of the "faithless and lawless" troublemakers. You were ready to implement some reforms that would have lifted up
the welfare of the people. I was very happy for that, and I wholeheartedly
approved of your policy. I was happy because I saw my people being governed
by such an exceptional genius as you. I approved of you for the artful way you
have displayed in the administration of a faraway colony.

During the past ten years or so, while meditating day and night, I hardly
stopped from commiserating with the Vietnamese people who have never had
the privilege of dealing with a genius. People who would not dare save the
country are not to be found, that's an understandable fact; but how come people
who revolt against the government are not to be found either? People who like
fervently the Vietnamese are not to be found, that's an understandable fact; but
why is it that people who are entirely devoted to further the French cause are
not to be found either? People who fight for mankind are not to be found, that's
an understandable fact; but how come people who fight against mankind are
not to be found either? That's why people become more and more ignorant,
more and more vicious, more and more miserable, to the point that today they
can no longer raise their heads above the ground. If among the people I
mentioned earlier one would have come to Vietnam, he would have modified
the colonial policy that was implemented at that time in Indochina with the aim
of harmonizing it with promises, instead of clinging stubbornly to the status
quo. In effect, if the colonial government preserves the status quo, the people,
being so ignorant, would not fail to have doubts concerning the measures
implemented by the government, however useful these measures could be. In
their minds the people think that the government is lying to them. That state of
affairs could eventually become a nuisance to the government, because the
people no longer trust the government; they do not readily listen to it, nor will
they execute its orders adequately. As a general rule, governments administer
through the people; now, if the people do not believe in their government, if
they do not obey it, then how can governments do their job? Ignorant people
have the propensity to listen to troublemakers. In fact, were not all the recent

troubles such as the poisoning, the uprising, the bombs all acts perpetrated by stupid people? In addition to all that, as soon as crises arose, it is difficult for government officials to remain calm. If they leave things as they are, they cannot fail to reduce the people to misery; and if the people are miserable, then where does the government find its revenue to tend to public affairs? Misery will drive people to burglaries, piracy that, in their turn, lead to internal instability. Under these circumstances how can the government pay any attention to foreign affairs?

If we apply a new policy, changes will undoubtedly occur in the legal and educational domains. If we modernize the laws, we shall surely apply only civilized laws; there indeed is absolutely no reason why we should apply barbarian laws. If the law is civilized, then the people of the country, whether nobles or villains, rich or poor, whether scholars, craftsmen, traders, or peasants, all will be treated as equals. Those who have riches will think of investing them for profit; those who have talents will use them in industrial and commercial enterprises; the nobles will guide the villains; the rich will help the poor; the clever will lead the clumsy; all will help one another in order to enjoy life and happiness; they no longer will have to bury their possessions or give up their arts and crafts to flee the country.

If the educational system is changed, then undoubtedly new methods are to be used, for example, in disciplines such as mining, electricity, medicine, literature, industry, commerce, agriculture, forestry. There will indeed be no reason to let the people behave in their own way, for example, to nurture hatred against foreigners or to learn how to despise others as in the past. Having learned the sciences from the government, the people will use them to improve the quality of their lives. There will no longer be husbands who owe their two meals a day to their wives and who roam everywhere aimlessly with their bundle of clothes under their arms as they do today.

What a privilege for Indochina to be governed this time by a man like you!

If from now on twenty-five million Vietnamese enjoy equality with other human beings, if fifteen thousand French citizens can live without fear of conflict, if the Indochinese colony becomes stable forever, that's owing to you; I beg you to remember that.

We hold no grudge against France, and, if we have revolted in the past against France, that was because the policy implemented by the colonial government was so cruel toward the Vietnamese people. If we had not revolted against that cruelty, the people would not have survived. That's why we have acted in such a manner.

Now that you have come and have shown interest in the indigenous people, now that you are ready to civilize them, then we no longer have any reason to ready ourselves painfully for revolution.

This time, coming to Europe, I had the firm intention to go all the way to

Paris in order to accomplish two missions: to meet with the ministers [of the French government] to expose to them the whole situation of Indochina and, second, to request a prolongation of your tenure in Indochina so as to allow you to implement the work you have undertaken. Unfortunately, as soon as I arrived here, I read in the local newspapers, and I also received letters from home to the effect, that the colonial government in Indochina was only interested in arresting as many Vietnamese as possible in order to prove its efficiency without any regards for humanity or any concern for the everlasting pacification of the country.

If the Indochinese government acts in such a manner, although I can plead my case right here in Paris with thousands and millions of words, all will be in vain.

Furthermore, if I arrive in Paris at the same time as the Indochinese government launches a brutal persecution of the Vietnamese people, I would give the impression that I have come to the end of my resources and that my presence in Paris would mean the willingness on my part to surrender to the French rather than the expression of my interest in the situation of the kingdom of Annam and the plight of my people. That's why I stopped over here [in Germany] rather than going all the way to Paris. Although I dare not present myself [to the French ministers in Paris], the hopes that I entertained in you for such a long time have not vanished. I, therefore, would like to tell you that I sincerely wish that you may be able to return to Indochina a second time.[3] And if ever you go back to Indochina, then I beg you to spread the following ideas among the civil servants of Indochina:

—it is advantageous to act in such a way that all the people volunteer to serve the government, because if the government had to count only on the service of salaried spies [to govern the people], as it is doing at the present time, that will divert the government from its right path without bringing any useful result.

—it is advantageous to act in such a way that the people think of nothing else but to remain quiet, to perform their own work, and not to commit crimes. If the government were only interested in arresting as many people as it possibly can in order to prove its efficiency, as it is doing at the present time, then it accomplishes nothing but makes everything worse.

—it is advantageous to be tolerant in form and extremely severe in substance. If the government were severe in form and tolerant in substance, as it is at the present time, it will worsen a situation that is already bad.[4]

In terms of colonial administration the English are much better off than you. Take Australia, for example, one of England's colonies. The entire population of that colony (I understand by this all classes of the population) serves the protecting government. The attitude of that colony with regards to the English government can be explained by the fact that the happiness of the [colonized] people is intimately related to the happiness of the colonial government whether in peace or in danger. If the government is calm, so is the population. If the government is threatened by some danger, so is the population threatened by the same danger. Year in year out, the people think of nothing else but of their work, and one never hears even a murmur about revolution. If, by any chance, someone nurtures some hostile ideas against the government, the people consider them rebels and repress them without any need for any intervention from the government: is it not advantageous to act in such a way?

To spend money to pay spies is simply to stray away from the right path. Over the last years the government sent an army of spies into the countryside. But nature has endowed human beings with a conscience. The government mistreats a people, who then revolts against that government, which, in turn, sends agents to spy on its own compatriots. That's nonsense. It is simply because they have nothing to eat that these agents agree to serve you. In the final analysis, if they are quick to welcome your generous presents, they will also be quick to betray you, for they do not loathe their compatriots. How could they subject their own compatriots to punishments meted out by the government? Furthermore, they may even provide you with false information. So, is it not equivalent to straying from the right path without any redeeming advantage?

When I mentioned colonized populations who think only about an eventless life, I had in mind English colonies like Australia or Canada. These colonies are on the same level as England in terms of industry, wealth, [military] strength. They possess ample means to sever all relations with the English government in order to acquire independence. Year in year out, however, they think only of their industry, their trade, their agriculture, asking themselves what the best conditions are for the development of their businesses without any need for a revolution or demand for autonomy. On the other hand, the English government has no need to increase its army contingent by one single soldier or to recruit one more spy, and yet the colonies enjoy the most complete calm; the colonial administration is based on solid foundations: is that not a good thing?

To arrest as many people as possible in order to prove the government's efficiency is tantamount to misunderstanding the data of a problem. Yet that predicament prevailed in Indochina during the past few years: no months passed without the arrest of some revolutionaries; no year passed without the deportation of patriots. If it were true that the more one arrests, the better one eradicates revolutionaries; the more one deports, the better one reforms revolutionaries; the more one decapitates, the better terror spreads around, then how come in spite of continuous arrests, deportations, and decapitations, the number of revolutionaries has not only not decreased, but it has even increased with every passing day? One revolutionary creates ten revolutionaries; ten revolutionaries create a thousand; the multiplication here looks very much like a sowing ceremony.

It is better to be tolerant in the form and severe in the substance. For example, a few years ago the people from Cochinchina were permitted to go to Hong Kong or to Japan to study. As long as they were allowed to go, they knew they would not be harassed upon their return. As neither the foreign countries' customs or their climate suited them adequately, they returned en masse to their own land: not a single one stayed on in a foreign country. The government spent no effort or money to send anyone to look for them. They came back on their own accord to lead a tranquil life under the government's protection in their own land; not a single one of them dared ask anything about Cuong De or Phan Boi Chau. Is that not an advantage?

To be too severe in the form and too tolerant in the substance is to hurt oneself needlessly.

The way the government treats the people in the rice fieds of Annam and Tonkin is really too rough. Not only does it not allow them to go to foreign countries; it even creates thousands of difficulties for them to travel simply from one province to the other [within Vietnam]. And yet the number of emigrants increases every day. That's because, as the government does not permit them to leave legally, once outside, even if they have to face tremendous hardships, they still feel obliged to endure these hardships in the foreign country rather than come home. And, while they stay outside, there is no reason why they should remain idle. They must try to get rid of the government that prevents them from coming back. If they cannot organize a general uprising, then they are satisfied with a few attempts at assassination. If they cannot set up adventurous movements, they are satisfied with bombs. In other words, they must unite their efforts in order to agitate constantly.

In the world, when one wants to do something, one looks for a favorable ground, like a peasant who plants rice would wish that everyone else have a bad crop. A silkworm breeder would wish that all the other breeders incur losses so that he alone can earn big profits. Similarly, the revolutionaries would wish that the government mistreat the people so that they have a fertile ground to recruit supporters. Up to now no one dared to profess those truths.

Whatever we are doing now, we cannot escape the fact that we live under a tyrannical regime. But if we don't act, the people will be very unhappy: so we become activists, but . . . against our will. We wish only one thing: that the people be happy. We ask for absolutely no personal reward if we succeed in our undertaking.

Over the last few years I have always wanted to talk to the government of Indochina. I have, however, done nothing toward achieving that goal, because I have not yet encountered the person of the day. Furthermore, after serious reflections I have always convinced myself that my proposals would not be heeded anyway: that's why I have refrained from unveiling them.

Today, in you, I am persuaded that I have encountered a worthy person: I, therefore, open my heart to you. I beg you to believe that I have done all this for the cause of the people and not for the private interests of Cuong De.

The art of governing a people is similar to that of curing a sick person. In order to overcome a sickness, the physician examines its causes, its origins; he looks for the appropriate remedies at the same time as he studies the temperament of the patient. In order to govern a country well, the good administrator scrutinizes the sentiments of the people, their habits, their needs, before he fine-tunes his policy; he makes it more liberal or more strict, depending on the circumstances. He modifies it according to his people's degree of evolution or to external circumstances. It is, indeed, not a good policy to treat a defeated people roughly while favoring one's own nationals.

The government has taken very harsh measures over the past few years against the Vietnamese people because they have communicated with foreign countries in search of the means to reconquer their independence. Those measures, which were appropriate at that time (i.e., a few years back), are absurd today, for the Vietnamese no longer think of their independence, because it appears to them impossible to attain. We ask only for a more liberal policy. Is it not time now to satisfy our moderate demand? Is our plea not legitimate? I am personally convinced that if in the near future you will not improve the conditions of the Vietnamese, Annam and Tonkin will undoubtedly witness the same events the memory of which still lingers in our mind. On the other hand, the government will gain much if it tries to alleviate the pain of the people, right now. It is to be feared that, when the Vietnamese start to appreciate France, it will be too late.

I have the honor to submit here to your high consideration some of my ideas, which I beg you to examine with kindness.

I end my letter wishing you a long life. I also send you my best wishes for the prosperity of France.[5]

Notes

1. People who supported Cuong De for the reason of his untainted bloodline seemed to have forgotten that it was Prince Nguyen Anh, the future emperor Gia Long, who had sent his son Prince Canh, Cuong De's ancestor, along with Bishop Pigneau de Behaine, to Europe in order to seek military assistance from France in his struggle against the Tay Son brothers. It is in fact the Gia Long emperor himself who is the target

of the popular dictum: "Bring the [outside] snake to bite the family chicken." Consequently, there was to be no "untainted" member of the Nguyen royal family.

2. See David Marr, *Vietnamese Anticolonialism, 1885–1925* (Berkeley, 1971); and *Viet Nam 1945: The Quest for Power* (Berkeley, 1995). For both books, check under the name Cuong De for all the passages related to him. See also my essay "The Japanese and the Disruption of Vietnamese Nationalism," in W. Vella, ed., *Aspects of Vietnamese Culture* (Honolulu, 1972), 237–69.

3. The original of this letter shows the date of 1 December 1913. At this date Sarraut was still the governor-general of Indochina. Officially, his tenure did not end until 4 August 1914, although he had left Indochina and arrived in France on 4 January 1914. This sentence leads us to believe that Cuong De knew already, in December, that Sarraut had completed his first tenure as governor-general of Indochina and was on his way back from Indochina to France. Sarraut was, in fact as Cuong De wished here, to be reappointed to a second term as governor-general of Indochina from 7 November 1916 to 9 December 1919.

4. I do not grasp the full meaning of this paragraph. The author will come back later to these same ideas of "being tolerant in form and severe in substance." In my opinion what he wants to say here is that the colonial government should decree moderately mild regulations (tolerant in form) while applying stricter corrective measures (severe in substance) rather than having too harsh laws and adopting less harsh punishments. But this does not sound right, because Cuong De would then advocate for harsher punishments.

5. The original of this letter written in Vietnamese is in ANSOM, Indochine, Nouveau fonds, 166: *Personal File of Albert Sarraut.* The letter was signed by Cuong De with his seal affixed next to his signature. The French translation, written in a very rough style and dated January 1914, can also be found in the same file. Another copy of the French translation can be found in ANSOM, Indochine, Nouveaux fonds, 28, no. 3.

DOCUMENT 8

The Thai Nguyen Uprising

Proclamation
(1917)

On 30 August 1917, corresponding to the fifteenth of the seventh month of the lunar calendar, a sizable group of indigenous guards mutinied against the French administration of the penitentiary of Thai Nguyen, where hundreds of Vietnamese political prisoners were confined. The mutineers freed the prisoners, and together they occupied, for six days at least, not only the penitentiary but also the administrative buildings of the provincial capital city. Governmental reinforcements dislodged them from the city, but they scattered around for a few more days and opposed a fierce resistance to the French mopping-up operation.

 The mutiny was led by a noncommissioned officer of the indigenous militia, Trinh Van Can. Sergeant Can—as he is popularly referred to—had enlisted, in the early years of the French conquest, in the French-commanded indigenous militia and had participated in the "pacification" of the northern region of Vietnam, the ruthlessness of which instilled in him a bitter resentment against the French colonialists. He must also have been egged on by Luong Ngoc Quyen, son of Luong Van Can, the founder of the Tonkin Free School (see Document 3), and one of the many political prisoners confined at the Thai Nguyen penitentiary. Luong Ngoc Quyen was a faithful follower of Phan Boi Chau in Japan, China, and Thailand. With Phan Boi Chau he founded the Association for the Restoration of Vietnam, or Viet Nam Quang Phuc Hoi (see Document 5), and became its military advisor and a member of its Executive Committee. Luong Ngoc Quyen was arrested in Hong Kong by the British police, who extradited him to the French colonial authorities. After having been confined in a number of jails, he was ultimately sent to Thai Nguyen, where he was put in iron shackles most of the time and constantly tortured by its infamous and sadistic administrator, a certain Darles. It was undoubtedly under Luong Ngoc Quyen's influence that the rebellion took the name of Empire of the Great Restoration and that it adopted a five-star flag, which was the emblem of the Restoration association. In fact, the proclamation eloquently mentions so many events related to the struggle against the colonial authorities that it was very likely composed by Luong Ngoc Quyen himself.[1]

On the fifteenth day of the seventh month in the first year of the Empire of the Great Restoration, we, the undersigned, Trinh [Van Can], Great Commander of the Liberation Army of the Province of Thai Nguyen, have the honor of bringing the following proclamation to the knowledge of the people of the country of Vietnam.

Alas! After a series of unfortunate events willed undoubtedly by Heaven, our country has become poor and weak. From the time the evil Western wind blew toward the East, it devitalized our race and almost extinguished it. For thirty years now our country has been turned into a desert. Our men of talent live in the deepest distress; our forty million compatriots survive in shame, rousing pity in the heart of the true patriots. But all the misfortunes that Heaven had sent us have come to their end today. That same Heaven who made us suffer in the past now has mercy on us and wants to transform our misery into prosperity.

Overseas we have men of value who study in schools so that they may become our guides. Within our frontiers we have capable persons who are ready to act. In the year of the Monkey [1908] did we not kill our enemies in Hanoi and sow terror within their ranks?[2] In the year of the Chicken [1909] the uprising in the province of Lang Son brought comfort to our oppressed hearts.[3] On another level the Tonkin Free School opened our minds [1907], while the province of Quang Nam resisted the imposition of a head tax [1908]. A student risked his life throwing a bomb in Hanoi.[4] [Phan] Xich Long rebelled in Annam.[5] In fact, we have struggled for more than ten years now to preserve our civilization. Our cause is strengthened everyday. All the efforts we have made to take back our country terrified the enemy, while at the same time they kindled our desire for independence.

In addition to all that, Europe is now in turmoil. Our enemies, the French, are attacked right on their soil. The English and the Russians have signed a separate treaty with Germany, thereby depriving France of her indispensable partners. Turkey and Austria have marched through Italy, intending to attack the underside of France. Paris will soon be indefensible. How can the French protect us here when they are threatened right at home? Let us take advantage of this weakness of France. Let us capitalize on this opportunity, unique in a thousand years. Let us use this rare occasion to cleanse off our shame and avenge ourselves.

Obeying the imperial order,[6] we train our troops, determined to chase away the enemy by combining our efforts within and without the country. We have contracted an alliance with China.[7] Our soldiers and officers learned their military strategy in schools belonging to our powerful neighbors: China and Japan.[8] These soldiers and officers are well trained and ready to give their lives for their beloved fatherland. With one hundred thousand cases of rifles and ammunition, ten thousand planes, we are going to launch lightning attacks. Soon, victory shall be ours.

Our troops behave well; they do not steal from the people. Wherever they go, their only preoccupation is to reconquer the land of our ancestors and to exterminate the race that is foreign to us.

Compatriots! Let us redouble our efforts to accomplish our great mission so that we may proudly raise our five-star flag in the five continents of the world. We should not fall short of the expectations of our country.

O! The life of a new nation that will last for thousands of more years begins today. It is incumbent upon us to free ourselves of the slavery that has oppressed us for too long already.

Such is our proclamation written in very clear terms.[9]

Notes

1. See Tran Huy Lieu, *Loan Thai Nguyen* (Hanoi, 1935) and *Lich su tam muoi nam chong Phap* (Hanoi, 1956), 1:186–200. See also Thiet Can and Hai Khanh, *Loan Thai Nguyen* (Hanoi, 1935); and Dao Trinh Nhat, *Luong Ngoc Quyen va cuoc khoi nghia Thai Nguyen 1917* (Saigon, 1957).

2. This sentence alludes to the attempt made by various anticolonial groups to attack the French garrison in Hanoi. These groups included the followers of Phan Boi Chau's Dong Du movement and the troops of De Tham, who commanded an anti-French resistance force whose headquarters were located in the northwest province of Yen The. The attack would come after French soldiers were poisoned during their dinner on 27 June 1908. The cooks and waiters did succeed in putting poison in the food for the French soldiers. But the uprising never took place. According to the current rumor, a French priest had heard in confession about this attempt and had warned the colonial authorities, who had disarmed, for precaution sake, all the Vietnamese militia. This episode reminds us of the beginning of the Philippine Revolution of 1896, instigated by the Katipunan. See Teodoro A. Agoncillo and Milagros C. Guerrero, *History of the Filippino People* (Quezon City, 1977), 195.

3. According to Thai Bach, *Thi van quoc cam . . . ,* this uprising was engineered "in 1909, by a group of Dong Du students, with the assistance of revolutionary Chinese cadres. That uprising took place in the province of Lang Son and killed a great number of French troops" (428 n. 2.) This uprising might have been lumped together with the resistance put up by De Tham in various provinces of North Vietnam in response to the general attack generated by the colonial government against him beginning in January 1909. For more information about De Tham, see Tran Huy Lieu, *Lich su tam muoi nam . . . ,* 1:110–27, and ANSOM, Indochine, Ancien fonds, 2 and 9.

4. A bomb exploded in the Hanoi Hotel in Hanoi on 26 April 1913, killing two French officers and injuring many other people.

5. Phan Xich Long did not really rebel in Annam; he was, rather, arrested in 1913 by the French authorities in Phan Thiet, which is, indeed, situated in Annam. His area of activity was in the province of Cho Lon, southwest of Saigon, where most of his followers came from. Phan Xich Long claimed that he was endowed with supernatural powers, and he signed his appeals with the title of emperor. He maintained that he was a descendant of the emperors of the previous Le Dynasty and that he wanted to chase away the French in order to regain Vietnam's independence. His followers, armed with the most primitive weapons and dressed up all in white—white turban, white tunic—raided the city of Cho Lon during the night of 27–28 March 1913. Again, during the night of 14–15 February 1916, three hundred of his followers, all dressed up in white pants and black jackets, with white headbands, attacked the palace of the lieutenant governor and the Central Prison in Saigon with the hope of liberating Phan Xich Long, who was there serving a sentence of forced labor for life. The rebels killed one French soldier and wounded three others. According to a letter written by the governor-general of Indochina to the French minister of colonies, it was "a serious attempt to put in execution a vast plot that has been prepared carefully and for a long time by a secret society which grouped together with professional bandits all the enemies of our domination . . . Cochinchina was therefore declared in a state of siege. A military tribunal was the only means available in such circumstances to bring about a quick, severe and efficient repression." ANSOM, Indochine, Nouveaux fonds, 8, 28(1) and 28(2).

6. This is an unsubstantiated claim. The Vietnamese court would have never endorsed the Thai Nguyen mutiny and rebellion, unless this "imperial order" refers to the order from the emperor of the Empire of the Great Restoration, mentioned in the first sentence of this proclamation.

7. This again is an unsubstantiated claim.

8. This is correct, as the Dong Du movement placed quite a few of its students in Japanese military schools. After they were expelled from Japan in 1909, Phan Boi Chau shifted his "theater of operation" to China and sent many Vietnamese students to Chinese military schools. It is also a well-known fact that later on, many Vietnamese students were enrolled in the Whampoa Military Academy, and quite a few of them ended up as high officers in the Guomindang's (KMT) army.

9. A French translation from the original written in Vietnamese is to be found in ANSOM, Indochine, Nouveaux fonds, 56, 646. A Vietnamese version of this document may be found in Thai Bach, *Thi van quoc cam . . . ,* 420–31.

DOCUMENT 9

Nguyen An Ninh (1900–1943)

France in Indochina
(1925)

Nguyen An Ninh was one of the best-known anti-French activists of the 1920s. He was a good enough student to earn a seat in the French lycée Chasseloup Laubat—a school established mainly for French children—in Saigon. He was subsequently sent through a colonial government scholarship to study law in France, where he obtained his master's degree in 1920. He returned to Vietnam on the same ship as Phan Chu Trinh, on 28 May 1925. A report filed by a French security agent alleged that Nguyen An Ninh, while in France, had joined the French Communist Party and had been an active member of the Intercolonial Union, a communist organization. Nguyen An Ninh vehemently denied these allegations, although he readily conceded that he approved of communist theory and practice, for, should that party one day seize power in France, it could mean complete freedom for Indochina. The French agent had his own assessment: "It is of little significance that Nguyen Van Ninh [an alias under which Nguyen An Ninh was known] be a nationalist or a communist: he is anti-French, that's all."[1] Whatever he was, the British authorities of Singapore judged his writing to be dangerous: during the stopover in that free port, the British police confiscated all the copies of a pamphlet he had published in French under the title France en Indochine, *the translation of which follows, along with many other books by him, some of which were doubtlessly of communist inspiration.*

Once back in Vietnam, Nguyen An Ninh published a rather radical anti-French daily, which he named La Cloche Fêlée *[The Cracked Bell], which appeared intermittently from 1923 to 1926: the few interruptions were caused by the publisher's lack of funds.[2] For his anticolonial activities Nguyen An Ninh was arrested several times and imprisoned for long periods. In 1928 he was sentenced to three years in prison for founding a secret society called the Cao Vong Thanh Nien (High Hopes of the Youth), the purpose of which was to free Vietnam from the foreign yoke. According to a report from the Indochinese*

190

Security Service, that society established an army divided into three sections; each one of them had its own complete general staff with ranks rising from simple second-class soldier to general. Admission requirements included the obligation of every member to keep the strictest secret about the society's activities; failure to do so could result in death. Along with Nguyen An Ninh, the Indochinese Security Service arrested more than 250 people: 110 of them received sentences ranging from three to fifteen years in jail. Nguyen An Ninh's last arrest came in October 1939, when he received a sentence of five years in prison. He was sent to Poulo Condore, where he died in 1943.[3]

The following text describes the colonial situation of Vietnam in very realistic and precise terms: how it clashes with the Vietnamese national character and how it confers on the French residing in Vietnam enormous privileges that they have used to abuse the Vietnamese people as well as Vietnam's economic resources.

It was not to carry out a sentimental deed that France came to Indochina, after crossing a distance of fifteen thousand kilometers. And those Vietnamese who, over the last few years, have talked about humanitarian motives on the part of the French, in order to humor the colonialists, are as naive as those Europeans who still believe in the civilizing mission of Europe. On the other hand, today, if one were to recall all the horrors of the time of conquest with the simple purpose of perpetuating the hatred that the Vietnamese people entertain toward their conquerors, one would show a narrow mind, completely insensitive to the sufferings, the real aspirations, and the future of the Vietnamese race. To complain ceaselessly about the destiny of the Vietnamese people or to expect every benefit to come from the colonial government or from the many ministries that have succeeded one another in the mother country amounts to a public confession of powerlessness as well as to an incapacity to face reality.

Before accepting the fact, however, that in order to eliminate the regime of slavery imposed by France on Indochina there is only one way, and that way is to combat violence with violence as in a bulls' fight, the Vietnamese youth of today, fully conscious of its responsibilities toward its own society, tries first to reconcile French interest with Vietnamese wishes. It tells the mother country— which is too far away from Indochina—the truth about what happens in this colony. The mother country will then decide whether it is in her own interest to abandon Indochina to its own fate or to legislate in favor of the colony a few laws that will grant its citizens some basic rights.

The Independent Character of the Vietnamese People

The independent character of the Vietnamese people has manifested itself very clearly in history. China has seen it. She was never able to dominate Vietnam in spite of her several occupations, which lasted altogether for more than a thousand years, and in spite of her repeated attempts at conquest, which were at times more violent than others. The French soldiers have of course encountered the strength of that independent character at the time of their conquest.

Even today, the Vietnamese have not yet accepted French domination. Notwithstanding the arbitrary division of their country into three different parts, they hold true to the unity of their territory— that is, the idea that they all belong to one people. The colonialists here know well that rebellious character. About six months ago I heard, during a trial at the Tribunal of Saigon, a prosecutor of the republic blame Mr. Ganofsky, a troublemaking journalist, in the following terms: "In the presence of the indigenous people, who are fast to revolt, etc., etc." A single pistol smuggled into the colony suffices to terrorize the entire European community. The colonial government of Indochina maintains an enormous local and external ring of spies. It uses every brutal method of repression to the point of drowning all rebellions in a bloodbath, even if these were peaceful. Evidence: the 1908 movement, when unarmed marchers were shot at point-blank range. Should we mention the pacification of the mountain people carried out through bombs launched from planes? During the seventy years of French domination, revolts have followed one after another at regular intervals:

—The Five Tigers who punish the West
—The plot of Thay Chim
—De Tham, a patriot and bandit with legendary exploits, and other rebels trained in the same school
—The revolt of the adzes
—The 1908 movement headed by Phan Chu Trinh
—The Dong Kinh Nghia Thuc
—The bomb in Hanoi
—The Gilbert Chieu affair
—The Thai Nguyen rebellion
—The Phan Xich Long conspiracy
—The attack of the Saigon prison
—The flight of Emperor Duy Tan, etc., etc.
—The recent bomb attack in Canton was launched by a Vietnamese, according to Chinese newspapers.

The peasants, while remaining close to their soil, are looking for favorable circumstances to regain their independence, using only their sharpened bamboo sticks or their long knives as weapons. Other Vietnamese, unwilling to suffer under a colonial regime, leave their homeland to gather in foreign countries. Still others, although remaining within the country's confines, refuse to collaborate with the dominators. Even Vietnamese civil servants whom dire circumstances and their own weaknesses oblige to serve the colonialists receive with great joy signals that herald the liberation of their race.

Only a clique of former servants or office errand boys who have been raised to higher ranks through largesses of the colonial government extols the benefits of French domination. They attempt to show the so-called loyalty of the people of Vietnam by organizing banquets of two hundred to three hundred guests, to which they force village notables, canton chiefs, and district and prefecture mandarins to attend. All these people, in any case, are the employees of the colonial government.[4]

If the people remain silent or if, on the contrary, they foment rebellions, it is because they are willing to abide by the rules of war, which ensure either the brutal triumph of the winner or the unmerciful humiliation of the vanquished. On the battlefield of the past they have been deprived of their right to life; now they are determined to claim back that right, on the battlefield of the present. They have struggled, for the last ten years, supported by big landowners, led by Confucian scholars. Today, among the latter, some accept their fate and give it up as an unequal fight; others flee to foreign countries. Consequently, the people give their trust to ignorant adventurers such as Phan Xich Long, a former house servant. Since they have no planes loaded with bombs, nor do they possess cannons or machine guns, not even a good rifle, they believe in the power of charms or talismans that are supposed to protect them from bullets and bayonets. Urged by their distaste for injustice, they simply go on fighting against bullets coming out of machine guns that await them, concealed in the bushes. That's how bad the rebellious spirit of the people is.

That kind of blind violence, the conception of a ruthless struggle, is condemned by Westernized Vietnamese as well as by Vietnamese scholars. But the stupid bullet cannot distinguish between good and evil. In an equal struggle the one who knows that his cause is right rebels at the eventuality of having to submit it to the judgment of hazard. In an unequal struggle the one who can claim justice on his side has all the chances of being defeated; in that case blind violence constitutes the weapon of those who live in despair.

To a Modern Form of Violence, a Modern Form of Resistance

When a people has reached the point where they must choose between death and slavery, to taunt death is more virile. Violence ought to be condemned when it is unnecessary. But there are cases when violence must be accepted, for it represents the only recourse.

If the masses taunt death rather than accept injustice and, on the other hand, if the colonialists refuse to give up their policy of oppression and exploitation without scruples, it is then the duty of the more courageous and the more devoted Vietnamese to think of methods of struggle that fit the time and to devise a form of resistance that is capable of fighting oppression. The prisoner who attempts to escape does not think about the death that may befall him during the evasion. The threat of Japan is insufficient to compel the Vietnamese to give up their liberty.

The Gallicized Vietnamese Youth Attempts Reconciliation

Yet, if the masses revolted, it is because of the oppression that weighs heavily upon them, not because of the hatred they feel for the foreigner. The masses simply followed Phan Chu Trinh to fight against corrupt mandarins. Mr. Albert Sarraut, a former governor-general of Indochina, owing to his lies and his hypocrisy, was able to earn the sympathy of the people for a short time. That is testimony to the fact that Vietnamese peasants do not spare even their own brothers if they are found to be unjust. A government, therefore, that is slightly concerned about justice would easily calm all attempts at rebellion. Such a people are capable of accepting the possibility and the advantages of an evolution toward political freedom, under French sovereignty, with the condition that this sovereignty be generous and loyal.

Such is the thinking of today's gallicized youth, who, because it prefers nonviolent action, attempts to reconcile colonial interests with Vietnamese aspirations. If, in two or three years, it comes to realize the uselessness of its efforts, it will then keep silent and yield its place to those who will be judged more useful to the Vietnamese race.

In the last few years, in spite of all the efforts of the colonialists to confine the Vietnamese to their own country, some of them have succumbed to the temptation that pushes many Asian masses toward Europe, so they went to France to observe, as they say, European life as well as the secret of the material power of Europe. They brought back from Europe ideas of democracy, a critical mind, a strength and a faith that are reinvigorated by the Western spirit. They received from the hands of metropolitan Frenchmen the condemnation of the political regime imposed upon Indochina by the French colonialists, who, after all, cannot prevent them from reading Montesquieu, Rousseau, and Voltaire . . .

Already there are people who try to persuade the masses to abandon their hope for revenge through violence and guide them toward a new kind of struggle. They demand only those basic liberties that protect the human dignity; they seek only such reforms that would harmonize the democratic tradition of the Vietnamese people with European ideals. They do not accept, as the masses have hitherto done, the rules of the struggle. They no longer fight in secret and out of sheer patriotism. They fight openly, in the name of humanitarian ideals and the principles of [the French Revolution of] 1789. The colonialists, on their side, no longer dare use the pretext of "French sovereignty in danger" to send these Vietnamese to prison or to the execution post.

Thus is heralded the unavoidable bankruptcy of the policy of exploitation of man by man as implemented in Indochina, a policy of a vendor of bad faith who sells at discount because of the imminent bankruptcy. Maybe oppression, even frustrated by its repeated failures, and despite signs announcing its impending demise, will persist in persecuting its prey, which continues to resist. It then will result in a common catastrophe that will make France lose her reputation and her interests and will cause the "civilizing mission" of Europe to be seen under its real light and will create conditions for Vietnam, after so much pain and so much anguish, to emerge freer, to realize its own destiny. Or maybe republican France will come to Indochina to replace colonialist France; then not only France's interests but also her reputation will be saved.

About fifteen years ago, responding to the complaints of those whom they had oppressed, the colonialists wrote in their newspapers: "France did not come here with the sword and the law. She brought here only the sword." It seems to me that, after seventy years of French domination and French influence, now that the Cochinchinese land has been declared French territory, the Vietnamese have the right to demand that France bring to Indochina the law and the sword that protects the law.

The fusion of French republican institutions with the democratic tradition of a society based on Confucian ideals will not foster, as the colonialists would like us to believe, a natural evolution. The emancipation of Asia will not follow the same process as the slow evolution that took Europe from a primitive community to a modern society. One must be a colonialist in the most stupid meaning of that term to believe in the civilizing mission of the Europeans who colonized Indochina. In India the proclamation of the civilizing mission of Europe elicits in a Tagore the conception of a civilizing mission for . . . Asia. In China the youth who has studied in Europe asked in their newspaper a question that sounds like a challenge to Europe: "Would you tell us whether civilization exists in your country?"

The Main Causes of the Social Ailment in Indochina

One may observe in the colonial policy in Indochina:

1. That not only does France not apply to Indochina the noble principles she has herself proclaimed; she also destroys the democratic tradition of Vietnamese society.
2. That France, which has granted freedom and the rights of the citizenship to men who, till yesterday, were still slaves, imposes slavery on a free people who already possessed a civilization at the time that the French were living in caves.

The European Prestige

Frenchmen who do not know much about things Indochinese think that it would be more correct to say French prestige. In Indochina two peoples meet each other: the French and the Vietnamese. It is a Franco-Vietnamese problem. But, in spite of all the efforts deployed by the French to prevent the Vietnamese from establishing contacts with other peoples of Asia, through the invisible and invincible strength of some great social law, the Franco-Vietnamese problem in Indochina is lightly veiled in the general atmosphere of a European-Asian problem. Owing to some inexplicable gaps in the wall built by the colonialists, the same law that presides over the transformation of China in contact with Europe presides over the transformation of Vietnam in contact with France. Except for the nuances due to local differences, the evolution of the thought, the uncertainties, the anxieties, the reactions, are clearly the same in the two countries.

The Vietnamese call the French "tây," meaning "Westerners," a word that designates all Europeans. Only the Vietnamese living near some important port cities can distinguish an Englishman from a Frenchman. For the French any white man of whatever nationality he may be who begs in Indochina puts to shame the whole French community in the colony. The Russians who pull rickshaws in Tianxin or who work in the bellies of big ships next to Asian seamen injure the self-esteem of the French in Indochina.

The European prestige is based neither on the moral nor the intellectual superiority of the Europeans over the Asians. It is based on the color of the skin alone. In Indochina it adds to the "prestige of the conqueror." It is also based on the arrogance and the egotism of the slave who becomes the master through brute force. It is nurtured by the colonial government because it is the only moral strength that sustains that government.

It is the European prestige that proposes that a European, as idiotic as he can be, could be a boss over a Vietnamese; the reverse situation is unacceptable. It is the European prestige added to the prestige of the conqueror that explains the advantages and privileges granted to Frenchmen: high salaries, innumerable scholarships given to European children for schools in the colony or in the metropole, while at most one or two Vietnamese can obtain a scholarship to finish their studies in France; the right to monstrously immense concessions of land, a thousand acres for a European and forty for a Vietnamese, etc., etc.

It is the European prestige that kills justice in the courtrooms; that prevents the judges from giving the same sentence to a Frenchman and a Vietnamese indicted with the same offense; that metes out very light sentences, sometimes even suspended ones, to Frenchmen who kill indigenous people. We shall not talk about the violence inflicted on indigenous people, violence that frequently ends in death. We cite two recent cases of homicide committed through "imprudence." In order to wake up a Vietnamese servant to accompany him in a hunting expedition, a Frenchman tickles him with his rifle. The rifle fires, and the Vietnamese was killed instantaneously. The case resulted in a fine of one hundred francs for homicide committed through imprudence. In Hanoi, a few days after the inauguration of the reconstructed Doumer bridge, the automobile of a certain David, employee at the Central Post Office, crushed a Vietnamese by the name of Do Van Ngoc. The owner of the automobile was fined one hundred francs—a suspended sentence—for homicide committed through imprudence. The attenuating circumstance is based on the ill health or the fragility of the pancreas of the victim: that is a classic case. It is in the name of the European prestige that the "bandit" Darles, a former resident of Tonkin, who had been the cause of the revolt at Thai Nguyen, was fined one hundred francs for all the monstrosities and the crimes of which he was officially acknowledged as the offender. Luong Ngoc Quyen was confined, Phan Chu Trinh told me, in a one-meter-high cell, where his limbs rotted in chains.[5] Through the pressure of events Darles was dismissed from his office, it is true. But he was given in compensation, so as not to harm the European prestige, an important position at the Distilleries Fontaine in Cochinchina. He could no longer reign in Tonkin, so he came to rule in Cochinchina. He rides every evening in an automobile with the governor [of Cochinchina], and he is satisfied with having the occult powers of a hidden eminence.

Individual Freedom

On the opposite side of the privileges granted to the conqueror there is something known as the "indigenat." It is a collection of regulations to which only the indigenous people are subjected. Thus, the governor-general [of Indochina], the governors or residents superiors [of each of the five different parts into which Indochina was divided], or simply the residents or administrators [chiefs of the provinces] have the right to put the indigenous people in jail without trial, for a certain period of time fixed by a legal text.

Upon an accusation, whether founded or unfounded, a Vietnamese can be thrown into jail even if he is seriously ill. That was how Thuan, accused of having contacts with the emigrants,[6] died in prison, because he had been incarcerated even though he was seriously ill. Thus, for instance, one was arrested during a severe illness and fortunately released later: Nguyen Van Hai of Ba Diem (Gia Dinh), former clerk in the service of the colonial government. Elsewhere they have confined for six months without trial a group of notables in My Tho. Phan Chu Trinh, the soul of the 1908 movement, was condemned to death. His sentence having been commuted, he was sent as a vulgar criminal to the penitentiary. Released, he was invited to visit France, where he was received by the more important officials and treated like a king. While he was being paid back for the injustices he had suffered and while he was enjoying his freedom, those who were accused of the same crime rotted in penitentiaries and died on a land reserved for bandits and assassins.[7] Phan Chu Trinh, when he was still in Annam, was locked up by a [French] customs agent with one of his students because of a trifling point of etiquette; they did not remove their hats when they passed by that agent's house.

Freedom of Thought

The freedom of the press does not exist in Indochina. In Cochinchina, where journalism has made some progress, there are two kinds of Vietnamese newspapers: the ones that are written in French and the others, written in Vietnamese.

The Vietnamese newspapers written in French are read only by the Gallicized minority. Because the law regulating the freedom of the French press does not apply to newspapers written in Vietnamese, Vietnamese newspaper publishers could always use the name of a Frenchman or a naturalized Frenchman to apply for the publication of a newspaper written in French. They then enjoy an unforeseen flexibility vis-à-vis the law; they are thus able to write freely, if, indeed, they have the courage to do so, for freedom of expression must pay a heavy price and the independent spirits are accused by the government of being anti-French, revolutionaries, communists, anarchists, bolshevists. I have to add quickly that it would be difficult, almost impossible, to find a Vietnamese who would be capable of giving a clear definition of communism or bolshevism.

The government tries to find a thousand reasons to fight against Vietnamese newspapers written in French that do not flatter it. For example, they could issue an interdiction to all the printers preventing them from printing the newspapers; they could also forbid officials of the government from reading them. And Vietnamese officials constitute a readership one cannot not take into account: nine out of ten Vietnamese who read newspapers in French are officials. As for those who read French and who are merchants or landowners, the administrators-chiefs of provinces could always call them into their office and advise them not to read certain newspapers. They would say things like this: "I think that wisdom advises you that it is in your own interest not to read this or that newspaper." The government reads the mail addressed to these newspapers in order to know the names of their subscribers.

La Cloche Fêlée, a newspaper I founded and to which I gave the subtitle "Medium of Propaganda for French Ideas," has gone through all these hassles. I must say that the means used by the government to harass the newspaper aim at exhausting the financial resources of the newspaper, which usually lacks capital and cannot afford not to have regular subscribers. One might add certain other dangers as well: I have been called a communist and threatened with violence by French journalists. I have been accused by the most-read French newspaper in Cochinchina, *L'Impartial,* a newspaper published by Representative Outrey,[8] of having fomented the assassination of Governor-General Merlin in Canton. It can be frankly stated that *La Cloche Fêlée* has not been the only victim.

Newspapers written in Vietnamese reach the masses, although they have no freedom whatsoever. In fact, all the newspapers written in Vietnamese "belong" to the government. Vietnamese have the right to apply for the foundation of a Vietnamese newspaper. There are, however, three conditions:

1. Authorization by the governor-general.
2. Each issue must be submitted to censorship before being circulated.
3. Interdiction to deal with political topics.

In fact, the permission from the governor-general is not easy to obtain. Only one permission has been given to a Vietnamese, Mr. Nguyen Kim Dinh. And yet he obtained it with the help of an influential Frenchman. All the other Vietnamese newspapers are "farmed out": a Frenchman applies for permission to publish a Vietnamese newspaper; he then yields the right to publish it to a Vietnamese with the condition that he may terminate the contract at any time it pleases him.

No regulation limits the power of censorship. The people at censorship cannot read a sentence without suspecting it to either have a second or third meaning or hide a clever invitation to rebellion. While the scandal about the concession of the Port of Saigon was going on, Mr. Lam Hiep Chau, the young editor-in-chief of the newspaper *Nong Co Min Dam,* was blamed by the chief of the Censorship Bureau for having offered a humorous compliment to those colonial councilors who had voted in favor of the concession. For making some far-fetched but unpleasant allusions to the same councilors and for speaking about "The Bell That Wakes People Up," the director of the *Dong Phap Thoi Bao* [French Indochinese Time] was threatened twice with the closing down of his newspaper.

The censorship bureau prevents newspapers from publishing anything concerning a flood in Cochinchina. It forbids printing certain news that it does not like from foreign countries, for example, news about the emancipation in some European colonies.

The third condition bordered on the ridiculous, for nothing defines precisely the word *politics.* The magazine *Nam Ky Kinh Te Bao* [Cochinchinese Economy] was closed down for having written an article attacking the concession of the Port of Saigon. The colonial government has simply decided that the question of the Port of Saigon belongs to the political domain and not the economic one.

As for the right to write books, I hereby publish the translation of a letter written by the former editor of the *Nong Co Min Dam* of whom we spoke earlier:

Saigon, 4 October 1924

With the collaboration of Tran Huy Lieu, I had the project of writing a series of books. To the first work in the series, we gave the title *Iron Pen*. No sooner had the first book been published than the Prosecutor of the Republic demanded that I come to his office on 13 September at four o'clock in the afternoon. That invitation shocked me to no end, as I could not guess its reason. I knew that it was about *Iron Pen* only after I arrived in the Prosecutor's office.

—What have you written here? he asked me.

—A book, I replied.

—This is not a book. It is a magazine. A book does not deal with so many topics. A book, from beginning to end, must deal only with one topic.

—No, Mr. Prosecutor. In a magazine or a journal, you see many signatures. In my book, you see only one signature . . . I write on diverse topics. This does not come from a group of writers. This is not a magazine.

—And are you going to publish this kind of works at regular intervals?

—That I cannot predict. Whenever I have finished writing a book, I bring it to the printer to publish it.

—Then, your work is a periodical. When a book is published twice a week or once or even twice a month, then it earns the qualifier *periodical*. It is the law here. Read it for yourself. If you transgress this law, you'll go to jail. If you want to publish a magazine, you would need a permission from the governor-general, or you submit it to censorship.

Subsequently, the Prosecutor wrote a text in French and asked me to sign it. He dismissed me right after, so that I did not have time to read everything that was written on that sheet of paper.

For the second volume of *Iron Pen* I followed to the letter all the directives given to me by the Prosecutor. I wrote on a single topic from beginning to end. Even then, the director of the printing office, Mr Testelin, told me to bring the galleys to the censor's bureau—that means to Mr. Arnoux, the chief of the Security Services. I yielded to the requirement and brought the galleys to the censorship bureau. Mr. Arnoux refused to sign them. He wrote a note to Mr. Testelin to the effect that the edict of the governor-general did not allow him to censure books. And he dismissed me.

I related all that to the director of the printing office, but he insisted that he dared not print my book without the signature of Mr. Arnoux on the galleys. The medical doctor blamed the sorcerer, and the sorcerer imputed the doctor. All that resulted in the fact that I could not publish my book.

I went afterward to the printing office of Mr. J. Viet, who informed me that he had just received a note warning him about the fact that he was forbidden to print any book written by Mr. Lam Hiep Chau. I asked him to show me the note. He refused, saying that he had no right to show secret papers from the government.

I ran right away to a Chinese printer in Cho Lon, the Asian Printing Office. The director told me:

—You have no permission from the governor-general. I don't dare print your book. I am afraid of going to prison.

I write to you this letter to demonstrate to you how just and right the French colonial government is.

The Prosecutor of the Republic has also ordered my collaborator, Mr. Tran Huy Lieu, to come to his office; he also threatened him. I'll tell Tran Huy Lieu to write to you so as to provide you with some new insights.

Yours

Lam Hiep Chau

Voilà where stands the freedom to write in Indochina!

The freedom of thought entails the freedom to speak and to assemble. Once, the Mutual Society for Education of Cochinchina invited me to give a talk at its headquarters. I accepted the invitation; officials who attended the conference were reprimanded. I received orders from the governor of Cochinchina, Mr. Cognacq, to come to his office. During our conversation in his office the governor declared with great authority: "There must be no intellectuals in Cochinchina." That sentence is in accordance with the program of "the horizontal plan in the development of education," as advocated by Governor-General Merlin.[9] It also bares the policy implemented by the colonialists in Indochina. In addition, the same Mr. Cognacq threatened to "use the last resorts," if I continued my propaganda. What "last resorts" did he allude to? As for the Mutual Society for Education, it received orders to "cut me down" (that's the word used by Mr. Cognacq) or to face dissolution. It could, however, not disavow me, since it had invited me. But the subsidy of three thousand piasters that had been regularly given to it by the government was discontinued.

I must add here that Chinese books have to be smuggled into Indochina, even when they were translations [into Chinese] of works by Rousseau or

Montesquieu. And if one keeps in mind the fact that the Far East is the only part of the world where people can be understood everywhere through a common system of writing—that is, the Chinese—and that, through it, a harmony of the mind could be created that united all the yellow races, one realizes the seriousness of that policy of isolation.

Acquisition by the Indigenous People of the Rights of French Citizenship

Of all the countries that compose Indochina only Cochinchina had been declared a "French territory." That's why some Cochinchinese have claimed for their compatriots living in Cochinchina the privilege of mass naturalization. It is rather intricate to satisfy this claim. The people, the peasants as well as the literati, are alien to that idea. They know nothing about the rights and duties of the French citizen. No preparation whatsoever has ever been made even by those who demanded that "mass naturalization." The masses themselves are opposed to that measure. Neither the peasants nor the literati could accept the label of "French citizen" without feeling morally ill at ease because of an old prejudice anchored in the race. The Vietnamese of the north and center share with them that feeling. That demand for mass naturalization, which is motivated by the desire to emancipate the Vietnamese race, has probably been suggested by some books in French law.

Here is how in reality the question of the indigenous people acquiring the rights of French citizenship arose in Indochina. Those Vietnamese who graduated from French primary schools were relegated to secondary positions reserved for them in the administration. Those who received a higher degree of education or who are trained in technical schools that constitute what they pompously call the University of Indochina occupied positions within the "lateral branches"[10] created especially for them. But there are those who have studied in France, in French universities, or in Higher Technical Schools in France. These people, once back in Indochina, in possession of their degrees, are not allowed, however, to apply for positions that are reserved only for French citizens with the same academic degrees. And so a Vietnamese with a master's or even a doctoral degree in law is not allowed to be a judge or even practice law. The legal reason for that situation is this: Vietnamese from Tonkin and Annam are French "protégés," while Cochinchinese are "subjects" of France; as such, they cannot enjoy the rights of French citizenship. They, therefore, cannot judge French citizens. In civil courts in Indochina there is a clear division between indigenous and European cases. I would like to bring in an observation. The English are reputed to be less liberal than the French. And yet, in India, Indians who have earned degrees in law not only can practice law as judges or lawyers; they also can judge British citizens, with the condition that the jury be entirely British.

In fact, as only two or three naturalizations are given out each year to the indigenous people and as these are not granted to graduates from institutions of higher learning in France, a class of dissatisfied intellectuals claims for itself the rights that come with the high academic degrees it has earned. In order to solve the problem of indigenous naturalization in its present situation, the Vietnamese who have been trained in French academic institutions must be given the right, not only the possibility, to be naturalized.

Freedom of Travel

Vietnamese are not allowed to travel to foreign countries. They cannot even go freely to France, nor can they travel without constraints within their own country.

Vietnam, since the French conquest, has been arbitrarily divided into three regions officially designated with the names of Tonkin, Annam, and Cochinchina. Until a few years ago one needed a passport in order to go from one region to another. That requirement of the colonial government elicited a few attempts at revolts. So they did away with the passport. But now, in order to go from one region of Indochina to another, we need a newly created identity card.

The widespread indignation of the people has also compelled the colonial government to do away with the passport for those who want to go to France. Today the identity card I mentioned earlier is sufficient. But a visa from the police is required. That visa is a ploy to hide the reality [that the colonial government puts up obstacles to travel to France by Vietnamese] from the metropolitan government. That visa can indeed be denied. [And that is how] the colonialists prevent the Vietnamese from going to study in France. They all say: "The more the Vietnamese study, the more they become anti-French." In reality, the Vietnamese who have been molded by French schools no longer feel, as the popular masses do, the hate of the conqueror, although almost all of them have become anticolonialist. The *Saigon Courrier,* a French newspaper published in Saigon, has publicly commended the colonial government for restraining as much as possible the exodus of Vietnamese students so as to block the way to what it called the "anti-France syndrome."

Individual Freedom, Freedom of Thought, Freedom of Travel

When a reform is needed for the life or the progress of a people, that people soon enough rises to claim it. But when these three freedoms are denied to the people, only silence and revolt remain. I know, however, that in 1789 the Rights of Man were proclaimed in France, and that's why I hope to be able to move the French people in the Metropole by showing clearly to them the absence in Indochina of these basic rights that protect the dignity of mankind. I know that in her present situation France cannot take care of her colonies unless it derives from it an immediate and material profit. I also know that present-day Europe has come to the point where human destiny is bound to the fortune of economic machineries over which mankind has no power, that the people's representatives of France have entrusted Indochina to its own fate and to a bunch of rapacious colonialists. But Indochina still finds itself at a sentimental stage in which the human will can still accomplish much.

No more in Indochina than anywhere else can human beings prevent events from occurring, but they are capable of avoiding foolish catastrophes. And there are twenty million people in Indochina. Not much determination is needed to administer Indochina and to avoid too many mishaps; what it takes is simply a small amount of goodwill.

It seems to me that it is not necessary to show to the French of the Metropole how the colonialists administer and exploit Indochina; how they constitute in that colony a real absolute monarchy with its royal court, its courtiers, its famous favorites, its feudal privileges, and its absurd wastes.

"Is it necessary," writes Henry Daguerbier, author of *Kilometre 83,*[11] "to quote again the endless series of follies committed in the name of [Governor-General] Beaudouin le Bokkhor: 3.600.000 piasters for a bath tub in silver, an electric piano, and paints that had to be scraped before it dries so as to harmonize them with the color of the skin of a new female occupant?" Must I also mention [Resident Superior] Robin's eccentricities: entire buildings that have been purchased at outrageous prices to serve as residences for his relatives and friends who do not even qualify for official housing; an important fleet of automobiles kept in the governor's garage, sometimes wrecked by the reckless driving of his kids. Probably, these are a few extravagant expenses that, in other times, would have looked like trifles. They would have elicited nothing more than a frowning of the eyebrows from the financial auditor, and then everything would have been forgiven and forgotten. But we live in a time when any unnecessary expense, however small, constitutes a serious mistake, when the dilapidation of the tiniest portion of the very hard-earned national treasury deserves a harsh penalty.

The absolute "monarchy" [in Cochinchina] is dominated by a group of financiers. Dr. Cognacq, the governor of Cochinchina, is assisted by the Grey Eminence Darles, the infamous "bandit" of Thai Nguyen, a real barbarian, more intelligent than the governor but blood-thirsty and endowed with a cruelty that is no less intense than that attributed to the most backward indigenous tribes of Africa. That Darles finds himself under the control of the Fontaines of the Indochinese Breweries—the same Fontaines to whom the monopoly of production of alcohol has been renewed without any consultation of the indigenous representatives [in the Colonial Council]; the Fontaines who, with the help of the official police, set the quota for the consumption of alcohol. That "trinity" represents the symbol of the power that subjugates Indochina.

There exists in Tonkin, Annam, and Cochinchina a council on which the indigenous people are represented. In Tonkin and Annam that council is called the Consultative Chamber, and in Cochinchina it is named the Colonial Council. The Consultative Chambers in Tonkin and Annam are purely consultative, and we fully know what that word *consultative* means in the mind of the colonialists.

The example I just cited of the renewal of the license to distill alcohol in Tonkin without any consultation whatsoever of the Consultative Council shows the importance accorded to that body by the government. The Colonial Council of Cochinchina enjoys a higher moral authority. It cannot go beyond the stage of making "wishes," however. In that council, furthermore, the Vietnamese delegates are always in the minority. Anyway, if one knows how the indigenous official candidates are chosen by the government to run for seats on the Colonial Council, how these same candidates are supported by that government during the elections, then one cannot say that the indigenous people are represented in the most important council of Indochina at all. For example, in the last colonial elections Mr. Huot, the unofficial candidate of the province of Tra Vinh, accused the government of having rounded up the Vietnamese notable-electors and confined all of them in a boat. They then anchored it in the middle of the river so as to immunize them from the propaganda of the unofficial candidates and to persuade them forcefully to vote for the official candidate, Mr. Phat. Mr. Huot went as far as accusing the government of electoral frauds. In spite of these accusations, and owing to smart maneuvers that the distance between Indochina and the Metropole allows them to operate, the official candidate, Mr. Phat, continued to represent the indigenous population of his electoral district.

As for the one person people call the deputy from Cochinchina, who sits in the National Assembly in Paris, he is but the representative of the majority of the European colony in Cochinchina. That majority is composed of French civil servants and eight hundred Hindus whom the colonialists have brought from India in order to defraud the electoral process. These Hindus, strangers to the life of the country in which they reside, contribute to the triumph of those who maintain them in life.

I will say nothing about how the colonialists destroyed the democratic ideal of Vietnam existing in the village. I will say nothing about the rotten royal court or about its ignorant mandarins, who are maintained in power as instruments of oppression. I will say nothing about the educational system in Indochina, from the primary school to the University of Hanoi. The Vietnamese who have been trained in European schools want for their country a slow but sure evolution, under the suzerainty of France, toward a constitutional regime as practiced in European nations. Among them a few enlightened patriots devote their efforts to attempt to show to the masses of the people the dangers of vengeance and the advantages of a patriotism that accepts, under the suzerainty of France, an evolution toward the political liberties promised in all the official speeches. They believe in a possible collaboration between the French and the indigenous people. But, if the colonialists stubbornly persist in refusing to the Vietnamese their basic liberties, they no longer can dissuade the masses from having recourse to violence, nor can they disapprove the action of the emigrants.

The long series of rebellions that have occurred since the establishment of French domination in Indochina testifies to the fact that the masses have not been paralyzed. The recent bomb launched in Canton by a Vietnamese, according to Chinese witnesses, shows that the revolt of the masses has found a base outside the Indochinese frontiers. Without doubt, the colonial government has taken all the measures to protect itself from revolts. Military duty will be required of all Vietnamese, except for the "civil servants." But the Tonkinese rifleman who poisoned the French garrison in Hanoi had served for ten to fifteen years in the Indochinese troops. And one day, in the face of all the other riflemen, he tore apart the medals granted him by the colonial government.

The absence of basic liberties unites all the educated Vietnamese for one common demand. Any important happening in eastern Asia will be likely to provoke a revolt by the masses.

Let France think about all these forces that are stretched to their utmost.[12]

Notes

1. SLOT III, 144.

2. It is interesting to note that the first motto of *La Cloche Fêlée* was "Medium of Propaganda for French Ideas. We are Frenchmen; anything that is grand, generous and noble is ours." Later in November 1925, when the political direction was given to Phan Van Truong, the motto then changed to "The people are everything; the State has but a secondary importance; the prince is nothing" (Mencius).

3. SLOT III, 55.

4. Their show of loyalty, therefore, can't really be considered as genuine.

5. See Document 8, in this volume.

6. The author probably means Vietnamese nationalist leaders who fled to China to escape French repression of their movement.

7. The author refers here obviously to the penitentiary located on the island of Poulo Condore, or Con Son. Sadly enough, that is precisely the penitentiary where Nguyen An Ninh was sent in 1940 to serve a sentence of five years. He never recovered his freedom, for he died there in 1943.

8. In addition to being the publisher of the newspaper *l'Impartial,* Ernest Outrey was also the representative of Cochinchina to the French National Assembly in Paris.

He was of course elected only by French citizens residing in Cochinchina. This is what the one-time governor-general of Indochina Paul Doumer remarked already back in the early years of the century. Speaking for Cochinchina, the only French colony of Indochina, which had the privilege of voting for its own deputy to send to the French National Assembly, the governor-general stated: "Thus, on a population of 3 million inhabitants, there were less than 2,000 voters and 3/4 of those voters were civil servants. That is what people call universal suffrage!" P. Doumer, *L'Indochine Française (Souvenirs),* 2d ed. (Paris, 1930), 72.

9. Horizontal plan of education: to develop education in the lower level (primary) rather than paying attention to the higher levels (secondary and tertiary) of education.

10. Lateral branches: within the civil service of the French administration there were different branches. The ones reserved for French citizens paid much more handsome salaries than branches reserved for the indigenous people. Under pressure from the newly educated native people, who were as well trained as the French but had to earn much less than their French counterparts, Governor-General Varenne instituted the "lateral branches," which are branches placed on the side of the French branches with remunerations not too much lower—but still lower—than those earned by French citizens.

11. I have not been able to locate this book.

12. The original, in French, published in the form of a pamphlet under the name of Nguyen An Ninh and the title *La France en Indochine,* by the Imprimerie A. et F. Debeauve, 35 rue Tournefort, Paris 5è, 28 pp. [April 1925], Prix 0.fr 50. This same text in French was also serialized in *La Cloche Fêlée* from 26 November to 7 December 1925.

L'Echo Annamite

The Wish List of the Vietnamese People
(1925)

In 1925 the French minister of colonies appointed Alexandre Varenne, a social-
ist deputy from the French National Assembly, to the position of governor-
general of Indochina. Before the governor-general's arrival in the colony,
Vietnamese intellectuals, politicians and journalists from Saigon got together
under the sponsorship of a committee composed principally of the indigenous
members of the Colonial Council, of the Municipal Councils of Saigon and
Cholon, of the Chambers of Commerce and Agriculture, and a group of con-
cerned citizens to draft a document in which they listed all their aspirations.
They presented it to Varenne on 27 November 1925 in what a headline in a
local newspaper proclaimed to be "A Grandiose Demonstration."[1]

This text is exactly what its title says: a list of reforms that constituted
essentially the political platform of a semipolitical party, semisocial club,
called the Constitutionalist Party, formed in 1917 by a group of Western-
educated and rich Cochinchinese landlords. The desired reforms amounted to
a sort of constitution to be granted by the colonial government that would
include drastic changes in the educational and judiciary systems, the acknowl-
edgment of basic human rights such as the freedom of the press, freedom of
association, freedom of travel, the reduction of the military service, and a
liberalized method of granting French citizenship to meritorious people from
Cochinchina.

Before taking up at length the questions that concern us here and in order to
broaden your understanding of them, it is necessary that we dispel a fundamental rumor you are going to hear repeated ceaselessly around you. That rumor
will attempt to persuade you of the inopportune or, at least, the premature
character of the reforms we request from you on behalf of our countrymen.
Indeed, people won't fail to inform you and to reiterate it to you ad nauseam in
private conversations as well as in newspaper articles that the minority, which

pretends to express the people's aspirations, is composed of a handful of agitated individuals and instigators, of a few modernized specimens of the elite class, or of a few disappointed but ambitious agents who only speak out their own personal opinions, while the mass of the Vietnamese people, satisfied with their daily bowl of rice, live in complete indifference, asking for nothing more.

But we, who come from all the regions of Cochinchina, who have ties with all the social classes of the population, we can assert that no reform, whether political or administrative, will leave the Vietnamese masses indifferent.

Bashful of authorities and distrustful of foreigners, the people enclose themselves in a prudent silence; if and when they come out of that muteness, it is only to say what they think will bring pleasure to these same authorities and foreigners. That's what makes the authorities think, probably with reason, that the people are satisfied with their conditions, upon which they absolutely wish no improvement. Of us, however, who are a part of them, whose long-range interests coincide with theirs, the people have no reason to be distrustful. They freely voice their opinions. We have summarized their aspirations here, in this wish list, which we respectfully submit to your kind examination.

In doing this, we are only guided by the concern for the interests that, from now on, will be common to both France and Indochina; our ultimate goal is to dissipate whatever feeling could provoke a mutual distrust between the French and the indigenous peoples. We try to move the two peoples closer together, aiming at realizing between them a sincere collaboration without which the development of our country is not possible. The most ambitious of our wishes are designed to obtain in favor of our countrymen the application of French metropolitan legislation to Indochina. To the eyes of the generous person that you are and to whom we submit this request, may our wishes appear in the entire sincerity we intended to put in them. They are naturally devoid of any subversive intention, and they carry with them not a shadow of a nationalistic thought. May they also make us appear as friends of France without any other ambition than the desire to see France realize, in the interest of Indochina, the civilizing mission she assigns to herself. May they not make us look like revolutionaries who receive their orders from Moscow.

I. Education

In Indochina, where education has always been highly regarded, questions related to it convey a very particular importance; they have generated impassioned controversies. Sixty-five years after the French conquest of Cochinchina, people are still bickering about the medium of instruction. They are still wondering whether to organize a system of education that is purely Vietnamese or whether it should be modeled on the system in use in the mother country. They still ask themselves about the aim that French education intends to attain in the colony, whether that system will instill in the indigenous people the real French culture while forming, at the same time, men of character, or will it solely deliver degrees to those who at best would fill subordinate positions in the various departments of the administration?

It seems to us essential to agree first on the real aim of public instruction. If it were true to the genius of France to spread the intellectual enlightenment all around, to share widely her culture and to train men—the word *train* is understood here in its noblest meaning—then one could draw a useful inspiration from some local examples with regard to the organization of education. We want to allude to the genuinely democratic organization of the teaching of Chinese characters applied in Vietnam before the French conquest. We also want to mention the example of some other countries in the Far East that, while being deeply committed to the old Chinese culture, have nevertheless succeeded in a relatively short time—that is, within a half-century—in assimilating the European culture without giving up a single characteristic of their national past.

The ability of the Vietnamese race to be educated and to assimilate a foreign culture—for example, the Chinese culture—is an undeniable fact; the ground is, therefore, very fertile for such a trial with a European culture, and that trial ought to be sincerely attempted.

Before the French establishment in Vietnam, the teaching of Chinese characters could be represented by a large pyramid; at its base are the many village schools, which are then complemented by those set up in the capital cities of each province. All that led to the examinations in the country's capital city: Hue. Instruction was free. It was accessible to all, and the humblest child of the common people could expect to be appointed to the highest position in the state government after he had successfully passed these competitive examinations. We regret we cannot say that much of the organization of our education in the present time.

Moreover, the example given by the countries still immersed in the old Chinese culture but willing to assimilate European sciences and technologies is no less suggestive. They started from the lowest level by spreading primary education widely among the popular masses. They hired as many teachers as were needed to teach all the children who were capable of learning. At the same time, they opened many secondary schools so as to select as great a number of students as capable of taking advantage of the higher education level, which then comes to crown the entire system. In the beginning technicians were recruited from Europe, while the elite elements selected from the student population in secondary schools were sent, with governmental scholarships, to be trained in schools in Europe and America. These students will, in time, become masters themselves, and, when they return to their native country, they will fill in these teaching positions.

That's the history of the countries of the Far East that are in possession of a doctrine in educational matters and determined to put that doctrine into practice so as to obtain a concrete result. Let us now turn our attention to Indochina.

1. The Question of Language

Should one use French or Vietnamese in primary education? Both languages have been suggested and with good reasons. These reasons, however, have in common one shortcoming: they are too absolute, and they do not address all the facets of the problem.

Those who advocate a wide diffusion of the French language are unaware of the difficulties Vietnamese students encounter in studying a language, the characteristics of which are totally different from their national idiom. Those who demand that the medium of language in primary education be Vietnamese forget the practical usefulness of French in a society that opens itself wider and wider to the influence of France. The director of education, caught between these two tendencies, has swung alternately from the one to the other, resulting in trials and errors within a domain that can ill afford to remain indefinitely an experimentation field. The effort Vietnamese children make in order to remember a foreign vocabulary will hinder their understanding of its essential properties so that, in the end, they will retain in their head, which becomes more and more confused, one incongruous jumble of broken formulas. They know nothing and recite by rote like parrots words and sentences, the meaning of which they are unable to comprehend. On the other hand, one cannot deny the fact that French, with its elegance, clarity, and precision, offers the ideal tool for the diffusion of Western culture. Those who want to modernize the old Vietnamese country are perfectly right to demand a wider use of the French language.

It would be possible, in our opinion, to reconcile these two divergent tendencies if the Franco-Vietnamese primary education were to be organized along the following bases:

a. Moral and practical knowledge will be taught in Vietnamese with an intensive use of textbooks written in the indigenous language. (In order to be plainly understood by Cochinchinese and Tonkinese students, the authors will use the local linguistic variables.)

b. French will be taught in the five grades of the primary cycle, simultaneously with Vietnamese. An increasing number of hours, at least five hours a week in the first year, will be devoted to it. In the beginning

French vocabulary is essentially of a practical level, but, as its scope is broadened over time, it will be used in all oral and written exercises of translation.

c. An examination called the Certificate of Primary Franco-Vietnamese Studies will be the sanction for this phase in the educational system. That examination consists of several written and oral tests in Vietnamese and at least one in French.

2. *The Necessity to Disseminate Primary Education among the Popular Masses*

It is a notoriously well-known fact that primary education in Cochinchina is not available to ensure the instruction of the 600,000 children of school age in a population of three million inhabitants. The 1924 statistics show a total of 72,000 children who were attending schools and taught by 500 teachers, of whom 125 are Europeans. It ensues that almost 90 percent of school-age children receive no other form of instruction than that given them in the families. It is, indeed, unreasonable to ask of the heads of families, the majority of them being simple farmers who are preoccupied with the earning of the family's daily food, to become teachers or schoolmasters at the same time. It would be, therefore, indispensable that our Vietnamese children be allowed to obtain some form of instruction from teachers and textbooks that are written in their mother tongue. If the French government is sincere in its desire to instruct and civilize the Vietnamese masses, then we earnestly request that it make up for lost time in putting a serious effort to promote primary education among the entire population.

The elementary level of primary education should be organized in the following fashion: establish teachers' schools to train as many indigenous schoolmasters as it needs to educate the mass of the Vietnamese youth of school age; open in every village or group of villages an elementary school that consists of the three first years in the primary education cycle. One should take the best advantage of the existing premises: communal house or pagoda. Everything will be done without complications, exaggerated expenses, or unnecessary red tape. The real education of the people begins in these schools, where, besides the common practical subjects such as reading in Vietnamese, arithmetic, and moral philosophy, the teacher will make room for physical education and hygiene. He may also extend his sphere of influence by instituting a few classes for adults in the evening.

Finally, next to primary education, which brings some culture to the mass of the children and allows them to pursue further studies, it is highly desirable that professional education also be developed. This education will be practical and shall be adjusted to the local needs of each agricultural or industrial region;

it will principally train workers and foremen, whom the country urgently needs if it wishes to improve the quality of its workforce in order to ready itself for the economic struggles of tomorrow.

3. *Superior Primary and Local Secondary Education*

The shortage in teaching staff we suffer in the elementary level of primary education is encountered again at its superior level. Each year, on average, of 1,200 students who pass the examination of the Certificate of Primary Studies, hardly 250 can find room in governmental schools. The rest of them attend private religious or nonsectarian schools.

At the end of four years of studies at the superior level of primary education, the Vietnamese students will still have to put in two more years to prepare for the local baccalaureate, which they absolutely need in order to get admission into the superior schools in Hanoi. Altogether the students must spend eleven years (five years of primary studies, plus four years of superior primary studies, plus two preparatory years for the local baccalaureate) before they can present themselves to the Hanoi schools, and only to the Hanoi schools, for the local baccalaureate is devoid of any value in the mother country and will not give access to any college or technical school there. Under these conditions wouldn't it be better to leave the organization of education as it is, as it caters to local needs, while at the same time institute a genuine secondary system that will be widely open to all children?

This system will be similar to the one in operation in the mother country and will, in ten to twelve years of studies, transform our youngsters into men, in the true meaning of that word. It will shape their mind, build up their character, as well as inculcate in them an authentic European culture. One can conceive for the Indochinese such an intellectual and moral education that will not uproot them from their environment and in which, in addition to the scientific knowledge, the Greco-Latin humanities will be replaced with the study of the languages and civilizations of the Far East.

Because that education will be given to our young in a language that is not theirs, it might be fair, in the beginning, not to impose any age limit for admission. In order to obtain a safe margin, one might institute an allowance of about two to three years.

4. *Higher Education*

At the apex of Indochinese education one finds what is called somewhat bombastically the "University" of Hanoi. It is less a university, in the European meaning of this word, than a collection of technical schools that train indigenous people to serve as assistants in the various departments of the government. It is the "nursery" for native civil servants.

Until such a time as a reorganized secondary education system would allow us to select without difficulties a great number of young students capable of receiving a superior education, we feel that it is better not to play with words. It is good to keep and improve the Hanoi technical schools to fulfill the aim assigned to them. The real superior education can only be found in France. We suggest that each year a number of elite students chosen through competitive examinations among the students of our secondary schools be sent there and that these students be dispersed among different Faculties and Grand Schools in the mother country. The development of Indochina and of its economic infrastructures demands the service of many technicians. It is necessary that they receive a full-fledged training. Until things change that training can only be obtained, in the best way possible, in the mother country's schools.

5. Private Education

In the previous pages we have insisted at length on the shortcomings of the government schools system in dispensing instruction to the Vietnamese youth. Because of this, a private system of education was created, and it developed daily in spite of obstacles put against its growth. If the pursued aim of the administration is the development of education in Indochina, then we formulate the wish that, as long as all the needs in educational matters are not yet fulfilled, a great liberality be adopted with regard to the opening of private schools.

II. The Reduction of the Military Draft

One of the reforms that stands closest to the heart of the Vietnamese is the reduction in the duration of the military draft. Presently it lasts four years. The military profession has always suffered from a low esteem among the Vietnamese, a people of essentially peasant extraction. In the past they took up arms only in the defense of their native land. Aside from cases of absolute necessity, they have always viewed military service as a form of slavery. Many of them, therefore, use all possible subterfuges in order to evade the draft: false vital statistics, corruption of the notables or civil servants, provoked or pretended illnesses, desertion, and the like. We must also acknowledge an obvious unfair practice through which frequently richer or more manipulative youngsters succeed in shirking their military duties, thereby throwing the entire burden on the shoulders of the less privileged. We must also observe the fact that the majority of the draftees are peasants, having two or three children at the time of their induction. For these poor souls to be away from their family for four long years represents a terrifying prospect, principally when they incur the risk of being sent out of Indochina, to Syria or Morocco, for example. Upon their return home they might very well find their families totally split up. Moreover, these rural persons become basically uprooted, and generally they do not go back to their agricultural work in the fields. They will be lost forever to agriculture, and that fact ought to be seriously taken into consideration when we envisage the future of this country, which is essentially an agricultural one.

In all fairness the Vietnamese people should be exempted from the military draft, since they are only French subjects, benefiting from none of the privileges that constitute the natural attributes of French citizenship. In case of necessity, wouldn't it be sufficient to require of them a reduced service of eighteen months or simply one year, as demanded of French citizens? Mr. Violette [a member of the French Parliament] has thought up that measure on behalf of the Algerians.

It would also be highly desirable to enlist the service of volunteers who can be attracted by the lure of large bonuses, even at the risk of having to establish a lottery system so as to fill up the contingent.

III. Freedom of the Press

Freedom of the press published in the Vietnamese language is earnestly and unanimously desired by the Vietnamese people. Being instrumental in the education of the masses, the press also effectively contributes to the advancement of the people. Furthermore, by allowing the public or the "man in the street" to express his opinion without any restrictions other than those imposed by social convention, for which the Vietnamese have an innate respect, the government secures for itself the surest means to know at any given moment the general tendencies, the frame of mind of the population, as well as its feelings on any particular problem. By establishing prior censorship on the media in the Vietnamese language, the government voluntarily denies itself an important source of information. Among the Vietnamese public opinion came into existence only very recently. In spite of the precautionary measures taken by the Censorship Bureau, that public opinion has become very strong particularly in 1919, at the time of the Chinese commercial boycott, and in 1923, on the occasion of the Monopoly of the Port of Commerce of Saigon-Cholon. The administration, however, systematically disclaims its existence so as not to have to deal with it, while, at the same time, trying to obstruct its expression. Under the pretext of forestalling attacks against French sovereignty, which has, in fact, never been put in question, and of safeguarding French prestige, the administration confines that public opinion within the narrow bounds of a regulation that is obviously inspired by a distrust of the people and a lack of generosity on the part of the government. All that contradicts the general tune of official utterances. The application of that regulation keeps the indigenous people in the belief, which is unfortunately often justified, that their aspirations and their grievances, being deprived of all means of expression, leave their government indifferent.

With increasing impatience, they bear the burden that heavily oppresses their thought and keeps them captive in a cage rendered narrower each day because of the forward evolution of their minds. Even new intellectual and moral needs cannot find their way of expression through the press. At the precise moment when Vietnamese society, influenced by modern ideas and French culture, finds itself prone to an important transformation, when social, economic, and political reforms are discussed everywhere, restrictive measures sentence the Vietnamese to silence.

The indigenous press, as well as the foreign [non-French] press, is regulated by the decree of 30 December 1898, which stipulates in its Article 2 that "the publication in Indochina of newspapers or other periodicals written in Vietnamese, Chinese, or any other foreign language shall not take place without the prior authorization of the Government General, which shall act only on the recommendation of the Permanent Section of the Superior Council of Indochina, replaced afterward by the Permanent Commission of the Council of Government of Indochina." Thus, the Vietnamese, who enjoy a few rights of French citizenship because they are considered French subjects—that is the case of the Cochinchinese, who are considered French subjects by the decree of 25 May 1881 relative to the naturalization of the indigenous people—are treated in their own country, which is placed under the tutelage of France, on the same footing as the foreigners.

The provisions of the decree of 30 December 1898 are made more restrictive by the institution of prior censorship, authorized by an administrative regulation that is warranted by no legal text whatever. It surely constitutes a very exceptional measure that is out of tune with repeated proclamations of "French peace" directed at a people whose loyalty has been highly praised.

Everything has been said about the disconcerted harshness of censorship in general. The censorship, imposed on Indochina, is much more arbitrary in its decisions than the one that existed in France during the war years. The evidence of that is provided by the scrupulously rendered translation of the enclosed front page article that was to be published in the issue of 6 November 1925 of the *Dong Phap Thoi Bao* [Time of Indochina], a newspaper from Saigon. In vain have we looked in this article for what could have incited the censorship to suppress it. Would it be because the article's first lines alluded to the joy felt by the Vietnamese at the news of your [Governor-General Varenne's] impending arrival in Indochina and to the hope it kindled in them, or could it be that because the article's author, while rendering homage to French colonial policy, later in the article put in question the intentions and projects of the "socialist" [Varenne] who is called upon to preside over the destinies of Indochina? We know not. At any rate the evidence is clearly established that politics, defined intentionally in its vaguest meaning, is positively off-limits to the press written in Vietnamese. Violations of that prohibition, which immediately results in the erasing of the faulty passages or of the entire article, may ultimately entail the temporary suspension of the newspaper or even its permanent closing. Obsessed by the threat of censorship, the reporters for the indigenous newspapers try to avoid in their writings even the least offensive words that may lend themselves to equivocal interpretations. They are thus reduced to indulge in dissertations about moral behavior when, whether out of their own interest or under order from their director or from the chief of the local administrator, they are not composing panegyric editorials in tribute to the master-distributor of administrative favors or of his friends or supporters.

The application of metropolitan legislation to Vietnam would fulfill the Vietnamese people's dearest wish. The law of 1881 and subsequent ones that anticipate and punish all the violations likely to be committed in this matter would suffice to prevent all the possible abuses. The local administration cites these possible abuses as pretexts for delaying the application of metropolitan regulations.

The abolition of administrative subscriptions, no matter what budget they are deducted from, constitutes the first step toward freedom of the press. The disguised favoritism shown by the administration [by subscribing] to some local newspapers leads to a double inconvenience of snuffing out their independence vis-à-vis the government or more precisely vis-à-vis the governor; it is simply a question of persons and also of placing them in a privileged position that makes competition impossible.

Administrative subscriptions to Cochinchinese newspapers alone amount to approximately 120,000 piasters, which are deducted from the irregular expenditures of several different budgets. The circular letter of interim Governor-General Montguillot, relating to the preparation of the 1926 budget, asked for an end to all these subscriptions; that request has not been acted upon so that favoritism and wastage still go on in Cochinchina while simultaneously persecution against the rare independent newspapers continues its way.

IV. Freedom of Association

While reproaching the Vietnamese for their lack of foresight and their egoism, the administration does nothing to stimulate or encourage their inclination toward association. Furthermore, everything seems to indicate that the administration even seeks to stop the development of that penchant. That's why, in spite of the vogue that sports enjoy among the indigenous people, the administration definitely shows, over the last years, a distaste for the creation of sporting societies. The same difficulties await the formation of regional associations of mutual help. All these organizations obtain with great difficulty or are simply denied the approval of their statutes, which need to be sanctioned by the chief of the local administration. In addition to the fact that the Vietnamese are allowed to found only these two kinds of associations, a formal provision contained in the statutes forbids them from discussing politics during their meetings. In the penal code that applies to the Vietnamese and other Asians the government has revived Articles 291, 292, 293, and 294 of the metropolitan code; these articles have been abolished in France. Their provisions have even been made more rigid by the addition of jail penalties.

The Cochinchinese population has demonstrated enough of its loyalty toward France so that France can now, in return, show her confidence by applying a more liberal regulation in matters concerning associations; why not apply to Cochinchina simply the metropolitan legislation?

V. Freedom of Assembly

In Cochinchina this matter is regulated by the law of 30 June 1881, which was made applicable to the colony by the order of 20 September of the same year. That law has been abrogated by that of 28 March 1907. But, as the last law was never promulgated [in the colony], it is still mandatory to issue a declaration before holding a public meeting.

Because of an erroneous interpretation of Article 291 of the Penal Code, which, in fact, concerns only permanent associations with daily meetings or with meetings on fixed dates, public meetings are practically forbidden for the Vietnamese people. The prior declaration stipulated by the law of 1881, which is still in effect, is different from an application for a permit, which is totally dependent upon the mood of the administrator, who may at his own sweet will reject or accept the request without any further procedure. Under these circumstances the promulgation of the law of 28 March 1907 in Cochinchina, which after all is a French territory, would be the most desirable solution. The people would receive that measure with gratitude, seeing it as a mark of liberalization on the part of the Protecting Nation vis-à-vis its subjects.

VI. French Naturalization

This is one of the many questions that interests very deeply the Vietnamese community of Cochinchina. In addition to the political, legal, and administrative privileges it confers to its bearers, naturalization constitutes a concrete criterion according to which people could fathom the liberal intentions the French government has toward the indigenous people. Is naturalization not the last stage toward total emancipation, a stage that confers to those who yesterday were still subjects the rights of man and those of the citizen? It allows them to take their place within the great French family.

In Cochinchina, after sixty-five years of French occupation, only three hundred indigenous people over a total population of three million inhabitants have been granted their rights as French citizens. That gives us a ratio of one to ten thousand. And the present policy of allowing only one or two naturalizations each year—it is what people refer to somewhat maliciously as the "constipated naturalization"—does not help in dissipating the uneasy feeling caused by their lack of confidence.

We must, however, first dispel a false rumor. The opponents of a liberal colonial policy have, for a long time now, raised the specter of "naturalization en masse," which we have never requested. If, indeed, naturalization does grant you rights, it also brings with it duties, and it would be but fair to admit only those who would be able to discharge of these duties. What are in fact the kinds of French subjects or French protégés who would be judged good enough to be admitted into the French city? Once these categories are well defined and the required conditions satisfied, then would naturalization still be a favor or simply a right?

To avoid arbitrariness and favoritism, we suggest that naturalization be granted de jure to those indigenous people who satisfy the conditions required by the law and who are willing to take advantage of it.

The attraction that naturalization exerts on the gallicized portion of the Vietnamese population can be readily understood if one considers the numerous and substantial privileges it brings to its seekers: freedom of thinking and writing; freedom of assembly and association; freedom of travel; freedom to bear firearms for hunting or for the defense of one's possessions against the raids of bandits when one lives in the middle of the Cochinchinese boondocks; the right to vote and to participate in all electoral consultations; a legal status defined by French law instead of by the insecurities of the indigenous civilian legal system with its courts of exception, the regime of "indigénat"[2] and of debt bondage; administrative privileges that prescribe that a naturalized French citizen earns, as a civil servant, five or six times more than a colleague of his who remains a French subject, even when the two of them have the same professional degrees, the same technical and working know-how. The simple listing of these privileges can explain the determination with which those of the Vietnamese population who are highly gallicized struggle to obtain them. As the civilizing mission of France in Indochina goes on, the following dilemma will impose itself on the colonial power: either to adopt a more liberal naturalization policy that grants citizenship to those who deserve it according to the law without distrust or reservation or to embark on a reform program of the status of the Indochinese subjects that would consist of more freedom; to bestow on the indigenous people a new legal status that guarantees to them the freedom of possessions and of persons; to perform a revision of the employment conditions for civil servants so that the masses can enjoy privileges hitherto reserved to a minority.

The problem of French naturalization in Indochina raises a number of political questions, even if one examines it only from the point of view of equity. There is no uniform law, as one could expect it, that regulates the naturalization of indigenous people in French colonies. Those living in Martinique, Guadeloupe, in the four French communes of Senegal, or in those of India are de jure French citizens according to an old law. Especially in India, in order to become French citizens, the natives have only to perform an act of renunciation, a simple formality in a court of justice, while in Indochina, in addition to certain academic degrees and anywhere from ten to fifteen years of loyal and good service, one still must go through complicated procedures, inquiries and counter-inquiries with opinions to be expressed by five or six layers of administrative offices, before an application for naturalization can be introduced to the Ministry of Justice in France. The consequences of that kind of policy are being felt soon enough. Owing to a great influx of Indian immigrants arriving in the Cochinchinese colony, they constitute an important block that overlaps with the European contingent to dominate the electorate in Cochinchina. It results in a rather paradoxical situation in which, under the protection of republican France, three different races live together in Asia; their political power is in inverse proportion to their number. Concretely speaking with figures, the electorate of Cochinchina for the legislative elections consists of three thousand voters, of whom two thousand are Europeans, seven hundred Indians, and three hundred naturalized Vietnamese French; the latter are supposed to represent a population of three million. Of the three ethnic groups that form the electorate, the European component is made up by a majority of civil servants who never think of settling down in this colony. The harshness of the climate, periodic paid vacations, numerous changes in the place of work—all that incites them to rather think of a well-earned retirement in the home country. The Indians have always looked at Indochina as a colony of transit. As for the three million Vietnamese who are riveted to their land and who provide all the revenues for the budgets, they have no say in the matter. Since the colonies are represented in the French Parliament, since the colonized people such as those of Martinique, Guadeloupe, Senegal, or India have been allowed to send their representatives to the mother country, what's wrong if the Vietnamese people have a representative of their own to take care of their interests in the metropolitan government? Are those interests not those of the entire country? If the future of Vietnam is tightly bound to that of France, why, then, the discrimination that deprives numerous people of an effective representation in the parliament?

The government has been apprehensive about the fact that with a great number of naturalizations, the elected assemblies in the colony will be dominated by the Vietnamese majority, and, thus, the interests of the French minority run the risk of not being well cared for as far as local politics are concerned. That fear is not properly founded at all as long as the country lives under the regime of decrees and as long as the legislative and executive powers are centralized in the hands of an administration that is powerful and jealous of its own prerogatives. That same administration can at any time exercise its rights of tutelage and accommodate the particular demands with the general good.

On the other hand, if the government were sincere enough in its policy of association, then that policy must not remain a noisy but empty concept; it'd better be based on the reality of facts. The Vietnamese are principally interested in the unending progress and prosperity of their country. The naturalization of a greater number of their fellow countrymen ought not be seen as a threat. On the contrary, the Franco-Vietnamese collaboration should be a strong factor of progress in all areas, and that collaboration will be all the more effective and widespread if it is freely adhered to. Then there is no need to oppose, as many have done, French to Vietnamese interests, which are really interdependent and strongly bound together. No European business could prosper if the country were in a recession or if the misery and starvation rendered the resources scarce that feed the diverse budgets and reduce the purchasing power of the Vietnamese consumers.

Another aspect of the naturalization problem concerns the would-be civil servants. It is feared that, subsequent to a liberal policy of naturalization, the mass of naturalized Vietnamese will fill in all the positions hitherto reserved for the French. If one looks at it in terms of social equity, how can one react to the following dictum that brings up a conclusion that is irrefutable in its logic? The dictum says: "To equal work, equal salary." Here one must take into consideration the general good that dictates that a great portion of budgetary resources not be set aside to maintain an army of civil servants. These resources should be devoted, rather, to the economic development of the country, to the improvement of the people's health, and to its intellectual and moral betterment. There should then be a budgetary adjustment so as to fairly pay the technical competence that the colony sorely needs while, at the same time, apportion to useful activities the remaining resources of the budget that cannot go on increasing without heavily burdening the taxpayers. The means to prevent an overinflation of civil servants, it seems to us, are numerous: the creation of "lateral" ranks for the indigenous functionaries; the abolition of subordinate employments for Europeans and Indians of French citizenship; the revision of salaries; and, most of all, the organization of competitive examinations for the recruitment of civil servants so as to eliminate incompetence or favoritism. Thus crashes down a long-held objection against a more massive naturalization program.

It might be possible that liberal reforms for the people in general and adoption of the principle of competitive examinations open to all competent people for the recruitment of civil servants would render moot the problem of French naturalization in Indochina.

VII. Justice in Indochina

A. Codification of the Vietnamese Civil Law

France, which committed herself to maintaining order in Cochinchina for the Vietnamese people, has promulgated there the French penal code. So, for penal affairs there is a code of law that the Vietnamese can easily consult. It is not so for indigenous civil matters: no code of law exists here. In principle colonial courts must apply, in civil cases concerning the indigenous people, the laws promulgated during the reigns of Vietnamese rulers such as the kings of the Le Dynasty [1428–1789] or the emperor Gia Long [1802–20]. Those laws, in addition to being unknown to most of the Vietnamese people, no longer reflect the customs, the mentality, of the Cochinchinese people of today.

For the lack of a precise text that would be considered a legal code, the judges themselves are placed in an embarrassing situation: their decisions in indigenous civil cases are not systematized; their sentences are at times contradictory. This simply confuses the Vietnamese people.

To improve upon the situation we suggest that a commission be empowered to prepare a draft of a civil code for the indigenous people to be applied to Cochinchina. The commission shall be composed of three French judges, who would have practiced law in Cochinchina for more than five years, two Vietnamese judges, one high official of the government, and two judiciary clerks, selected from among the highest-ranked interpreters of the court administration. That commission will prepare, without delay, a civil code applicable to the indigenous people.

B. Abolition of the Debt Bondage

Debt bondage has been abolished in France by the law of 22 July 1867, which has been proclaimed applicable to Cochinchina, French territory, by the decree of 12 August 1891. The promulgation of that law was done in the colony on 9 October 1893. From these texts it is very clear that the intention of the French Parliament is definitely to abolish debt bondage not only in France but also in the French colonies.

Taking back with one hand what the law has given out with the other, the decree of 31 July 1893 and the ordinance of the governor-general of 16 March 1910 proclaim that debt bondage is applicable only to the Vietnamese and other assimilated Asians. Foreign debtors, French or Indians, continue to enjoy the immunity regime. The Vietnamese in their own country are not protected by the courts against usurers of all races; ironically, they are in fact far less privileged than the indigenous people of Madagascar or Equatorial Africa.

We therefore request that, in the name of equity, the law should apply equally to all as far as debts are concerned and that debt bondage be abolished in Indochina.

C. Reform of the Jury in French Criminal Cases

When a criminal case, instead of concerning only French citizens, involves French and Vietnamese, it is the criminal court that is declared competent. That court's composition is as follows:

—3 career judges
—4 French jurors or French assessors.

Such a composition of the jury has frequently led to legal decisions that deeply confuse the simplistic mind of the indigenous people as well as shake their innate sense of justice. We should like to mention the numerous acquittals or very light sentences pronounced against Europeans who have committed murder against indigenous persons.

To put an end to such a situation, in fact, very detrimental to the good name of French justice, which should reign serene, impartial, equal for all, we wish that the reform of the jury in Franco-Vietnamese cases that are heard in criminal courts be studied and put into effect. We advocate the formation of a mixed jury, composed of an equal number of Europeans and Vietnamese, the latter may be either French subjects or citizens.

D. Free Access to the Bar

Under the present system indigenous law degree holders are not allowed to open a law office outright in order to practice law. They are instead required to work for three years as a secretary in an established office of a French attorney-at-law. Under these conditions the Vietnamese have no free access to the Cochinchinese bar because either the attorneys need a secretary who one day will become their partner or they want one who will be able to stand in for them during their absence from the colony. In either case, they hire a French lawyer.

It is, however, no less legitimate a complaint for the Vietnamese to hold that the present bar system leads to unjust consequences for them. To satisfy their rightful wish, why not make access to the bar free by abolishing the compulsory training stage? Free competition will by itself eliminate those who are incapable, if any.

VIII. The Representation of the Indigenous People

The general directives of French colonial policy as well as your own plan call for a wider and deeper participation of the Vietnamese in the management of the affairs of their own country. That principle being accepted, we dare present a few wishes that will make its application more certain.

The first wish concerns the equality in the number of elected French and Vietnamese members in the local assemblies. It is a fact that, speaking in their mother tongue, invested with the prestige of a winner, a prestige that is difficult to define but nevertheless very real, in possession of a greater personal and educational value, drawing upon an undeniable experience in public affairs, the French representatives in these assemblies enjoy as compared to their Vietnamese colleagues a genuine superiority made even more noticeable by their greater number. For example, at the City Council of Saigon, the French population is represented by twelve members and the Vietnamese people only by four. The Chamber of Agriculture is composed of four indigenous members elected by eighteen hundred voters representing one million cultivators and twelve French members elected by seven hundred voters. The Chamber of Commerce counts also four indigenous and twelve French members.

The composition of the Colonial Council is, we must admit, well on its way toward equality between French and indigenous membership: it consists of ten French and ten elected indigenous members. But when two delegates from the Chamber of Agriculture and two delegates from the Chamber of Commerce are added to the council, then they tip the scale in favor of the French side.

In the Dutch East Indies and in the Japanese colonies (Formosa and Korea), the indigenous people occupy the same number of seats in the elected assemblies as the colonizers. Is France, which always boasts about her long tradition of liberalism, going to be overtaken by two nations that are in fact latecomers in the area of colonization?

We, therefore, request that, in the local mixed assemblies, the French and indigenous populations be represented by the same amount of deputies. Especially for the Colonial Council, we would reach that equality by simply adding to the elected members two indigenous delegates, one each from the Chambers of Agriculture and Commerce. These two chambers will then send to the same council one French delegate each, instead of two, as previously done.

After that general reform are the changes we should like to see brought into the organization of the existing assemblies, which follow.

A. Provincial Councils

As of the present day, the provincial councils do not enjoy the desirable degree of independence from the chief administrator of the province who represents the central government. The majority of the council members do not speak French; they also tend to be shy and intimidated as they come from the countryside. They are elected by the village notables, who are easily influenced by the suggestions, usually turned into orders, coming from the provincial chief. Impressed by this provincial chief, who by right presides over these assemblies, the elected members sheepishly endorse the views of the administration. They know too well that a nonconformist attitude, even if it were mitigated with politeness and with the traditional respect for authority, would likely not be beneficial to their career. It all results in a restrained attitude deriving from their timidity. In order to allow the Provincial Councils to express their genuine and sincere feelings as well as the wishes of the people to the administration, we request that they be elected by an electoral college similar to that of the Colonial Council but restricted within the borders of the cantons where the elections take place.

The president of the council will be chosen from among the members of the council and elected by them. The chief of the province will continue to play a supervisory role in the discussions and workings of the assembly as the representative of the government. Finally, the meetings of the council will be open to the general public.

B. Colonial Council

The limited powers of the Colonial Council have been further reduced by the decree of 9 June 1922, which reorganizes the highest elected assembly in Cochinchina. It would be too long to enumerate here all the reasons why that reduction had been imposed upon the assembly.

It seems to all concerned, French and Vietnamese alike, that it would be necessary to request for the council the same attributions enjoyed by the General Councils in the mother country. The French Colonial Councilors [of Cochinchina] have been elected precisely on that platform. Over the past four sessions of their tenure they have made and reiterated that wish, which has been endorsed by the indigenous members as well.

Moreover, in the new and poor provinces, where education is still not really available to the people, not enough candidates seek elections, while too many of them run for office from rich and more developed provinces. That situation restricts drastically the choice of the voters, who, for the lack of good candidates, give their votes to those who are not well qualified. Not very confident in their own merits, these same candidates have the tendency to purchase votes that can ensure them success at the polls. At the last elections the division of Cochinchina into five districts facilitated that kind of manipulations. It seems to us, therefore, high time to request, in the interest of the country and in order to preserve the value of the votes, the establishment of a single electoral college and the adoption of an electoral list. Each voter will vote for ten indigenous members instead of three, as in the past. The significant number of voters (forty to fifty thousand) will make electoral frauds impossible or at least reduce their occurrences. The experiment made in the last elections of the Chamber of Agriculture has yielded conclusive results: no corruption attempt worthy of notice occurred. Furthermore, the request we express here has been adopted by a great majority, almost unanimously, by the Colonial Council at its session of 24 November 1925.

C. Council of Government of Indochina

Cochinchina sends to the Council of Government, along with the other components of the [Indochinese] Union, only one indigenous member; generally that member is an old retired civil servant, appointed by the administration.

This part of the country that contributes the most to the income of the general budget should be more effectively represented in the highest assembly of Indochina. It would befit it to be given three indigenous deputies elected by a restricted electoral college composed of the indigenous members of the Colonial Council, of the Saigon City Council, of the Municipal Commission of Cholon, of the Provincial Councils, and of the Chambers of Agriculture and Commerce. Their tenure should last four years.

VIII. Assistance to Agriculture

A. The Agricultural Credit

Hitherto, unlike what happens in France and in other colonies, the agricultural credit has not benefited from fees imposed on the bank of emission, in this case the Bank of Indochina. When the license for this bank is to be renewed, the government has suggested, with the accord of the Bank of Indochina, the creation by this bank of an Agricultural Bank with an initial capital of one million piasters. We request that such a project not be lost sight of and that it receive, when its time comes, a satisfactory solution to the benefits of Cochinchinese agriculture.

Meanwhile, one could improve upon the availability of credit given by agricultural unions by simplifying the procedures of application for loans. The measures taken by the administration in view of this should be executed as soon as possible. They will familiarize the indigenous with a loan they have not been able to appreciate until now at its right value. They don't know the real advantages of that loan for which they rarely apply because of the complex and loathsome procedures for its application.

B. Regularization of Land Concessions

In order to stimulate the exploitation of this country and to give to the cultivators the necessary guarantees over the lands they have reclaimed from the bushes and forests and which they have watered with their own sweat, there is a great need to regularize without delay their situation by granting them definite concessions or by selling those pieces of land to them. Many applications for concessions have remained unsolved for many years in the offices of the inspectors. It behooves you to have them examined and acted upon as soon as possible so as to prevent acts of seizure and eviction on the part of the unscrupulous few who make light of the rights of other people and the social peace of the country.[3]

Notes

1. *L'Echo Annamite,* 28 November 1925.

2. *Indigénat:* as defined by Nguyen An Ninh, in *France en Indochine,* Document 9, in this volume. "It is a collection of regulations to which only the indigenous people are subjected." It is therefore some sort of a special code of law with binding effect only on the natives: it represents, as one could guess, the supreme form of discrimination.

3. The original text of this document, which was written in French, was serialized in *L'Echo Annamite,* 28 and 30 November; 1, 2, 3, and 4 December 1925. It has also been issued in the form of a pamphlet with the same title, published in Saigon in 1925.

Pham Tat Dac (1911–35)

An Appeal to the Soul of the Nation
(1926)

The author of this long poem, Chieu Hon Nuoc *(An Appeal to the Soul of the Nation), is a fifteen-year-old high school student. Before the publication of this appeal, he had been involved in the student protest movement following the trial of Phan Boi Chau (1925) and the death of Phan Chu Trinh (1926). As soon as the poem was published, it was immediately banned by the colonial authorities and its author arrested and detained in the Central Prison of Hanoi for two months before being put on trial for subversive activities. He was acquitted, probably because of his young age, by a correctional tribunal for acting without full knowledge. The publisher of the pamphlet, however, being a full-grown individual, was sentenced to six months in prison. Although acquitted, Pham Tat Dac was nevertheless ordered to spend three years in a penitentiary colony for minors, the length of time for him to attain his majority. For bad conduct, inciting other inmates to beat up the guards and to vandalize the installations of the penal colony, Pham Tat Dac was subsequently transferred back to the Central Prison in Hanoi, from which he was released in 1930. According to the rumor that circulated around Hanoi, while under detention Pham Tat Dac was given some slow poison that devitalized his health beyond any possibility of restoration. He died five years later, in 1935, at the age of twenty-four.*

Following are some excerpts from his poem, which is undoubtedly one of the best known among Vietnamese patriotic texts of the twentieth century. It became very famous principally because of what happened to it and its author. In my opinion the poem is rather lengthy and repeats itself in many places. The enthusiastic reception of this document by the people of the time apparently did not result from the quality of the writing but from the youth of its author and from the general atmosphere of patriotic fervor kept alive by many eventful happenings.

A journalist wrote the following comment on the fate of the young poet and his poem in L'Annam, *on 23 June 1927: "So the young poet was acquitted by law; he was, however, condemned in fact . . . This is a political trial in which, in spite of all the bias one could muster, one was unable to find the slightest trace of a crime. The poem,* Appeal to the Soul of the Nation, *constitutes a cry of despair, let out by a seventeen-year-old voice that tells of the tribulations of the fatherland and the lethargic sleep of the countrymen . . . Our French protector, feeling threatened to be thrown into the sea by the Vietnamese any day, see powerful revolutionaries even in our young children, capable of rousing with one scream an entire people . . . Until he is twenty, the young writer will live among a perverted youth . . . For three years, he will be removed from the affection of his parents; he will receive no education and will be assigned to vile tasks under the yoke of brutal guardians."[1]*

> Twenty-five million children and adults, men and women
> For four thousand years, we descend from the Hong Bang[2]
> We have homes, where have they vanished
> We have a country, why is it now lost
> O Heaven!
> A look at our conditions induces laughter then tears
> We want to turn to action
> Tear the sky with an echoing shout
> Melt our bodies the same as our country and homes.
> O compatriots, children of Dai Viet[3]
> You have a body but no mind,
> You while away days and months, waiting for opportunities.
> Frustrated, you rely on others
> But who will help you?
> Now that wind and waves from all four corners are raging more
>   violently than ever
> Are you going to cling to your old habits?
>
> Wake up fast lest it be too late.
> In the past, our many heroes
> Brought their exploits everywhere on earth and ocean
> In one hand they held the destiny of our land
> Their reputation has lived through thousands of years
> Their glory showered the children of Lac Long[4]
> Our mountains and rivers remain picturesque,
> Our grass, our trees grow strong and green
> Our people look like people
> With ears, eyes, the same as anyone else
> Such is the landscape, such are the emotions
> Why live, to what purpose?

In such quandaries, what is left of human dignity
In such state, what remains of the land?
The present predicament makes my heart wither
Our mountains and rivers prompt my tears to roll down
Alone, in the loneliness of the night
I yearn to paint with my blood our mountains and rivers
The wind drifts into the room and sways the bleak lamp
The bird with its cry "Fatherland" shames the heroes
Gnawing my teeth, swallowing my pride
I summon the old soul to come home to our mountains and rivers

Soul, o soul! The children of Hong and grandchildren of Lac[5]
Have long gone astray; they have endured hunger and thirst
For a long time, their bodies have decayed
For a long time, their vitality has crumbled
Because of you, soul
Gazing at the four seas, our heart aches
Scanning the five continents, soundless, we cry
The night is late; all is quiet; the sky serene
If really sacred, o soul, you will come home.
Once back home, stop being lost in dreams
Right away, you must improve upon your past behavior
Back home, try to help
The children of Hong Lac and their land
What is more glorious
Than to die in battle?
Back home, you do whatever you will
Not a moment of hesitation or it will be too late
Success and failure dwell usually in everything
No indecision, or your mission will slip by
Soul, once back home, you must give up all your rights
Give yourself entirely to our country
Even if your flesh be thrashed, your bones crushed
Enthusiasm and determination should remain the same as in the past

Here now, soul, you should strengthen your courage and sharpen your
     intellect
Don't be tempted by delicate food
Everyday, be satisfied with pickles, salt, vegetables, bean sauce
They are our own, much better than wine and meat provided by others.
Soul, this is what our country looks like
Let me tell you what has happened to the race of Lac Hong while you
     were away

At night, people never ceased weeping
Daytime, they didn't stop moaning
Ready to shed their blood, yet they hid themselves in the mountains
Others chose exile in faraway lands
Some forsook families, homes
Worries turned the hair of still others into snow
There are also those who are willing to be buffaloes and horses
Servants and even slaves
And those who sell out their country, their race
Sacred soul, you will observe all that for yourself
Our mouths are unable to speak up
They tied them up, our arms and legs
In darkness, we could not distinguish good from evil
We hardly understood what went on around us
In this silent and late night, do you feel any bitterness, resentment at
    what I've described to you?
In my veins flows the same red blood as in my compatriots'
Also made of flesh and bones, the same descendants of Dragon and
    Immortal.
Observing the state of our country, I lose my mind
Our people's disposition drives me crazy
Yet I cannot remain calm
So, with all my heart, in only a few sentences
I sent you my invitation
You received it; you read it; your heart was troubled
You heard it, and you accepted to come home
O, soul, do not be half-awake, half-dreaming
Don't lose your time fathoming what's shallow, what's deep.
Soul, simply come back to your old land.

You shall eradicate the greedy and the cruel
You shall do away with those who harm their fellow compatriots
Those who lined their pockets with the people's silver and gold

Once you are home, people will wake up
No longer will they be stupid and idiots
No longer will they labor from early morning till late at night
No longer will they be exposed to sun and rain.
Please, soul, hurry, hurry up back
I am waiting
I look forward to your return
Please, come back so we may together adorn our land

You will educate the children of the Dragon and the grandchildren of
   the Immortal.
The long night will soon be over but the wind's still blowing
No more oil for my lamp, though my tears are still a plenty
Questions for you pile up in my mind like mountains
Whenever you are ready, I am ready to help you
It is true that I'm not too intelligent
But not a complete idiot either
My heart simply is filled with love
That's why I hope, I wait, I call for your return
The night is almost over, the place deserted, silence everywhere
If really sensitive and sacred, you will certainly return
Here I end my letter
My ears are attentive to what my mouth utters
But when my mouth stills, then my eyes swell up with tears
The tears blotch the written letters
We decide to print a thousand copies of the smeared text
And distribute them to the public
After reading the text, the public will be transformed
Transformed, they will wake up other people from near and far
Urging them to pay their debts to our mountains and rivers.[6]

Notes

1. SLOT V, 17.
2. The Hong Bang was the legendary dynasty that was supposed to have ruled over Vietnam from 2879 B.C.E. to 258 B.C.E. through eighteen kings, all of whom bore the name Hung. Ironically enough, as in France, but centuries later with Louis the Eighteenth, the Hong Bang king who lost his throne was also King Hung the Eighteenth.
3. One of the many names of Vietnam.
4. Lac Long: name of the legendary first ancestor of the Vietnamese people. His full name is Lac Long Quan. According to the legend, he was the founder of what was to become Vietnam and, therefore, the first ancestor of the Vietnamese people. Lac Long Quan married a fairy by the name of Au Co, and from their union were issued a hundred eggs; one hundred children hatched from these eggs. One day the couple decided to separate. Lac Long Quan then said to his wife: "You issue from the race of fairies or immortals, so why don't you take fifty of our children and go to live in the mountains. As for me, I am from the race of dragons [his name has the word *long,* which means "dragon"] I take the other fifty children and live on the plain along the shores." This gives the Vietnamese the reason for saying that they are children of a dragon and grandchildren of an immortal: "con rong, chau tien."
5. *Hong* and *Lac: Hong* stands for *Hong Bang,* the legendary dynasty of Vietnam. *Lac* is the tribal name of Vietnam; the full name of the tribe is supposed to be Lac Viet.

Lac can also represent the first name of Lac Long Quan, the first ancestor of the Vietnamese. See notes 2 and 4.

    6. To do this translation I have relied on two texts that are slightly different from each other. One can be found in *TVYNVCM,* 542–46, and the other in *Tho Ai Quoc* (Hanoi, n.d.), 5–17. The last-mentioned title is preserved in the National Library, Paris, and also in the National Library in Hanoi.

DOCUMENT 12

Phuc Viet and Vietnam Hon

An Appeal to the League of Nations for the Right of
Self-Determination of the Vietnamese People
(1926)

The years 1925–27 marked a turning point in the anticolonial struggle of the Vietnamese people, which saw the Confucian generation of scholars-activists being replaced by the Western-trained young professionals. Phan Boi Chau was arrested, tried, and condemned to death in 1925. Although his sentence was commuted, the trial did not fail to arouse the sympathy of the Vietnamese masses. The emotion had not had time to subside when Phan Chu Trinh died, a mere three months later, in March 1926. His funeral, combined with the sentence against Phan Boi Chau, elicited a general reaction by the population resulting in strikes by the workers, walkouts by the students, boycotts of French merchandises and merchants by the consumers. A year later, as people congregated to celebrate the first anniversary of Phan Chu Trinh's death, their patriotic fervor was further rekindled by the passing away of Luong Van Can, one of the founders of the Dong Kinh Nghia Thuc (Tonkin Free School) (see Document 3). The colonial authorities, as expected, forcefully repressed these activities, arresting thousands of people, incarcerating them without trial, dismissing students from their schools, and discharging hundreds of workers. All these represent the "serious events" mentioned in this appeal. The authors of this appeal, as listed at the end of the document, are the Phuc Viet (or Parti Annamite pour l'Indépendance Nationale [PAI]: Vietnam Party for National Independence) and Hon Viet Nam *(Soul of Vietnam), a newspaper that changed to another title because the French authorities prohibited its publication under the old one. These titles were* Phuc Quoc *(National Restoration),* L'Ame Annamite, La Nation Annamite, Quoc Hon *[National Soul] or* Viet Nam Hon *[Vietnamese Soul] or simply* Viet Nam. *There were, however, no more than one or two issues under each title. The newspaper was printed and circulated in France, but quite a few copies were smuggled back into Vietnam.*

The serious events that occurred recently in Indochina, the news of which has shocked the public in the mother country, are caused solely by the national oppression and the social exploitation of a people of twenty million souls who have been subjugated for a half-century by colonialists and administrators.

Our Political Situation

We do not have the freedom of thought, of publication, of education, of travel and emigration, of association and assembly. A special kind of justice system is reserved for the indigenous people, who are not able to exert any effective control over the budget of their own country. Most of our schools have been destroyed and few of them replaced. Finally, racism crushes us.

Upon Mr. Varenne's arrival in Saigon on 27 November 1925, seven hundred Vietnamese representing all the social classes and full of confidence in the collaboration policy advocated by this new governor-general presented to him a wish list. Unfortunately, Mr. Varenne has not complied with the wishes of the representatives of our people.

Our Social Situation

We are subjected to the poll tax, to forced labor, and to the salt tax. No legislation protects our workers, and it is a well-known fact that children less than twelve years old, of both sexes, are employed on rubber plantations and in coal mines.

The government compels our humblest villagers to buy opium and alcohol in big quantities.

As seven-eighths of the Indochinese budget goes to the maintenance of civil servants, public works of the first necessity are neglected. That is why our dykes have never been cared for by the state to the point that, every year, the rural population of Tonkin has their crop, their houses, and their cattle wiped out by flood.

This is approximately the present condition of our people.

Comparison with Our Neighbors and with Our National Past

Completely different is the condition of our neighbors who have remained independent. Siam, for example, maintains an army of 400,000 men, enjoys a stable government, and possesses a railroad network that crisscrosses its territory. Yet, fifty years ago, the Siamese were not more advanced than the Vietnamese.

On the other hand, try to visualize how Vietnam was before the French conquest. It was an independent country that knew how to earn the respect of its neighbors, although it despised war and military matters. For its national defense it relied solely on its militia. It was a democracy that, though under the appearance of an absolute monarchy, was endowed with the autonomy of the villages, with an unencumbered and free education system at all levels. It had also gotten rid of feudalism as well as the clergy. It was a nation based on the unity of language, religion, race, and customs. Finally, even from the testimonies of French scholars, the Vietnamese possessed from time immemorial a very high moral civilization.

Where are we today, under the tutelage of France? You have seen it. Where could we have been, without France? You may guess it. Anyway, we repeat it again to you: the present situation of our people invites disastrous consequences.

Toward a War in the Pacific? Toward a War in Indochina?

Given the very serious character of the recent happenings in Indochina, it is of course not fanciful to anticipate, in the very near future, a general uprising by the indigenous people. In such a case it would mean that France, which is already beset by two colonial conflicts[1] and a financial crisis and whose fleet is second-rate, would, in addition, be involved in a third war.

And who knows if the war in Indochina shall not spark a conflagration in the Pacific and thereby provoke an unprecedented cataclysm for the universe?

Our Demands

On behalf of the true friendship that exists between the French and Vietnamese peoples, on behalf of the interests of both countries, on behalf of peace in the Far East and in the world, on behalf of the sacred principle of the right of self-determination for peoples, a principle proclaimed right after the Great War by the Allied Forces, including France, we demand, in the presence of the Society of Nations, the complete and immediate independence for the Vietnamese people. Once our country is free, we commit ourselves to:

1. Pay, in money or in kind, in a certain number of yearly installments, a part to be determined from the war debts taken out by France from America and England.
2. Conclude a treaty of political and commercial alliance with France.
3. Draft a political and social constitution, inspired by the principles of sovereignty of the people, of respect for ethnic minorities and respect for work. That constitution shall serve as a basis for the creation of a Federal Republic of Indochina.
4. Build up a national army, according to our traditional system of militia, that shall be responsible for internal order and external security.

5. Send a delegation to the Society of Nations on the same footing as Siam and China.

Hanoi, 25 July 1926   Paris, 30 August 1926

—The "Phuc Viet," or Vietnam Party for National Independence.
Honorable members: Phan Boi Chau and Phan Chu Trinh: formerly condemned to death.
Delegate member in Paris: Nguyen Van Ngoc: 27, rue Sommerard, Paris (5)

—The "Viet-Nam Hon," or the Vietnamese Soul. Free platform for Vietnamese students and workers.
Founder: Nguyen Ai Quoc. Administration: 7, rue Galleron, Paris (20)[2]

Notes

1. The authors refer here to the colonial conflicts in Morocco and in Syria.

2. Printed leaflet written in French to be found in SLOT V, 15. This text is reproduced in Daniel Hemery, "L'Immigration Vietnamienne en France," in *Le Mouvement Social* 90 (1975): *Annexe III,* 51–53; and also in Dang Huu Thu, *Than the va su nghiep . . . ,* App., xiv, 134–37.

DOCUMENT 13

The Vietnamese Party
for Independence

Memorandum to the French Minister of Colonies
(Paris, 1927)

The Vietnamese Party for Independence—or the Parti Annamite de l'Indépendance (P.A.I.) as they called it in French—was founded in France in 1926 by a group of Vietnamese students residing in France. As the signatures and the identifications at the end of this document show clearly, the founders of this party belonged to several different organizations operating in Vietnam and in France. The manifesto of the party states that "it is neither separatist, nor communist, nor even nationalist. It is simply that we are slaves and that we want to become free; we are twenty million oppressed people who desire to establish an independent nation. Being nothing more nor less, our party is what it is: a party for independence, democracy and peace." That party was banned by the tribunal of Paris on 21 March 1929.[1]

The PAI must be closely associated with the various anticolonial movements founded by Phan Boi Chau while in exile in southern China and before his arrest in 1925. In any case, Phan's name appeared first on the list of members of the Commission for Evacuation that the PAI promoted in this document. The many references to China suggest that the authors were very familiar with the situation of the Vietnamese nationalists operating in southern China, who maintained a close cooperation with both the Chinese Communist Party as well as with the Guo Min Dang of Chiang Kai Shek. In fact, many young Vietnamese were enrolled in the Whampoa Military Academy. Another interesting point to be noted is the idyllic representation the authors made of the "old empire of Vietnam." The suggestion for a commission of evacuation is indeed an interesting one, for it offers a concrete and realistic plan for future relations between France and her former colony of Indochina once the latter became independent from the former. The anticipated relations belong to the best kind—amicable, nonadversarial, cooperative, harmonious.

The scandals occurring recently in Cochinchina in which were involved, among others, the representative of France in our country [the governor-general] and the representative of the French citizens residing in our country to the Chamber of Deputies in Paris have shaken up the French Parliament as well as the world public opinion.[2] All the smear splashing from those scandals has no other effect than to stain the Vietnamese people, who are but a massive and innocent victim of so much mud slinging and shame.

At stake are the honor and national interest of France. May the generous people who, in the past, have put an end to slavery and who, in the present, refuse to take any part in the oppression and the exploitation of millions of other human beings; may the people who do not draw any real profit from colonization but who will have to bear its disastrous material and moral consequences; may these generous people react with all their strength against the handful of colonialist sharks with their suspicious fortunes. These sharks are not even all Frenchmen (their leader, Mr. Homberg, was born in Austria), but they use the name, the money, and the blood of the French people to steal, poison, and brutalize twenty million Indochinese.

It is not only in the Darlac Province [the region where the land concessions took place] but in the entire Indochina; it is not only today but for a half-century already that international financiers, in the name of false civilization, have exploited a people who have been civilized for thousands of years.

The Vietnamese people have today reached the end of their patience. Their peasants rebel; their workers strike; their students demonstrate in the streets. After the wars in Morocco [the Rif War of Abd El Krim in Morocco, 1924–26] and Syria [rebellion of the Druses, 1925–27], at the very moment when the victory of the Cantonese Army [the Northern Expedition conducted by Chiang Kai Shek, 1927] resounds loudly across our borders, it is the Indochinese war that will occur with its retinue of mournings and ruins for our two peoples, who are in fact made to understand and help each other. The ultimate end of that conflict will, therefore, not necessarily be to the advantage of French imperialism.

What to Do?

In order to avoid the imminent catastrophe, is the government of the Republic going simply to limit its reforming measures to shuffling around the governors, to changing its methods, to starting a policy called "close collaboration with the indigenous people"? What a utopia! What a demagoguery! What an aggravation of the danger!

From the time of the initial conquest until today, the government has changed fifty-four governors, and each one of these governors has come to make thousands of promises. The collaborationist policy was proclaimed by

Mr. Doumer, the man who imposed the salt taxes, and by Mr. Sarraut, the man who introduced the state monopolies of alcohol and opium, and, supreme irony, by Mr. Varenne, whose recent and scandalous attempt at a "socialist" colonial policy has forever dissipated the ultimate illusions of the Vietnamese people.

The fact is this: colonization will continue to be essentially implemented for and by financiers who will continue to rule as absolute masters as long as colonization exists. It, therefore, serves no purpose at all to change either its methods and/or its agents.

The present commission of inquiry [into the scandals mentioned earlier] formed by the metropolitan government will, consequently, be totally useless. Have we not had to suffer, three years ago, a very sad experience, that of parliamentarian missionaries [this refers to an earlier mission of inquiry composed of French congressmen]? Don't we have to suffer, at all times, the supervision of colonial inspectors whose presence constitutes in itself an already permanent commission of inquiry set up by the metropolitan government itself? Even if one conceded that the present extraordinary commission would succeed in conducting a serious inquiry and thereby in imposing heavy sanctions, these will concern only recent past and immediate future but not all concessions. *Yet it is our entire country that has been pillaged. It means that immense concessions should be stopped and abolished in their entirety.*

Composition of the Commission of Evacuation

The Commission of Evacuation will have the same number of Vietnamese and French members. Among the Vietnamese who would be the most representative and the most able to take part in the commission, we don't hesitate to advance the following names:

—Phan Boi Chau (Annam): former political convict; great scholar.
—Huynh Thuc Khang (Annam): great scholar; former political prisoner; president of the Chamber of the People's Representatives [in Annam].
—Ngo Duc Ke (Annam): well-known scholar; former political exile; director of the magazine *Huu Thanh.*
—Le Huan (Annam): well-known scholar; former political prisoner.
—Phan Van Truong (Tonkin): former attorney at the Court of Appeals of Paris, France; former political prisoner; director of the newspaper *Annam.*
—Luong Ngoc Can (Tonkin): great scholar; former political exile.
—Phan Trong Kien (Tonkin): former political prisoner.
—Bui Quang Chieu (Cochinchina): former student of the Agronomical Institute of Paris; former inspector of the Agricultural Services; vice president of the Colonial Council.

—Nguyen Van Thinh (Cochinchina): former intern of hospitals in Paris; member of the Colonial Council.

—Luu Van Lang (Cochinchina): former student at the Central School for Arts and Manufactures of Paris; deputy director of the Service of Public Works in Cochinchina.

Principal Tasks of the Commission of Evacuation

The commission will study the peaceful conditions for a French military, administrative, and economic evacuation from Indochina. It also will work out the basic principles for a customs and military convention to be negotiated later between France and Indochina.

1. Military Evacuation

The French army of occupation will be sent back to France. Vietnamese troops that have been sent to France, Morocco, Syria, and China will be recalled to Indochina. A national Vietnamese army will be raised according to our old system of communal militia; it will be placed under the command of Vietnamese officers who are presently fighting within the ranks of the Cantonese army.[3] The Vietnamese government will be entitled to make use of French military attachés, technical advisors, and professors for our arsenals as well as for our military, naval, and aeronautical schools.

A military alliance between the two countries will be considered.

2. Administrative Evacuation

The positions of governors, residents, prosecutors, inspectors, and directors of Customs and Monopolies will be abolished. Of the other civil servants whose enormous number, to say nothing about their quality, consumes the seven-eighths of our budget, a handful will be retained. French engineers, technical agents, foremen, physicians, nurses, professors, and schoolteachers will be maintained in their present positions.

The Vietnamese-elected bodies such as the Colonial Council, the Chambers of People's Representatives, and the Consultative Chambers will be renewed in accordance with the principles of universal franchise free of all pressure from the administration. These bodies will form the Vietnamese Parliament, which will write a constitution, a legal code, and also will appoint a provisional government of Vietnam.

The court of Hue and its mandarinate, which are more than ever corrupt and, at the same time, debased by the French administration and standing low in the estimation of the people, will be abolished and replaced by municipalities [whose administrators] will be elected according to the principle of universal suffrage. The municipalities will regain their autonomy, which they used to enjoy under the old Vietnamese empire.

The French community in Indochina will receive the same treatment as the Indochinese in France with one special advantage: if they are employed by the Vietnamese state or if they exercise a liberal profession in Indochina, they are not required to take the Vietnamese citizenship. In fact, naturalization did not exist as an institution in Vietnam before the French conquest: foreigners were automatically treated on equal terms with the indigenous people.

Free of all pressure from either the Vietnamese or French administration, the Commission of Evacuation will organize a plebiscite in Cambodia and Laos to determine whether their people want to remain under the French colonial yoke or to form a federation with Tonkin, Annam, and Cochinchina or to become independent states altogether.

With regards to China, the Vietnamese government not only will forbid any arms traffic to go through north Vietnam and destined for the antirevolutionaries in Yunnan, it will moreover begin negotiations with the government of Canton in view of a mutual recognition of each other and a pact to be concluded between South China and a free Vietnam, as it has existed in the past.

3. Economic Evacuation

The tax on salt, unknown in the past, will be abolished, as will be the monopolies of alcohol and opium, which will result in the interdiction of the latter and the industrialization of the former. The monopoly of money printing will be abolished, and that privilege will be transferred to a bank belonging to the state of Vietnam. The state monopoly in transportation will be abolished, and the control over foreign trade will be given to the Vietnamese state. Railroads and mines will be nationalized. The assets of all the big foreign companies will be impounded, while these same companies will be placed either directly under the management of the Vietnamese state or under that of Vietnamese and French individuals or groups of Vietnamese businessmen, employees, or workers under the supervision of the Vietnamese state. All properties belonging to the foreign religious missions will be expropriated as all concessions of land to foreigners will be canceled. This will be done with the aim of giving back that land to the peasants. Small foreign businesses may continue their operations under the supervision of the Vietnamese state. In order to bring about drastic changes in the present regime of agricultural concessions, the Vietnamese government will draw inspiration from our old agrarian system, which was based on the respect for the interest of the community but also on the dignity of labor.

The Vietnamese government will keep in its service the French technicians, employees, and workers who were employed by the impounded big foreign companies. It will also offer employment to the people who are out of work in the mother country.

A treaty over customs between the two countries will be considered.

The Urgent Tasks of the French Government

While waiting for the results of the work done by the Evacuation Commission, the government of the French Republic will:

1. Abolish the exceptional jurisdiction imposed upon the indigenous people and will proclaim a general amnesty in favor of all political prisoners.
2. Grant to the Vietnamese people all the basic political freedoms that they have been requesting for a long time now and that they have enjoyed under the old Vietnamese empire: freedom of the individual, freedom to travel, freedom to write, to form associations, to teach, etc.
3. Grant to the Vietnamese workers the right to unionize and to strike. It will also effectively extend to the Vietnamese workers the benefits of social insurance and of worker's compensation. It will forbid the massive and forced emigration of the Vietnamese labor force to Oceania. (Emigration was not allowed in the past when Vietnam was independent.)
4. Levy taxes on the profits made by all the big colonial companies in order to build the dykes immediately that will protect the people from the return of the flood in the very near future. The government will also exempt the victims of this year's flood from all taxes; it will give them not the usual refundable but the absolutely free assistance as used to be the practice in the old Vietnamese empire.
5. Reorganize and expand the University of Hanoi, the Lycée of Hanoi, the Collège Chasseloup-Laubat in Saigon. It will also set up technical institutes and professional schools. Public education will become, as it was in the old Vietnamese empire, secular and tuition free at all levels. Education will be spread everywhere, primarily in the national language (*quoc ngu*); Chinese characters will be taught as part of Vietnamese humanities, whereas French will constitute the first foreign language.
6. Abolish those contributions from Indochina to the mother country that only serve to cover the military expenses of the mother country: 32,300,000 francs for the French air forces and navy in the colonies; 700,000 for the maintenance of the Colonial School; 225,000 for the

General Agency for the Colonies; 830,000 for the Colonial Agricultural Institute; 203,000 for the Corps of Inspectors of colonies; 40,000 for the Superior Council of Colonies, etc. . . . It will also abolish the Economic Agency of Indochina in Paris and the Indochinese section of the Colonial Service established at Marseille.

Approximately 40 million francs would thus be saved. Half of that amount could be used to assist French unemployed workers and the other half to grant a thousand scholarships to poor Vietnamese students who would like to come to France to study.

In the past, when our country was a vassal state of China, our emperors used to send to the Chinese rulers yearly presents such as elephant tusks, tiger paws, or peacock feathers in exchange for which the Chinese emperors sent us precious gifts like vases, compasses, or old pens. There were no other contributions.

7. Abolish the service of postal control and the service of assistance to the Indochinese people in France. It will also put an end to the scandalous subsidies it has been giving to the shipping company Messageries Maritimes, and it will not agree to appropriate any part of these subsidies unless the shipping company commits itself to extend a 40 percent discount to Vietnamese students and workers traveling to France.

8. Recall the Vietnamese troops that had been sent to China and prohibit all arms traffic through the territory of Tonkin destined for Yunnan.

Conclusion

If all these requests were to be fully satisfied, then what would be the nature of the relationship between our two countries?

For a long time now the Vietnamese people have had a strong social organization and a true democracy, although the latter has been placed under a monarchical regime. (The autonomy of the villages and the uniform system of education, however, are evidence that the institutions were really democratic.) They also have achieved unity in races, customs, and languages and, therefore, will be capable of living in peace and harmony: our past will be the best guarantee for our future.

Our state will know how to deal with our own economic, housing, and employment crises.

Being endowed with a long tradition of peace, we would never envisage the possibility of killing millions of our compatriots nor borrow billions from foreign countries in order to make war.

Therefore, there will be no chaos within our frontiers, and there will be no adventurous or foolish acts beyond our frontiers.

We turn now to the relations between our country and France:

1. The military accord that will be signed between France and Indochina, while Indochina is an ally of China, will prevent our two peoples from ever attacking the Chinese people. The accord will allow our two countries to reveal all the cruel plots fomented by the international financial oligarchy in the Far East, and, at the same time, it will ensure to our two countries the friendship of four hundred million of China's people; with that friendship, peace will be a guaranteed condition in the Pacific.

   In the hypothetical circumstance that France will be attacked by an imperialist power, a fascist power for instance, what then will be its destiny? We shall witness hundreds of thousands of Vietnamese citizens, whether military people or manual workers, hundreds of thousands of Indochinese piasters [units of Indochinese currency], rallying to the aid of France. And this assistance would be fully voluntary, not forced assistance as was the case during the war of 1914–18.

   As for the Vietnamese people, after attaining their national independence, they will be free to arm themselves. With the military training provided to them by their ally, France, they will be more than able to defend themselves and not let America or Japan attack them at will as they do it at present. [?]

2. The restrictions put on the employment of European civil servants and the fact that they are required to obey the law and to live on the same footing as the Vietnamese people will send back to France a substantial workforce hitherto wasted in their offices. It will also spare the state of Vietnam humiliation and hatred, at the same time as it will tremendously reduce the expenditure of our budget, thereby allowing us to devote that money to projects that would be highly useful to the people, such as construction of railroads and dykes, the electrification of the country, improvements in our port installations, etc. . . . But if the number of French civil servants is reduced, by contrast a greater number of technicians, foremen, and unemployed workers will be invited to come to Vietnam so as to participate actively in the building of our country. That undertaking will not benefit the international financial oligarchy but the entire people of our two countries.

3. The convention on customs and the regulations of external trade will benefit the great majority of the small businessmen as well as the retail consumers in our two countries, because the big middlemen and those merchants who stockpiled goods or who hoarded French francs and Vietnamese piasters will be put out of business. Bizarre transactions will no longer be seen, such as coal from North Vietnam being shipped

to Hong Kong, to Great Britain, before reaching France, or rice from South Vietnam arriving in Genoa, Antwerp, Hamburg, before entering Marseille.

The cost of living, the financial crisis, and the unemployment rate will be automatically reduced and reduced drastically as compared to the situation today.

4. The Vietnamese people will be free to send thousands of their children to study in France, and, as their traditional university system will be revived and modernized, the people of Vietnam will be free to invite thousands of French professors and teachers to come to propagate French civilization in Indochina. The obscurantist policy of old will be replaced with a free-flowing communication of ideas between French and Vietnamese, by spreading those ideas among the peoples and by exchanging the benefits coming from the civilizations of the two countries.

Then and only then will we see, appearing at the horizon, a new era, and that era will really be the true era of "harmonious collaboration" between our two countries.

For the Vietnamese Party of Independence:
—Hoang Quang Giu (Tonkin): delegate of the Vietnamese Restoration Party (or Vietnamese Party for Independence [PAI, Phuc Viet]) in Europe: 32 rue des Ecoles, Paris 5è.
—Bui Cong Trung (Annam): delegate of the Young Annam (Thanh Nien) Party: 6 rue de Brosse, Paris 4è.
—Tran Van Chi (Cochinchina): president of the Mutual Association of Indochinese Residents in France: 15 rue Sommerard, Paris 5è.[4]

Notes

1. See SLOT III, 1 and 3. According to a letter sent by the French minister of the interior to the minister of colonies dated 1 July 1927, the first number of the newspaper with the title *Vietnam* (this refers to the newspaper *Hon Vietnam,* etc., mentioned in the introductory part of Document 12, in this vol.) was published on 1 June 1927. "It claimed to be the European [as opposed to the Vietnamese version] publication of the PAI with Nguyen The Truyen as the political director, Nguyen Van Luan as its Chief Editor and Bui Ai as the secretary of the editor. It bears the address of Nguyen The Truyen at 6, rue Saint Louis en l'Isle, Paris." From the same source it appears that the PAI had started to publish its newspaper as early as 1926, in which "it openly encouraged the Indochinese people and the Vietnamese soldiers to revolt against the Administration. That propaganda has already had its results because last February, in Algiers, a number of Indochinese soldiers and officers of the 19th Infantry have committed an act

of collective insubordination." For more details on the PAI, the protean newspaper *Viet Nam,* and its political director Nguyen The Truyen, see Dang Huu Thu, *Than the va su nghiep nha cach mang Nguyen The Truyen* (Paris, 1993).

2. The scandals mentioned here related to the concession of the Port of Saigon, which was granted without bidding to a group of French industrialists headed by Homberg of the Bank of Indochina, and also to a series of oversized land concessions granted to French citizens. These measures had been intensely debated in the Colonial Council of Cochinchina, and the media had very closely monitored the maneuvers leading to these concessions.

3. These were Vietnamese students sent to be trained at the Whampoa Academy by various Vietnamese nationalist organizations. Some of these students were to go back to Vietnam to work for their respective organizations; some others enlisted in the Cantonese army, which launched the northern expedition under the command of Chiang Kai Shek.

4. The original of this document, written in French, was sent with a cover letter to the French minister of colonies on 26 March 1927. The authors of the cover letter purport to be prominent members of the Vietnamese Party for Independence (Phuc Viet) and Young Annam. That letter was signed by the three persons whose names appear at the end of this document (SLOT III, 52). The French text has been published by several newspapers in Saigon: see *La Tribune Indochinoise,* 29 and 30 May 1927, *L'Annam,* 13 May 1927. Some of the newspapers' clippings are to found in SLOT V, 39. A similar text is reproduced in Dang Huu Thu, *Than the va . . . ,* app. 25, 203–12. A translation of this document into Vietnamese can be found in Tran Huy Lieu, *Hoi Ky* (Hanoi, 1991), 88–96; and SLOT V, 1 and 3. The bylaws of the party, written in Vietnamese, can be found in SLOT V, 45.

DOCUMENT 14

The Nationalist Party of Vietnam
(Viet Nam Quoc Dan Dang)

Proclamation to the People
(1927)

The Nationalist Party of Vietnam, or Viet Nam Quoc Dan Dang (VNQDD), was founded in 1927 by a group of young professionals, many of them still students, who had received a Westernized education. Its political platform was deeply influenced by the three principles of democracy advocated by Sun Yat Sen for his Guo Min Dang (KMT). It was one of the more successful and more popularly based than any other anti-French revolutionary movement to date. It had nevertheless a short existence. Because of its success, the leaders of the movement grew too confident in the strength of the party and called for an armed uprising for the night of 9–10 February 1930 in the northern part of the country. The center of operations was located at Yen Bai (Yen Bai Province). The uprising failed lamentably, however, due to bad communication between the various sections of the party and also due to infiltration by agents of the colonial security services. A special court called the Criminal Commission was set up immediately after the suppression of the uprising with the express purpose of trying its participants. Only in 1932 did it cease its operation, after meting out hundreds of death sentences and thousands of years of imprisonment and banishment to the Poulo Condore or the Guyana penitentiaries. The most famous execution was that of thirteen leaders of the party, among whom was Nguyen Thai Hoc, its founder, on 17 June 1930 at Yen Bai, when each of them, before submitting themselves to the guillotine, shouted loudly for all to hear the slogan "Long live Vietnam."[1]

The English oppressed the American people, and the revolution led by Washington was its consequence. The Chinese, under the leadership of Sun Yat Sen, have risen against the Manchu, their oppressors. These are famous examples that are not easy to forget. It is clear, however, that, in order to put an end to the

248

misery of the people, it is indispensable to do away first with the pirates of the nation.

The French, although they are of a different race from ours, came to conquer our country. Under the pretext of protecting us, they made a colony of our country. They have at their service corrupt mandarins and civil servants who behave like hunting dogs toward the people. They tried to destroy us with drugs and alcohol. Their cruelties equal only those of snakes and wild beasts. They steal all our possessions, including our real estate. Many a time taxes have increased. The French never cared whether our people were miserable or that they remained in ignorance. Their educational system is indeed very narrow: it aims simply at training slaves. Their laws are offensive: they are enacted in order to gag our mouths and to shackle our limbs. Publications are forbidden, correspondence censured. Those who found associations are thrown in jail. Students who go overseas are punished. It is the rule of force. Is this political regime not the replica of the one that existed under the reign of King Louis? Where is justice? Why are sentences pronounced against political detainees so heavy?

Oh! Our freedom is lost. We expect nothing from the concept of equality. The more we speak up, the more we suffer. And yet the twenty-five million of Hong Lac's[2] children are as intelligent as anyone else. What a shame that they have accepted for more than seventy years the role of beasts of burden. To live in these conditions is a shame. It is better to die rather than to lead such a life. We only wait for the opportune moment to strike.

Following directives that have been approved by the general public opinion, our party has decided to raise a revolutionary army. This is not some device thought up to intimidate the people. On the contrary, the time has come: we can no longer hesitate to strike.

At present the French find themselves in a difficult situation. Indeed, they had hardly settled their quarrels with Germany[3] when the Moroccans rose up in arms against them.[4] All these events have left their country in ruins. Their external debt amounts to several billion, from which they will surely not be able to free themselves for many years to come. Moreover, the number of their soldiers under arms has decreased: their armed forces are, therefore, drastically reduced. Against that background we have our means, within the country as well as outside. It only takes some action on our part to obtain good results. We shall gather in our party good commanders and courageous soldiers, and our action will be such that bamboos will split up and tiles will be shattered. As soon as a battle is fought, its repercussion will ripple throughout North Vietnam. If we gather all our forces together, we shall obtain favorable results, without the shadow of a doubt.

Such is my proclamation. I beg our people to think about their country. Let them draw their sword out of its sheath. Let them raise their rifle. We must kill the enemy in order to regain our rights. We shall govern our country ourselves, and we shall bring happiness to all. Let all the people remember this: death will be dealt unto those who do not act accordingly.

Such is the proclamation.[5]

Notes

1. See the letter that Nguyen Thai Hoc wrote to the members of the French National Assembly in which he explained to them the aims and demands of the Vietnamese nationalists, in Harry Benda and Jack Larkin, *The World of Southeast Asia* (New York, 1967), Document 48: "Radical Nationalism in Vietnam," 182–85. It would also be interesting to read the account of a member of the party and a participant in the Yen Bai insurrection, in Hy Van Luong, *Revolution in the Village,* 23–50.

2. See notes 2, 4, and 5 of Document 11, in this volume.

3. The author refers here to the Versailles Treaty, which did not settle any of the problems existing in the relationship between France and Germany after World War I to the satisfaction of either contracting party.

4. The author refers here to the revolt of Abd-El-Krim, which broke out against French rule in Morocco from 1921 to 1926. This war was also known under the name of the Rif War.

5. I have not been able to locate the original of this proclamation, which must have been written in Vietnamese. The translation offered here is made from a French text found in SLOT III, 8, which is preserved together with other documents in a file sent by the governor-general of Indochina to the French minister of colonies in Paris on 3 August 1927. At the end of the French translation, which I use here, there is a note probably written by the translator that says: "The handwriting is of Nguyen Khac Nhu." Nguyen Khac Nhu was a high-level leader of the Viet Nam Quoc Dan Dang, who, after the failure of the insurrection and before the French Security Service agents could arrest him, had committed suicide.

DOCUMENT 15

Tran Huy Lieu (1901–69)

A Bag Full of Confidences
(1927)

Tran Huy Lieu led an eventful and extremely interesting life. Born in northern Vietnam (Tonkin), he was attracted at age twenty-two to Cochinchina, probably for its less restrictive regulations concerning the freedom of the press, for Tran Huy Lieu had discovered in himself some journalistic talents. He, indeed, soon landed editorial writing jobs at prestigious newspapers of the time, such as the Nong Co Min Dam, Dong Phap Thoi Bao, *and* Phap Viet Nhut Gia. *He quickly involved himself in political activities. He was among the organizers of numerous demonstrations to demand the commutation of Phan Boi Chau's sentence. With others, he turned the funeral of Phan Chu Trinh, a year later, in 1926, into a powerful popular show of force against the colonial government. He founded or actively participated in several clandestine political groups.*

For the role he played in the underground anti-French organization Vietnamese Nationalist Party (VNQDD), he was to be deported from Cochinchina back to Tonkin, when he was condemned to five years in prison and sent to the Poulo Condore penitentiary from 1928 to 1934. After his release from the penitentiary, he joined the Indochinese Communist Party (ICP) in 1936 and was assigned to a journalistic team in charge of the publication of the party's many newsletters. In 1939, he was again arrested by the French authorities and confined until 1945, when he started writing for the party's newspaper Cuu Quoc. *Tran Huy Lieu was appointed minister of propaganda and mobilization in the first provisional Vietnamese independent government. Besides holding many important positions in the government of the Democratic Republic of Vietnam (DRV), Tran Huy Lieu doggedly pursued his research and writing: the list of his works constitutes no less than 645 titles of books and articles covering a great variety of topics from economics to anthropology, history, and political thought.*

The translation that follows is made of substantial excerpts from a pamphlet, Tran Huy Lieu, *issued in 1927 in the collection of books published by the*

251

Nam Dong Thu Xa, a commercial enterprise established by the VNQDD with the aim of using its revenue to finance the activities of the party. In these pages Tran Huy Lieu offers a sharp analysis of Vietnamese society of the period and urges the people to search for a remedy to all their ailments in order to attain, as soon as possible, freedom for the Vietnamese people and independence for the Vietnamese nation.

Reasons for the Loss of Our Country (Stories of the Past)

Politics caused the loss of our country.

Although the monarchy reigns over a country, it really consists of a family: the family of the king in which only the king exists. While the monarch is respected, the people are held in contempt; while the king is prominent, the people insignificant. In the past the Siamese ambassador advised the king to learn from the West. The king retorted: we learn from China, we refuse to learn from the barbarians. People like Pham Phu Thu, Ha Ton Quyen, and Nguyen Truong To, who advocated modernization and Westernization, were accused of the crime of lese-majesty. We lost our country because our political life was depraved by a horde of autocratic mandarins. If the mandarins were abusive, it was because we, the people, did not know how to exercise our rights. We have but ourselves to blame.

Education caused the loss of our country.

We never study to become better human beings; we studied to become mandarins. We discarded Confucius and Mencius to end up with this conservative Confucianism that caused the loss of our country today. Whom can we blame but ourselves?

Ethics caused the loss of our country.

People were so obsessed with the five relationships of kings to subjects, parents to children, husbands to wives, brothers to brothers, friends to friends, that they forgot all about more important connections. To devote all of one's efforts to filial piety, one came to neglect one's duty as human being toward mankind and one's duty as citizen toward the fatherland. It is generally held that, while the parents are still living, it is impious for the children to go anywhere far away, but then, after the parents have died, it is equally impious to be away because nobody will take care of their graves. What then became of our spirit of adventurism, exploration?

Customs caused the loss of our country.

Happiness is not leaving your village. Every resource should be devoted to securing a place to stand on in the village. Nothing is bigger than the village: no canton, no province, no country—no desire to go even to a foreign country to study.

The belief in spirits or magical powers is balanced with a total disbelief in oneself. Last year in Phu Tho (North Vietnam) there was a group of people, completely unarmed, coming to fight against French soldiers; they simply wore talismans, waved their flags, and fully believed that they were invulnerable to bullets.

Religion caused the loss of our country.

Every country should follow a religion so that the people have something to believe in. The leaders have an easy task guiding a religious people because, although the people's intellect differs greatly, their religious belief stands on the same level so that the smart leaders may change their zeal for martyrdom in the name of religion to martyrdom in the name of the "cause." The success of Gandhi's noncooperation movement was due to the fact that the three hundred million Indians who supported him were also three hundred million believers. Had it not been so, his supporters would have had, each one, his or her own mind and would not have listened to his appeals or followed his example. Our country is a country without a religion. Our scholars follow Confucianism, but Confucianism is not a religion. As for Buddhism, it remains a private matter between the monks and the nuns, who are endowed with such a narrow mind that they do not understand at all the doctrines of their religion. Bandits kill you to rob you of your possessions, of your house, but you do not dare even touch them, for you do not want to violate your "nonkilling" principle. With a country without a religion and a people without belief, what can we hope to achieve? Whom can we blame but ourselves?

Conclusion.

A strong, intelligent country will subjugate a weak country. The strong will dominate the weak; the intelligent will dominate the stupid; such is the motto of the powers, while autonomy and self-strengthening are the aims of the dominated. Today our people are dangerously sick. I am afraid that if we cannot find good doctors soon, our annihilation is near. I cannot refrain myself from lamenting: Are our compatriots causing the loss of our country?

Our Compatriots Cause the Loss of Our Country
(Stories of Our Time)

Our country is already lost. Our compatriots have lost their country. A lost country no longer has any status; a person without a country can no longer find any source of joy. Are autonomy and self-strengthening not concepts that remind us of our situation? How come when I observe the behavior of my compatriots I only see a deplorable spectacle! There are those who squander fortunes bequeathed upon them by their parents on good food, expensive clothes, lavish entertainment. They are fully satisfied to earn the title of the "noble playboy." They have no idea whatever about their duty toward family or fatherland. There are others who are filled with egoistic preoccupations: besides their own selves, they have no concern for their compatriots; besides their own families, they have no regard for their country, their society. If they are reminded of their duty toward their country, they let out a painful sigh: I can't even take care of myself or of my family, let alone the compatriots or the country. Those words, we hear them very frequently. But do these people think they would still be able to enjoy their family if their country were totally destroyed? In the past, if our heroes neglected their family to serve their country, that was not because they did not care about their family but because they knew that their family would live in peace only when their country was well governed, and, conversely, if their country were in disorder and their compatriots in disarray, how do they expect to enjoy their familial pleasures? Then, there are the cowards. They do feel the pain resulting from the loss of their country, but because their cowardice is so inveterate they are terrified by the slightest sign of danger. They act as if they were mentally disturbed: they do not dare do anything for their country, even speaking about its problems or listening to people talking about its troubles. That ailment hits principally the rural people, who, although governed by the French for more than seventy years now, yet still cannot look at a Frenchman without shuddering, still cannot encounter a secret agent without being petrified with fear. Affairs of the state sound like thunder in their ears: they are scared of being put in jail, sent to Poulo Condore, or guillotined. Alas! How laughable and yet how painful to see citizens who dare not talk about the problems of their own country!

After I resigned from the newspaper *Dong Phap Thoi Bao,* I moved my family and myself to a village in the province of Ben Tre. It took only two days for me to notice some uneasiness about our presence there. I queried the deputy chief of the place, who stated that my presence may attract trouble to his constituency, because when I wrote for the newspaper many of my articles were censured by the government. What a sad fact: to have had your articles censured constitutes sufficient cause for people to ostracize you! What if you are involved in more violent activities?

Another time, while on a trip, I stopped to visit a friend who was an educated person, with a reputation of a decent man in his village. But on that day, upon seeing me, he clearly showed signs of discomfort, apprehension. He ultimately confessed that as he had been recently elected to be the chief notable of his village, my presence was not welcome there because of my involvement in the affairs of the state: the secret agent is likely to create difficulties for his career.

How sad it is to witness such cowardice in my compatriots! I can understand that they are afraid of real dangers, but why are they frightened by fictitious threats?

Another category includes people I would qualify as "living drunk, dying asleep." In this world of intense competition people would be proud to have a rich country and a strong population, but not our people here. They pursue, rather, empty honorary titles, spend hundreds and thousands to buy the lowest degree in the mandarinate, to subject themselves to untold humiliations in order to secure a medal of distinction. That is, I must say, partially the fault of our society, which confers importance only to those who are in possession of some title, particularly when that title comes from the emperor. Little do they know that the emperor himself has been reduced nowadays to a "wooden sculpture" without any value, without any power.

Another group of people do empathize with the situation of their country, but they would say: They have big ships and powerful cannons, while we do not possess even an inch of steel; they have competent generals and strong soldiers, while we do not have even one able body; they have everything ready, while we lack everything so that, even though we are motivated by anger or enmity, eggs cannot clash with stones, nor can grasshoppers ever hope to overturn a carriage. The result will certainly be our annihilation, so why not accept the current situation and be at peace with ourselves? This way of reasoning is totally incorrect. What is expected of us now is not to launch ourselves into any audacious adventures but simply to remind ourselves of our duties as citizens who dare protect the rights we actually possess. If we respect ourselves, no one will treat us with contempt; if we train ourselves to become strong, then no one will oppress us. Nothing is impossible in life, and there is no life that we cannot turn around.

There are ignorant people whose eyes cannot see very far ahead and whose ears are immune to noble tales. They compare the Chinese colonial regime of thousands of years ago, which they find to be cruel and inhumane, with the present colonial policy of the French, which they say is lenient and benevolent. They would reason in the following way: had the French not come here, we would not have had all those grandiose monuments, running water or electricity in our lofty houses, automobiles to drive wherever we want to go, elegant clothes to dress our bodies, and varied forms of pleasurable entertainment. This place, which yesterday was a dense forest, now shelters a beautiful and prosperous city; that area, which yesterday was a dangerous and unhealthy spot, has now become the center of a network of communication lines. When they look back at the past, they see banditry or piracy everywhere, whereas now peace reigns all over the country. Furthermore, with the Franco-Vietnamese Collaboration policy, everybody is so satisfied and happy to the point that they all are frightened by the thought that one day the French will go back to their own country, leaving no one to govern Vietnam, which then will revert to the state of unrest, instability, and turmoil of the past! These people forget one thing: the more oppressive the policy, the more violent and forthcoming the reaction, for the cruelty is so patent that all the subjugated people endeavored to find ways to put an end to that policy. Today's imperialist countries all implement a much more dangerous policy: under false pretenses of morality, generosity, and humanity, they persuade the colonized people that they have no intention of occupying territories or exploiting the riches of the colony; they are here only to respond to their divine mission of civilizing the colony, and once that mission is accomplished they will return to their country empty-handed, leaving in the colony the seeds of civilization. This kind of policy has been compared to tuberculosis: its germs have already devoured the lungs and liver of the patient, who, nonetheless, does not feel any discomfort, until the day when he succumbs to the illness without even being aware of his impending death! Brothers and sisters, the tuberculosis germs have already invaded our heart and lungs, and yet apparently you do not feel it, because you continue to praise their policy as generous and benevolent; because you continue to claim that we should feel lucky to live in comfort under the colonial yoke. It seems to me that we all have lost our souls, our willpower. If our soul has died, how are we to save our country?

[A long section here deals with the Franco-Vietnamese Harmony or Collaboration policy advocated by the French governor-general of Indochina toward the end of World War I, the role played by Phan Boi Chau in that controversial policy, and the big mistake made by some Vietnamese nationalists who looked up to Japan for its help to fight against French colonialism. For Japan will dominate Vietnam and will apply to Vietnam the same cruel and inhumane policy as it has implemented in Korea and Formosa. Furthermore, once Japan has colonized Vietnam, there will be no hope for Vietnam to ever regain her independence.]

In the previous pages I have listed all the categories of people who, either by ignorance, by egoism, or by weakness of character, have completely ignored the needs and wants of their country and compatriots. Judging them with the standards of our national law, we may absolve them of any wrongdoing. There are, however, others who willingly and intentionally have committed the same misdeeds. Their crime is of the utmost seriousness. I am calling them to the popular tribunal so that the entire people may judge them.

1. *The corrupt mandarins and the venal civil servants.*

People complain: in addition to the exploitative policy of the foreigners, citizens of a lost country must suffer also the exactions of the native officials. In today's Vietnam the mandarinate and the people seem to have aligned themselves into two opposing factions: the former look at the latter as scrumptious prey, while the people consider the mandarins as thieves, as bandits. The saying "thieves of the night are called bandits; those in broad daylight are called mandarins" has become an "honorable" label of the administrators. Both Phan Boi Chau and Phan Chu Trinh have warned us against the abuses of the mandarins.

2. *Those who sell out their country.*

A country is a place founded by our ancestors; it is a place where we are born, where we grow up, where we live, where we die. There is nothing more shameful, more painful, than being accused of selling out your own country! We have already lost our country, and yet there are compatriots who still want to sell it. They have exchanged their nature as children of dragons and grand-children of immortals for that of hunting dogs and baiting birds. As secret agents in the service of the colonial government, they report right away to the authorities those among their compatriots who say something right or do something good [for the national cause] as rebels or traitors so that the govern-ment can indict them, put them in jail, send them to Poulo Condore. Some of them have even been executed. The secret agents, those hunting dogs and baiting birds, have all forgotten about their ancestors, whom they perfunctorily worship on the altar; about their compatriots, who live around them. They spare no one, neither their own parents nor their siblings. They have no con-science. They have severed all relationships with other human beings. You find them not only within the country but also in foreign countries: in China, in France.

Next to them we have these false patriots who proclaim in public their love for the country. They infiltrate all organizations; they participate in all discussions about future activities; they are made privy to all secrets, which soon enough reach the ears of the authorities, who clamp down harshly on the activists. As for the false patriots, they simply use these denunciations as steps to climb up the ladder of officialdom. Next there are the successful false patriots: they are those who are wearing already the mandarins' robes and the officials' beard. They now can sell their country in public, without restraint or disguise. They petition the government to raise the people's taxes so as to defend the value of the French franc; they suck the people's blood; they carve out the people's bones and offer them as trophies to the colonial government.

There are soldiers in the service of the French who, in order to demons-trate their loyalty to their masters, turn their rifles against their own com-patriots. By doing so, they claim that they have pacified the rebels and that they have, therefore, served well the mother country! During World War I many left their country, abandoning parents, wives, and children to volunteer to defend the mother country. Except for those who died in battles, the people who returned from the war displayed with great pride the insignia of officers, and the medals that covered their chest proclaimed for all to hear their valor and their courage. To tell you the whole truth, I think there are not a few of our compatriots who would look up to them with respect, admiration, and envy. Who can fathom the sentiments of people? A Frenchman has the following insult: "Until the time Vietnamese dogs cease eating excrements, the Viet-namese people also stop basking in slavery."

3. *The fake patriots.*

These are more dangerous than the country sellers. We can easily recognize these country sellers for what they are, whereas we must have very sharp eyes in order to see through the fake patriots, who have the country sellers' soul but who display the appearance of patriots. That's the danger, and it is frightening! Poor Vietnamese people who had their limbs cut off by the country sellers; now their inside organs are savagely bitten by the fake patriots. Will the people be able to survive?

The fake patriots know well that the people today have heightened their awareness so that they can no longer apply the same tactics as the country sellers; they must change their method, which always consists of selling out their country, now doing it stealthily. They pretend they care for the people and love the country so as to acquire the confidence of their compatriots. They claim today to be the leaders of such a party, the next day the representatives of another association. After they have acquired the confidence of the people, then they betray them so as to be able to ride in automobiles, to live in palatial houses, to gamble all through the nights. Is it true that these people have no patriotic feelings? From hearing their public declarations, from reading their newspaper articles, one would have to conclude that they represent true patriotism and authentic care for the people. Have these people accomplished anything to the benefit of the people? Yes, they have, from time to time, and that is how they are able to lure the people into thinking they are true patriots, and that is how the people are committing a serious mistake in placing their confidence in them!

So what have these "leaders" or "representatives" done for the people? Write an article in French about national politics published by a newspaper? Deliver a speech on politics during a public banquet? In spite of that meager achievement, our people still count on these "revolutionary" leaders to obtain their autonomy, to free them from slavery. These leaders start to raise funds: today twenty thousand francs to send a delegate to Paris to deal with the affairs of state; the next day twenty thousand francs to publish a newspaper in order to defend the interests of the Vietnamese people. These fake patriots have piled up the corpses of our people, whom they use to climb up to the highest rings of the scale of power and wealth. There are some real patriots who intend to expose the fake ones, but they are isolated, devoid of weapons, without organizational support, so that their opponents can easily muzzle them, render them totally ineffective. At times some activists would appear on the political arena who seem to have succeeded in mobilizing the people, in garnering the popular support. The fake patriots make right away a move to quash them or at least to prevent them from having too big an influence on the people.

Who among us does not know that our people are lacking everything? What to do in order to attain independence? What to do in order to obtain autonomy? When we look at our people, we realize that what we have studied up to now is how to be slaves. In agriculture we count on the natural phenomena, while the industrial and economic profits remain in the hands of foreigners. Here is a multitude of children in search of schools. There are the peasants, the artisans, the merchants, who desire to improve their trade, but nobody is showing them the way. Why don't the fake patriots take them by their hand and lead them on the way of progress, instead of spending all their time raising funds?

The three culprits I have exposed in the previous pages are the corrupt mandarins, the country sellers, and the fake patriots. They are no different from three bacteria that are devouring the lungs and heart of our people, who, consequently, have become gravely sick. How much longer can the patients survive? Looking around the world, we see that practically every country and every people are practicing self-strengthening. The revolutionary flame is burning in Syria and Morocco. The autonomous wave is engulfing India, the Philippines. Back in our country, we witness a sorry state of affairs: our people are divided into factions fighting against one another. The bandits have come to rob our house, and yet the brothers pay no attention to them because they are absorbed in their struggle against one another. We are not avenging the murder of our ancestors; our hatred is directed, rather, against our own people. Our people are weakening everyday, and our country is suffering more and more, and yet it is devastated here by flood, there by epidemic; each year the number of victims increases dramatically; if the situation is not contained, it is sure that the end will be the annihilation of our people. The state of affairs in foreign countries is not brighter. Don't you think it is time for us to worry? In the past there were many causes for the loss of our country. Now we are the causes. What hope do we have to recover? Compatriots! Our soul has gone astray; our bodies have become emaciated; our sickness is life threatening.

How are we to cure our sickness? To call doctors from foreign countries? No, that would not do. To take medicines with violent aftereffects? Where can we get such medicines? Furthermore, can our weakened bodies tolerate them? These are important questions I would like to ask of twenty-five million patients. We are sick, so we must seek remedies. But if we do not have the right doctors or the appropriate medicines, our illness may get worse. I hope that if any among our compatriots have come to some solution, then let them speak up, and we shall together discuss it so that we can avoid the danger of extermination of our race.

If you have any ideas conducive toward curing our illness, please send them to me. I shall publish them in my next book to present them to our people. In my next book I shall also publish a pharmaceutical prescription—that is, another bag full of confidences to see whether it would be proper for all of us who suffer from the same illness to use that remedy.[1]

Note

1. The book from which these excerpts are translated is written in Vietnamese and published as Dau Nam Tran Huy Lieu, *Mot bau tam su,* Nam Dong Thu Xa (Saigon, 1927).

A quatrain printed on the cover and qualified as "My Most Intimate Thoughts" serves as a subtitle:

Who is going to receive my confidences
A long time I have waited for a friend
The country stirs up anxieties
Who is crying in silence and because of whom

DOCUMENT 16

Huynh Thuc Khang (1876–1947)

**Speech Delivered at the Opening Ceremony of the Third
Session of the Chamber of People's Representatives in
Annam Held in Hue on 1 October 1928**

*This chamber was a representative institution established by the French col-
onial authorities in 1925 in order to advise the government of Central Vietnam,
called at that time Annam, on various matters of public interest; it had, however, no legislative power. The government of Annam, one of the three administrative units into which Vietnam was divided during the French colonial
period, was a hybrid one. The Vietnamese emperor ruled directly over it with
his cabinet of ministers and his provincial mandarins. The Imperial Privy
Council (Co Mat Vien), composed of the emperor's ministers, was presided
over by the French resident superior, who, by the same token, became the
highest executive officer in the territory. He governed it through the imperial
government but also through a number of French administrators placed at
strategic points in the central as well as the provincial administrations.*

*Huynh Thuc Khang was elected as a member of that representative in-
stitution in 1926, for its first session; he also became its first president. A
Confucian scholar, Huynh held the highest degree in the traditional educational system. Implicated in the peasants resistance against high taxes in 1908,
the same movement that sent Phan Chu Trinh to the penitentiary on the Con
Son Island, or Poulo Condore, and later into exile in France, Huynh Thuc
Khang was condemned to twenty-three years of imprisonment and deported to
the same penitentiary of Poulo Condore. The government released him in 1921
for good behavior, and in 1926 he founded the most popular newspaper of
Central Vietnam, entitled* Tieng Dan *(Voice of the People), wherein he professed a loyal opposition to the government of the French protectorate. It
should be noted that Huynh Thuc Khang became the vice president of the
Democratic Republic of Vietnam, which was proclaimed on 2 September 1945;
Ho Chi Minh was its president.*

In this eloquent speech Huynh Thuc Khang apprised the French resident superior for Annam of three important problems Annam had to face at the time: inadequate educational institutions; exhaustion of resources due mainly to frequent increases in taxes; and the complexities of the penal code. Huynh Thuc Khang ended his address with a political wish, that France would grant Annam a constitution,[1] which was a daring act, for members of representative assemblies were not allowed even to formulate wishes concerning political matters.

In form and substance this document reminds us vividly of the open letter written by Phan Chu Trinh and addressed to the governor-general of Indochina twenty years earlier. (See Document 2.)

His Excellency the Resident Superior,
Their Excellencies the French and Vietnamese Ministers,
Gentlemen,[2]

This is the third session of the Chamber of People's Representatives of Annam and also the last one of our tenure. Next year there will be new elections. The meeting today is placed under the presidency of Mr. Jabouille, the resident superior, who governs this part of the country in the name of France. The ministers of the Imperial Privy Council, the French as well as Vietnamese dignitaries, have generously come to take part in this session. Other French and Vietnamese officials are here as observers. The atmosphere in this chamber is indeed dignified and solemn. We have obediently responded to the call of the resident superior to gather here today. First of all, I would like to express my heartfelt thanks to the government, which has gracefully accepted to cooperate with our chamber. Second, I would like to describe with the assistance of a few sincere words the situation of the people in this part of the country.

Entrusted with the confidence of my constituents, I have assumed, thanks to the civilizing policy of the government, the responsibility of a people's representative for the past two years. I know that the remarks I have made during the two previous sessions have all been simple and well defined; how inadequate they were, though, when compared, on the one hand, to the grand policy the government proposes to implement in this region and, on the other, to the aspirations of the people. Nonetheless, they do manifest clearly the confidence we have in the government's generous policy because we have not hesitated to speak up about the aspirations of the people. We did so in the hope that our chamber does not wear an empty title and that we deserve the trust placed in us by the people: there were no other motives.

Yet, during the last two years, the government has not once given heed to any of our requests, failing thereby to reassure the people that this new institution is different from the absolute rule they had experienced in the past. The people, consequently, have lost their confidence in us. Neither did they believe any longer in the government. We ourselves have often heard uttered by our constituents comments such as the following: "The name does make use of the words representatives of the people, but the reality simply yields a new mandarinate."

We, indeed, find ourselves in an equivocal situation: we have been unable to achieve anything positive in favor of the government; as for the people, we naturally cannot fulfill their aspirations with the empty title of "people's representatives." At night we cannot help but think with shame and sadness about this quandary of ours, and our ultimate hope is to make this third year of our tenure last more than a half-century. Such is the plain truth.

Then all of the sudden came the call for this third session. We have thus arrived at this conclusion: it is the government's duty to implement such and such proposals, but for us, who have been elected by the people in order to contribute our ideas to the improvement of this region's affairs, our duty is to report to the government all aspects of the people's situation that we are able to discern. Our responsibility, therefore, should remain at all times within the bounds of law and order. Seizing upon the occasion of the opening of this session, I would like to present with the greatest sincerity the following observations.

The difficulties encountered by the people in Central Vietnam are many. They spring, however, from three essential causes.

1. The first one stems from the restrictions imposed on education. If one's eyes could see clearly, one would not lose one's path. There would be no misunderstanding if the ears were sensitive enough. Only an educated man can distinguish between right and wrong. One must know how to earn a living if one wants to survive in this world. The people of Central Vietnam have had a culture for hundreds of generations. Everyone recognizes the importance of education. People regard education as their life, their legacy; without it, they cannot live. In this highly competitive period, without education, what more can be said? In Annam today the old educational system has been completely abolished; the new one has hardly started to function. There are not enough public schools, and there are no private ones to speak of. The curriculum is limited, and the law restricts initiative of any kind. While the people regard education as their very life, the government looks at it as its enemy; public schools are constantly modified by decrees, whereas red tape makes it so difficult to obtain a permit to open up private schools.[3]

Recently many people have been implicated in various crimes simply for setting up private schools. Today many children see their education terminated because they are unable to secure admission into a higher school. Later in life, how are they expected to find any job? As for those who are about to commence their education, they will have to while away their youth, facing the outer walls of the schools, for lack of space inside. The parents will look at their children in distress; the brothers will look at one another in anger. Such a loss and such a pity! The first word of the government is *civilization;* its second word is *collaboration.* And yet, in education, it has consistently refused to adopt an appropriate policy without which it will be impossible for thousands of Vietnamese youngsters to find jobs. It is difficult for the people to believe that the government's aim is to lead a throng of jobless people on the road toward progress. It is indeed useless to guide a blind person onto the street as it is a wasted effort to persuade a deaf to listen to good singing. Ignorance constitutes a calamity for the Vietnamese people, and it may later become a hindrance to the collaborationist policy advocated by France.

In educational matters, therefore, would it not be advisable to implement compulsory education and grant the people the freedom to open up private schools?

2. The second cause consists of the exhaustion of resources. The water will not dry up if it is supplied by streams; the fruits will develop normally only if the tree is well rooted. In a country with a low level of productivity, if the expenditures are too high, then it is not surprising that difficulties will set in one day. Central Vietnam has a small territory; its people are poor. Communications are not well established yet. Local industrial production is practically nil. Commerce is in the hands of foreign traders. Commodities such as silk, sugar, tea, cinnamon, etc., are transported by Chinese peddlers from one region to another, and it is they who unilaterally determine the prices of these goods. Because they are not allowed to move freely around, the Vietnamese have to accept the conditions set by the Chinese, however hard these conditions may be.

The majority of the people in this region live on agriculture. And yet severe droughts occur every year. Land, rice fields, production, all remain stagnant. Yet the tax rate increases every year. Not only does the government depend on taxes to draft its fiscal policy; the mandarins collect them over-zealously and the local potentates abuse their power. Each year at the time of tax collection people run amuck. Drums and gongs resound. The rattling of shackles and handcuffs deadens the people's screams and cries. Disorder reigns everywhere. That is not to mention the abuses of the corrupt officials and the treacherous notables who collect more than the taxes due, squeezing the last drop of tears and sweat out of the people. The tax money has not had time to reach the state treasury when it is spilled along the way and lands in the pockets of these greedy officials. In the final analysis the state stands to lose a great deal of revenue while at the same time earning a bad name. By drying up the pond to capture fish, one may catch some fish, but the pond will remain dry. By felling trees to collect fruits, one may gather a great amount of fruit, but when the next season comes the orchard will turn into a desert. The government keeps repeating that it is humane, that it is generous. But in its fiscal policy, it finds no other way to raise revenue except by increasing taxes. The poverty and misery of the Vietnamese people, indeed, will not constitute an asset for France.

In fiscal matters, therefore, would it not then be advisable to tax only luxury items? Wouldn't it be better to fix, once and for all, the rate of the head taxes?

3. The third cause pertains to the complexities of the penal code. One cannot avoid shaking the nervous system of a normal person if one treats that person with medicines destined to a mental patient. Passersby may not avoid falling into a pit dug up to trap wild animals, if that pit were located right in the middle of the road. Law in a country is written so as to punish criminals, for example robbers and rebels, with the ultimate aim of maintaining order in that particular country. But if an innocent person may at any time suffer punishment or if he runs the risk of being falsely accused of a crime and may even be thrown in jail before a judgment is meted out to him, then how can one avoid misjudgments? Even those who have always conducted a spotlessly clean life would not know how to avoid these miscarriages of justice. In recent years Central Vietnam has received a few stimuli from the outside world, while its internal affairs were not in total order. For the sake of security the government has had to implement a rigorous penal code: newspapers and books were banned, individual houses searched, people who spoke in public or who intended to open up private schools were arrested. It is normal that criminals should be punished, but is it normal that so many innocent people suffer chastisement? In addition, many are accused of obscure crimes, without much evidence. In Central Vietnam, when someone is arrested, not only is he not told of his crime; he is not even allowed to discuss it at all with anybody. This is indeed a very strange regulation, to say the least. People who would like to show their zeal would not hesitate to resort to false accusations. One tip-off, and five or seven houses are searched. How many promising careers has the simple word *suspect* already ruined? The government is too credulous of all the rumors, accusing some people of seditious acts, some others of rebellious activities. In fact, there is usually not much of any real substance to these rumors, which, by nature, tend to exaggerate things. But, because of that, the ignorant and some young people have fallen into the net of the law without being conscious of it and, therefore, without the possibility of avoiding it. How pitiful can that be! A child who falls into a well would deeply move even a passerby. A moaning and groaning patient will not let the doctor sleep quietly on his pillow. How can a government that talks always of humanity and justice leave the Vietnamese people in such a plight? That would not do any good to the reputation of France.

On the issue of the penal code, therefore, would it not be advisable to implement the recommendations we made during the first two sessions of this chamber? We would request simply the application in Annam of the same legal code that has been promulgated in Tonkin.

The three causes mentioned here constitute the main torments for the people of Central Vietnam. For a long time now, because of a paranoid mentality, because also of the habit of crushing inferiors while adulating superiors, no one has had the courage to bring the sufferings of the people to the knowledge of the government, which, consequently, has remained in the dark. Furthermore, the government has also made a few awkward decisions: today it issues a decree to be contradicted by another one the next day; the people never know against what standard they are being measured; their ears and their eyes can no longer hear and see anything very clearly. The mandarins, then, heap abuses upon the people, who, in their turn, pile resentment against the government. By disliking the mandarins, the people also distrust any policy statement coming from the government. Profiteers can take advantage of the situation to sow seeds of dissension. All this is indeed very detrimental to the civilizing mission of the government.

We have observed that mess. We have heard and seen everything quite distinctly. That is why today, standing in front of the government and in the presence of French as well as Vietnamese officials, we dare say the following with total frankness:

If the protecting power sees it as an advantage for France to use force to treat the Vietnamese people, so that with every passing day they become poorer and more ignorant to the point of suicide, then I would not add one more word. But, on the contrary, if the government were willing to consider what constitutes the advantages and disadvantages to the future of our two peoples, and if it sincerely desired to guide the Vietnamese people on the way toward progress and to allow them to cooperate with the government, then the three causes we have discussed must be changed in a way that should be simple, clear-cut, well balanced, and yet not too drastic. These changes shall be in total harmony with the people's aspirations. From then on, other decisions may be implemented, one after another, without much difficulty.

If the government did not act as proposed, then, even if its policy were perfect, even if the mandarins endeavored to promote it, even if the press publicized it, and even if all of us, people's representatives, went from house to house, from individual to individual, to try to persuade them, the people would still think that the government's policy is simply an empty promise. They would no longer believe in anything coming from the government.

The Vietnamese have a saying: if the water is far away, it cannot extinguish a nearby fire. The points we presented here are the close-by fire, while the measures the government proposes to implement, such as forest inspection, etc., represent what the people see as the "faraway water." The mind of the indigenous people of this country has been deceived so many times already. If the government does not immediately enforce one or two radical changes so that the people can see them with their own eyes and hear them with their own ears, their resentment will not subside.

Such is the situation in which the people of this country find themselves. What follows now is an essential point concerning politics.

In the last session I raised the question of a constitution. The governor-general, in his reply, stated that he was ready to bring that topic to the attention of the Vietnamese Imperial Court. After that, the resident superior, Mr. Fries, wrote to this chamber to inquire about its position on the same subject (Communication no. 990A of 15 November 1927).

If today we again raise the question of a constitution, that is because we realize clearly that, although Annam has become a protectorate for almost a half-century, its political regime still remains vague; the rights of the people are not defined, nor are their duties explained. Hundreds of difficulties derive from that ill-defined regime. The government has become an object of resentment. Although the country has its king and the king has his mandarins, whenever the people encounter difficulties, they all complain: "This is the French era. This is the business of the French," meaning the indigenous administration is powerless to solve their problems. The political regime being thus unclear, it is but natural that the people do not know where to turn to. That is why, if peace in the country were to last long, if the relations between France and Vietnam were to endure, then the country must build itself into a body politic, the members of which must receive well-defined responsibilities; their power should be limited but real so that the country can benefit from it. The essential basis for all that is indeed a constitution.

Obviously, we cannot consider lightly such an important issue for three reasons.

1. According to articles 1, 5, 7, and 11 of the 1884 treaty,[4] Annam is placed under the protection of France; the internal affairs of the kingdom, however, are in the jurisdiction of the Vietnamese Court. The governor-general reiterated that position again in his speech to this body in its last session:

France has signed an unequivocal treaty with the Court of Annam. If we went back on some of its articles, it would sow dishonor onto France. . . .

If that's so, then the old treaty still forms the basis for the political regime of this country. In reality things have changed drastically over the past thirty years, and the present situation by no means reflects that which was agreed upon in the treaty.

2. Article 1 of the convention of 1925 reads: "The time has come for the people to participate in public affairs." When in his speech to the first session of this assembly Governor-General Pasquier attempted to describe the responsibilities of the people's representatives, he had the following words to say:

What you should do is to make the peasant, the woodcutter, the worker, the notables in the villages, the merchants and the handicraftsmen realize that the future of their country resides entirely in their own hands.

According to that declaration, the political regime that the government proposed to implement would be timely and would respond adequately to the aspirations of the people; it would conform to the spirit of the convention of 1925. The reality, however, is quite different. Not to mention other things, we have suggested in the bylaws of this Chamber of Representatives a few changes here and there; to this day this chamber still functions exactly in the same manner as the old Privy Council. The people, therefore, cannot have faith in the chamber.

3. Such is the situation with the treaty of 1884 and its relationship with the convention of 1925. The three basic elements of a constitution are the territory, the people, and the public affairs. The respective delimitations between these three elements in our country being very blurred, a constitution, therefore, would have no solid foundation. Furthermore, since it is difficult to enforce the constitutional separation of power into the executive, legislative, and judiciary, even if a constitution is drafted on paper, it is doubtful that it will have any positive effect under the present circumstances.

For all these reasons we cannot commit ourselves yet to any solution. We only ask for one thing. If the government decides that a constitution is a political foundation that will be firm and long-lasting in this country and in harmony with the aspirations of the people, then:

1. The governor-general should put this question to the scrutiny of the Judiciary. First of all, he should obtain a decree from the regents and an edict from the young Emperor Bao Dai;[5] the purpose of both documents is to promise and to proclaim to the people that Annam must now adopt a constitution.
2. A Constituent Assembly should be created in such a way that the entire population of the country can participate in its activities and help draft the constitution.
3. In the period of preparation the Chamber of People's Representatives should be granted more power, and the mode of electing the representatives should be more carefully studied so that the people will be free to vote, without encountering any obstacle. (In the previous years people took very lightly the election regulations, which are the same as for the election of the mayors of villages or chiefs of cantons.)

The authorities might counter our suggestion by saying: "But the people are not ready for a constitution." We agree with that assessment; we would, however, like to add: "One reaches one's destination only by walking on the road; one becomes literate only through learning."

Now, if you are not allowed to walk, and at the same time you are told that the road will not lead you to your destination and if you are not allowed to learn and yet people reproach you for being illiterate, then, even if you are given a hundred thousand years, you will never reach your destination, nor will you ever be able to read.

Your Excellency Mr. Resident Superior,

Your Excellencies,

We have described to you the situation of the people and the political state of the country. We have done it with few words but with a great sincerity. The aim of this speech is simply to convey the remarks of my last tenure in this chamber. We again appeal to the good sense of the government to implement our suggestions; the people of Annam will forever be grateful.

On the occasion of the opening of this session, on behalf of the people of this region, we beg of you, Mr. Resident Superior, to transmit our regards to the governor-general, to the newly appointed Governor-General Pasquier, to His Excellency the Minister of Colonies, to His Excellency the Regent, and to His Majesty Bao Dai.

We thank you.

6 October 1928.[6]

Notes

1. We are fortunate to have the reaction of the French resident superior to this speech in the words of a Vietnamese journalist: "Mr. Jabouille [the resident superior] replied to Mr. Huynh Thuc Khang. He looked a bit irritated and that was why one or two passages of his reply sounded rather harsh! He said that the Vietnamese people should not blame the protectorate government because it is thanks to the protectorate government that Annam has reached today such a degree of prosperity: the people are busily working in total peace. According to Mr. Jabouille, the Vietnamese people have beautiful houses, good roads with shining lights on which automobiles are able to drive fast. People should feel really happy. As for mental happiness, it is not necessary to have it at all!" (*Duoc Nha Nam,* 5 Oct 1928). From the issue of 8 October 1928 of the same newspaper we learn that Huynh Thuc Khang resigned from his position as president of the chamber.

2. It is to be noticed the absence of any female participant in the activity of this chamber.

3. See in Le Quang Hong, *Recueil des décrets et arrêtés relatifs à la réglementation de l'enseignement privé au Tonkin* (Hanoi, 1926), the regulation of 14 May 1924, stating that "No one can open a private school in Indochina without an advanced authorization from the relevant administrative authorities. That authorization is granted by the Governor General for any secondary and high education establishment and by the

Resident Superior for any other establishment. Authorization may be withheld for reason of public security; in that case, the refusal is definite and not susceptible to any further recourse."

4. This refers to the Patenôtre-Nguyen Van Tuong Treaty of 1884, which regulated relations between France and Vietnam until it was superseded by the 1925 convention signed after the death of Emperor Khai Dinh.

5. From the death of Emperor Khai Dinh in 1925 until 1933, when Emperor Bao Dai came back from his schooling in France, a Council of Regents ruled the country on behalf of the young emperor.

6. The text of this speech can be found in the following publications: Nguyen Q. Thang, *Huynh Thuc Khang, Con nguoi va tho van* (Saigon, 1972), 323–29; in *Tieng Dan,* 6 Oct. 1928; Thai Bach, *Tho van quoc cam . . . ,* 486–97; and Chuong Thau, *Tho van Huynh Thuc Khang (chon loc)* (Danang, 1989), 349–63.

DOCUMENT 17

Duy Tan Tho Xa (Modernization Publishing House)

Manifesto
(1928)

In the latter part of the 1920s several publishing houses were established that would promote books written in the new romanized system of writing, quoc ngu. *These books encompassed principally works of fiction, which constituted a novel literary genre highly fancied by a Western-educated readership. A rash of works of nonfiction aimed at spreading among the general public the basic concepts in the humanities or social sciences were also widely distributed. The translation of the manifesto of one of these publishing houses, Duy Tan Thu Xa (Modernization Publishing House), is given here as a sample of what these publishers intended to accomplish. Besides the Modernization Publishing House, other publishers flaunted names such as Tu Do Tung Thu (Freedom Collection), Ton Viet Thu Xa (Survival of Vietnam Publishing House), and Tan van Hoa Tung Thu (New Culture Collection). These publishing houses offered Vietnamese readers books written by Phan Boi Chau, Phan Chau Trinh, and others but also essays composed by a younger generation of scholars, among whom were included Dao Duy Anh, Tran Huy Lieu, and Tran Huu Do. The New Culture Publishing House, for example, issued several treatises written by Tran Huu Do with titles such as* Dialectic, Historical Materialism, Imperialism, *and* The Philosophy of the Proletariat. *Tran Huu Do himself headed the Freedom Publishing House, which printed his own works:* The Roll of the Freedom Drum, Readings for the Youth, The Soul Awakening Bell, *and* An Affidavit about the Loss of Freedom. *The Modernization Publishing House printed novels with engaging titles such as* A Very Strange Marriage in the Pacific, Dissatisfied Dead Souls, The Tears of Heroes, *and* Eternal Regrets. *It also issued pamphlets on more serious subjects—for example,* The Great Russian Revolution, Three Heroines from Russia, The Youth and the Present Situation, Sino-Vietnamese Harmony, Women and the Nation, *and* Scholars and Businessmen. *Tran Huy Lieu, who would become the minister of propaganda in the first government of independent Vietnam formed by Ho Chi Minh in 1945, also had his own publishing house, Cuong Hoc (Strengthening Study), which printed mainly works written, edited, or translated by himself or written in collaboration with another writer, whose initials were DKH:* Memoirs from Prison, The Heroes Who Save the Country, The Great People Who Founded the Nation, *and* Let's Offer our Lives to the Nation.

The manifesto translated here was printed inside the covers of a book entitled Guong Ai Quoc *(Examples in Patriotism). It gives a somewhat Marxist interpretation of imperialism and emphasizes the Darwinian doctrine of survival of the fittest. The author waves those ideas in order to encourage the people to promote modernization, which consists of reviving the national spirit to fight against French colonialism.*

How to act?

Brothers and Sisters, how are we to act?

Today the drama of the "competition of nations" is unfolding with more brutality than ever; imperialism has practically reached its zenith. What does imperialism mean? Any country that uses its political and military superiority to control the economy of another country, region, or people. Since the nineteenth century strong countries of Europe, with the invention of their machines, the development of their industries, and the extraordinary explosion of their population, have manufactured so many goods that they could not consume them all by themselves. They, therefore, had to find less-developed countries to exploit them as consumers' markets. There is more. In order to produce goods, one needs raw material, and, if one's own country does not have enough raw material, then one must find weaker countries to use them as raw material providers. That indeed constitutes the major aim of colonization.

To command a "consumers' market" consists in exchanging manufactured goods for the money, sweat, tears, and raw material of equal value that belong to the people of weaker countries.

To seize raw material is to capture all the products of the land, all the labor of the weaker people, who then become the buffaloes and horses in the service of the stronger countries.

So what will the imperialist countries do when the weaker peoples rise up against them to voice their opposition? They have anticipated that situation. If it concerns a country that they have marked as a target for colonization, then the first thing they will do is to enhance their political position. If the weaker people persist in opposing them, they will then use brute force, which means they will use brute force to consolidate their political position, with the aim of occupying the market, and to pilfer the raw material. They would sign unequal treaties with other countries, so as to realize their imperialist designs. Still, with some other countries they simply reduce them to the status of colonies. Immediately, they become the owners of the country, while the indigenous people turn into buffaloes and horses to serve them. In order to prevent the colonized peoples from challenging their rule, they invent all sorts of evil schemes: they instill in us, the colonized people, the mentality of slaves, obliterate in us the sense of patriotism, remove from us our national consciousness, destroy the soul of our nation. They also eliminate all human rights: freedom of speech, freedom of thought, freedom of publication, freedom of association, freedom of education. They forbid overseas travels; they impound us in our own countries as they impound dogs in kennels; they treat us like buffaloes. Because they reserve for themselves all economic rights, we have no food to feed our bellies, no clothes to hide our shame. Our means of subsistence are reduced with every passing day. The birthrate of our population is so low that our race is threatened with extinction every day. Genocide by economic onslaught is in fact one hundred times, if not one thousand times, worse than genocide by swords, guns, or bombs. It puts us out of existence in the same mild manner as tuberculosis germs chisel and puncture the liver and lungs of their victims. Let's look around us: the red-skinned people of America are almost all exterminated so that the white race can now proclaim: "We must preserve some red-skinned people in order to exhibit them in anthropological museums." Alas! The strong people will win over the weaker ones; the intelligent people will triumph over the dumb: such is the law of survival in this world.

The might of imperialism is indeed overwhelming. Five races coexist in this world, and three and a half have already been annihilated or reduced to slavery. Five continents share the space on this globe, and three and a half have already been occupied as colonies. Countries that subscribe to imperialism are England, which occupies India and Egypt; America, which rules over the Philippines; and France, which controls Morocco and Vietnam. China and Turkey are big countries, and yet they are preys to a flock of hungry ravens that are fighting over them as over a putrid corpse of a dead buffalo. Let's face it: imperialist countries are like knives and cutting boards, while weak countries are seen as meat and fish.

In order to avoid extermination India, Egypt, the Philippines, Morocco, China, and Turkey all have risen up to wage revolutions. Some of them are still bathed in a sea of blood; others have succeeded in marching on that glorious road that leads them to the creation of a new nation, to bring in a new dawn.

What, then, forms the basis of revolution? It is the national spirit. What is the national spirit? It is the spirit that derives from the sharing of the same nation, partaking of the same compassion, suffering together in silence the same pains, the same humiliation, the same fear. It is the spirit that is aroused by the same anger to a point of generating a fighting spirit, of building up together a powerful mass organization that will not refuse any kind of sacrifice, that will be of one mind, determined to liberate their members from the fate of buffaloes and horses, to free them from the destiny of extermination. The national spirit constitutes in fact a first-rate sacred medicine that is capable of resurrecting the weaker peoples from death.

At present our people find themselves in the position of "a tenuous hair that must hold a thousand pound weight"; our national spirit is catching its last gasps, whereas the threat of extermination has already begun to unfold in front of our own eyes. How to act? Brothers and Sisters, how to act in this situation?

We must awaken our national spirit. How are we going to wake up our national spirit? We must strengthen our virtues, open up our minds, nurture the thought of our people. How are we going to strengthen the virtues, open up the minds, nurture the thought of our people? We must have many books in order to spread widely the new thought, the new scholarship, the new ideologies; in one word we must disseminate the ideology of Renovation. First of all, we must build up a strong mass organization so as to use it as a symbol, as a vanguard army that will prepare the way for the people. It is, indeed, a painful and humiliating fact to mention it here: today, in our country, there is no such organization.

In spite of the fact that our abilities are limited and our knowledge scarce, but because we have hoped for so long and yet no person of talent has appeared, we dare, in the most sincere way, to bring out whatever we have learned from new books to first educate ourselves and afterward to spread that knowledge among our compatriots.

Presently, as our financial situation is still fragile, our publishing business still imperfect, we, therefore, respectfully request our brothers and sisters to inform us of any mistakes we may have made, albeit unknowingly. And if among our readers there are some who nurture the same ideas, we would ask them to come forward to collaborate with us.

"Help thyself and Heaven will help thee."

Brothers and sisters! If we have a fighting spirit, then eventually, one day, the national soul will be resurrected. Our people will be freed from annihilation and ready to march on the road toward Modernization. The four words *The New Viet Nam* will appear in the world.[1]

Note

1. This text, written in Vietnamese, is printed on the inside cover of the book entitled *Guong Ai Quoc* by Ngoc Son and Doan Hiet, published in Saigon, 17 December 1928 (1,500 copies of this book were printed).

DOCUMENT 18

Do (Red) Newsletter

The Communists Must Organize Themselves into a
Single Party
(1929)

*The following document is an article presumably written by Nguyen Ai Quoc-
Ho Chi Minh under the pseudonym Ly Thuy in* Do *(Red), a newsletter published in Canton. While in Canton with the Russian mission to the Guo Min
Dang, Nguyen Ai Quoc's most crucial task was to unite all the Vietnamese
groups with some communist leanings to form a single communist party. In this
article he tried, quite convincingly in fact, to persuade his readers of such a
necessity. The subtitle of the newsletter reads as follows: "The newspaper* Do
*is the organ of a communist section that nurtures the hope of persuading the
communists and their sections in Vietnam to quickly unite and form a single
communist party."*

Today society is evolving into another phase. The economic foundation of
capitalism and imperialism can no longer boast of a quiet life; it is, on the
contrary, in a state of crisis. The forces opposing capitalism increase in intensity with every passing day. Imperialist wars are about to break out. The
imperialist powers all want to form a coalition to overthrow Soviet Russia.
They still prefer to fight against one another, principally Britain against America. The revolutionary movement is thereby making big progress, the proletariat becomes more motivated, and the colonial people's uprisings more
frequent and more threatening.

 In Vietnam the French imperialists are busily preparing for the war, attracting to their side the big landowners and the intellectuals, oppressing the
peasants and workers, while terrorizing the revolutionaries.

 The peasantry is deeply divided among itself because of the capitalistic
measures taken by the French imperialists such as the Torrens policy,[1] the
agricultural credits, the irrigation program, etc. . . .

 The number of workers has grown tremendously due to the increase in the
number of factories established by French imperialists. The workers also have

275

become better organized, and owing to the ideas that were fashionable in the world at the time, to their own experience, and to the massive unemployment, they have developed a consciousness in their strength and have transformed themselves into a struggling social class. The revolutionary movement in Vietnam has indeed already gone beyond the intellectual and petit bourgeois stages. All of their parties and factions have failed to instill an ounce of confidence in the population. Furthermore, they have all been decimated by French imperialists.

The artisans or small capitalists have lost their businesses and been ruined by capitalistic measures taken by the French imperialists such as increases in taxes, raises in the price of raw materials, and the absence of custom duties to protect locally produced goods.

The revolutionary movement in Vietnam has now begun the stage of proletarian leadership. Vietnam, therefore, must have a communist party. The Communist Party is the avant-garde of the proletariat, and the peasantry is the leader of the proletariat, so the peasantry will overthrow the French imperialists, seize political power, and set up the dictatorship of peasants and workers in order to achieve a communist society.

The urgent task of the Communist Party in Vietnam is to lead the ongoing movement of the peasants and workers against the fascist policy of the French imperialists and to be prepared to transform the international war between the imperialists into an internal rebellion.

In such dire straights, if, as Communists, we are so isolated from one another, if each of us is active only in a specific area, if each of our cells covers only a specific region, how can we expect to fulfill the historical mission of the proletariat? How shall we be able to lead the revolutionary movement in Vietnam?

We, therefore, should found as soon as possible a unified and official Communist Party that will be recognized by the Communist International. Only then will we master the circumstances and be able to shoulder the present-day revolutionary task.

We should not imagine that it suffices for a communist agent or for a communist cell to operate alone in a specific region and to "penetrate the masses" for them to find each other ultimately. We should not simply recognize twenty or thirty communist members or twenty to thirty communist cells as representing the Communist movement and, consequently, feel no need for other communist agents or cells. Why can we not see the example of the government of the French imperialists? How stable, how centralized, it is! We intend to use the proletariat to overthrow that government, and yet we don't have a solid or a centralized party. How do we expect to achieve that goal? We should not use the excuse that this agent is immature or that cell's composition or activities are unknown to us so as to overlook the most urgent task in the present situation—that is, to have a unified party in Vietnam. Otherwise, we don't have the revolutionary spirit.

Despite all that, we should nevertheless not consider any one member as a comrade, nor should we ally ourselves with any one cell. What we must bear in mind is the benefit or the loss to the revolutionary movement not only for today but also for tomorrow.

Comrades! The urgent task is, therefore, to found a unified Communist Party. If we failed to realize that goal, how can we claim to be the followers of the scientific socialism of Marx and Lenin? If we did not do that, then circumstances will bury us. We shall die if we remain inactive.

How to Found a Communist Party

To found a Communist Party it does not suffice to work at it for five or seven months. Nor would it be sufficient to have twenty or thirty members in order to declare the formation of an official party. An official party must have a systematic organization from the cells to the Central Committee, according to the principle of democratic centralism. It must count among its members peasants and workers. It must also be recognized by the Communist International.

So what is to be done now?

a. First of all, we must take the unit of production (the factory, the mines, the agricultural colonies, the schools, the railroads, etc.) as the basis of organization.
b. After a cell has been organized, then it must shoulder the responsibility of creating two, three, or more cells. After two, three, or more cells have been created, the task of expanding them must be continued.
c. After the creation of two or three contiguous cells, then a district cell can be founded. After two or three contiguous district cells have been founded, then a provincial cell can be established. With two or three provincial cells, an interprovincial or regional cell can be created. With three or more interprovincial or regional cells, we may hold a grand congress of representatives to elect some of them to the Central Committee for them to be responsible for the affairs of the whole country. We may then ask to adhere to the Communist International.

Such are the basic principles of organization. Let the Vietnamese Communist comrade think fast. Wherever he is, he must found a cell there, so that, later on, all the cells can be welded together into an official Communist Party.

Why Must Vietnam Have a Communist Party?

Should Vietnam have a Communist Party? To answer that question we must first ask ourselves whether Vietnam has poor workers and peasants. If the number of poor peasants and workers has increased, it means that the suffering resulting from the exploitation by the capitalists has become all the more intolerable. Their class consciousness is heightened and the class struggle all the more acute. If the workers already have engaged in the class struggle, it is inevitable that they may encounter with defeat or failure: from that derives the need for an overall organization.

The Communist Party in Vietnam is organized by the workers and peasants who have had their consciousness raised; it is the forerunner of the proletariat in Vietnam. Revolution in Vietnam, because the world revolution has not yet been successful, will be achieved through the cooperation between the proletariat and the peasantry together with the small capitalists in a united front so as to fight against imperialism. But in the formation of that front the strongest component must be the proletariat, which must also be the most revolutionary. The proletariat, therefore, must hold the commanding role among the fighting forces, and the leadership of the revolution must remain with the party of the proletariat, which is the Communist Party.

In Vietnam now there are many political parties; all of them are parties of landowners, capitalists, intellectuals, petit bourgeois; all of them are either false revolutionaries or anti-revolutionaries. No party represents the true interests of the proletariat; no party is able to assume the leadership of the revolutionary movement in Vietnam. As a result, Vietnam must have a Communist Party.

The Communist Party always takes the interests of the proletariat to heart. In the first place, it will not sacrifice any interest, even the slightest, of the proletariat to serve the interest of any other social class. The Communist Party, however, continuously monitors the oppression exerted against the other social classes so that it is able to forge daily slogans to mobilize these social classes against French imperialism.

Some Reflections on the Situation in Vietnam

Recently, the French repression has been going full blast. Home searches, arrests of people according to the cruel and barbaric laws of the French imperialists, have occurred everywhere in North, South, and Central Vietnam. The searing screams wrought out of tortures are daily occurrences. Poulo Condore, Lao Bao, Tuyen Quang, etc. [all names of infamous prisons], are overcrowded with political prisoners. From the cities all the way to the countryside, everywhere the people are anxious, terrified.

Watching that situation, those who have conscience, those who nurture revolutionary intentions, cannot help but feel pain, anger, and determination to fight the French imperialists once and for all.

And yet the Vietnamese revolutionaries remain silent, expressing no compassion for that kind of oppression. Do they think that such an attitude will have no influence on the future of the revolution?

The revolutionary fervor is not negligible in Vietnam now. From North to South no region is in want of it. If we could gather all that energy for a movement to protest against the repression, do you think the French imperialists will continue to prosecute it for much longer? If they kill one of us, can we not kill one of them? They arrest, torture, shoot to kill our people every single day; are we then unable to use swords, knives, rifles, grenades, so as to prevent them from eating their good food and from sleeping soundly in their comfortable beds?

How pitiful! Although the revolutionary fervor is high, it is nevertheless split into five factions, seven parties. The revolutionary ideology may be one, but when it comes to action, then each person goes his or her own way. While the enemy is united, cohesive and solidly organized, our revolutionary side can be compared to a handful of sand, the grains of which the wind scatters in all directions.

If this situation persists, the French will naturally continue their repression. Our comrades will continue to be arrested. And where there are no more comrades, the French will arrest the common people. When we reach that quandary, the revolutionary fervor will no longer be there, and the people will no longer have any confidence in the revolution. They will also cease to believe in the "Party."

We should, therefore, immediately

1. Constitute a unified Communist Party.
2. The Communist Party will gather all the revolutionary forces together into a front to protest against the repression.
3. The Communist Party will stand on the side of the proletariat.[2]

Notes

1. I have not been able to find any information about the Torrens policy.

2. This article was written in Vietnamese and published in the first issue of the newsletter *Do,* 1 September 1929. The original copy of that first issue can be found in SLOT V, 26.

DOCUMENT 19

Tran Phu (1904–31)

The Political Theses of the Indochinese Communist Party
(October 1930)

(Draft to be discussed within the Party)[1]

The Dang Cong San Viet Nam (Vietnam Communist Party [VCP]), which was founded in February 1930 following the fusion of several communist splinter groups, was apparently not satisfactory to the Comintern, which denounced it as "unprincipled" and in violation of its directives. The VCP's program of action was spelled out in a document entitled Summarized Strategy of the Party,[2] *which urged the Vietnamese proletariat, under the leadership of the party, "to do its best to maintain relationship with the petit-bourgeois, intellectual and middle peasant groups."[3] In October of the same year the First Plenum was convened of the VCP's Central Committee, which, at the same time that it harshly criticized the documents produced a few months earlier, adopted a new set of political theses written by Tran Phu, then secretary-general of the VCP. At that same plenum the name of the party changed from Dang Cong San Viet Nam (VCP) to Dang Cong San Dong Duong (Indochinese Communist Party [ICP]).[4]*

This document represents the orthodox line at the time. The role of the proletariat, peasants, and workers in waging revolution is emphasized. All the other classes may ally themselves with the vanguard of the revolution, but, when the revolutionary fervor gains momentum, these classes tend to close ranks with the enemy of the revolution.

I. The State of the World and the Revolution in Indochina[5]

1. Since the end of the imperialist war of 1914–18, the state of world affairs can be divided into three phases:

   a. In the first phase (1918–23) the war devastated the capitalist economy, which then found itself in a crisis. The European proletariats rose up to seize power in many countries. Finally, the Russian proletariat succeeded in overcoming the imperialist powers that besieged it from the outside, while within its borders it subdued the entire revolutionary forces in order to establish a stable dictatorship of the proletariat. But other European proletariats have floundered, as in the case of the German proletariat in 1923.

b. In the second phase (1923–28), seizing upon the recent failure of the proletariat, the imperialists have deployed all their energy to exploit the proletarian class and the colonized peoples. Owing to that exploitation, for a while, the imperialist economy attained a degree of stability. Because of their past failures, the proletariats in the imperialist countries kept a defensive position. In the colonies, however, revolution exploded everywhere. In the Soviet Union the economy was stabilized and the doctrine of communism spread to the whole wide world.

c. The third period is the present time, which has the following characteristics:

The temporary stability of capitalism can no longer be maintained; on the contrary, it has relapsed into a crisis situation. The imperialists, therefore, must fight against one another over their markets with even more viciousness, making the next war between the powers totally unavoidable.

The Soviet Union's economy, on the other hand, has surpassed prewar levels; it has very successfully built up socialism, and that is the reason why the imperialists resent it all the more and want to destroy it, because it constitutes the bastion of world revolution.

The proletariats in the imperialist countries struggle with great fervor (strikes in Germany, Poland, etc.). In the colonies revolution has increased its intensity (particularly in China and India). If revolution has reached that degree of intensity, it was because, in crisis, capitalism exploited the people without restraints, putting millions and millions of workers out of their jobs. The workers and peasants are in utter misery.

In this third phase the proletarian and colonial revolution has reached very high levels. In some places they are at the point of seizing power.

At the moment Indochina has linked its revolutionary vigor with the clamorous struggle of the world, thereby widening the front line of the battle fought by the workers and peasants against imperialism. Conversely, the intensity of the revolutionary movement in the world (particularly in China and India) influenced deeply the struggle in Indochina by speeding up its pace. The world revolution and the Indochinese revolution are thus very intimately connected.

II. Characteristics of the Situation in Indochina

2. Indochina (Vietnam, Cambodia, Laos) is a colony of exploitation of imperialist France. The Indochinese economy is, therefore, subordinated to the econ-

omy of imperialist France. The two most important characteristics of the Indochinese economic development are:

a. Indochina should have developed an independent economy, but because it is a colony, it cannot generate an independent economy.

b. The contradiction between the social classes reaches a higher level of intensity every day. On one side we have the workers, peasants, and other wretched people; on the other stand the feudal landlords, the bourgeois, and the imperialists.

3. The Economic contradiction

a. Agricultural production is mainly destined for export by the imperialists while it remains essentially in a feudal mode. The majority of the plantations (rubber, cotton, coffee) belong to the French capitalists. Most of the rice fields are properties of the indigenous landlords, who manage them in a feudalistic mode, which means that they lease their plots of land to poor peasants for very high rents. The yield of rice fields in Indochina compares unfavorably with other countries: one hectare in Malaya produces 2,150 kilograms of rice, in Thailand 1,870 kilograms, in Europe 4,570 kilograms, and in Indochina only 1,210 kilograms. The exported volume of rice increases every day, but that does not necessarily mean an increase in its production; what it does mean is that the capitalists steal the rice from the peasants in order to export it.

b. The oppressive policy of the French imperialists has prevented Indochina from improving its productivity. They have not established heavy industries such as metallurgy or tool-making machines, etc., because the implantation of these industries in Indochina would have impaired the monopoly of French industry. They only introduced industries that could boost their controlling power and their commercial interests to the maximum, such as railroads, small ship-building arsenals, etc. The principal aim of imperialist France was to turn Indochina into a country that depends on France's economy. France, therefore, established in Indochina only industries that were more profitable to establish in Indochina than in France. The exploitation of raw materials did not seek the goal of making an independent Indochina but simply of making France independent from other imperialist countries.

c. The export business rests entirely in the hands of French capitalists. That's why trade and productivity of the country depend exclusively on the export needs of imperialist France. Consequently, the more export increases, the more natural products are siphoned out of the country by imperialism. Another special point is that French banks (such as the Bank of Indochina and the Real Estate Bank, etc.) gather capital from the indigenous people for the benefit of French exporters.

In brief, the economic backbone of Indochina is agriculture, where feudalistic practices still reign supreme. These conditions prevent the Indo-chinese economy from evolving in an independent direction.

4. The social classes contradiction

The French imperialists allied themselves with the indigenous landlords, businessmen, and moneylenders to exploit the peasants in the cruelest way. The imperialists export local agricultural products to foreign countries and sell their manufactured goods to the local people. They impose such heavy duties and taxes that the peasants are reduced to famine and misery, while craftsmen in countless number go jobless.

More and more rice fields and land are appropriated by the imperialists and landlords. Furthermore, there are people who lease big expanses of land and then turn around to sublet them to other tenants; these tenants, in turn, rent these lots out to still other tenants; after a few turns, these lands come finally to be rented to the poor peasants with rents that reach sky-high.

The peasants, in need of cash, must borrow money from usurers, who exploit them to the point that they must sell their own land or their children to pay their debts.

Dykes are erected in order to prevent floods, but the state pays them scant attention. Irrigation works belong to a handful of capitalists who charge astronomical fees, so that poor tillers must make do without water. Bad crops resulting from flood or drought become very frequent happenings. The peasants, therefore, are not only unable to improve their own economic position; they depend more heavily every day on the capitalists. Their living condition deteriorates, and more and more of them suffer from joblessness and from famine.

The old economic structures are fast disappearing, and the new industrial development marks slow progress. The hungry and jobless people cannot work, so they remain idle in the rural areas, causing them to become places of utmost misery.

In the factories and plantations the capitalists exploit and oppress their workers in the most savage manner. The workers' pay is insufficient to feed them, and yet they are swindled up and down. Their working hours average eleven to twelve a day. They are humiliated; they are beaten. When they are sick, instead of medicines, they receive their dismissal papers. The workers benefit from no social security insurance whatsoever. In plantations and mines the owners confine their workers to barracks and forbid them to leave their place of work. They rely on the contracts that the workers have signed to move them to any place they see fit. They retain complete control over the workers, including the power to judge them. Due to these horrifying working conditions, many workers catch devastating diseases such as tuberculosis, malaria, eyes disorder, etc. More and more workers are dying young.

The Indochinese proletariat is not numerous, but the number of its members increases every day, principally among workers in the plantations. The workers' struggle, therefore, has acquired stronger driving momentum. The peasants have also awakened and are fighting forcefully against imperialism and landlordism. The strikes of the years 1928–29, the forceful struggle of the workers and peasants this year [1930], demonstrate that the class struggle in Indochina has gained much in breadth. A special and important characteristic of the revolutionary movement in Indochina can be seen in the fact that the struggle of its peasants and workers encompasses a very clear measure of independence. It no longer is influenced by simple nationalism as in earlier times.

III. The Nature and Mission of the Indochinese Revolution

5. All the contradictions described here favor the maturing of the revolution in Indochina. In the beginning the Indochinese revolution will be a bourgeois-democratic revolution, for the revolution is still unable to solve by itself and directly the organizational problems of socialism: the economy of the country is still too undeveloped, the fetters of feudalism too many, the proletariat relatively too weak; the country, after all, finds itself under the oppression of imperialism. Due to all these factors, in the present situation the revolution cannot be anything else but agrarian and anti-imperialist.

The bourgeois-democratic revolution constitutes but a preparatory stage for the socialist revolution. With the victory of the bourgeois-democratic revolution a government of workers and peasants will be established, industry in the country will improve its situation, the proletarian organizations will be enhanced, the leadership of the proletariat will be consolidated, and the class strength will lean on the side of the proletariat. The struggle, at that time, will acquire more intensity, a wider scope, steering the bourgeois-democratic revolution on the way toward a proletarian revolution. That period will be the period of the worldwide proletarian revolution and the period of building up socialism in the Soviet Union. Indochina will receive the assistance of the dictatorship of the proletariat from other countries in order to skip the capitalist stage and advance directly toward socialism.

In the bourgeois-democratic revolution the proletariat and peasantry constitute two crucial moving forces, but only if the proletariat seizes the leadership role will the revolution be successful.

6. The essential role of the bourgeois-democratic revolution is to fight for the abolition of all feudal fetters, for the removal of all forms of precapitalist exploitation, and for the implementation of a radical agrarian revolution. On the other hand, its goal is also to overthrow French imperialism in order to attain full independence. These two aspects of the struggle are intimately

connected, for only after imperialism is eradicated can the landlord class be destroyed and can an agrarian reform end in success. Similarly, only after the feudal regime is abolished can imperialism be eradicated. To realize all these conditions, a government of soviets formed by workers and peasants must be established; this constitutes the only effective weapon to overthrow imperialism, feudalism, landlordism, so that the peasants will have land to till and the proletarians will have laws to guarantee their own rights.

The essential role of the bourgeois-democratic revolution is:

1. To overthrow French imperialism, feudalism, and landlordism.

2. To establish a government of workers and peasants.

3. To confiscate all landed properties belonging to foreign or indigenous landlords and to various religious organizations with the goal of distributing them to middle and poor peasants and to make the government of workers and peasants their rightful owner.

4. To appropriate all properties belonging to foreign capitalists.

5. To abolish all present duties and taxes and, at the same time, set up a progressive tax system.

6. To initiate the institution of an eight-hour working day and, therefore, to improve the living conditions of the workers and poor people.

7. To make sure that Indochina is fully independent and the people endowed with self-determination.

8. To create an army of workers and peasants.

9. To implement equality of the sexes.

10. To support the Soviet Union, to ally with all the proletarian classes of the world and with the colonial and semicolonial revolutionary movements.

7. In the Indochinese revolution the status of the social classes is not equal:

a. The *capitalists*. For imperialism all capitalists do not occupy the same position.

The commercial capitalists, because they share common interests with imperialism, ally themselves with imperialism and landlordism against the revolution.

The industrial capitalists, while maintaining contradictory interests with imperialism, but because

a. they lack strength;

b. they are linked with landlordism (some of them are even landlords);

c. they are afraid of the proletarian movement and are influenced by the Chinese and Indian capitalists, they cannot afford to side with the nationalist revolution; they can only support nationalist reformism. When the movement of the masses reaches higher levels, and when the proletarian revolution comes in sight, then they take the side of imperialism.

b. The petite bourgeoisie is divided into many categories, the position of each of these categories is different, and that position varies with each phase of the revolution.

1. The craftsmen do not favor imperialism because their products cannot compete successfully with merchandise imported from imperialist countries. They also dislike the proletarian revolution because they want to continue to exploit their apprentices. Because of that contradiction, their attitude toward the revolution is, to say the least, wavering.

2. The businessmen, because they are involved in the exploitative activities of trade, usury, and because they desire to continue these activities, they, therefore, do not approve of the revolution.

3. The bourgeois intellectuals, students, etc., are nationalists. They represent the interests of all the classes of indigenous capitalists and not only those of the bourgeoisie. They cannot foster the interests of the peasants because they have strings that attach them to the landlords.

4. The poor people who live in cities, such as vendors of vegetables in the streets, small craftsmen who do not have hired workers, unemployed intellectuals, etc., because they lead miserable lives, all support the revolution.

8. The strength of the revolution

a. In its majority the proletariat in Indochina is made up of peasants or of unemployed craftsmen. The proletariat is still young and in possession of a narrow mind while not liberated yet from feudal practices. As most of its members are illiterate, the raising of the class consciousness meets with a few obstacles. That class, nevertheless, attracts people, and its membership increases every day. Furthermore, as the colonial exploitation and oppression become more cruel, the proletariat is compelled to break out of these obstacles rapidly in order to fight more effectively against the imperialist capitalists. That is why the proletariat has turned itself into the principal and very strong moving force of the revolution in Indochina and the leading class of the revolutionary peasants and poor people.

b. The peasants constitute the majority of the population of Indochina (more than 90 percent); they play a crucial role in the bourgeois-democratic revolution. But they are not the same throughout Indochina. While it is struggling against landlordism and imperialism, the proletariat may nurture the hope of attracting all the peasants to the side of the revolution. When the class struggle becomes more intense and spreads more deeply into the countryside, and when the agrarian revolution expands more widely, then the rich peasants walk over to the side of the counterrevolutionaries.

The land question is the pivotal point in the bourgeois-democratic revolution. Only if the proletariat accepts to act as the vanguard of the peasants or to struggle alongside with them in order to protect their daily rights and to

implement a radical agrarian reform can the proletariat claim to be the leader of the peasantry. The allies of the proletariat are the middle and poor peasants.
9. Attitude toward the diverse classes

a. The local capitalists can be divided into two factions. The first faction has collaborated with the imperialists (by participating in their political and economic organizations); the second faction represented by such people as the Huynh Thuc Khang, the Pham Quynh, the Ngo Bao,[6] etc., are trying to find a way to accommodate the imperialists. They use the revolutionary movement to wring out of the imperialists advantages for themselves, while, at the same time, they abuse the people by declaring in public that they are demanding certain reforms from the imperialists, but in reality they try to sabotage the revolution of the workers and peasants. The strategy of the party is to expose clearly the reformist and nationalist tendencies of these elements. Their aim is simply to lull the people with dreams and to divert them from the revolutionary path. If, from now on, the party is not doing its utmost to wean the people from the nationalist-reformist influence, that influence will become a danger to the growth of the revolution. The party will have to make it very clear to the people that all the nationalist-reformists want is to compromise with the imperialists, that they have time and again fought against the revolution, and that they have opposed all demands of the people.

b. The party must indicate clearly the nature of the bourgeois political parties and their position within the revolutionary movement. They are the Nationalist Party (VNQDD), Nguyen An Ninh,[7] etc. Right now they can be seen as revolutionary nationalist parties, but soon enough they will become nationalist-reformist. All these parties have connections with the indigenous landlords and capitalists. As far as imperialism is concerned, the bourgeois intellectuals are the leaders of these political parties, and they do promote nationalist revolutions. But their only real aim is to fight for the development of capitalism in Indochina. As the anti-imperialist revolution emerges, they turn against imperialism in defense of the rights of the local capitalist class. But as the revolution reaches higher levels, when it is time to solve fundamental problems, especially the problem of agrarian reform and the establishment of the dictatorship of workers and peasants, these political parties will desert the revolution to run toward reformism by collaborating with imperialism.

That is why, from the political and organizational point of view, right from the beginning, we must draw a very clear boundary between the Communist Party and the bourgeois political parties; we must primarily thwart bourgeois tendencies such as assassination, lack of confidence in the people, etc., which exist within our party.

If we wanted to use every opportunity to widen the scope of the revolutionary movement, then our party may temporarily collaborate with these political parties, provided that they sincerely fight against imperialism and that they not impede the communist propaganda among the people. Without these conditions we should not have anything to do with these political parties. While we collaborate with them, the party must strive to preserve the class character of the workers and peasants movement. That means that the party must reserve for itself the right to agitate, propagandize, organize, and mobilize the people to struggle according to the slogans of anti-imperialist and pro-agrarian revolution of the party.

At the same time, we must denounce the unenthusiastic and reluctant attitude of the other political parties and the intolerant understanding of their nationalism. We must anticipate their reluctance so as to know how to fight it. We must do whatever is in our power to eliminate their influence on the masses and to free the masses from their control so as to retain in our hands the leadership of the proletariat.

10. The essential condition for the success of the revolution in Indochina is to have a Communist Party that has a correct political line, that has a centralized discipline, that is intimately related to the masses, and that grows through the experience of the struggle. The party is the vanguard of the proletarian class, using Marxism and Leninism as its basis to represent the principal and long-lasting interests of the proletarian class of Indochina and to lead the Indochinese proletarian class in the struggle toward the final aim of the proletariat, which is the communist ideology.

In order to achieve its mission in the revolution the party must first of all organize independent groups (trade unions, agricultural associations, etc.).

a. The party must attract to its ranks the majority of the members of its own class; that is the reason why its main responsibility is to set up and enlarge the trade unions in the essential factories and the larger cities. The trade unions must be united and at the same time centralized according to the nature of their production and their locales. We must organize unions in the factories and particularly mobilize the workers in plantations and mines. The party will be active not only in communist trade unions but also in workers' organizations that are still influenced by reactionaries or reformists in their attempt to mobilize the masses. The party must combine closely its secret with its public activities so as to boost the mobilization of the workers.

b. In order to establish the dictatorship of workers and peasants, the proletarian class must lead the majority of the poor people, principally the peasants. The party must therefore follow closely the process of land concentration and the class contradictions in the countryside. Right from the beginning, the party must lead the peasants against imperialism and landlordism. Poor and middle peasants participate enthusiastically in the agrarian revolution; they must, therefore, be organized throughout the country. The essential point is to set up consolidated unions for agricultural workers and groom them into becoming leaders of the peasant masses in the revolution.

As for the rich peasants, we must pay attention to them already now and not let them mingle with the unions and thereby influence the poor and middle peasants.

11. The way to struggle

In the designing of a strategy, the party must carefully examine the situation within the country and in the world, the strength of the enemy, the fighting spirit of the masses, the attitude of the various categories of people toward the revolution, etc. Based on these data, the party should determine the strategy for leading the people in the struggle. In ordinary times, according to particular conditions, we must disseminate "minimum slogans" in order to defend the interests of the masses, such as Increase the salaries; Reduce the working hours; Cut down taxes; Fight against taxes; Fight against the high cost of living, etc. That will widen the scope of the revolutionary struggle. We must, however, subordinate these "minimum slogans" to the principal slogans of the party, such as Down with Imperialism, Feudalism, and Landlordism; Full Independence for Indochina; Establish a Government by Workers and Peasants, etc. It is a serious mistake not to pay special attention to the needs and the daily struggle of the masses. It is, however, an even more serous mistake to pay attention only to the daily needs and not to the important goals of the party.

The duty of the party is to use the daily needs as the first steps to lead the proletarian class and the peasants to the battlefield of the revolution. When the revolutionary fervor reaches its zenith, when the ruling classes are shaken, when the middle classes lean toward the revolutionary camp, and when the masses of the workers and peasants fired up by the revolution are ready to sacrifice for the struggle, then the party must immediately lead the masses to overthrow the enemy's government and to establish a government by workers and peasants.

At that time the party will use transitional slogans such as Establish Soviet Governments; Establish Councils to Confiscate Lands; The Means of Production in the Control of the Workers; Arm the Workers and Peasants, etc. At the same time, the party must organize or amplify all the techniques of the struggle of the masses, such as strikes, strikes and demonstration, strike and armed demonstration, general strike and uprising.

An *armed uprising* is not an ordinary act; it must not only be organized according to the prerevolutionary condition but also according to the military model: that is why we must be very cautious. While we do not have prerevolutionary conditions, we must still go on struggling with ardor. But if we continue to struggle with ardor, it is not to organize adventurous or premature actions but essentially to mobilize the masses toward demonstrations, manifestations, strikes, etc., in order to prepare them for any future armed uprising.

12. Protest against imperialist wars

This period is the period of crisis among all the imperialist countries of the world, while workers' movements sprout vigorously in all countries as well as in Indochina. The threat of war between imperialist countries is nearer every day. The party, therefore, must promote the movement of protest against the arms race; we must at the same time mobilize the soldiers in the army and set up self-defense groups among the workers and peasants; we must spread the slogans far and wide among the masses against imperialist wars, such as Transform Imperialist Wars into Revolutionary Wars; Down with Imperialism and the Exploitation of the Classes; Defend the Soviet Union and the Revolutionary Movement in the World; etc.

13. Establish contact with the proletariat and the colonial peoples of the world

The Indochinese proletariat must establish contact with the proletariats of the world, particularly the French proletariat, so as to set up a mother country's and colony's front in view of increasing the strength of the revolution.

In the anti-imperialist struggle the Indochinese revolutionary masses must remain in contact with the revolutionary masses of the colonies and semi-colonies, particularly those in China and India, etc.

In its activities the party must be in close contact with the French, Chinese, and Indian Communist Parties.[8]

Notes

1. This notice, within parentheses, does not appear in the title on the cover or on the title page but only on the first page of the text itself.

2. One may read the complete text of this in *Ho Chi Minh Toan Tap, 1925–1930* (Hanoi, 1981), 2:297–98; along with *Summarized Theses of the Party,* 295–96; *Summarized Platform of the Party,* 299; and *Summarized By-Laws of the Party,* 300–302.

3. See Huynh Kim Khanh, *Vietnamese Communism, 1925–1945* (Ithaca, 1982), 125–26.

4. The rationale for changing the name of the party was given in the resolutions of the plenum in the following terms: "Calling the Party the 'Vietnamese Communist Party' would exclude Cambodia and Laos. At the same time, it is wrong to leave the working class of those two countries outside the framework of the Party, for, although the Vietnamese, Cambodian and Laotian proletarians differ in their linguistic, customary, and ethnic backgrounds, in political and economic aspects, they must maintain intimate relationships." Huynh Kim Khanh, *Vietnamese Communism,* 128.

5. All the subdivisions into numbered subchapters and paragraphs are in the text that I have used to do this translation.

6. Huynh Thuc Khang: see Document 16, in this volume. Pham Quynh: see Document 20, in this volume. *Ngo Bao:* title of a newspaper published in Hanoi from

1927 to 1936. It purported to advocate reforms but pursued essentially financial advantages for itself.

7. Nationalist Party: see Document 14, in this volume. Nguyen An Ninh: see Document 9, in this volume.

8. This translation is made from an official version of the original text brought out by an official government publishing house (Su That) in a pamphlet entitled *Luan cuong chanh tri nam 1930 cua Dang* (The 1930 Political Theses of the Party) (Hanoi, 1983).

DOCUMENT 20

Pham Quynh (1892–1945)

Open Letter to His Excellency the Minister of Colonies
(1931)

Pham Quynh wore many different hats in the Vietnamese literary and political arena—minister of education and of the interior in the royal government of Vietnam, director of the cabinet of the last Vietnamese emperor, publisher of a widely read literary-political magazine, Nam Phong *(Southern Wind), one of the founders of an organization, Hoi Khai Tri Tien Duc, with the aim of opening the mind of the people in order to foster their virtue. He has also requested permission to start a political party named Dang Dan Tien (Peoples' Progress Party) but without success. Pham Quynh was said to have been the "cultural lackey" of the French. Certainly, he was no revolutionary, and the role he played in the propagation of the Vietnamese romanized script was, to say the least, prodigious. In politics, however, Pham Quynh appeared immature, or rather self-serving, and his attitude toward the French colonial regime is plainly obsequious, servile.[1]*

The following letter was written on the occasion of a visit made to Indochina by Paul Reynaud, the French minister of colonies, in 1931. In a style that is at the same time pompous, sycophantic, and uselessly flowery, Pham Quynh unveiled his ideas concerning the future of a Vietnamese nation, "for ever bound to the Great and Noble Protecting Nation," which is, of course, France.

Your Excellency,
Under the regime of absolute monarchy of the past, its humblest citizen had the right to communicate with the people who held power so as to apprise them of the situation of the country and the wishes of the people. That citizen could even go farther, higher, to present to the emperor himself his requests and petitions. Thus, the people who cared or were responsible for the government could receive, without any intermediary, the wishes and requests of the masses and assess for themselves the state of the people and the nature of their needs; the voices of the multitude were capable of reaching at any moment the August steps of the throne.

Minister of the Great and Noble Nation that has taken upon herself to guide this country toward better destinies, deign, Excellency, allow a humble scholar from Annam to inform you in all sincerity about what his fellow countrymen expect of your visit.

He will not offer to you a notebook filled with wishes that are carefully numbered and labeled. He will not provide you with the platform of such and such a party or the demands of such and such a group.

He will not present to you a detailed and circumstantial list of all sorts of freedoms and franchises the people of this country are said to expect from the generosity of the French government.[2]

Your Excellency, you are more than informed about all these petitions that, because they have been repeated again and again, have acquired almost the characteristic of a ritual. But, on the other hand, you might be eager to know what lurks behind these emotionless faces, which, all along the Mandarinal Route, will bow with great respect each time you pass by them. You may want to scrutinize the bottom of those hearts that, under their blue and black gowns, have been beating more forcefully since they learned about your impending arrival.

In a triumphal voyage you have gone across the southern and central parts of Indochina. Of the three Vietnamese countries, you have already visited two, and today you set foot on the Tonkinese land. Here stands the cradle of our race. From here, the descendants of the Giao Chi[3] launched their conquest of Indochina that lasted for several centuries. From here departed those human waves that slowly submerged Champa and pushed the Cambodians away from the rich plains located along the Mekong River that have become the beautiful Cochinchina of the present day.

In effect, we also have been a conquering people. We have been, ourselves, "imperialists" in our own way.

After we liberated ourselves from the domination of China in the tenth century, we have bit by bit conquered all of present-day Annam and all of present-day Cochinchina at the expense of our neighbors, in spite of the fact that they themselves were resourceful and tough. That expansion along the coastal plains of Indochina combined with the victorious resistance we opposed to the Mongol invasion in the thirteenth century constituted one of the most flattering and the most glorious pages in our history.

A great French scholar, the late director of the French School of the Far East, Léonard Aurousseau, has summarized the history of that famous expansion in the following catching lines:

"The Vietnamese," he says, "will [*sic*] triumph, in 1471, over their Indianized rivals and continue to expand further south until they reach the region of Qui Nhon toward the end of the 15th century, that of Song Cau in 1611, Phang Rang in 1652, Phan Thiet in 1697, Saigon in 1698, Ha Tien in 1714. Finally, during the first half of the 18th century, they will complete the expansionist task undertaken by their race by occupying the entire territory of present day Cochinchina. After they have clearly defined the limits of their national territories,[4] as they are today, the Vietnamese will then stop, certain that they have well honored their ancestors from the Chinese coastal plains,[5] and fully satisfied with a fatherland they have created over twenty centuries of struggle, a land that seems to fit perfectly the genius of their race."

Our people, therefore, have shown vitality and energy in the past. But, since the end of the eighteenth century, internal dissension, including civil strife, has profoundly weakened us as the breaking up of our country combined with unrest have brought about such a state of affairs that could justify the French encroachment first against Cochinchina, and subsequently against Tonkin and Annam, in the latter half of the nineteenth century.

And such was our destiny. From then on Vietnam was for ever bound to France!

For sure, we are not complaining about our destiny. We even came to ask ourselves whether that destiny could have been different from or better than what it was. It looked like French tutelage was working well and was even beneficial to us. In a half-century she has helped us achieve considerable progress in all areas. She has above all maintained for us order and peace, resulting in a sense of security that allows our mind to open up, our conscience to be strengthened, our personality to bloom at the revitalizing breeze of liberal ideas blowing from the West. Then spawned in us new needs, further desires, that were less immediate than the preoccupations of material life.

Looking at the future with confidence and reminiscing with pride about a past that was not devoid of glory, we came to the ambitious idea that not only can we have a national life, but we would furthermore be able to live it, fully and intensely, under the tutelage of France. For that national consciousness, a long time in lethargy, has begun to live again in us; it even acquires a new vigor with every passing day. That fatherland that our fathers have created so painfully and of which we have at times forgotten the souvenir, that fatherland is now haunting our imagination with all its hidden power and all the obsessive strength of a fixation.

The confrontation between that fixation and reality yields a profound and indefinite anxiety that grips our hearts and fills our souls with a vague disquietude.

We are thus suffering from an affliction that apparently nothing can justify but which, nevertheless, constitutes the very consequence of the progress we have made under the protection of France.

The intellectual and moral evolution we have accomplished during a quarter of a century has the effect of forcing us to become conscious of our identity and of our nationality. And that new consciousness fits badly into a regime that is not made to give it satisfaction.

These circumstances give rise to the affliction we suffer, which consists really of a crisis of identity and nationality.

From the national point of view that crisis can be summarized in the following manner: *we belong to a people who are in search of a fatherland and who have not found it yet.*

That fatherland, Honorable Minister, cannot be France for us. Let that sentence not offend you. It connotes no ill will whatsoever toward France; it, rather, constitutes the expression of an exact truth. The Vietnamese people cannot consider France as their fatherland because they had one of their own. And France is in a position to grant that fatherland back to them by endowing them with a political status that will develop their personality as a nation and will provide them with a national life, worthy of that name, within the parameters of the French Empire.

In that way France will be more than a fatherland to us. She will forever be our benefactor, who will have lent us her assistance in reconstituting a defaulting fatherland.

It does not behoove us to determine the way France can accomplish that. Sovereign France must make her decision herself in the fullness of her rights and powers.

Her most authoritative delegates, several times already, have made very clear to us her intentions, which, we hasten to say, are extremely generous and partially meet our own wishes.

Your eminent predecessor, Your Excellency, Mr. Pietri, the Honorable Minister, declared last year in a resounding speech:

Indochina generates a problem concerning its administration and another concerning its sovereignty. What is the position of France? It can be stated in two words: *the respect of the Indochinese nations within the boundaries of a French federation.*

To clarify his thought about the Vietnamese nation, he added:

No one thinks with reason of assimilating the Vietnamese. Yet one must not fall into the error of disassimilating them from Vietnam itself, by driving them away from their traditions, their customs, from their ancestors and from their kings. What would remain for them of their moral and political foundation?

It would seem that the most appropriate solution would consist of endowing the Vietnamese people with a national status that would serve as their moral and political foundation and in integrating that renewed and strengthened Vietnamese nation into an Indochinese federation, which would form an integral part of the French Empire.

A Vietnamese kingdom endowed with a modern constitution within the limits of an Indochinese state, itself invested with an appropriate federal charter and placed under the high hegemony of France: that, Your Excellency, is a reform or an accomplishment that would satisfy both our intimate national wishes and our need for security under the watchful protection of France.

Our eminent governor-general, undoubtedly one of the people who knows us the best, has perfectly realized the importance of such a measure that, incidentally, at least for Annam and Tonkin, strictly conforms to the spirit of the treaties that bind us to France. And the governor-general has made the following very clear declarations in his speech of last year before the Council of Government:

> I do not want to initiate a new quarrel between the ancient and modern schools; I don't want to place in opposition those who advocate a loyal protectorate against those who promote an annexation, more or less in disguise. For me, my position is to honor the given word, to show respect for the signature of France. Implementing our promises is the most legitimate way to *respond to the wishes of the Vietnamese nation, to help raise the consciousness of its personality. The aim of the political reorganization of Annam-Tonkin ought to be a modern readjustment of the internal sovereignty of Annam to the 1884 treaty . . . France will restore [the Annamese monarchy] instead of weakening it, and she will restore it according to the Vietnamese national tradition.* After such a long dynastic past, the country of Annam cannot cease to be a kingdom . . . The young king, who pursues his brilliant studies in France, will be the first modern monarch of Annam.[6] He will come home with an intellect that is mature enough for him to understand the nobility and the perils of his task. He will have an advisor in the representative of France. Selecting his ministers by himself, organizing a renovated administration, he will help us to implement fully the regime of the protectorate. A new Annam is taking shape and its face shines among the countries of Indochina, of which the ultimate constitution will be an association of states placed under the suzerainty of France. Then the indigenous people of Indochina—I add here that I speak particularly of the Annamese [Vietnamese]—will be at the same time citizens of their own country, invested with special political rights, and also citizens of a federation in which their social advantages will be enhanced.

These declarations are clear and unequivocal. They define the policy of France toward at least the two countries that live under the protectorate regime

[Annam-Tonkin]. That policy will return to the Vietnamese people the fatherland they have lost while at the same time integrating that reconstructed fatherland into the structure of an Indochinese Federation.

What we expect of you, Your Excellency, is the unmitigated implementation of that policy; you may do so by building up a Federal State of Indochina in which each of the federated states, and in particular the kingdom of Annam-Tonkin, which would have been reconstituted according to the treaty of protectorate, will be endowed with a national status capable of satisfying all the wishes of the people.

With regard to the Vietnamese, they have, therefore, only one wish to express to you, Your Excellency, a wish that is very close to their heart and that transcends all others: *they ask of you a fatherland for them to serve.*

That request is not unreasonable; it is legitimate; it is a homage rendered to the generosity of France. It is a shining testimony of our total confidence in the protecting nation. It does not connote any secessionist intention or ulterior motive. On the contrary: that fatherland that France will reconstitute for us, we offer it back to France, with our two hands, so as to ask France to integrate it forever into the French *commonwealth* [*commonwealth* in English in the original].

But the Vietnamese people do not have that fatherland yet, and they are suffering. They will be very happy to have it. France is in a position to give it to them; she will be able to give it to them through you, Your Excellency, by implementing a thorough reform, of which we have just recalled to your attention the general outlines.

Your name, Your Excellency, will be honored by our people as the restorer of the Vietnamese nation.

Please accept, Your Excellency, the expression of my profound respect.

Pham Quynh[7]

Notes

1. For more on Pham Quynh, see his writings: *Essais Franco-Annamites (1929–1932)* (Hue, 1937); *Le Viet Nam à la croisée des chemins (Essais, 1922–1932)* (Paris, 1985); *Le Viet Nam: problèmes culturels et politiques (Essais, 1922–1932)* (Paris, 1985); *Thuong Chi Van Tap* (Saigon, 1962).

2. Pham Quynh must be referring to the document that was presented to Varenne, the governor-general of Indochina, in 1925. The said document was entitled *The Wish List of the Vietnamese People.* See Document 10, in this volume.

3. Giao Chi: one of the many ancient names of Vietnam or of the Vietnamese.

4. The author, L. Aurousseau, uses the plural form here to indicate that Vietnam encompasses three different territories.

5. The author implies that the original habitat of the Vietnamese was situated on the coast of China.

6. This speech must have been delivered sometime between the death of Emperor Khai Dinh in 1925 and the return of Emperor Bao Dai in 1933.

7. This letter was published both in French and Vietnamese in a pamphlet entitled *Lettre ouverte à Son Excellence le Ministre des Colonies. Buc thu ngo trinh quan Thuoc Dia Tong Truong* (Hanoi, 1931). It can also be found in Pham Quynh, *Essais Franco-Annamites (1929–1932)* (Hue, 1937), 463–72.

Bibliography

Archives

Archives Nationales de France. Section d'Outre Mer. Abbreviated as ANSOM.
Service de liaison avec les originaires des territoires d'Outre Mer. Abbreviated as
  SLOT.
Indochine. Anciens fonds.
Indochine. Nouveaux fonds.

Periodicals

I have skimmed through the following periodicals but have concentrated in greater
  detail on the periods covered by the dates placed within parentheses.

Argus Indochinois (Feb.–Dec. 1922)
La Cloche Fêleé (1924, 1925, 1926)
Dong Phap Thoi Bao (1923, 1924, 1925, 1926)
Duoc Nha Nam (1928, 1929)
L'Echo Annamite (1920, 1921, 1926)
L'Indochine Enchainée (1925–26)
Nam Phong (1920–27, 1930–31)
Nong Co Min Dam (1919)
Le Paria (1922)
Phu Nu Tan Van (1929, 1930)
La Presse Indochinoise (1924, 1925)
Than Chung (1929, 1930)
Tieng Dan (1927, 1928, 1929, 1930)
La Tribune Indigène (1918)

Publications

Ajalbert, Jean. *L'Indochine par les Français.* Paris, 1931.
Ajalbert, Jean. *Les Nuages sur l'Indochine.* Paris, 1912.
Anh, Tho. *Ben giong song Huong.* Hanoi, 1986.
Anh Van and J. Roussel. *Movements nationaux et lutte de classes au Vietnam.* Paris,
  1947.

Appel à la Société des Nations pour le droit du peuple Annamite à disposer de lui même. Paris, 1926.

Bach, Dien. *Nguyen Thai Hoc va Viet Nam Quoc Dan Dang.* Hanoi, 1950.

Bac Ho, Hoi ky. Hanoi, 1960.

Baudrais, G. *La Politique coloniale française en Indochine.* Paris, 1920.

Beau, Paul. *Situation de l'Indochine, 1902–1907.* Saigon, 1908.

Bernal, Martin. "The Nghe-Tinh Soviets Movement, 1930–1931." *Past and Present* 92 (Aug. 1981):148–68.

Bernard, Paul. *Nouveaux aspects du problème économique indochinois.* Paris, 1937.

Bernard, Paul. *Le Problème économique indochinois.* Paris, 1934.

Boudarel, Georges. "Bibliographie des oeuvres relatives à Phan Boi Châu éditées en quoc ngu à Hanoi depuis 1954." *BEFEO* 56 (1969): 151–76.

Boudarel, Georges. "Marxisme et Confucianisme." In René Galissot, ed. *Les Aventures du Marxisme,* 321–56. Paris, 1984.

Boudarel, Georges. "Phan Boi Chau et la société Vietnamienne de son temps." *France-Asie/Asia* 23, no. 199 (winter 1969): 354–36.

Boudarel, Georges. "Phan Boi Chau: Mémoires." *France-Asie/Asia* 22, nos. 194–95, (fall 1968): 3–210.

Boudet, Paul, and André Masson. *Iconographie historique de l'Indochine française.* Paris, 1931.

Brébion, A. *Dictionnaire de bio-bibliographie générale, ancienne et moderne de l'Indochine française.* Vol. 8. Paris, Académie des Sciences Coloniales, 1935.

Brocheux, Pierre. *Histoire de l'Asie du Sud Est: révoltes, réformes, révolutions.* Lille, 1981.

Brocheux, Pierre. "L'Implantation du mouvement communiste en Indochine française: le cas du Nghe Tinh (1930–1931)." *Revue d'Histoire Moderne et Contemporaine* 24 (Jan.–Mar. 1977): 49–77.

Brocheux, Pierre. *The Mekong Delta: Ecology, Economy and Revolution, 1860–1960.* Madison, 1995.

Brocheux, Pierre. "Le Prolétariat des plantations d'héveas au Vietnam méridional." *Le Mouvement Social* 90 (Jan.–Mar, 1975): 55–86.

Brocheux, Pierre, and Daniel Hemery. *Indochine, la colonisation ambiguë.* Paris, 1995.

Bui Quang Chieu. *France d'Asie.* Toulouse, 1925.

Buttinger, Joseph. *Vietnam: A Dragon Embattled.* 2 vol. New York, 1967.

Cahier des voeux annamites présenté à Mr Alexandre Varenne, Ancien Vice-Président de la Chambre des Députés, Gouverneur Général de l'Indochine, au cours de l'audience accordée à la délégation de la population annamite le 27 novembre 1925 à Saigon. Saigon, 1926.

Cao Huy Thuan. *Les Missionnaires et la politique coloniale française au Vietnam (1857–1914).* New Haven, 1990.

Chesneaux, Jean. *Contributions à l'histoire de la nation Vietnamienne.* Paris, 1955.

Chesneaux Jean, et al. *Tradition et révolution au Vietnam.* Paris, 1971.

Co Nhi Tan. *Nguyen Thai Hoc.* Saigon, 1969.

Copin, Henri. *L'Indochine dans la littérature française des années vingt à 1954.* Paris, 1996.

Coulet, Goerges. *Les Sociétés secrètes en terre d'Annam.* Saigon, 1926.

Coyle, Johanne Marie. "Indochinese Administration and Education: French Policy and Practice, 1917–1945." Ph.D. diss., Fletcher School of Law and Diplomacy, Tufts University, 1963.

Dang Huu Thu. *Than the va su nghiep nha cach mang Nguyen The Truyen.* Melun, 1993.

Dang Thai Mai. *Hoi ky.* Hanoi, 1985.

Dang Thai Mai. *Van tho cach mang Viet Nam dau the ky XX (1900–1925).* Hanoi, 1964.

Danguy H. *Le Nouveau visage de la Cochinchine.* Saigon, 1929.

Dao Duy Anh. *Dan toc.* Hue, 1929.

Dao Duy Anh. *Nho nghi chieu hom.* Ho Chi Minh City, [1989?].

Dao Trinh Nhat. *Dong Kinh Nghia Thuc.* Hanoi, 1937.

Dao Trinh Nhat. *Luong Ngoc Quyen va cuoc Khoi nghia Thai Nguyen 1917.* Saigon, 1957.

Dao, Van Hoi. *Ba nha chi si ho Phan.* Saigon, 1957.

De Francis, John. *Colonialism and Language Policy in Viet Nam.* La Haye, 1977.

Delamarre, E. *L'Emigration et l'immigration ouvrière en Indochine.* Hanoi, 1931.

Detay, A. *Les Sociétés commerciales indigènes en Indochine.* Paris, 1932.

Devilar, C. *Comment on perd une colonie.* Paris, 1927.

Dorgeles, Roland. *On the Mandarin Road.* Trans. Gertrude Emerson. New York and London, 1926.

Dorsenne, J. *Faudra t-il évacuer l'Indochine.* Paris, 1932.

Doumer, Paul. *L'Indochine française (Souvenirs).* 2d ed. Paris, 1930.

Duchene, Albert. *La Politique coloniale de France.* Paris, 1928.

Duiker, William J. "The Red Soviets of Nghe Tinh: An Early Communist Rebellion in Vietnam." *Journal of Southeast Asian Studies* 4, no. 2 (Sept. 1973): 186–98.

Duiker, William J. "The Revolutionary Youth League: Craddle of Communism in Vietnam" in *China Quarterly* 51 (July/Sept. 1972): 475–99.

Duiker, William J. *The Rise of Vietnamese Nationalism, 1900–1941.* Ithaca, N.Y., 1976.

Dumarest, Andre. *La Formation des classes sociales en pays annamites.* Lyon, 1935.

Duong, Ba Trac. *Tieng goi dan.* Hanoi, 1925.

Duong, Kinh Quoc. *Chinh quyen thuoc dia o Viet Nam truoc cach mang thang tam 1945.* Hanoi, 1988.

Duong Quoc Anh. *Viet Nam: nhung su kien lich su 1858–1945.* Vol. 3: 1919–1935. Hanoi, 1988.

Duong, Van Giao. *L'Indochine pendant la guerre de 1914–18.* Paris, 1925.

Dupré, J. *L'Assimilation des indigènes aux nationaux.* Montpellier, 1913.

Durtain, Luc. *Dieux blancs, hommes jaunes.* Paris, 1930.

Ennis, Thomas. *French Policy and Development in Indochina.* Chicago, 1936.

Exposition coloniale nationale de Marseille, Compte-rendu et Rapports. Marseille, 1922.

Fenn, Charles. *Ho Chi Minh.* New York, 1973.

Ferry, R. *Le Régime douanier de l'Indochine.* Paris, 1912.

Fontaine, A. R. *Essai de politique indigène en Indochine.* Paris, 1926.

Fraternité, (La) Tonkinoise. *Nos vues et notre action en matière de politique indigène.* Hanoi, 1930.

Frederick, William. "Alexandre Varenne and Politics in Indochina." In W. Vella, ed., *Aspects of Vietnamese History,* 96–159. Honolulu, 1973.

Galembert, J. de. *Les administrations et les services publics indochinois, Gouvernement de l'Indochine (Office Indochinois de la Propagande).* 2d rev. ed. Ed. E. Erard. Hanoi, 1931.

Garros, Georges. *Forceries humaines: l'Indochine litigieuse.* Paris, 1926.

Girardet, Raoul. *L'idée coloniale en France de 1871 à 1962.* Paris, 1972.

Gobron, Gabriel. *Histoire du Caodaisme.* Paris, 1948.

Gourdon, Henri. *L'Indochine.* Paris, 1931.

Gourou, Pierre. *Le Tonkin.* Hanoi, 1931.

Gouvernement Général de l'Indochine. *Direction des affaires politiques, Continuité de la politique française du protectorat en Annam-Tonkin avant et après l'avènement de sa Majesté Bao Dai.* Hanoi, 1933.

Ha Huy Giap. *Nguyen An Ninh, mot lanh tu hung bien.* Saigon, 1989.

Hanh, Son. *Cu Tran Cao Van.* Paris, 1952.

Hemery, Daniel. *Ho Chi Minh, de l'Indochine au Vietnam.* Paris, 1990.

Hemery, Daniel. *Révolutionnaires Vietnamiens et pouvoir colonial en Indochine.* Paris, 1975.

Henry, Yves. *Economie agricole de l'Indochine.* Hanoi, 1932.

Ho Chi Minh. *Revendications du peuple annamite.* Paris, 1918.

Ho Chi Minh. *Toan tap.* 7 vols. Hanoi, 1995.

Ho Huu Tuong. *Bon muoi mot nam lam bao; hoi ky.* Saigon, 1972.

Ho Huu Tuong. *Tram tu cua mot ten toi tu hinh.* Saigon, 1965.

Ho Ta Khanh. *Lich trinh tranh dau cua cac nha cach mang quoc gia chan chinh dau the ky XX, Thong su Cong ty Lien Thanh.* Paris, 1983.

Hoang Trong Thuoc. *Vua Duy Tan.* Laguna Hills, Calif., 1984.

Hoang Van Dao. *Viet Nam Quoc Dan Dang.* Saigon, 1970.

Hodgkin, Thomas. *Vietnam: The Revolutionary Path.* London, 1981.

Hong Lien va Dong Tung. *Mot gia dinh cach mang. Tai lieu lich su cach mang Viet Nam.* Saigon, 1970.

Hop tuyen tho van Viet Nam. 2d ed. in 6 vols. Hanoi, 1978.

Hop tuyen tho van yeu nuoc. Tho van yeu nuoc va cach mang dau the ky XX (1900–1930). Hanoi, 1976.

Huynh Kim Khanh. *Vietnamese Communism, 1925–1945.* Ithaca, N.Y., 1982.

Huynh Ly. *Phan Chau Trinh, than the va su nghiep.* Danang, 1992.

Huynh Ly. *Tho van Phan Chau Trinh.* Hanoi, 1983.

Huynh Ly et al. *Hop tuyen tho van Viet Nam (1858–1920).* Vol. 2. Hanoi, 1985.

Huynh Phu So. *Biography and Teaching of Prophet Huynh Phu So.* Saigon, 1966.

Huynh Thuc Khang. *Phan Tay Ho tien sinh lich su.* Hue, 1959.

Huynh Thuc Khang. *Tu truyen.* Translated from a Chinese manuscript by Anh Minh. Hue, 1963.

Huynh Xuan Canh. *Le Crédit indochinois.* Paris, 1929.

Indochine Française. *L'Administration des Douanes et Régies en Indochine.* Hanoi, 1930.

Indochine Française. *Le Centre de formation professionnelle de Hue.* Hanoi, 1931.

Indochine Française. *Contribution à l'histoire des mouvements politiques de l'Indochine française.* Hanoi, 1930–33.

Indochine Française. *Documents officiels.* Paris, 1931.

Indochine Française. *Exposition coloniale internationale.* Paris, 1931.

Indochine Française. *L'Organisation de la justice en Indochine.* Hanoi, 1930.

Indochine Fançaise. *Les Services militaires en Indochine.* Hanoi, 1931.

Indochine Française. *Les Services de l'Instruction Publique en Indochine en 1930.* Hanoi, 1930.

Isoart, Paul. *Le Phénomène national vietnamien.* Paris, 1961.

Jacnal, Jean. *Mémoires de Son Excellence Huynh Con, dit Dan Truong, Ancien Ministre des Rites à la Cour d'Annam My Hoa Tu.* Hanoi, 1924.

Kelly, Gail P. "Franco-Vietnamese Schools, 1918–1938." Ph.D. diss., University of Wisconsin, Madison, 1975.

Lacouture, Jean. *Ho Chi Minh: A Political Biography.* Trans. Peter Wiles. New York, 1968.

Langlois, Walter. *André Malraux: The Indochina adventure.* New York, 1966.

Le Breton, H. *Le Budget et l'Instruction Publique en Indochine.* Hue, 1932.

Le Fèvre, G. *Démolisseurs et bâtisseurs.* Paris, 1927.

Le Quang Hong. *Recueil de décrets et arrêtés relatifs à la règlementation de l'enseignement privé au Tonkin.* Hanoi, 1926.

Le Tung Son. *Nhat ky mot chang duong.* Hanoi, 1987.

Le Van Kim. *Les Travaux publics en Indochine.* Paris, 1926.

Le Van Thu. *Hoi kin Nguyen An Ninh.* 2d ed. Saigon, 1961.

Lebel, R. *Histoire de la litérature coloniale en France.* Paris, 1931.

Lebrel, G. *Deux aspects de l'évolution du protectorat français en Annam-Tonkin.* Paris, 1932.

Leclerc, J. *De l'évolution et du développement des institutions annamites et cambodgiennes sous l'influence française.* Rennes, 1923.

"Les Lettrés devant l'histoire." *Études Vietnamiennes* 56. Hanoi, 1979.

Lévi, Sylvain, ed. *Indochine, Exposition coloniale internationale de Paris.* Paris, 1931.

Liauzu, Claude. *Aux origines des tiersmondismes: colonisés et anti-colonialistes en France, 1919–1939.* Paris, 1982.

Lockhart, Bruce McFarland. *The End of the Vietnamese Monarchy.* Lac Viet Series 15. New Haven, 1993.

Luong, Hy Van. *Revolution in the Village: Tradition and Transformation in North Vietnam, 1925–1988.* With the collaboration of Nguyen Dac Bang. Honolulu, 1992.

Luong Van Can. *Au hoc tung dam.* Hanoi, 1929.

Ly Binh Hue. *Le Régime des concessions domaniales en Indochine.* Paris, 1931.

Malleret, Louis. *L'exotisme dans la litérature française depuis 1860.* Paris, 1934.

Malraux, Clara. *Les Combats et les jeux.* Paris, 1963.

Marr, David. *Vietnamese Anti-Colonialism, 1885–1925.* Berkeley, Calif., 1971.

Marr, David. *Vietnamese Tradition on Trial.* Berkeley, Calif., 1981.

Maspero, Goerges. *Un Empire colonial français: l'Indochine.* Paris, 1929.

Mathieu, E. *Evolution intellectuelle et sociale des Annamites sous l'influence française.* Saigon, 1930.

Maybon, A. *L'Indochine.* Paris, 1931.

McHale, Shawn F., "Printing, Power, and the Transformation of Vietnamese Culture, 1920–1945." Ph.D. diss., Cornell University, 1995.

Merimée, J. *De l'accession des Indochinois à la qualité de citoyen français.* Toulouse, 1931.

Metin, A. *L'Indochine et l'opinion.* Paris, 1916.

Monet, Paul. *Annamites, au travail.* Saigon, 1926.

Monet, Paul. *Entre deux feux.* Paris, 1928.

Monet, Paul. *Français et Annamites.* Paris, 1925.

Monet, Paul. *Les Jauniers.* Paris, 1931.

Moneta, Jacob. *La Politique du Parti Communiste Français dans la question coloniale, 1920–1963.* Paris, 1971.

Montaigut, D. de. *La Colonisation française dans l'Est de la Cochinchine.* Limosges, 1929.

Morel, J. *Les Concessions des terres au Tonkin.* Paris, 1912.

Morlat, Patrice. *La Répression coloniale au Vietnam (1908–1940).* Paris, 1990.

Munholland, Kim. "The French Response to the Vietnamese Nationalist Movement, 1905–1914." *Journal of Modern History* 38 (1975): 655–75.

Munier, P. *Les Poètes français d'Indochine.* Hanoi, 1932.

Murray, Martin J. *The Development of Capitalism in Colonial Indochina.* Berkeley, 1980.

Murray, Martin J. " 'White Gold' or 'White Blood'? The Rubber Plantations of Colonial Indochina, 1910–1940." In *Plantations, Proletarians and Peasants in Colonial Asia,* ed. E. Valentine Daniel et al., 41–67. London, 1992.

Mus, Paul. *Le Destin de l'Union Francaise.* Paris, 1954.

Mus, Paul. "The Role of the Village in Vietnamese Politics." *Pacific Affairs* 22 (1949): 265–71.

Mus, Paul. "Vietnam." *Sociologie d'une guerre.* Paris, 1952.

Mus, Paul. *Le Vietnam chez lui.* Paris, 1946.

Mus, Paul, and John McAlister. *The Vietnamese and Their Revolution.* New York, 1970.

Naturalisation (La) française en Indochine. Paris, 1921.

Ngo Nhan. *Dan toc.* Hue, 1929.

Ngo Nhan. *Xa hoi.* Hue, 1929.

Ngo Tat To. *Hoang Hoa Cuong.* Saigon, 1929.

Ngo Van Hoa and Duong Kinh Quoc. *Giai cap cong nhan Viet-Nam nhung nam truoc khi thanh lap Dang.* Hanoi, 1978.

Ngo Vinh Long. *Before the Revolution: Vietnamese Peasants under the French.* Cambridge, Mass., 1973.

Ngo Vinh Long. "The Indochinese Communist Party and Peasant Rebellion in Central Vietnam, 1930–1931." *Bulletin of Concerned Asian Scholars* 10 (1978): 15–34.

Ngoc Son and Doan Hiet. *Guong ai quoc.* Duy Tan thu xa. Saigon, 1928.

Ngoc Son and Doan Hiet. *Guong cach mang,* vol. 1. Duy Tan thu xa. Saigon, 1929.

Ngoc Son and Doan Hiet. *Than tu do,* vol. 1. Duy Tan thu xa. Saigon, 1928.

Nguyen Ai Quoc. See Ho Chi Minh.

Nguyen An Ninh. *Cao vong cua bon thanh nien, An Nam dan toc.* Saigon, 1926.

Nguyen An Ninh. *La France en Indochine.* Paris, 1923.

Nguyen An Ninh. Saigon, 1988.

Nguyen Chanh Sat. *Am muu khoi loan* [in Chinese characters]. *Toa quan vu xu Nguyen Huu Tri va noi bon ve toi an cuop kham lon trong dem 14 rang ngay 15 thang Fevrier 1916.* Tan Dinh, 1916.

Nguyen Cong Binh. *Tim hieu giai cap tu san Viet nam thoi Phap thuoc.* Hanoi, 1959.

Nguyen Cong Binh et al. *Lich su Viet Nam.* Hanoi, 1976–85.

Nguyen Dai Dao. *Ong Nguyen An Ninh duoc tha, 7 janvier 1927.* Saigon, 1927.

Nguyen Dang Manh, Nguyen Ha Thu, and Huynh Ly. *Hop tuyen van hoc Viet Nam (1920–1945).* Hanoi, 1987.

Nguyen Hai Ham. *Tu Yen Bay den Con Lon.* Saigon, 1970.

Nguyen Hien Le. *Dong kinh nghia thuc, phong trao duy tan dau tien o Viet Nam.* Saigon, 1968, 1985.

Nguyen, Hien Le. *Muoi cau chuyen van chuong.* Los Angeles, 1986.

Nguyen Khac Hieu. "Cai tinh than ai quoc . . ." *An Nam tap chi* 3 (1926): 1–4.

Nguyen Khac Hieu. *Giac mong con.* Hanoi, 1926.

Nguyen Khac Hieu. *Giac mong lon.* Haiphong, 1930.

Nguyen Khac Hieu. *Khoi tinh con.* 2d ed. Haiphong, 1922.

Nguyen Khac Hieu. *Tan Da tung van.* Hanoi, 1922.

Nguyen Khac Ngu. *Viet Nam, nhung hinh anh xua.* Montreal, 1986.

Nguyen Khac Ve. *Les Institutions représentatives des intérêts des habitants de l'Indochine.* Paris, 1922.

Nguyen Khac Ve. *La Naturalisation française en Indochine.* Paris, 1921.

Nguyen Kim Dinh. *Bon lam nguy tai tinh Bien Hoa. Toa quan chanh xu ngay 27 avril 1916, nham ngay 25 thang tu annam.* Saigon, 1916.

Nguyen Kim Dinh. *Gai anh hung nuoc Nam.* Saigon, 1929.

Nguyen Kim Dinh. *Nguyen Huu Tri et consorts se révoltent et attaquent la prison centrale de Saigon dans la nuit du 14 au 15 février 1916. Jugement des rebelles.* Saigon, 1916.

Nguyen Ky Nam. *Hoi ky 1925–64.* Saigon, 1964.

Nguyen Luong Bang. "Mes rencontres avec l'oncle Ho." *Souvenirs sur Ho Chi Minh.* Hanoi, 1962.

Nguyen Manh Bong. *Hien than tho nuoc.* Hanoi, 1923.

Nguyen Manh Bong. *Tay Ho Phan Chu Trinh tieu lich su can dai Viet Nam.* Haiphong, n.d.

Nguyen Phan Long. *Le Roman de Mademoiselle Lys.* Hanoi, 1921.

Nguyen Tan Duoc. *Discours prononcé au Conseil Colonial par Monsieur Nguyen Tan Duoc, Séance plénière du 24 novembre 1925. Interventions de MM. Gallet et Monin, Conseillers Coloniaux. Carence du governement.* Saigon, 1925.

Nguyen Tao. *Chung toi vuot nguc.* Hanoi, 1977.

Nguyen Thanh. *Bao chi cach mang Viet Nam (1925–1945).* Hanoi, 1984.

Nguyen Thanh Khiet. *La Cochinchine française.* Montpellier, 1915.

Nguyen The Anh. *Monarchie et fait colonial (1875–1925): le crépuscule d'un ordre traditionel.* Paris, 1992.

Nguyen The Anh. *Phong trao khang thue mien Trung nam 1908 qua cac chau ban trieu Duy Tan.* Saigon, 1973.

Nguyen Thuong Hien. *Mot tap van lo nuoc thuong dan.* Hanoi, 1926.

Nguyen Thuong Huyen. "Cu Phan Boi Chau o Hoang Chau." *Bach Khoa* 73–74, nos. 1–2 (1960): 29–40.

Nguyen Tien Lang. *Pages françaises par un jeune élève annamite.* Lycée du Protectorat, Hanoi, Enseignement secondaire local. Hanoi, 1929.

Nguyen Trieu Luat. *Bon muoi bai quoc su.* Hanoi, 1929.

Nguyen Trong Hoang. "Chinh sach giao duc cua thuc dan Phap o Viet Nam." *Nghien Cuu Lich Su* 96, no. 3 (1967): 13–25.

Nguyen Van Dien. *Notions sommaires sur la justice indigène au Tonkin.* Hanoi, 1923.

Nguyen Van Hau. *Chi si Nguyen Quang Dieu, mot lanh tu trong yeu trong phong trao Dong Du mien Nam.* Saigon, 1964.

Nguyen Van Kinh. *Chung quanh van de suu tap dan nguyen va cuoc meeting o rap Thanh Xuong.* Saigon, 1927.

Nguyen Van Lich. *Mot tui chan doi.* Hanoi, 1927.

Nguyen Van Loc. *Ve xu tu 38 nguoi, 22 fevrier 1916.* Saigon, 1916.

Nguyen Van Nghi. *Etude économique sur la Cochinchine française et l'infiltration chinoise.* Montpellier, 1920.

Nguyen Van Ngo. *Trente deux leçons d'instruction civique, Cours Moyen, 2è année.* Saigon, 1938.

Nguyen Van Trung. *Chu dich Nam Phong.* Saigon, 1975.

Nguyen Van Trung. *Chu nghia thuc dan Phap o Viet Nam: thuc chat va huyen thoai.* Saigon, 1963.

Nguyen Van Trung. *Truong hop Pham Quynh.* Saigon, 1974.

Nguyen Van Vinh. *Thuc tinh dong bao.* Saigon, 1926.

Nguyen Van Xuan. *Phong trao Duy Tan.* Saigon, 1970.

Nguyen Xuan Giac. *Le Régime économique de la Cochinchine.* Paris, 1920.

Nhuong Tong. See Pham Hoang Tran.

Olichon Mgr. *Le Baron de Phat Diem.* Poitiers, 1931.

Ong gia ben Ngu. Hue, 1982.

Pasquier, Pierre. *L'Annam d'autrefois.* Paris, 1930.

Pasquier, Pierre. *La politique de la France en Indochine.* Paris, 1928.

Pelletier, G., and L. Roubaud. *Images et réalités coloniales.* Paris, 1931.

Petit, R. *La Monarchie annamite.* Paris, 1931.

Pham Hoang Tran. *Nguyen Thai Hoc.* Saigon, 1949.

Pham Nhu Thom, ed. *Hoi ky Tran Huy Lieu.* Hanoi, 1991.

Pham Quynh. *L'Evolution intellectuelle et morale des Annamites depuis l'établissement du protectorat français, Conférence faite à l'Ecole Coloniale le Vendredi 31 Mai 1922.* Paris, 1922.

Pham Quynh. *Lettre ouverte à Son Excellence le Ministre des Colonies.* Hanoi, [1931?].

Pham Quynh. *Vers une constitution.* Hanoi, 1930.

Pham Quynh. *Le Vietnam: problèmes culturels et politiques (essais 1922–1932).* N.p., 1985.

Pham Tat Dac. *Chieu hon nuoc.* Hanoi, 1945.

Phan Boi Chau. *Loi hoi . . .? cac anh em thanh nien.* Le Phuoc Thanh alias Le Van Thinh, ed. and trans. 2d ed. Saigon, 1928.

Phan Boi Chau. "Nguc Trung Thu." In David Marr, ed. *Reflections from Captivity,* trans. C. Jenkins, Tran Khanh Tuyet, and Huynh Sanh Thong. Athens, Ohio, 1976.

Phan Boi Chau. *Phap Viet ai huu chanh kien thu.* Nguyen Huu Tien, trans. Hanoi, 1926.

Phan Boi Chau. *Toan tap,* Chuong Thau, ed. 10 vols. Hue, 1990.

Phan Boi Chau. *Van tho Phan Boi Chau chon loc.* Chuong Thau et al., ed. Hanoi, 1967.

Phan Boi Chau. *Viet Nam vong quoc su.* Nguyen Quang To, trans. Saigon, 1969.

Phan Chau Trinh. *Tay Ho va Sante thi tap.* Le Am, comp. Saigon, 1961.

Phan Khoang. *Viet Nam Phap thuoc su.* Saigon, 1971.

Phan Thien Chau. "Transitional Nationalism in Vietnam, 1903–1931." Ph.D. diss., Denver University, 1965.

Phan Van Hum. *Ngoi tu kham lon.* Saigon, 1957.

Phan Van Truong. *Essai sur le Code Gia Long.* Paris, 1922.

Phan Van Truong. *La "Fraternité," association d'Indochinois. Note pour nos compatriotes.* Paris, 1913.

Phan Van Truong. *Viec giao duc hoc van trong dan toc An Nam.* Saigon, 1925.

Phuong Lan Bui The My. *Nha cach mang Nguyen An Ninh (1899–1943).* Saigon, 1970.

Phuong, Lan Bui The My. *Nha cach mang Ta Thu Thau (1906–1945).* Saigon, 1974.

Pietri, François. "L'affaire de Yen Bay." *La Revue des Deux Mondes,* 15 July 1960, 278–88.

Pike, Douglas. *History of Vietnamese Communism, 1925–1976.* Stanford, Calif., 1978.

Popkin, Samuel. *The Rational Peasant: The Political Economy of Rural Society in Vietnam.* Berkeley, 1979.

Portoukalian, Leon. *Le Conseil Colonial de la Cochinchine.* Marseille, 1931.

Pouvourville, Albert de. *L'Annamite.* Paris, 1932.

Pouvourville, Albert de. *L'Annam sanglant.* Paris, 1912.

Pouvourville, Albert de. *L'Asie française.* Paris, 1911.

Pouvourville, Albert de. *Griffes rouges sur l'Asie.* Paris, 1933.

Pouyanne, A. A. *Les Travaux publics en Indochine.* Hanoi, 1925.

Remy, E. *Monographie du cadastre en Indochine.* Hanoi, 1931.

Robequain, Charles. *L'Indochine française.* Paris, 1935.

Roubaud, Louis. *La Tragédie indochinoise.* Paris, 1931.

Rousset, Pierre. *Communisme et nationalisme vietnamien.* Paris, 1978.

Sarraut, Albert. *Grandeurs et servitudes coloniales.* Paris, 1931.

Sarraut, Albert. *La Mise en valeur des colonies françaises.* Paris, 1923.

Saumont, Jean Baptiste. *L'Oeuvre de Klobukowski en Indochine.* Hanoi, 1910.

Schultz, Y. *Dans la griffe des jauniers.* Paris, 1931.

Scott, James. *The Moral Economy of the Peasant.* New Haven, Conn., 1976.

Serge, Victor. *Les Coulisses d'une sureté générale.* Paris, 1931.

Simoni, H. *Le Role du capital dans la mise en valeur de l'Indochine.* Paris, 1929.

Smith, Ralph. "Bui Quang Chieu and the Constitutionalist Party in French Cochinchina." *Modern Asian Studies* 3, no. 2 (April 1969): 131–50.

Smith, Ralph. "The Development of Opposition to French Rule in Southern Vietnam, 1880–1940." *Past and Present 64* (1972): 94–129.

Smith, Ralph. "An Introduction to Caodaism: Origins and Early History." *Bulletin of School of Oriental and African Studies* 33, no. 2 (1970): 335–49 and 33, no. 3 (1970): 573–89.

Son Nam. *Thien dia hoi va cuoc Minh Tan.* Saigon, 1971.

Suignard, J. *Les Services civils de l'Indochine.* Paris, 1931.

Taboulet, George. *La Geste française en Indochine.* Paris, 1955–56.

Tai Hue Tam Ho. *Millenarism and Peasant Politics in Vietnam.* Cambridge, Mass., 1983.

Tai Hue Tam Ho. "The Politics of Compromise: The Constitutionalist and the Electoral Reforms of 1922 in French Cochinchina." *Modern Asian Studies* 18, pt. 2 (July 1984): 371–92.

Tai Hue Tam Ho. *Radicalism and the Origins of the Vietnamese Revolution.* Cambridge, Mass., 1992.

Taittinger, P. *Le Rêve rouge.* Paris, 1930.

Talon, Vital. *Le Régime douanier de l'Indochine.* Paris, 1932.

Tessan, F. de. *Dans l'Asie qui s'éveille.* Paris, 1922.

Teston, E., and M. Percheron. *L'Indochine moderne.* Paris, 1931.

Thai Van Kiem. "Un Grand patriote: le prince Cuong De." *France-Asie Asia* 11, no. 106 (Mar. 1955): 484–88.

Thanh Nam. *Phong trao dau tranh cach mang cua cong nhan cao su mien Dong Nam bo.* Hanoi, 1982.

Thep Moi. *Thoi dung dang.* Paris, n.d.

Thich, J. M. *Van de cong san.* Quy Nhon, 1927.

Thiet Can and Hai Khanh. *Loan Thai Nguyen.* Hanoi, 1935.

Thompson, Virginia. *French Indochina.* New York, 1937.

Thu Trang Cong Thi Nghia. *Hoat dong cua Phan Chau Trinh tai Phap, 1911–1925.* Paris, 1982.

To Hoai. *Hoi ky: Gio bui chan ai.* Hanoi, 1992.

To Hoai. *Nhung guong mat.* Hanoi, 1988.

To Hoai. *Tu truyen.* Hanoi, 1985.

Touzet, A. *L'Economie indochinoise et la grande crise universelle.* Paris, 1934.

Tran Huu Do. *De quoc chu nghia.* Saigon, 1937.

Tran Huu Do. *Hoi trong tu do.* Saigon, 1926.

Tran Huu Do. *Hon doc lap.* Saigon, 1926.

Tran Huu Do. *Thanh nien tu doc.* Saigon, 1928.

Tran Huu Do. *Tieng chuong tri hon.* Saigon, n.d.

Tran Huu Do. *To co mat quyen tu do.* Saigon, 1926.

Tran Huy Lieu and Bui Cong Trung. *Viec Ong Phan Boi Chau.* Saigon, 1926.

Tran Huy Lieu and Nguyen Thanh Lam. *Hoi kin . . .* Hanoi, 1935.

Tran Huy Lieu. *Dang Thanh Nien, 1926–27. Tap tai lieu va hoi ky.* Hanoi, 1961.

Tran Huy Lieu. *Hoi ky.* Tran Nhu Thom, ed. Hanoi, 1991.

Tran Huy Lieu. *Loan Thai Nguyen.* Hanoi, 1935.

Tran Huy Lieu. *Mot bau tam su.* Saigon, 1927.

Tran Huy Lieu. *Les Soviets du Nghe Tinh de 1930–1931 au Vietnam.* Hanoi, 1960.

Tran Manh Nhan. *De quoc chu nghia.* Saigon, 1928.

Tran Tu Binh. *The Red Earth: A Vietnamese Memoir of Life on a Colonial Rubber Plantation.* John Spragens Jr., trans.; David G. Marr, ed. Athens, Ohio, 1985.

Tran Tuan Khai. *Tho van A Nam Tran Tuan Khai.* Xuan Dieu, intro.; Lu Huy Nguyen, comp. Hanoi, 1984.

Tran Van Chuong. *L'Esprit du droit sino-annamite.* Paris, 1922.

Tran Van Giau. *Giai cap cong nhan Viet Nam. Su hinh thanh va su phat trien cua no tu giai cap "tu minh" den giai cap "cho minh."* Hanoi, 1957.

Tran Van Giau. *Gia tri tinh than truyen thong cua dan toc Viet Nam.* Ho Chi Minh City, 1993.

Truong, Buu Lam and Maivan Lam. *Rebellion, Resistance and Revolution: The Power of the Rural Masses in Vietnamese History.* Singapore, 1982.

Truong, Thi Sau Madame Nguyen An Ninh. *Con duong giai phong.* Hanoi, 1976.

Tuck, Patrick. *French Catholic Missionaries and the Politics of Imperialism in Vietnam, 1857–1914: A Documentary Survey.* Liverpool, 1987.

Valat, Charles. *L'Indochine actuelle et son avenir.* Hanoi, 1924.

Vanlande, R. *L'Indochine sous la menace communiste.* Paris, 1930.

Varet, P. *Les Dieux qui meurent.* Paris, 1932.

Vella, Water, ed. *Aspects of Vietnamese History.* Asian Studies at Hawaii, no. 8. Honolulu, 1973.

Viollis, Andrée. *Indochine S.O.S.* Paris, 1935.

Vivies, A. *L'Ame de la Cochinchine.* Saigon, 1924.

Vo, Nguyen Giap and Truong Chinh. *The Peasant Question.* Christine P. White, trans. Ithaca, N.Y., 1974.

Werth, Leon. *La Cochinchine.* Paris, 1926.

Woodside, Alexander B. *Community and Revolution in Modern Vietnam.* Boston, Mass., 1976.

Xuan Dieu and Nguyen Khac Xuong, eds. *Tuyen Tap Tan Da.* Hanoi, 1986.

Index

Abd El Krim, 239, 250n. 4

Administration, 129, 214–15, 217, 221, 225, 226, 241–42; agency, 50; artful, 180; central, 261; colonial, 3, 24, 25, 31, 41, 45, 49, 51, 69, 70, 141; court, 222; departments, 210; Doumer, 89; English, 182; favoritism, 217; French, 17–18, 41, 74, 76, 186, 241; foundations, 183; indigenous, 9, 15, 267; Indochina, 295; local, 15, 19, 217–18; officials, 133; opponents, 157; parallel, 15–16; penitentiary, 186; positions, 12, 51, 96, 203; powerless, 16; provincial, 126, 129, 261; renovated, 296; royal, 15, 69, 125

Adzes, revolt of the, 192

Aéronautique, 20, 35n. 31

Africa, Equatorial, 223

Agent provocateur, 22

Agrarian: reform, 285, 287; revolution, 284, 286, 288; system, 242

Agricultural: associations, 288; colonies, 277; credits, 275; estates, 90; exploitations, 41; implements, 47; parks, 89; production, 282; products, 283; reform, 284, 286, 288; schools, 73; society, 28; system, 242; workers, 289

Ai quoc, 6

Air Force. *See* Aéronautique

Alcohol, 97, 165, 249; company, 172; consumption, 172, 206; cost, 48, 87, 172; distillers, 48, 172, 206; distribution, 25, 86; French, 48; importation, 25; kind, 172; monopoly, 24–25, 47–48, 97, 172–73, 240, 242; moon-

shiner, 172; outlets, 97; poison, 72; production, 172, 204; provider, 117; purchase, 172, 235; quality, 48, 63n. 26; quantity, 25; taste, 48; taxes, 89, 92, 100, 172; traditional, 48

Algerians, 21, 215

Algiers, 246n. 1

Alsace, 54

Am Vo, 179

Ame Annamite, L' (newspaper). See *Viet Nam Hon*

America: ambassadors, 108; artifacts, 151; bombing, 36n. 32; cities, 123; consul, 66n. 54; debts, 236; England, 175, 248, 275; imperialist, 273; independence, 176; Indochina, 245; influence, 175; newspapers, 151; people, 114; red Indians, 136; red race, 176; red-skinned, 273; scholar, 65n. 44; students, 210; teachers, 114, 163; threat, 119; trade, 118; training, 122; unequal, 118

Anarchist, 198

Annam, 6, 7n. 3, 17, 19, 20, 60, 198, 240, 246, 261, 263, 292, 296–97; administration, 15–17, 19, 50; code, 266; constitution, 262, 267–68; consultative chamber, 13, 14, 206; court, 267; education, 263; encroachment, 31, 293; federation, 242; government, 17, 261; justice, 22, 23, 95; monarch, 295; monarchy, 9, 16, 31, 296; new, 295; part (of Vietnam), 204, 261; people, 184, 203, 269; policy, 183, 267, 295; problems, 262; protectorate, 8,